CW01497194

RISE OF THE VILLANS

RISE OF THE VILLANS

Inside Unai Emery's Aston Villa Revolution

GUILLEM BALAGUÉ

SEVEN DIALS

First published in Great Britain in 2025 by Seven Dials,
an imprint of The Orion Publishing Group Ltd
Carmelite House, 50 Victoria Embankment
London EC4Y 0DZ

An Hachette UK Company

The authorised representative in the EEA is Hachette Ireland,
8 Castlecourt Centre, Dublin 15, D15 XTP3,
Ireland (email: info@hbgi.ie)

1 3 5 7 9 10 8 6 4 2

A CIP catalogue record for this book is
available from the British Library.

ISBN (Hardback) 978 1 3996 2504 3
ISBN (Trade Paperback) 978 1 3996 2505 0
ISBN (eBook) 978 1 3996 2507 4
ISBN (Audio) 978 1 3996 2508 1

Typeset by Input Data Services Ltd, Bridgwater, Somerset

Printed in Great Britain by Clays Ltd, Elcograf, S.p.A.

*For William, who once served the Word
and now helps shape mine.*

CONTENTS

CONTENTS

FOREWORD

MERVYN KING

Unai Emery has transformed Aston Villa in little more than two years. From the brink of relegation he built a winning team that in 2024–25 reached the quarter-finals of the Champions League with thrilling victories under the lights at Villa Park against Bayern Munich and Paris Saint-Germain. Since November 2022, when he took over as manager, he has piloted Aston Villa through the shoals of the Premier League as a major disruptor of the established order. One of the hardest tasks in any management role – whether football, business or in government – is to shake a team out of a sense that it is performing well enough and to energise the players and team to perform at a higher level than they themselves thought possible. How has he done this?

Guillem Balague has produced a fascinating description of how a top manager goes about managing world class players with egos and agents to match, creates a team structure with balance and instils belief in his players. It requires a relentless work ethic, rare enough in itself, as well as a deep knowledge of football and psychology. Players are not machines. Some are geniuses, others journeymen. Ideally a team has more of the former than the latter, although in practice both will be needed.

My own experience with organisations as diverse as central

banks, investment and commercial banks, orchestras, museums, as well as sports teams in tennis, cricket and football, is consistent with Balague's analysis of the qualities that are necessary for success and that characterise Unai Emery: passion, total commitment and hard work, and deep analysis of the challenges ahead, setting aside conventional wisdom and clichés. As with most major roles in an organisation, there are two key ingredients. First, you must have a clear vision of where you want to take the organisation or team, and to communicate that to everyone involved. Second, you must pay attention to details. If the person at the top combines those two attributes, then success will follow. By dint of dedication and hard work Unai has done this. I particularly like his philosophy of continuous improvement – every day to work on something and improve. There is room for improvement in every individual or team. And only players who respond to this call for greater aspirations, and avoid the trap of complacency, will rise to the heights needed to win trophies. Look at how Roger Federer changed and improved his game when he saw the rise of opponents such as Novak Djokovic and Rafael Nadal. Emery did the same after he was sacked by Arsenal. He evolved new tactical approaches while retaining his basic beliefs developed over many years as a coach. Standing still is not an option – only continuous improvement will keep you at the top.

Many football club owners fall into the trap of allowing a new manager to buy 'their' players and sell the players brought in by the previous manager. There is a policy of buying high and selling low. Inevitably, it is financially disastrous. Unai Emery transformed the Villa team with very much the same players he inherited. Only gradually has he added depth to the squad as the demands of European competition have created the need for a larger pool of first-team players. By making players understand that they must improve in both physical and mental discipline, Emery has helped them realise that their potential is higher than what they had become accustomed to. And players who remain content with their current level will be sold on. In the best possible way, Emery has been a disruptor in the Villa dressing room.

Emery is a disruptor not just on the playing side but in every aspect of how the club is run. And he has the full backing of the owners – Nassef Sawiris and Wes Edens – to do that. They too are disruptors – in their business careers and their ownership of Aston Villa. But they have been frustrated by the financial fair play rules which, based as they are on commercial revenues rather than, for example, team salary caps, give an advantage to teams based in London or with a track record of success. My own experience in the global financial crisis of recapitalising the banking system means that I empathise with the challenge facing Nassef, Wes and Unai of being a successful disruptor of entrenched conventional wisdom.

The trust between the owners and Unai Emery is fundamental to the transformation of Aston Villa. In any organisation, trust between the key people is crucial to success, and the experience at Aston Villa is an example to other organisations. Raising standards to a new level has often required the arrival of a disruptor. Think of the creation of franchises, such as the IPL in cricket, the English Premier League in football, the LIV tour in golf, and watch out for new initiatives in the world of tennis. To understand a disruptor requires us to understand their life in all its dimensions – background, beliefs, motivations and their families. Guillem Balague provides us with a picture of the journey which has taken Unai Emery from a modest background in the Basque country to international fame. Reading this book will help you understand the man and the reasons for his success.

Another key quality of Emery is the ability to use defeats as an opportunity to learn and improve. For many teams, an unexpected defeat lowers morale and performance levels. Not with Emery. In the final match of the 2024–25 season, with only 15 minutes remaining, the referee made a terrible mistake and disallowed a perfectly good goal by Aston Villa, thus depriving the club of Champions League football for the next season. Fans, players and neutral pundits were outraged. Emery, while understandably angry, will use it as motivation for the next season.

Understanding the way Unai Emery has transformed the sleeping giant of Aston Villa is a guide to success in any competitive or pressured environment. In this fascinating study of a highly successful top manager, Guillem Balague's task, as he puts it, 'was to observe and report the pursuit of excellence'. We can all learn from his description and analysis of the journey that Emery has taken with Aston Villa. Something special is stirring at Villa Park. The club that founded the Football League, and was for many years its most successful team, has returned from the wilderness and is once again one of Europe's top teams. Under the leadership of Unai Emery, and its two owners Nassef Sawiris and Wes Edens, Aston Villa is coming home.

INTRODUCTION:

THE TREASURE TO UNEARTH

Have you ever watched Tibetan Buddhist monks meticulously create intricate sand mandalas, only to destroy them moments after completion? These geometric masterpieces, crafted with coloured sand, symbolise life's impermanence and the beauty of the present moment. In many ways, football mirrors the essence of a mandala. Just like a tactical meeting before a match, each mandala begins with chants and prayers to sanctify the space and set intentions. The monks prepare a wooden board, typically covered with fabric to help the sand adhere – their pitch for artistic expression. The monks outline their designs with precision; concentric circles, squares and lines representing spiritual teachings. Similarly, coaches draw up patterns and formations. The soft, rhythmic vibration of the *chak-pur*, the funnel used to guide the sand, mirrors the hum of fans filling a stadium, their collective voices rising in anticipation. The calm before the storm. Each grain of sand is placed with meticulous care, the colours representing different qualities, such as purity, passion, wisdom. Just like football shirts. The creation of a mandala takes days or weeks. Repetition hones their craft to mastery, the same foundation of footballing excellence. When the mandala is complete, prayers are offered before it is revealed, akin to a manager giving his final

1

instructions before kick-off. And when the final whistle blows, at the end of the design, whether the outcome is success or failure, the next step is always the same. In a profound act symbolising impermanence, the mandala is destroyed. Football, too, is ephemeral. The match unfolds, captivates and then fades, leaving behind insights for the next game.

Is creating beauty or evoking emotion essential for life? For the soul, it is. We can't do without football, or without art. Both teach us about transformation, respect and that true fulfilment lies in the journey itself. I plan to take you on a journey: a trip into the world of Unai Emery and his work at Aston Villa, where every decision is the culmination of an obsessive passage through layers of knowledge, endless conversations and meticulous preparations of football mandalas. The detail, the relentless hours spent strategising – that much I knew. I had seen it at Almería, Valencia, Sevilla, Paris Saint-Germain and Arsenal. Yet his evolution as a coach remained elusive. How had he refined his craft? What exactly was he doing at Aston Villa to achieve such impressive results so quickly? My task was to observe and report the pursuit of excellence. But before I could decode the man – and the method – there was something I had to do first.

This book is not a history lesson. It won't dwell on the past glories of Aston Villa's European Cup win in 1982 or the domestic triumphs of the 1980s and 1990s. Instead, it is a snapshot of now – a moment in time when Aston Villa seem to be waking from a long, restless slumber. A club with roots stretching back to the very foundations of English football, now roaring back into relevance with Unai Emery at the helm, new ownership driving ambition and fans who've weathered decades of frustration and heartbreak acting as the club's bedrock.

Social media is a wondrous thing. I put one simple message out on X looking to create a conversation about the Midlands club that would put me on the right path. Shortly after, I found myself in the heart of Birmingham surrounded by a group of Aston Villa fans, who shared something more profound than mere support for a football club. For them, it is a way of life. Some create content related to the club (like music or podcasts), while others wanted to share their story. But what began as a casual enquiry into what makes this club special and why the arrival of Unai feels so significant, ended with a meeting filled with memories and revelations. Thanks to the hospitality of the Malt House pub, we sat with cameras rolling and microphones ready to record it all for future reference – and hearts opened. We explored the very essence of Aston Villa Football Club, something I did not know enough about.

The conversation began with introductions and each person brought a different story. Joe, a young journalist who's been a Villa fan for as long as he can remember, set the tone with his first game: a classic Villa roller coaster. '1–0 down at half-time against Newcastle, then a Wilfred Bouma goal and a John Carew hat-trick. Classic Villa, but we were successful in the end.' There it was, in one tale: the unpredictability, the drama, the wild hope that defines what it means to follow this club. Then there's Baz, a lawyer who hosts the *Talk of the Trinity* podcast. His first Villa game came before the Premier League even existed. 'It was March 1992, against QPR. We lost 1–0. The most memorable thing? The cheese and onion crisps.' I learnt very quickly that dry humour, the acceptance of disappointment, are part of Villa's DNA. Supporting this club, as Baz puts it, is a lesson in life. 'You set the bar low, so when the good times come, you appreciate them even more.'

Ben, a blogger, speaks of trauma. 'My first game was a 2–0 loss to Manchester United. I think I've been traumatised by them ever since.' For Simon, from the *Holtecast* podcast, the journey began with triumph. His first memory? The 1996 League Cup final. 'We battered Leeds 3–0. I thought I'd picked the right club. Little did I know that that was the peak . . . for a while. In my second game we beat Liverpool 1–0. Before the match, my nan said, "You're not going to win every game" and I came back shouting "We're the best team in the world". She knew better than me.' The confusion of starting with glory and then enduring decades of struggle.

And then there's Gemma, from the Villa and Proud group, who embodies Villa's generational pull. 'I got married at Villa Park the year we got relegated [2016]. On the pitch, it was a disaster. Off the pitch, it was the best day of my life.' The common paradox of being a Villa fan. 'My wedding at Villa Park wasn't just about football; it was about family, tradition and identity.' The club, a backdrop for life's milestones. 'We had photos in the dressing room, on the pitch, by the pitch, in the dugout. They made us a shirt with our wedding date and our new double-barrelled name on it. At the same time, some of the staff were unfortunately losing their jobs, obviously due to the relegation.'

Aston Villa is not just a club; it is a reflection of Birmingham itself. The city's diverse, industrious spirit is mirrored in the club's identity. As Ben describes it, 'Birmingham has a mix of cultures, is vibrant and is home. And that's what Villa is too.' This connection runs deep, threading through generations and binding people together. In Birmingham, supporting Villa isn't always a choice – it's an inheritance. 'You don't choose to support Aston Villa; Aston Villa chooses you.' Sam is a musician who wrote an anthem for Villa. A fan since 1993, his first game was 'like for many people, a pretty miserable experience. My dad broke his rib that day. It was raining. It was cold. It ended up 0–0, nothing happened. We went home and the car broke down. My dad got home and he had a big row with my mum. My dad surely had one of the worst days of his life . . . but I thought it was amazing. I guess that is what happens when you are a kid, you just fall in love with a football club.'

Birmingham isn't a one-club city. Rivalries abound, from Birmingham City to West Bromwich Albion, even to nearby Wolverhampton Wanderers. As Baz describes it, 'Supporting Villa in Birmingham is like having siblings. You're always arguing, always fighting for the biggest piece of the pie. But we're the top dogs, and we always have been.' This tussle for supremacy within the city creates a unique dynamic – one of pride, defiance, identity. TJ, whose dad worked as a cleaner at Villa Park when his family first arrived in England, now runs a football media company in London and tells a story of connection. 'Villa Park, 2022. Villa nil, Arsenal one. After the match, I was on the train back to London with Arsenal fans. You know how rowdy they can be – they ended up wrecking the wagon, and we were kicked off at Coventry. On the next train, I pulled out my charger and my Villa scarf fell out. I looked around and quickly hid it. I looked up again, relieved that nobody had seen it. But two older women, probably in their late sixties, noticed. One winked and said, "Tough loss for us, right?"' One more defeat, though. 'We're always seen as the cuddly teddy bear of the Premier League. Rivals had been thinking, *Yeah, let's play Villa, we'll have a nice time and we'll go away with a win.*'

Those born in the 1960s are generally fourth-generation Villa fans. Their great-grandad would have been there when Villa were winning constantly in the 1890s, and their grandad could have been present at games during the 1910 First Division title win. Their dad might have been one of the 76,588 present at Villa Park on 2 March 1946 in an FA Cup sixth-round tie against Derby County, the stadium's record attendance. And, after visiting the ground for the first time before they had even reached ten, they would never forget the sights, sounds and smells of a Saturday afternoon match. And they would want to take their own children too. That generation from the 1960s, now in their sixties today, grew up hearing stories about a period of glory that saw Villa win six First Division titles between 1894 and 1910, and the FA Cup several times, before themselves watching their crowning achievement. Under the management of Ron Saunders, the club clinched First Division silverware in 1981, paving the way for the subsequent European Cup triumph in 1982 under Tony Barton, the pinnacle of Aston Villa's historic success.

Our conversation in the Malt House also allowed us to recall Villa's prominence in the early era of the Premier League, years that created the first memories for most of those present at the pub. In the 1992–93 season Aston Villa finished second in the league, a reminder of the club's once-competitive stature, and finishing in the top six was a regular occurrence during that first decade. The 1996 League Cup victory was one of the most one-sided finals ever in the competition (it turned out to be the last major trophy the club has won to date). It set the expectation of future success. Under the management of John Gregory in the late 1990s, Villa even topped the league during January 1999 and the club had a memorable FA Cup semi-final against Bolton, resolved in their favour following a penalty shoot-out in April 2000. Everyone re-members that one. It was in fact Luke's, creator of the *Up the Villa* fan channel, first memory: 'I was just a kid surrounded by eupho-ria.' An intoxicating feeling. 'Flags on cars, in the windows of our houses. After a 0–0 game in normal time, it went to penalties, me and my brother just cheering that it had gone to pens. About thirty Villa fans turned around looking at us like, *What are you on about penalties?*' Later on in his life, Luke would have the misfortune to discover the cruelty of those moments.

6

What followed that FA Cup final loss to Gianluca Vialli's Chelsea was a steady decline, starting with the ownership of Randy Lerner. Initially, there was ambitious talk and significant investment, with improvement in the Bodymoor Heath training ground, especially during Martin O'Neill's tenure between 2006–2010, when Villa finished sixth three times in a row and narrowly missed out on Champions League qualification. However, after O'Neill's departure, insufficient funding saw the club spiral downwards, culminating in the disastrous period under manager Rémi Garde, in charge for only 147 days, which fans described as one of the worst times in their lives. Managers came and went, as Gérard Houllier, Alex McLeish and Paul Lambert all tried to stabilise the club, but their efforts fell short. The squad weakened, investment dried up and the club gradually slipped into successive relegation battles. The 2015–16 season proved disastrous, leading to Villa's demise to the Championship; the club had not been in the second tier for twenty-nine years. They are not meant to be there. This marked one of the darkest moments in the club's history.

In the Championship, the club's struggles continued. The Midlands club failed in their first two attempts at being promoted back to the Premier League. 'In those Championship years,' Simon recalls, 'I was still living at home. I look back now and feel so sorry for my mum and dad. I would get back home on a Saturday completely miserable. There was a reason why they were out every weekend – they didn't want to have to deal with me.' Aston Villa was on the brink of administration under the tumultuous ownership of Dr Tony Xia, who had bought the club in a £60 million deal in 2016 following their relegation. However, a lifeline arrived in the form of new owners Nassef Sawiris and Wes Edens, who took over in 2018, injecting fresh ambition, financial muscle and stability. Dean Smith's appointment as manager later that year marked the beginning of a slow resurgence. Smith, a lifelong Villa fan whose father had been a steward at Villa Park, brought renewed passion, galvanised the fans and provided the foundation for future growth. With the leadership of the talented academy youngster Jack Grealish, Villa achieved promotion back to the Premier League in 2019 through the play-offs. 'When we were on that journey,' Luke remembers, 'that ten-game winning streak, getting to the play-offs, winning the play-offs, getting back into the Premier League, maintaining our position in the Premier League, it was just absolutely amazing.'

The return to the top-flight was a relief, but survival remained a challenge, as TJ points out. 'We've had how many owners in the last twenty years? From when I was thirteen to twenty-four, Aston Villa has been through three or four different periods, but it always felt as if nothing could make us stable.' Dean Smith was not able to break free from the lower half of the table. The sale of Grealish to Manchester City for £100 million funded changes in the squad, but the brief and ill-fated tenure of Steven Gerrard, who replaced Smith as manager in 2021, saw the club flirt with relegation once again. 'The month before Unai Emery came in, we played Chelsea at home,' Baz remembers. 'I got a free ticket from a mate of mine and I was thinking about demanding my money back at the end of the game. We were absolutely dreadful. After the match, Gerrard basically said, according to a fan, *What do you expect? It's Chelsea. They've got all these players, they've got all this money. Look at what I've got at Villa.* He didn't say we were a bunch of losers, but close. In the game before he got sacked, the 3–0 away defeat against Fulham, I thought, just after thirty seconds, *Yeah, we're gonna lose here.*' The end of hope, it seemed.

By late 2022, it was clear that Aston Villa needed a transformative figure – someone who could unlock the club's potential and return them to their former glory. Aston Villa's ownership was about to follow, perhaps inadvertently, the Gucci resurgence. The brand experienced a revival driven by visionary leadership, strategic reinvention and a renewed identity. Nearing bankruptcy in the early 1990s, it found salvation with Tom Ford as creative director in 1994. He redefined Gucci's image with bold, modern designs, implementing fresh strategies that revitalised the company. In the same way, Villa was aiming to recapture its historic footballing prestige, Gucci sought to reclaim its luxury trendsetter status. Its upturn influenced pop culture and luxury fashion.

The fashion brand's story, highlights the power of strategic leadership, and the need for rebranding and cultural connection to achieve a successful comeback. Aston Villa was replicating the strategy and hoping to achieve a similar outcome. The man chosen to turn around the fortunes of the club on the pitch was Unai Emery, a manager known for his tactical acumen and European success, and whose choice symbolised the ambition of the club. The sleeping giant wanted to stir again.

Emery arrived at a time of despair. His first game, a 3–1 win over Manchester United, was a statement of intent. Baz sums it up perfectly: 'He took the same players Gerrard dismissed and turned them into winners.' Where Gerrard saw limitations, Emery saw potential. He brought structure and tactical discipline that had been missing. The team, picked up by Emery in seventeenth, ended that 2022–23 season in seventh place, qualifying for European competition. In just a short period, Unai changed fans' expectations. 'I thought I knew football,' Luke confesses, 'but Emery has shown me things I never imagined. He's transformed us.'

'One of the biggest things for me in that first season he arrived happened around the January, February period, when he had been in charge three months or so and we lost three matches in a row,' Simon recalls. 'Defeats against Leicester, who would end up being relegated, Arsenal and Manchester City. Especially against Leicester, we expected to win. And we lost 4–2. But the team kept playing exactly the same way for the whole ninety minutes, building from the back and all that, that style was taking us a while to get on board with. I remember coming away from that game, thinking, *I'm glad they stuck to playing the way that he wants them to play, even though it didn't work today.* It was a turning point not just for the players on the pitch, but for the fans, too, to just accept that style and leadership. This is exactly what this man [Emery] wants us to do. We best buy into it, because it is not going to change. From that moment on, we all bought into it. And we went on a ten-match unbeaten run, with eight wins in the process, and clean sheets in most of them.'

But Emery is more than a tactician. There is ambition in everything he does. As Joe puts it, 'He's earned our trust. We believe in his vision, in his plan. He's not just a manager; he's a leader.' And yet, Emery remains something of a mystery. 'He often looks like shit, doesn't he?' Sam jokes. 'Like how a detective would look having spent all night away trying to find solutions to the latest crime.' His meticulous methods, his pursuit of improvement and his reserved public persona leave fans curious. What drives him? What does success look like in his eyes? Is this club his place in the world, has he been looking for something like this in order to shine, or to be happy? The language barrier accentuates Unai's status as an enigma. People know he is obsessed and tenacious. They see him walking along the Birmingham canals, his eyes set looking far into the distance, they know he lives in the city centre. They clearly get his message: *We are going to places, and you are coming with me.* But how is he doing it?

Simon captures this tension: 'He's a genius, but we're terrified he'll leave. We've waited so long for someone like him. Just give us a trophy, any trophy. We need it.' This fear underscores the fragile optimism Villa fans are learning to embrace. Emery has raised the bar, and the challenge now is to keep up, to support his vision on the pitch and off it as well. But with that ambition comes pressure. The goal is clear: to establish Villa as a consistent presence in European football. But how does a club with Villa's history but not with the recent success or equal finances of the biggest clubs, bridge the gap to the modern elite?

Adam, a marketing man who organised the pub meeting, lays bare the challenge: 'Our commercial revenue is miles behind the teams we're trying to compete with. We need strategic partnerships, smart investments. Increasing ticket prices alone won't cut it.' This commercial reality is the unglamorous side of football's modern arms race. 'This summer of 2024 we got into the Champions League and we only spent a net six million pounds on that squad,' Adam explains with a worried look. Fans feel the pinch, especially when Champions League nights come with a steep price tag. Most people, but not all, understand progress demands sacrifice. 'We're going somewhere, but we're going fast,' Luke observes. Can the ownership sustain this pace without alienating the fans who are the heart of the club?

As we wrapped up our conversation, more questions hung in the air. What is Unai Emery's ultimate vision for Aston Villa? How does he see his journey with the club unfolding? What would he consider a successful era? What are his core values? What happened in the eighteen months he was in charge of Arsenal? How do the players view Emery's methods? What is the club's plan for commercial growth? How will they balance ambition with the values and traditions that make Villa special? Why has he bought a football club in Spain, Real Unión? These questions will form the backbone of this book, so I'm looking to delve deeper than football tactics, business strategies and what qualities make Unai Emery special.

Aston Villa is waking up. The slumbering giant is stretching its limbs, eyes wide with the promise of glory. The fans feel it. The city feels it. There's a sense that something special is happening, a feeling that after years of wandering in the wilderness, Villa is finally coming home to where it belongs. This book is an attempt to capture the moment by listening to the people who make Aston Villa what it is: the fans, the players, the manager, the assistants, the personnel, the owners.

Every story begins with a hero – a figure with a bold goal and an arduous path. The higher the stakes, the more compelling the journey. Chaos strikes, obstacles block the way and tension mounts. Facing enemies constantly, the hero must fight and adapt, and his struggle keeps us hooked. In the end, he overcomes the hurdles, tension is resolved. But, to make the story relevant, the rise of Aston Villa should mirror, somehow, at some level, our own story.

To unearth that treasure, I must walk the corridors of Bodymoor Heath training ground.

So, come with me.

PART I:
THE LION

1

LANDING IN BIRMINGHAM:

THE FIRST WIN

Unai Emery once toyed with the idea of acquiring the trademark for 'Good ebening' and stamping it on T-shirts, mugs and notebooks. After all, his polite greeting to the media had become something of a phenomenon. A compilation of his 'Good ebening's on YouTube has amassed 4.5 million views. In Spain, 'v' and 'b' both sound like 'b', so in the beginning it was endearing, a gentle humour that celebrated his effort to speak English and revealed a glimpse of his personality.

Yet, football is a ruthless storyteller and narratives shift with results. What started as a symbol of charm turned into a tool for mockery. When Emery's promising start at Arsenal – one that included reaching the Europa League final in the first season of the post-Wenger era – began to unravel early in his second season, his accent suddenly became a weapon used against him. In the eyes of some, the way he said 'evening' was enough to undermine his competence. It was reductive, even xenophobic, to repeat that caricature of his pronunciation, reinforcing tired stereotypes of non-native speakers. Months later the derision spilled into real life when a group of teenagers spotted him stepping off Villarreal's team bus. 'Good ebening!' they shouted mockingly, adding sarcastic praise for his time at Arsenal. Emery, who is typically composed, responded with a half-smile – and a middle finger held long enough to ensure it was captured on camera. An act of defiance that carried layers of meaning.

Football, after all, thrives on simple statements – heroes and villains, successes and failures – crafted to engage emotionally rather than analytically. Most fans don't dissect tactics; they latch on to symbols. 'Good ebening' became one of those symbols, a convenient scapegoat for complex problems. It's reminiscent of a story from Kobe Bryant's rookie season in the NBA. Playing for the Los Angeles Lakers, Bryant, who was renowned for his intense search of excellence, missed four crucial shots during crunch time in the fifth game of the Conference semi-finals. After the game, Bryant sat on the bench, his hands on his head. When asked later about his feelings at that moment, his response was stark: 'Feelings? I was working out why I missed those shots. I now know why, and I can do something about it.' Emery's middle finger carried the same energy. It was his way of saying: *I know what happened. I know how it can be fixed. And I don't care what you think of my past.* The gesture is a fitting place to begin a book about the new era he is leading at Aston Villa. It sets the stage with a setback – a sacking – and the laughter of critics.

Clearly the story of Unai Emery could have started differently, with a list of his achievements. For instance: achieving promotion with Lorca Deportiva in his inaugural season as a coach; leading, well ahead of expectations, Almería to LaLiga for the first time in the club's history; still in his late thirties, qualifying for the Champions League three seasons in a row with the ever-demanding and financially restrained Valencia; winning three consecutive Europa League titles with Sevilla; lifting seven trophies with PSG in just two campaigns, where his team got numerous points and goalscoring records that still remain. Our story could also have begun by highlighting Emery's role in shaping some of the best talent in world football: David Silva, David Villa, Juan Mata, Jordi Alba, Ivan Rakitić, Neymar, Kylian Mbappé, Edinson Cavani, Marco Verratti, Pierre-Emerick Aubameyang, Bukayo Saka and Pau Torres, to name just a few. However, the middle finger is better. It's raw, unpolished and unapologetic – dedicated to those who see a sacking as a definitive failure rather than the start of something new.

Yet, that confidence in front of a phone camera had a backstory. It wasn't always so easy for Emery to look back at his time at Arsenal. Of course, it hurt, not so much because of the results or the sacking; it was the feeling that he hadn't been given the tools or the time to truly succeed. It took him months to fully process what had gone wrong and, more importantly, what he needed to do differently. His dismissal in autumn 2019 was met with relief by many fans, but Emery resented the story that emerged, portraying him as a figure of fun. This oversimplification ignored the deeper issues within the club. While he acknowledged his mistakes, he also pointed to a fractured leadership, an imbalanced squad and a lack of alignment, even support, between management and coaching staff. He felt isolated in the crisis, without the protection he might have expected from those in charge.

The Covid-19 pandemic that followed provided Emery with an unexpected opportunity for reinvention. By the time Villarreal came calling, eight months after his departure from Arsenal, Emery had taken the time to reflect deeply on his methods, on the evolution of football and on how best to position himself to catch the right train back to the elite. He was ready, not just to lead again, but to do so fully on his own terms.

He needed a club where he could rediscover himself and have full command of his surroundings, where every victory or defeat would be primarily his responsibility. At the same time, while recovering strength and confidence, he sought to improve his English. Unai also felt the need to return home. He longed for the pleasures of family stability, using the time to strengthen his bond with his son, Lander, who lived in Valencia. At seventeen, Lander was a young goalkeeper, following in the footsteps of his paternal grandfather and great-grandfather. Having missed much of his father's European adventures, Lander had reached that challenging stage of life where the relationship between father and son changes. So, moving to Villarreal, just 60 kilometres from Valencia, seemed like the logical next step for Unai. Although his representatives had doubts, he was convinced it was the right move. When Villarreal approached, he took charge, negotiating directly with the club's directors. He understood the risks. 'Either I stay where I am, achieving targets like regular European qualification, which would be amazing, or I decline, which could happen. Moving upward is very difficult,' he reflected at the time. Another question remained in his mind: *When will I be ready to return to the Premier League?*

In 2020, Villarreal had never won a major trophy in nearly a century of existence. It had been transformed by the vision of Fernando Roig, whom since taking ownership in 1997 had elevated the club from a modest team in a city of 51,000 inhabitants to the upper echelons of Spanish football and international recognition. The chemistry between owner and manager produced instant results and Emery cemented his reputation as one of Europe's top managers. In his first season, he won the Europa League, his fourth title in the competition. Villarreal defeated Manchester United in a dramatic final, which ended 1–1 and was decided by a penalty shoot-out (11–10). Gerónimo Rulli, Villarreal's Argentinian goalkeeper, scored the winning penalty. Emery had proven his worth once again on a grand stage and in front of the audience he longed to rejoin. Was the Premier League paying attention?

By November 2021, during his second season, Newcastle United expressed interest in Emery as a replacement for Steve Bruce. 'Tell them to call me directly and not beat around the bush,' he instructed when informed by an agent. Shortly after, Amanda Staveley, representing Newcastle's owners, contacted him. A Zoom meeting followed with Crown Prince Mohammed bin Salman, chairman of the Saudi Public Investment Fund (PIF), which owned 80 per cent of the club. The offer, promising control over sporting matters and substantial finances, was very compelling. The day after the call, Emery got confirmation that the English club wanted him to be their new boss.

Before Villarreal's Champions League home encounter against Young Boys, Unai met with Fernando Jr, the owner's son who oversees the day-to-day operations of the club. The coach shared the news of Newcastle's interest. 'Let's discuss it calmly after the game,' Fernando Jr told him. Still, a sense of uncertainty inevitably crept into the VIP seats. Just before kick-off, a story broke in the British media claiming there was an agreement between Newcastle and Unai. It stated that the Spanish coach would travel to England after the match and begin training his new team by Friday. The timing of the leak felt deliberate, but the information was false.

Unai was curious about Newcastle's plans, but no financial agreement or contract details had been discussed. Since the Roig family was aware of the conversations, it wasn't expected to cause any internal issues. Following Villarreal's 2–0 victory over Young Boys – which boosted their chances of progressing in the tournament – Unai was questioned about the situation just minutes after the final whistle. Emery was visibly surprised and annoyed. 'I have no news beyond their interest,' he told Cristina Bea of

Spanish TV station Movistar+, the first journalist he spoke to. 'I need to respect this squad and this club.' The press conference was tense, with questions assuming his departure. Newcastle, overly confident, had underestimated Unai's commitment to Villarreal. The leak and its fallout helped to clarify Emery's next step.

Emery felt he was a recognised manager but still needed a major success story in the Champions League. Progressing to the next round, in a group that included Manchester United and Atalanta, required a visit to Bergamo and a good result. Yet, he believed his team was competitive and capable of making a strong impression in Europe. That was crucial.

Unai met both Roigs after the match and assured them the final decision would be taken very quickly. It was a long night. On the drive home, Unai spent over an hour on the phone with Damià Vidagany, the former director of communications at Valencia and a close confidant ever since. His career had spanned journalism, club media, and by then representation work with DV7 Management, the agency led by David Villa. Unai had always valued Damià's deep understanding of football and knew he could be invaluable in helping him navigate the challenges he faced. The manager felt appreciated by Newcastle, but also realised that the way events had unfolded were not right. He decided to close the door on the Premier League club.

He called Villarreal's owner: 'Fernando, I am staying 100 per cent. Zero doubts.' At that point, it was crucial to dispel any external uncertainty to the outside world. Damià worked late into the night, making calls to ensure the story of Unai's decision to stay at Villarreal was promptly shared. The next day, Unai announced it all via a statement on social media. He told his inner circle: 'I will have my Premier League club, but it will be another time.' Feeling reinvigorated, he wanted to give the Champions League his all, testing how far Villarreal could go. Newcastle tried to reinitiate conversations, effectively asking him to name his price. However, Unai refused to engage any further. He told the English club he had given his word to Villarreal and would not go back on it.

From that moment, his authority within Villarreal grew stronger. Fearing he might leave in the future, players and staff rallied around him, fully committing to his leadership. In their final group match, Villarreal travelled to Bergamo but the game had to be postponed due to heavy snowfall at the Gewiss Stadium. The following December day Villarreal secured a dramatic 2–3 victory, sealing their runners-up spot and a place in the Champions League round of 16 at the expense of Atalanta. They went on to eliminate giants like Juventus (1–4 on aggregate in the round of 16) and Bayern Munich (1–2 on aggregate in the quarter-finals). Though they eventually fell to Liverpool in the semi-finals, Villarreal earned widespread praise for their intelligent performances. Unai took pride in having elevated Villarreal to punch above their weight in Europe's most prestigious competition.

By the end of that season, Emery had one year left on his contract. Many around him believed that if Villarreal offered him an extension, even for just one extra year, it would have been difficult for him to say no. However, Villarreal faced significant financial challenges. The club's stability depended on Pamesa Cerámica, the Roig family's main business, a prominent Spanish company specialising in the production of ceramic tiles, which was heavily affected by skyrocketing gas prices following the outbreak of war in Ukraine. While Villarreal could have improved and extended Unai's contract, keeping him required more than a renewal. It demanded a strengthened commitment to the project, retaining key players, making new signings. Unai thrives in environments where tangible progress is visible. He needs to believe the club has the resources to build on the previous season's success. For him, stagnation is unacceptable. But, known for their integrity, the Roigs were cautious and, as a result, they decided to wait before presenting a renewal.

Damià, as well as Unai, was close to Fernando Roig Jr so from time to time, he would convey what he thought might be good for both Villarreal and the manager. 'For Unai, leaving Villarreal was very, very hard,' Damià says. 'The calm, the structure, and the support he had there were incredibly important. He did not want to leave.' But it felt the door had been opened by the club. The real turning point came after the final match of his last full season at Villarreal, that ended with a victory at the Camp Nou and European qualification. Unai went to lunch with Fernando Roig Sr and Jr expecting a forward-looking conversation about the future of the club. Instead, what he encountered was something far more hesitant. Unai understood the broader socio-economic context, but he did not get a determined plan to continue building the project with ambition. He felt no disrespect. He knew Villarreal valued him highly. But he also sensed that, after their Champions League run and their qualification to the Conference League, with the financial hit that implied, the club was not in a position to sustain the level of investment his ambitions required.

So, four months later, by late October 2022, with the gas crisis still unresolved and before Villarreal could propose not just a contract extension but a renewed vision for the future, super-agent Jorge Mendes re-entered the picture.

Jorge Mendes had always nurtured a warm and close relationship with Unai Emery, built on years of trust and mutual respect that dated back to their time together at Sevilla. Mendes had been instrumental in shaping opportunities for Unai, ensuring he received offers from clubs such as Benfica and Napoli. When Rafa Benítez signed for Real Madrid, Emery's name had also been mentioned as a possible candidate for the job, which was Mendes's work too.

Yet, when Unai joined PSG, it was without the need for intermediaries. The call came directly from the club. The first words they said were: 'You'll have Neymar.' Later, they added: 'We're also going to sign Mbappé.' The whirlwind began. Unai first met with Mbappé's father, then with the player himself and later with his mother. At just eighteen, the young forward was already remarkable – not just on the pitch but also in his approach to his career. 'I want a team like Messi's,' Mbappé told Unai, 'where even if I have a bad day, I'm not easily dropped. I don't want to be the first one taken out.' His maturity was striking. Real Madrid had offered €180 million, a bid Monaco had accepted, and Jorge Mendes was acting as the intermediary between the two clubs. But in the end, Mbappé chose PSG, who offered the same €180 million but structured as a deferred payment to be finalised the following year. Unai's move to Arsenal, however, was handled by another agent, Arturo Canales. Mendes had, in fact, tried to push Julen Lopetegui for the Arsenal role, but the club chose Unai instead.

Fast forward to Villarreal, where Unai rebuilt his reputation with two strong seasons. Yet, the pull of returning to the Premier League remained an irresistible goal. So, after the remarkable 2021–22 Champions League, Unai turned to Jorge Mendes with a simple request: 'Let's see if you can find me a team.' Mendes's response was swift and confident: 'Challenge accepted.'

Manchester United and Chelsea were both searching for managers that summer, but ultimately passed on Unai. The shadow of his Arsenal tenure still loomed over him in England. Mendes then brought up Aston Villa to Unai – the club that had been quietly monitoring him for years but didn't initially seem like the right fit. However, Mendes had a strong relationship with one of Villa's owners, Nassef Sawiris, and knew there was genuine admiration there. Before buying Aston Villa, Sawiris had been a follower of Arsenal. There was a particular match that stayed with him: Villa at the Emirates, shortly after he and Wes Edens had acquired the club. Villa went 0–2 up. Arsenal went down to ten men. Yet, Unai made a series of brave, tactical substitutions that turned the game around. Arsenal won 3–2. The impact lingered. Sawiris continued following Unai's work at Villarreal, and with each passing year his admiration deepened. He saw beyond the tactician.

One October morning in 2022, Damià was out for a morning walk along the river in Valencia when his phone rang. It was Unai. Expecting it to be a casual call to arrange breakfast, Damià was caught off-guard by Unai's urgency: 'No, get dressed properly. We're going to Madrid. I'll explain in the car.' On the way, Unai informed him that Nassef Sawiris had asked Mendes to arrange lunch. 'No commitments, just an introduction,' he said. Emery's English, still a work in progress, added tension to the trip. As they drove, he and Damià rehearsed key talking points. This meeting wasn't about money; it was about structure. 'The difference between Manchester City and Manchester United isn't oil money – it's the people,' Damià said. 'City works because Ferran Soriano, Txiki Begiristain and Pep Guardiola form a triangle of understanding and protection. That's the blueprint.' Unai nodded. Damià and Unai shared the belief that a manager – who, unless you have a Messi or Ronaldo, is the most valuable asset at a club – must be surrounded by a protective circle. This circle should consist of people who understand him deeply, anticipate his needs before he even expresses them and clear the path for him, like steamrollers preparing the ground before the road is laid. Emery wanted to avoid the disjointed leadership he had experienced at Arsenal, where decisions like signing Nicolas Pépé and Sokratis Papastathopoulos had disrupted his intentions. Unai doesn't like the word 'project', they were not to use that word in the meeting. When he hears it, he pulls back because he knows that, more often than not, it's just a cliché of football jargon that rarely gets fulfilled. If you lose four games, the 'project' is over.

Jorge Mendes offered his home in Madrid for the encounter, and some members of his team were present. Nassef, with an unsettled stomach, flew in from London. Unai and Damià explained that the difference between success and failure often comes down to time. With the right ingredients, success can be immediate, but if it takes longer, you need time to make it happen. How do you secure that time? By putting in place safeguards against drastic decisions: a strong contract, a long-term agreement and a structure that keeps everyone informed about the steps being taken – one that is fully aligned with the ownership too. The manager should not be a scapegoat. Villa's issue, they pointed out, wasn't just a coaching problem, it went deeper than that; it was one of mentality. After twenty years without European football and fifteen managers in that time frame, something fundamental had to change.

Nassef wasn't there to offer a job. Or a 'project'. He wanted Unai to design one. Handing him a blank piece of paper, he said, 'Draw the club you need to succeed, not just the team, but everything. What do you need to make Aston Villa winners?' Not so much a proposal to *Sit on my bench*, but rather Nassef was saying, *Here's the key to the house.* Unai didn't fill the blank page during that meeting, but he was intrigued. Nassef's promises felt genuine. Still, something more was needed. Nassef picked up the phone and called Wes Edens. 'This,' Sawiris said, 'is not just a commitment from me, but also from my partner.' Wes' words carried weight, 'We're both fully behind this project. We promise to support you financially. I'm genuinely excited about the possibility of having you at the club, and I really hope we can convince you.'

Villa's storied history, loyal fans and potential resonated with Unai. *Villa is a sleeping giant,* Unai thought. At that moment, he wasn't considering leaving Villarreal, though his contract was set to expire in eight months' time. Still, he needed space to think. From Unai's perspective, the conversation was geared towards the following season, 2023–24. The interest from Liverpool, Bayern Munich and Manchester United was not converted into offers nor had it even led to conversations with decision makers within the clubs. What Aston Villa offered him, however, was total trust in his capabilities. But at Villarreal, Unai felt secure. The club was in the Europa Conference League, although performing modestly in LaLiga. He mentioned Aston Villa's interest to Fernando Roig Jr but didn't dwell on it. As Villarreal still hadn't offered him a renewal, and with just seven months left on his contract, it gave him some freedom.

Then things accelerated. During the following two weeks, Villa's results plummeted with a draw against Nottingham Forest, a loss to Chelsea, both at home, and a 3–0 defeat at Fulham leaving them seventeenth in the Premier League, level with the relegation zone. Mendes called Unai: 'They want you now. They'll pay your release clause.' When he joined Villarreal, he ensured his contract protected both sides: if Villarreal underperformed, they could release him without cost. If a major project came calling, he could leave for an agreed fee that felt generous. The release clause was €6 million. It wasn't the first time the signing of Unai Emery required a release clause to be activated either. Back in the summer of 2016,

PSG paid the €2 million stipulated in the Basque coach's contract with Sevilla.

Villarreal had gained millions in revenue during his leadership. The Europa League title and reaching the Champions League semi-finals had led to increased sponsorship deals. Letting him go wasn't ideal, but it wasn't catastrophic either. Villarreal had the chance to secure the equivalent of two years' salary for a top LaLiga manager to replace him.

For Unai, the decision to leave would eventually boil down to three factors. Villarreal weren't in the Champions League, the club couldn't offer a long-term project and the coach knew he was going somewhere he was not only wanted but also where he could grow. On the same day as Villa's defeat to Fulham, Villarreal mourned the passing of José Manuel Llaneza, a great supporter of Unai's, someone admired by all and a key figure in the club's modern transformation. After the funeral, Unai met with Fernando Roig Jr for a coffee. 'It's the Premier League,' he said. 'I need to seriously think about it.' Two days later, Villarreal beat Almería 2–1. The victory lifted them to seventh place. In the locker room, Fernando Roig Sr approached Unai: 'How can you leave now? What's happening?' Unai promised to decide by the next day.

He chose to leave. His relationship with the Roig family has not changed one bit since then.

On Monday 24 October 2022, Villarreal announced Unai's departure. That same day, Aston Villa confirmed him as their new manager, with his official start date set for 1 November 2022. Villa fans, desperate for a world-class leader, embraced him with hope. The target had been clear from the meeting with Sawiris: Aston Villa would aim to make up for lost time and restore the relevance the club held in the 1970s, '80s and early '90s.

Unai turned to Damià Vidagany with a straightforward question:

would he join him and help him settle into this challenge? Unai envisioned a structure that was clear and collaborative, populated by people who understood his vision and could execute it. His focus would remain firmly on football, but he also recognised that a club was more than the sum of its tactical moves. Damià and his chosen people could breathe life into the atmosphere. Without that motivation, the project would falter before it even began. His old friend agreed without hesitation. The specifics – role, salary, duration – were irrelevant. He would help Unai build a project, awaken the giant.

'Let's go,' Vidagany said, leaving his wife Montiel and his kids Roman and Gerard behind, only temporarily. From a distance they offered their constant support and reminded him of the many benefits of what he was about to embark on. 'We will join you soon,' Damià heard for a while. None of this is easy, one of the many realities football conceals behind its glamour.

Accompanied by his right-hand man, as well as Mendes, Unai flew to London for the formalities. Before heading to Birmingham, they stopped at Nassef Sawiris's home for a relaxed dinner brimming with discussions about the future. It felt to all like an opportunity to take a raw block of stone and sculpt it into something enduring. From London, Unai and Damià drove to Birmingham, ready to immerse themselves in what lay ahead. As the car turned on to the narrow road that leads to Bodymoor Heath, fences enclosing the training pitches came into view. A 20-mile-per-hour speed limit sign prompted Unai to smile softly, the job was not going to be done at that pace. This training ground was a canvas, his laboratory. The car turned left, where the security guard, Big Matt, greeted him at the main gate with a hearty Brummie welcome. Each handshake and introduction as he made his way to the main building felt like assembling tools for a craftsman's workbench.

The training centre was a state-of-the-art facility, and it soon dawned on Unai that it had its own established dynamics, routines and comforts. Emery's team of ten Spanish assistants, that he was originally bringing with him, would face a new reality they were more than willing to challenge. The massive gym offered everything from weight training to sprint tracks, its glass walls connecting players inside to the pitches outside. A hydrotherapy area nearby simplified water-based recovery, replacing the need for distant pools. Passing the boot room, the mingled scents of leather and freshly cut grass reminded Unai of the essence of this sport. Upstairs, his office awaited him. It was practical and well equipped, with a whiteboard, a table, a sofa, a shelf unit and a TV. Positioned with a clear view of the pitches, the adjoining balcony stretched across the first floor, providing a vantage point for Unai (as well as his team of assistants, analysers and data gatherers in nearby offices) to observe the men's first team. Further afield, separate facilities housed the Under 23s and the women's squad.

Before even stepping on to the pitch, Unai had prepared his first words to the players, who had been filtering in throughout the morning. He knew he didn't want to sound like a saviour or magician. In the gym, flanked by his new assistants, he gathered the group. He let a few seconds pass, studying their expectant faces, willing his English to hold steady. As a former player, he understood the weight of a first impression. 'I'm not happy; I'm sad because a colleague of mine, Steven Gerrard, has been sacked. He was not the only one responsible for what went wrong here. He's not the only one. You are responsible. You and everyone in the club. We cannot always put the blame on the coach. And something else: I didn't come here to waste my time. I've come here to win things.'

In those few moments, two things became clear to the players.

First, his message was direct, unyielding. Second, they would all need to raise their game. However, the real discovery would come in the four training sessions before their next game, a home fixture against Manchester United.

The arrival of Unai marked a departure from the old-school style, where a distant manager observed from afar. Instead, Villa now had a scientific army of football minds: Rodri, not the City player, but Antonio Rodríguez, a veteran coach in the second and third tier of Spanish football; Pako Ayestarán, who had Premier League experience; and Pablo Villanueva (known as Pablo Villa), a decade-long confidant who shared Unai's methodical, analytical approach. They had watched every single game of Villa's that season. The priority was not so much to assess the team's physical condition but to evaluate its organisation and structure. The coaches concluded Aston Villa weren't disorganised, but their approach relied heavily on chaotic end-to-end play – classic English football.

In theory, the new coaching staff had four days of training sessions to prepare for their first match, against Manchester United at Villa Park. The contract had been signed, and Unai Emery's assistants were able to step on to the pitch to lead training. However, Emery himself was not allowed to until the second day, he couldn't even wear the club tracksuit before then. Brexit-related paperwork remained unresolved, preventing him from officially taking charge. That limited the time he had to directly influence the team ahead of his Sunday debut. As a result, the first session was overseen by Pablo Villa, Pako Ayestarán and analyst Víctor Mañas. Unai asked them to focus the initial sessions on shape and control, urging the team to gain time by favouring more passes. Yet he knew there wasn't enough time to fully implement a perfectly advanced defensive line or to establish clearly defined roles and responsibilities. That level of understanding required consistency and, above all, patience – a winding road rather than a straight path. These would come later.

Training often revealed habits ingrained in the squad's style. Players would shoot from the edge of the box even when it wasn't the best choice. Crosses were delivered aimlessly without assessing whether a forward was in position. A cross, Unai repeated, had to be a pass. This was a change of perspective. Leaving the comfort zone was disorientating, even terrifying, for some. Unai wasn't just tweaking tactics; he was changing the way they thought about football. Yet a spark ignited almost immediately. First, the squad felt the weight of having a title-winning coach. Next, they saw a manager willing to roll up his sleeves, one they could learn from. Unai was from the start 24/7 football. His presence altered the atmosphere at Bodymoor Heath. Players arrived with a new sense of purpose, staying after sessions to discuss the work. 'We've gone from black-and-white football to full colour' was a statement heard in the canteen. Senior players like Emiliano Martínez, Ollie Watkins, John McGinn and Lucas Digne embraced the change. Their enthusiasm became contagious.

To keep that new feeling of harmony, one decision was critical: who would wear the captain's armband? In England, the role of captain carries profound significance. Johan Lange, Villa's sporting director, had travelled to Valencia to brief Unai on the squad and club dynamics. He suggested that a potential change of the captain could be positive, noting that Steven Gerrard's decision to strip Tyrone Mings of the captaincy had alienated a key player in the squad. It was a delicate issue that required careful handling. The opinion of Christian Purslow had to be sought. He was the club's chief executive officer and was also in charge of sporting decisions, although he was not always present as he didn't live in the Midlands. It was necessary to gather information and conduct a situational analysis before rocking the boat too much. John McGinn was serving as captain following Steven Gerrard's decision to appoint him earlier in the year, and Emery chose to maintain that leadership structure. The intention was to provide stability during a turbulent period of change.

In fact, danger loomed on the pitch. A negative result against Manchester United could push them into the relegation zone. The following game was against third-placed Brighton, the season's revelation. Two defeats would surely leave Villa in the bottom three heading into the six-week break due to the World Cup in Qatar. Some tactical variations for playing out from the back, as well as where and when to apply pressure, had been prepared with the intention to surprise Erik ten Hag's fifth-placed United. Villa started with two changes to their previous line-up: Lucas Digne replaced Ashley Young at left-back, and academy player Jacob Ramsey, 21, came into midfield. Leon Bailey, normally a winger, paired with Ollie Watkins in the attacking set-up. McGinn was on the bench. 'Guys, this is a new start. You can compete against anyone in this league,' Unai told his players before they walked out of the changing room and into the tunnel.

The atmosphere crackled with expectation. Unai, hands in his pockets, visibly focused, was loudly cheered as he stepped out just before kick-off. Giving a thumbs-up was perhaps not the most natural greeting to the fans, but that was what he did, perhaps feeling a bit uncomfortable with so much attention on him. The match erupted straight from kick-off and did not abate as Villa struck early. Leon Bailey, assisted by Ramsey and quicker to the ball than United's centre back Lisandro Martínez, scored in the 7th minute. Moments later, Lucas Digne's curling free kick doubled the lead as he slotted home at the near post.

32

Unai was highly active in the technical area, issuing instructions, arms outstretched, demanding full commitment and pointing to exactly where the next pass should go. The performance was impressive so far, but at this club, things are rarely ever easy. A deflected Luke Shaw shot pulled one back before half-time. Ramsey felt very comfortable with the new set-up and restored the two-goal cushion early in the second half. Villa played with confidence and limited United's chances until the end of the match, securing a 3–1 victory – their first home win over United in twenty-seven years. Villa Park exploded with joy. It felt like the club had finally broken free from years of gloom. It was not just any win. Baz was in the Holte End. His voice cracked as he described the scene. 'It wasn't just loud, it was primal. People weren't just cheering; they were screaming, crying, hugging strangers. When Bailey scored so early, it was like a dam had burst. We've had moments of joy before, but this felt different. It was like the entire stadium believed again, as if we'd collectively been waiting for this exact moment to breathe life back into the club.'

This was Unai's first eleven and substitutions for that match: Martínez, Cash, Konsa, Mings, Digne (Young 79'), Luiz, Buendía (Ings 79'), Dendoncker (Sanson 90'), Ramsey, Watkins (Kamara 78'), Bailey (McGinn 70'). The win moved Aston Villa up to thirteenth, 3 points clear of the relegation zone. The Spanish manager used the victory to set a target in the press conference. 'This win is special, not just because of the result, but because of the belief the team showed from day one. I want Villa Park to be a place where opponents feel something special. It's the first step. We have to be demanding.' The atmosphere was electric in the changing room. There were handshakes, hugs, singing, dancing and a sense that something new had just started.

Yet, amid the celebrations, Pako Ayestarán offered a sobering reminder: 'We've won, but this won't be easy, boys.'

Inside the coaches' dressing room Emery's technical staff, ever cautious – perhaps even pessimistic – saw things through the lens of their perfectionist boss. For Unai, victories weren't moments to revel in but opportunities to dissect every detail, to highlight areas for improvement. Damià was at the other end of the spectrum. 'Lads, let's celebrate! What we've achieved today is massive. Tomorrow, you can get back to work.' But even in victory, or especially in victory, Unai's methods loom large. Defeats? They are catastrophic, a funeral, the bad-tasting medicine you have to take if you want to get better, regardless of the bigger picture. At Valencia, they used to call Unai 'the cat with seven lives'. In Spain, the number seven is a symbol of luck, which is why Spanish cats are stuck with two fewer lives than their luckier Anglo-Saxon counterparts. Losing two matches in a row was almost unthinkable for him, as after every loss, with the world having collapsed, Unai found an unrelenting energy to ensure it wouldn't happen again. The cold, objective analysis after the United victory was clear: Villa had won, but on the players' terms. It had been an end-to-end affair, chaotic and uncontrolled. This wasn't the football Unai envisioned.

Before the World Cup break, Villa managed another victory, this time 1–2 away against a surging Brighton. But after the tournament, they returned with two poor performances at home: a 1–3 loss to Liverpool, during which they wasted several chances, and a 1–1 draw against Wolves. Sandwiched between these was a 0–2 away win at Tottenham, a glimmer of what was possible. Unai grew visibly restless with the way the Villa Park crowd demanded a style of football he didn't want to play. They wanted end-to-end sprints, frantic transitions. He wanted control, patience on the ball, deliberate timing, dominating the play. The gap between the two visions was vast.

But one morning, on the way to Bodymoor Heath from his hotel, he found himself smiling. He was ready to fight, but this time, it wasn't with the fans; it was *for* them. Instead of offering a middle finger, he wanted to extend his hand, to connect and make them see what was now required to win consistently. The work became all-consuming and the days felt shorter than ever. Winter nights arrived early, cloaking the training ground in darkness by late afternoon. For Unai, the idea of home became a distant memory. He spent three months living in a hotel, with no time to search for a house. For his coaching staff, separated from their families, it felt like an extended camp-out, like students on an endless field trip. Conversations began over the first cup of coffee at 8 a.m. and carried on late into the evening, often over the final sips of yet another coffee after dinner.

It was the only way. An entire world needed moulding.

2

FORGED IN THE BASQUE COUNTRY:

THE ORIGINS OF UNAI

It is January 2025 and the streets of the unassuming Basque town of Irún carry the crisp chill of a winter morning. Yet, despite everyone being bundled up in heavy jackets, as is typical at this time of year, the sky is clear and the sun shines brightly. A perfect Sunday for a football match to kick-off at 12 noon. At the edge of town, Real Unión's Stadium Gal, situated in the same place for almost one hundred years, stands quiet and practical, its modest facade flanked by a car park on one side and the slow-moving Bidasoa river on the other. In the water, boats lie moored, waiting patiently for something to happen – though little ever does.

Everything moves at a different pace. It's not just because it's Sunday. They do things differently here. The Basque Country is not only a region – it's a mindset. Tucked into the rugged folds of northern Spain, between the Bay of Biscay and the western Pyrenees, it has long stood apart. Its people speak Euskera, a language older than the Romans, unrelated to any other spoken tongue in Europe. It is both a means of communication and a declaration of identity – proud, private. The landscape breeds a certain resolve. The hills are steep, the weather often harsh, the villages remote. Generations have grown up surrounded by stone,

36

sea and silence – shaped by them. This is a people who value hard work, self-reliance and humility. From this soil, legends grow. According to Basque mythology, the *jentilak* – ancient giants – once roamed the mountains, shaping the land and passing down their wisdom to humans, until the birth of Christ when they were swallowed by the land, retreating into their caves, mountains and the underground, vanishing from the world of humans.

This land is older than history.

A short stroll from Real Unión's stadium takes you to the small Behobia International Bridge that connects Spain to France, marked only by a discreet sign at its midpoint. From there, you can see on one side Irún's tightly packed, functional, Spanish apartment buildings clustered together, with the stadium standing as a landmark among the huddled rooftops. On the other, Hendaye's spacious white houses with red inverted V-shaped rooftops are scattered across the green landscape. Refugees and exiles once crossed this bridge. Today, it's travellers and traders who walk its path. The border between the two countries, between their cultures, has softened in the Spanish and French Basque Country. Here, students grow up learning both Spanish and French as tools for connection, so from an early age people understand the value of tradition and heritage, but also that the world is vast and that borders are nothing more than artificial lines.

The Emerys, people that have lived in many lands, are no different. Their surname is of Norman origin, derived from Emmerich, meaning 'power'. The Normans, of combined Viking and Frankish descent who settled in Normandy, France, became known for their military prowess, most famously conquering England in 1066 under William the Conqueror, reshaping its language and aristocracy. So, today, the Emery surname can be found both in England, and France, from where the paternal branch of Unai's family comes. Unai's grandfather was one of four siblings who settled in Irún. His parents made their home just 12 minutes away by car, in Hondarribia. Nestled on the Bay of Txingudi and untouched by the real-estate frenzy, the town has grown around its colourful houses, which line the narrow cobblestone streets of the old quarter, still enclosed by fortified walls. Today, it is home to sixteen thousand people.

Unai still has a photo at home of him sitting at the feet of his grandad, Antonio Emery Arocena but doesn't have many more mementos of him. There are other photos, mostly hung on the walls of the Real Unión stadium, where Antonio played for the entirety of his career, dressed in the long-sleeved thick cotton jersey of a goalkeeper, heavy wool shorts that reached to the knees, knee-high wool socks and sturdy leather football boots. He wasn't particularly taller than the rest of the team, and he carried some extra weight. They called him 'Pajarito' (meaning 'little bird') and he died when Unai was eleven years old. The day he passed away, in 1982, the family started receiving telegrams of condolence from the most famous clubs in Spain, including Real Madrid, Barcelona and Athletic Club de Bilbao. Unai's dad and uncle would read those messages to him before placing them on a table around a photograph of Pajarito Emery. That image stayed with him. He had just discovered that his grandad was more than just a grandfather. In his young, impressionable eyes, he had become something greater. The reverence, the significance of his role, the universality of football, all carried a weight that the boy couldn't yet put into words. Now, looking back, he understands the impact of that moment.

What escaped him at the time was that football in Spain had been shaped in the land he inhabited, and many of their stars were from there. The Basque Country didn't just contribute to the rise of the Spanish game – it defined its early character. In the opening decades of the twentieth century, Basque clubs dominated the national stage, setting the standards of physicality, technical skill and competitive culture. Even before formal competitions, Basque teams were instrumental in spreading football throughout Spain – often taking the game south through exhibition matches and cup ties.

Real Unión was one of the most successful clubs of the 1920s. By 1927, they had already won three Copas del Rey, including a notable 1–0 win over Real Madrid. Athletic Club, founded in Bilbao in 1898 by workers and students returning from Britain, was one of the first clubs to institutionalise football in Spain. They won the first recognised Copa del Rey in 1903 and went on to claim nine titles between 1903 and 1923 alone. Alongside them, Real Sociedad (1909) and Arenas Club de Getxo (1909) emerged as early forces. All four were part of the original ten-team league launched in 1929. Stadium Gal even hosted the first-ever LaLiga match – a clash against Real Sociedad – in that inaugural season, which ran from February to June. Athletic Club quickly became one of the giants of Spanish football, winning the league title in 1930, 1931, 1934 and 1936 – often with squads made up entirely of local players. That philosophy later became a symbol of cultural resistance under Franco's dictatorship. Football was a coded expression of identity at a time when the Basque language and symbols were banned.

These early Basque sides were known not just for their success but for a style: tough, direct and disciplined, yet tactically sharp. In many ways, they helped shape the DNA of Spanish football long before the aesthetic of possession took hold.

The region has always been a factory of talent, producing players who combine intelligence with intensity and managers who obsess over belonging, structure and detail. From Pichichi (Rafael

Moreno Aranzadi), Athletic Club's legendary forward who scored Spain's first international goal at the 1920 Olympics and gave his name to the league's top scorer trophy, to Javier Clemente, who coached Athletic to two league titles; Txiki Begiristain and José Mari Bakero were key in Johan Cruyff's Dream Team at Barcelona. From Telmo Zarra to Xabi Alonso, from José Ángel Iribar to Unai Emery, the Basque legacy runs deep, not only in the teams of Bilbao and San Sebastián, but across Spain.

For decades, Basque players have formed the backbone of the Spanish national team. Jacinto Quincoces, Luis Regueiro (one of the great forwards of the pre-war era, from Irún), Periko Alonso, Andoni Zubizarreta – they were all crucial in different generations. And Xabi Alonso, Periko's son, became a pillar of the golden era that won Euro 2008, the 2010 World Cup and Euro 2012. Today, Unai Simón and Nico Williams continue that tradition.

That first league season was ultimately won by Barcelona, with Real Madrid finishing as runners-up. Real Unión's coach at the time was the Englishman Steve Bloomer, perhaps one of the earliest global stars, a pioneer who pushed for the professionalisation of Spanish football. Until it became legal to pay for players in 1925, he had to rely on local players who split their time on the pitch with work. Among them was nineteen-year-old Antonio Emery Arocena, a temporary worker on the railway who started as a left-winger but ended up as a goalkeeper, as well as a one-club man, during his twelve-year career. That is how football entered the world of the Emery family.

He was known as a goalkeeper who was fearless in every challenge and, according to Basque legend, seemed to fly among his opponents to fight for the ball. Despite standing only 1.72 metres tall, he was agile and courageous, often clearing the ball with his fists. 'They used to tell me my grandfather's nickname, Little Bird,' explains Unai Emery, 'was because he flew "high". But my father said it had to do with his debut in Santander against Racing. He joked that playing that match meant he had missed out on a lunch of game birds, a popular meal at the time.'

He never trained with the team during the week because he was also studying civil engineering in Madrid. On weekends, he would hop on a motorbike and ride to Irún. His talent made up for the lack of training. In fact, it was quality that defined Real Unión, a team made up mostly of Irún-born players, friends who played a style of football that captivated fans, much like a modern-day Barcelona of their era. He was in goal for the 1924 Copa del Rey final; Real Madrid couldn't get past him in a legendary 1–0 victory. Three years later, he won a second Copa del Rey, Real Unión defeating Arenas in the first all-Basque final. He also made history as the first goalkeeper to concede a goal in LaLiga, on 10 February 1929, at Sarrià, the old stadium of Espanyol. However, he never played for Spain, as his French father made him ineligible under the regulations of the time. When the rule changed, Ricardo Zamora, a legendary Spanish goalkeeper, was already in place.

Antonio was a father, grandfather and great-grandfather to goalkeepers, but Unai did not follow the family tradition. Yet, Unai's face always lights up when he speaks about either his grandfather or the career of his dad, Juan María. Grandad Antonio's son was a goalkeeper who stopped forwards all over Spain, from Deportivo de La Coruña to Recreativo de Huelva, and also at Real Unión, where he played in two different eras. Across sixteen years as a professional footballer, he wore the shirts of nine different teams, helping three of them achieve promotion to the top tier.

Clearly, football was ever-present in the Emery household. There was always a ball rolling around, and stories of past games were told as if they had just finished. Juan, known as a fair and kind man, would play with his four sons, even training them, and the family became known in Hondarribia as 'the footballing family'. Near Unai's home, there was a *frontón* (a pelota court) and a gravel football pitch. Football was played there for hours on end but also out on the streets as traffic was not an issue in Hondarribia. 'My dad used to kick a ball with me and my three brothers on a pitch near our house,' Unai recalls. 'I also loved going to stadiums and watching games. How old was I? Five or six years old? Back then, football interested me more than school. On Sunday nights, there was always football on TV. I would watch through the half-open living room door, catching as much as I could until my mother would appear and say, "Off to bed! It's late, and you have school tomorrow."'

Amelia was the only woman in the household, but anyone wondering how she managed with five football-obsessed men clearly doesn't know her. She has a strong character and never let herself be overrun. Everyone knows Amelia in Hondarribia. They see her sticking to her unique habit of going to the beach every single day, even in the coldest months of January and February.

On 26 April 1981, the Emery family gathered around the radio. Across the Basque Country, thousands of families were doing the same. Affordable and accessible, it was a trusted source of entertainment and news, especially in a Spain still emerging from Franco's dictatorship. They were listening to Real Sociedad chase a historic first league title; the game was not on television.

They needed a point, but they were losing away to Sporting Gijón, 2–1. Time was running out. Then, in the final moments, Jesús María Zamora scored the crucial 2–2 equaliser, securing the title at the expense of Real Madrid, who had already begun celebrating after their win against Real Valladolid only to be stunned by the radio broadcast of Zamora's goal. 'I was nine years old. I jumped up and down in excitement imagining how it had unfolded. I remember Zamora's goal at El Molinón as if it happened yesterday,' Unai says. Real Sociedad had suddenly become of special significance to him.

After retiring, Juan worked at a transport company. 'We never lacked anything, but we never had too much either,' Unai says. He also became a youth coach, earning his regional coaching licence and managing Real Unión's youth teams and other local clubs. Unai would often watch him plan training sessions, realising that nothing in football happened by chance. From the age of eight, Unai played in the town's youth team. One of his father's friends watched him in admiration. 'Look at this kid! The way he strikes the ball, what a talent!' The path started to be pinpointed. In fact, all four of Juan and Amelia's children played regulated football.

Koldo, the eldest, was born in 1968. Unai followed in 1973, then Andoni a year later, in 1974. Igor, the youngest, was born eight years after Unai in 1981. Sundays were a logistical puzzle for Amelia and Juan, as they shuttled their children to different matches across the region.

Juan's brother, Román, another former Real Unión goalkeeper and a passionate football lover whose life revolved around his nephews, often helped with the travelling. Only Unai made it as a professional. When he started to study and train with Real Sociedad in San Sebastián, Román would drive him so the boy could sleep a little longer before the long day ahead. Then, he would turn around and head back to work. He and Juan were employed by the same transport company, a business that had hired them through football, as it was one of Real Unión's main sponsors. Román suffered a heart attack at sixty but survived, living until he was ninety, but he passed away a couple of years ago. For Unai, it felt like losing a mentor, a father figure.

*

Real Unión's small club shop opens its doors shortly before 11 a.m. Its windows display the team's three jerseys, one bearing the Aston Villa colours, claret and blue, as a nod to Emery's connection. Inside, scarves hang neatly beside wine bottles sourced from local vineyards. Occasionally, the shopkeeper glances towards the door, anticipating arrivals, but it is empty at the moment. Two visitors, a couple of journalists who are following the story of Unai Emery, put their heads through the door and promise to return later.

Groups of people gather outside the stadium, mostly greeting each other by name. Some move towards the ground's entrance, others towards the nearby bar, which has opened early to cater to matchday visitors. Outside the bar, middle-aged men stand with cigarettes and small glasses in hand, likely filled with *carajillo*, coffee laced with a touch of brandy. Inside, fresh bread had arrived hours earlier, ready for the rush. *Bocadillos*, sandwiches neatly arranged and inviting, sit behind the glass display case. Old photos of Real Unión, including one of Pajarito Emery and one of a team that features Juan Emery, are hanging on the walls. Opposite the bar counter, through wide windows, the pitch opens up from the corner, its green stretching in front of you. That is the height a manager sees a game at from the touchline.

'Is he here yet?' The question ripples through the small crowd.

Word has spread. Unai is visiting today. They know he has flown in from Valencia that morning, after taking a couple of days off on the back of Aston Villa's hard-fought FA Cup victory over West Ham. A narrow 2–1 win, not their sharpest performance but a win, nonetheless. It is going to be a short visit: a chance to watch the game, have lunch with his brother Igor, president of Real Unión, the new manager Albert Carbó, the family lawyer Iosu Reta and some friends, plus to go and give his mum a hug before returning with his son Lander to Birmingham. The constant weight of decision has been left behind for a bit. Aston Villa are mostly performing well at this stage, but the challenge of balancing the Champions League and the Premier League is proving to be elusive; there are defensive frailties. Soon there will be another transfer market to take new steps forward; one key player seems determined to leave. But that is for another day. At fifty-three, you can't always keep pushing forward. He needs to take a breather, because so much depends on his clarity. If he stumbles, many stumble. The invisible tubes connecting Villa, Real Unión, the hotel and restaurants he owns – those waiting on his final call – they all get clogged with uncertainty. He is involved in so much, in so many people's lives. The club he has bought gives him space to step away. Football as a way to escape football.

Irún and Hondarribia are beach and mountain, stability and memories, sources of energy for Unai. A corner of security. Unai left home at twenty-five and often went six months without re-turning. He would only visit his family in the summer and at Christmas. Being a player, or more accurately being young, there was not much space for anything else but football. But as time went by, things changed. He married a woman from Málaga who even-tually settled in Valencia with their son Lander. So, in the middle of the season and all its storms, there was always Hondarribia and Valencia to escape to. Now, a stopover in Mallorca is also a wel-come retreat. But the Basque Country is where his roots are. Unai has a ritual when returning: he always takes the coastal road. 'I enter my town by the sea,' he says.

Water has always been a constant in Unai's and his siblings' lives; unsurprising in a town so closely tied to water. When they were little, Amelia and Juan would take them out on to the bay in a rowing boat. Juan would carry a large stone, tie it to a rope and once they rowed far enough, he would drop it overboard as an anchor. Then, they would all swim. That was when Unai's mum started the daily routine of spending 10 minutes in the sea. Later, when a knee injury threatened his career, Real Sociedad's physio advised Unai to walk into the sea up to his knees for recovery. He followed the recommendation religiously, even in winter, even in the rain. His mum next to him under the water. Now, whenever he can, he walks along the shoreline in Hondarribia, or Hendaye, where the beach is wider. Half an hour, alone with his thoughts, unwinding. Or, if the weather is good, he swims. This past year he didn't swim once, often rushing between appointments when he went home, and the sea simply waited. But then as time passed by it felt as if his mind were filled with clutter that needed to be cleared. The need to swim is also the need to cleanse.

These days, he returns home more often and the airport, 10 minutes from Hondarribia, makes it easier. Last September, he made it to the town's annual fiesta, something he had missed for fifteen years. The international break allowed him to go, his family by his side, wearing the traditional scarf, embracing it all. A dinner organised by Amelia and another with lifelong friends followed. He still keeps his childhood circle close – one is a painter, another a cyclist, another a fisherman. None of them are involved in football. When they meet, they talk, they laugh, they eat, they sing Basque songs. They never ask him for anything. 'You realise now that life is about those moments, being with your childhood friends, your *cuadrilla*,' Unai admits. 'And when you're away, when you get older, you appreciate them even more.'

Unai and his generation grew up and studied in the *ikastolak*, the Basque-language schools which preserve the language and culture. After Franco's dictatorship, during Spain's transition to democracy, it was a way of reclaiming a culture that had been suppressed, a statement of resilience. He recalls a time when speaking Basque with his family or singing songs with his dad and uncle wasn't always possible, especially when he lived in places like Toledo (where he spent four years), surrounded by teammates whose families were Guardia Civil (Civil Guards), often viewed as the enemy by Basque nationalists. They are a national law enforcement agency with military status which, during Franco's dictatorship, was used to suppress political dissent and enforce state control. But Unai also feels Spanish. He often tells his mother, 'Ama, Spain has given me so much in football and life.' If he had to be placed anywhere politically, it would be in the camp of common sense.

When he returns to his home town of Hondarribia, or Irún, there is little talk about politics. In the eyes of others, he embodies quiet success. In June 2021, he bought Real Unión, then in the third tier of Spanish football, not to remind those who stayed behind how well the kid who left was doing but as a tribute to his roots. More than anything, it was a homage to his grandfather. Unai's dream is to build a training centre in Irún and name it 'Pajarito Emery'. There you go, Irún. A gift from the family of footballers.

He will soon be surrounded by the warmth of those who have come to see him, those waiting for him. The visitors and fans make their way into the stadium. From the main entrance to the pitch, where half an hour before kick-off the buzz is at its peak, it's just forty steps. On the touchline, quiet conversations about Real Unión's struggling season unfold between well-dressed men, representatives of the club's main sponsors and of both teams, gathered around president Igor Emery. Middle-aged but youthful in appearance, impeccably dressed, he has the kind of face that belongs to someone who wouldn't hurt a fly. Nobody can step on the pitch, meticulously maintained by Andoni, the second eldest of the Emery brothers. Andoni's devotion to the grass reflects his need to embrace what life offers him, especially when it often seemed to take more than it gave. He learnt the trade from scratch, quickly becoming the protector of the ground, ensuring no one steps on it unnecessarily. Among the crowd are other members of Unai's family, their lawyer Iosu Reta, club media staff capturing everything on video, a couple of members of Aston Villa's coaching team – Alberto Benito and Rodri, and the two journalists, taking in the view of France just beyond the stands. Soon after, the players from both sides emerge to warm up. The new manager, Albert Carbó, a young coach who spent two years with Unai at Aston Villa as a member of the individual training team under Rodri, came in with the intention to turn things around. However, after an initial win, the team suffered two defeats. Now they face Zamora, a veteran-filled team. Heads turn as Unai arrives accompanied by his son, Lander. Dressed in a warm, modern jacket zipped to his chin, he moves with purpose. Igor greets him with a firm handshake and a brief hug. Iosu gets the same friendly treatment. Unai moves his head to greet other visitors whom he will talk to at some point, and he acknowledges the two visiting journalists, speaking to them briefly, before more handshakes.

Suddenly, unexpected music fills the stadium, not the usual football anthem but a nod to the owner. Eskorbuto is the band. It's no coincidence. Unai has a deep love for Basque punk rock of the 1980s. The song 'Cerebros Destruídos' (meaning 'destroyed brains') blasts through the speakers. It is a generational song, raw and defiant, a cry of despair and a rejection of social manipulation. Eskorbuto were one of the most iconic and controversial bands in 1980s' Spain. Hailing from Santurtzi, their vehement, aggressive music and lyrics filled with anger made them pioneers of radical punk. From the start, they rejected political labels, embracing an uncompromising anti-establishment but also self-destructive ethos. This irreverent defiance put them at odds with both the authorities and other sections of the Basque punk scene, which, of course, meant they were admired by the youth of the time. One of their most infamous moments came in 1983, when they were arrested and jailed in Madrid for lyrics deemed 'subversive'. By the late 1980s, heroin addiction had taken its toll on Iosu and Juanma, the band's leading figures. At that time, heroin devastated the Basque Country, and many believe the authorities turned a blind eye to keep young people away from radical politics. Rather than prevention or rehabilitation, the response was repression. Whether through negligence or intent, it became a form of social control. Both Iosu and Juanma died in 1992, just over four months apart, but their legacy endures as a refusal to conform.

The 1980s and early 1990s were a violent and deeply fractured period in the Basque Country. Spain was still adjusting to democracy after Franco's dictatorship, and tensions over Basque nationalism were at their peak. The armed separatist group ETA (Euskadi Ta Askatasuna) was founded in 1959 as a resistance movement against Franco's repression of Basque identity. But by the 1980s, with Franco gone, ETA evolved into a brutal paramilitary organisation that no longer just targeted symbols of dictatorship but anyone they saw as standing in the way of their ultimate goal: total independence of the Basque Country from Spain and France. ETA operated through a campaign of terror, assassinations, bombings and kidnappings. Their victims were carefully chosen: politicians, judges, business leaders, police officers, journalists and even civilians who opposed their methods. Fear became a weapon. Over

800 people were killed in attacks spanning decades, and thousands more lived under the threat of extortion via the so-called 'revolutionary tax' ETA demanded: blackmail or exile. The Basque Country became a region where political allegiances could be dangerous, where speaking out against ETA often meant putting your life at risk.

By the time Unai was twelve years old, he had stopped playing football in the streets and on nearby pitches with his brothers and dad. His talent had already been spotted by Mikel Etxarri, a prominent football thinker who had shared his expertise through various roles at both the Gipuzkoan and Spanish football federations. At the time, Etxarri was sporting director at Real Sociedad, and it was he who brought Unai into the club's youth system. From then on, his days started early, balancing his studies and training in San Sebastián.

Up at 6.30 a.m., suitcase in hand filled with books and his training kit, Unai would walk to the bus stop in Hondarribia for the 7.15 a.m. ride to San Sebastián, a 50-minute journey. He went to school, had a rushed lunch at the hostel where some of the younger players lived and if a teammate's bed was empty for whatever reason, he would take the opportunity to grab an hour of sleep. Then, another 20-minute bus ride to Lasarte, where the training ground was located. From the bus stop, a half-hour walk to the pitches. Then training, before two more buses back home, arriving at 9 or 10 p.m. Four days a week. His uncle Román would occasionally pick him up from training, sparing him the exhausting commute.

Football was a chance to find refuge from the confusion and conflict that ETA brought about during that time. And, also, it was an escape from drugs. Unai lost several friends to heroin overdose, an epidemic which plagued the Basque Country during the 1980s. HIV was another real threat, too. During that time, he knew many people who were into drugs and many others who weren't. Some were deeply invested in local politics, while others stayed out of it. At Unai's school in Hondarribia, four children of ETA members studied there. One day a different friend to those four invited him to take part in a political activity with their classmates, while the kids from his neighbourhood had made other plans. Unai remembers standing there, weighing up whether to join in. In the end, he turned it down. He had thought about it but preferred to go out with the group of friends from his neighbourhood who didn't want to get involved in politics. He ended up surrounded by friends who were primarily interested in sport. Unai's main focus was 'to play football'.

But you can never truly escape. 'Once or twice, while seated in the bus that took me from San Sebastián, passing through Rentería, Pasajes and other towns, I would be on my way home, carrying my bag, about 9 p.m. at night, after training, freezing in the winter . . . and suddenly, ETA would stop the bus, make you get off and burn it. But it got to the point where it just became . . . normal. Oh, they've stopped us again. Another bus gone,' Unai recalls with vivid detail. The reality of life in the Basque Country during that time.

Now, at Stadium Gal, Los Secretos play over the speakers, another of Unai's favourite bands. One of the most iconic groups in Spanish rock, their sound leant towards melancholic pop with country-rock influences, reminiscent of American bands like the Eagles. Their lyrics about heartbreak, loneliness and disenchantment became their trademark. But their story was also marked by tragedy. In 1984, drummer Pedro Antonio Díaz was killed in a road accident. Then, in 1999, came the hardest blow, the tragic death of their leader and main songwriter Enrique Urquijo, from a heroin overdose. The background is dramatic, but the music itself is softer, more reflective and fitting for the Unai who now sits in the stands, watching the match that's about to begin. Unai often says he has always wanted to feel secure, to have a job, to enjoy life. Today, he struggles to understand a world so full of extremes, a world where respect seems to have faded, where priorities have shifted. When he returns to his home town, his old friends, his *cuadrilla*, are a mix of every possible belief. In a group of twenty, maybe three still believe in Basque independence, while another three feel deeply Spanish, perhaps because their parents are from Murcia. Politics is rarely discussed, and if it does come up, it's quickly shut down.

The match unfolds with familiar frustrations for Real Unión. They fall behind early, struggling to find their best version. From the stands, Unai shares his thoughts on the performance with his best friend Alberto Benito, and Rodri. They are broadcasting the game.

'Be calm!'

'Good decision!'

'Push higher!'

'He's lacking physically.'

Alberto and Unai then share a quiet comment not meant to be heard by anyone. Followed by a big laugh. They were teammates at Toledo for three and a half seasons in the late 1990s, and in their final season together, Alberto and Unai even shared a flat. They also both played five games in LaLiga, Unai for Real Sociedad and Alberto for Valencia. Since then, their lives have remained closely intertwined. Unai trusts Benito's eye for talent, the information he can acquire. He knows his friend might get things wrong about a player, but he will never let him down. Loyalty, friendship and work, those are the foundations of their relationship, that became professional too.

Unai took Alberto to Almería to become director of football when the club had just been promoted to LaLiga. When Unai later moved to Valencia, Alberto remained at Almería for several years. Having failed to bring him to Arsenal, and coinciding with Alberto being unemployed, Unai took him to PSG – not to work with the club directly, but as his personal scout. Unai paid him out of his own pocket. Alberto will never forget that gesture. As new opportunities arose, Unai never stood in his way, such as when Alberto received a good offer from Real Betis. Although, after signing for Aston Villa, he called his friend again and Alberto didn't hesitate to accept Unai's offer. From the beginning, Alberto admired Unai as a coach, recognising one key thing that explains why he's gone so far: Unai has always won because he pushes people. In the past, he did it with less experience, but the same relentless energy. Now, with experience, he pushes with precision at Aston Villa. He never punishes mistakes, never singles out individuals, but he demands everything. Especially from his friends. Over the years, Alberto and Unai have debated football endlessly. He knows him inside out. Yet Unai is chameleonic, always adapting, always learning. That's why Alberto values being close to him, to see where Unai's evolution is heading and to advise him along the way. He still travels to games with him as they used to do all those years ago, back in Almería.

Real Unión equalise, which is celebrated with the high-energy punk anthem 'Nellie the Elephant' by Toy Dolls blasting through the speakers. Ultimately, Real Unión lose the match. After the final whistle, Unai and Lander make their way to the VIP lounge, a room filled with a modest sense of pride. Gleaming trophies line the walls, including the club's last Copa del Rey from 1927. During the week, it serves as a boardroom, but on matchdays, once the tables are pushed against the walls, it transforms into a gathering space. Plates of Ibérico ham, chorizo and fresh bread sit alongside bottles of Rioja, ready to be shared. His brother Andoni is there making loud jokes. So are Igor, Iosu and the two journalists. Some stories of the past are shared, and the latest Aston Villa result is discussed. Unai is predictably but also naturally friendly, nervous, jumping quickly from chat to chat, taking over the conversation so there are not uncomfortable silences. Eating what is left and keeping an eye on Unai's movements, some of the visitors that came to share a moment with him finally go over to shake his hand but others only manage to stand next to him. His niece brings her daughter for a photo, and everything is done quietly, almost embarrassedly. He is not Unai the famous manager who has lifted trophies. He is now the local boy made good, the boss. One of those men of integrity. Gracious yet grounded, respected by all and instinctively kind. Men who see it as their duty to correct injustices and restore order. Unai prefers to wait until the crowd, over a thousand on the day, has thinned before making his exit. Real Unión youth players, a couple of Unai's cousins, want to see him before he leaves the stadium.

The next stop is a bustling restaurant nearby, where Unai, Lander, Igor, Iosu, Alberto, Rodri and a disappointed Albert settle in. The young Real Unión manager knows what is coming. He is about to feel the weight of his boss's expectations. They gather around a long table, the heart of Basque culture. The air is thick with the aroma of grilled fish, roasted lamb and freshly baked bread. Bottles of red wine punctuate the scene. As always, Unai is animated, dissecting tactics with his trademark intensity, his hands painting the game in the air. As expected, conversations shift between light-hearted anecdotes and the stark realities facing Real Unión. Igor, more burdened than ever, listens in silence. The responsibility of running the club, of meeting the standards Unai sets not just for others, but for him, too, weigh on him.

Unai is the son of a way of life, one built on community, solidarity and tradition. Co-operation is central, from *txokos*, gastronomic societies, to *auzolan*, the tradition of voluntary communal work that strengthens neighbourhoods, or even industrial worker co-operatives like the Mondragón Corporation. This mentality extends to sport. In Basque pelota, rowing and football, teamwork and loyalty come before individual glory. Lifting stones, chopping wood, they are competitions born from labour itself. Farmers wagered their earnings, even their homes, on their own strength and endurance. To compete is to work hard, and to work hard is to succeed.

It is no surprise, then, that coaches from this small region, particularly from Gipuzkoa, Spain's smallest province, have a unique way of seeing the game. They are adaptable, hard workers, obsessed with learning and view themselves as just one cog in a larger footballing machine. Andoni Iraola, Xabi Alonso, Julen Lopetegui, Mikel Arteta, Juanma Lillo, Pako Ayestarán, Imanol Alguacil, Jagoba Arrasate, José Luis Mendilibar, Unai Emery ... The list of elite managers from this tiny corner of the world is disproportionately high. Perhaps there's something deeper that connects Basque culture with others that share the same work ethic? Scotland has seen its own golden generation of tough, uncompromising managers in David Moyes, Walter Smith, Billy McKinlay, Steve Clarke, Sir Kenny Dalglish, Sir Alex Ferguson and, going back further, Jock Stein, Bill Shankly, Sir Matt Busby, Bill Struth. Ferguson was shaped by the shipyards of the Clyde.

Shankly and Stein came from mining towns, their values forged in the hard realities of working-class life, not too dissimilar to Basque managers, moulded by an industrial socialist core built on teamwork and shared responsibility.

'Socialists never retire,' sports psychologist Michael Caulfield likes to say. 'They don't sit back on sun loungers, sipping cocktails. They need to work. It's in them. They can't let go.' In the Basque Country, hard work is not measured, it's expected. That sounds exactly like something Ferguson, Shankly, Stein and Busby would say, or even modern managers like Pep Guardiola and Jürgen Klopp. Wealth hasn't changed them. They are still workers at heart, still driven by the need to build, improve, compete.

The acquisition of Real Unión is rooted in all of that but also in solidarity and family heritage. The idea had been in Unai's mind for years. Among the newer Emery generations, just Igor had worn the club's badge, though only at youth level. By the end of the 2020–21 season, the club was drowning in financial trouble. Salaries had gone unpaid for four months, debts had spiralled to nearly €2 million and survival seemed unlikely. So, Unai made some calls. First to Igor, then to others. 'I want to try and save the club. It would be heartbreaking to let it go.'

The professional advice was clear: stay out. The club was a financial disaster. The logical move was to dissolve it and start over. Unai didn't care. He took responsibility, absorbing most of the club's debt and committing to reviving it. Since then, he has personally invested €1 million per year from his own pocket. This is now his fourth season doing so. 'If we do things right,' Unai explained, 'Real Unión has great potential. Maybe we can become Gipuzkoa's second club, behind Real Sociedad.' For years, the mighty rival had absorbed Real Unión, using it like a reserve team. That changed on 28 November 2023, when Aston Villa made a formal agreement to bring Real Unión into the V Sports network, alongside clubs like Vissel Kobe (Japan), ZED FC (Egypt) and Vitória SC (Portugal). The deal meant severing ties with Real Sociedad and stepping out of its shadow.

Shortly after landing in Birmingham on one of his regular visits to Aston Villa, Nassef Sawiris approached Damià Vidagany and asked him, 'How's Unai?'

'He's doing great. But you know what? Real Unión is what excites him. After working 23 hours of the day, that 1 free hour is spent thinking about Real Unión. I think he would appreciate your support, Nassef,' Damià told the Aston Villa co-owner.

Sawiris later flew to Hondarribia. He had lunch with Unai, walked through Real Unión's stadium and saw the club's potential. The agreement with Aston Villa started as a collaborative one but by taking a 25 per cent stake in Real Unión in December 2024, the English club replaced the financial support Real Sociedad once provided. The goal is to improve the club's infrastructure and develop young players who can later return to Aston Villa stronger, more mature, as well as helping Unai achieve his vision for the club.

'For an English player, Spanish football is tough. If they come here, they get closer to becoming players that can earn a living in the first or second division back in England. They grow, both as players and as people,' Igor explained. During Unai's visit that January, the club had goalkeeper James Wright, left-back Finley Munroe and Colombian centre-back Yeimar Mosquera on loan from the Midlands club.

Unai's ultimate dream? To see Real Unión reach LaLiga, but there is more. 'We want to build something with our own identity,' Unai said. 'I want to honour our past and rebuild this club. I want kids from Irún to play here, to have proper facilities, to make it a sports city with new pitches and modern dressing rooms. I want three or four thousand people in the stands, a professional team that belongs to the town. If we get promoted to the Segunda soon or eventually LaLiga, great, but that's not the only goal. This isn't just about football. It's about revitalising the community. We can create jobs. I don't make a profit, I don't live off this. It gives me satisfaction. It helps people.' That's what he told the mayor of Irún.

'It's a dream, yes. But why not? Modest Eibar did it.'

Real Unión isn't the only struggling business Unai has taken on. He's proactive in managing his assets, often stepping into troubled ventures to rebuild them. In Irún, he heard there was a hotel for sale near his family home and the club. He asked Iosu for advice and spoke to his mother, who liked the idea. He bought it, saving jobs and bringing it back to life. It was a way to build something for the family, and over time, his brother Koldo, a member of Beti Mugan, a rock band that sang in Basque, became involved as well. He enjoys being part of it, visiting and meeting people. Though a trusted manager oversees operations, Unai still suggests improvements, such as a pool and a renovated lounge. He greets the fifteen employees whenever he stops by. During the town's annual festival, the fair is set up right under his mother's apartment, making it impossible to sleep, so the hotel becomes their retreat. For Unai, it's not about business. 'My job is football. That's where my focus has to be.'

In Valencia, he rescued the restaurant La Casita de Sabino, run by a Navarrese couple hit hard by the 2008 financial crisis and personal circumstances. In fact, the decision was an act of kindness. The previous owner, Álvaro, had been diagnosed with cancer and, after his passing, Emery stepped in to buy the premises, ensuring his legacy endured. He even bought a flat for Álvaro's brother, allowing him to stay on as a tenant.

One day, while coaching Valencia, a man approached him for an autograph. They got talking and he explained that he was a former chef from Hondarribia, now out of work. As they said goodbye, Unai looked at Iosu and gave him a knowing glance. 'What do you think?' A week later, the man was working at Unai's restaurant. In 2013, Emery purchased Kailuze, an eatery specialising in Basque-Navarre cuisine, to go along with La Casita de Sabino. Then in Madrid, he invested in another La Casita de Sabino, keeping it afloat under similar circumstances. 'There has to be financial viability, but I always think about the people first. Can I help? I can pay it with my wages from football, it keeps people in a job . . . Then I figure out how to make it work.'

When he gets involved in something, he wants everyone to set and keep high standards. At Real Unión, he gave his younger brother Igor the chance to lead the project as president, but that came with high demands. Their relationship is often marked by debate and, lately, by one or two disagreements and by their love of the game. When Igor started playing football, the others were already focused on different things. In their childhood home, which had three bedrooms, he shared his with Unai, while Koldo and Andoni shared another. Every Saturday night, they all gathered to watch the only televised match of the week. Even though only Unai became a professional, football remained a big part of Igor's life. As a child, he often went with their parents to watch Unai play for Real Sociedad's youth and B teams. He also visited him in Toledo with his uncle Román when he played there. Igor himself played in the youth teams of Real Unión and Hondarribia FE, later coaching their reserves and youth teams after earning a coaching licence. After studying in Hendaye just across the border from Irún, he earned a journalism degree from the University of Navarra, hoping to become a sports journalist. For over fifteen years, he worked in radio, TV and print. Then he transitioned into personal management, becoming Unai's communications and scouting co-ordinator for six years. He built Unai's website while he was at Valencia and from then handled his public image. In July 2021, he took on the new challenge as president of Real Unión. So, Unai is his brother and his boss.

Igor reminds Unai of his true role in Real Unión while having lunch after the Zamora defeat. 'Unai, you're not just the owner. You're the mentor. The direct connection to the manager of Real Unión. That's your biggest value.' Igor represents Unai at the club but feels the weight of his expectations, having stepped into a role that demands far more than he originally anticipated. Financial pressures, the legacy of their family name and the push for professionalism all add to the challenges they face. At one point, Igor tried to make Unai understand the realities of running the club, but Unai isn't there every day and he watches games with the mindset of a top-level coach, but keeping up that level of scrutiny from a distance became unsustainable. Last year, Igor told him, 'The only solution is for you to coach the team yourself.' After a heated argument, Igor stopped speaking to Unai for months.

They had never quarrelled like this prior to the acquisition of the club. 'I'm arguing with you to protect you,' Igor told him. 'You don't see it, but this is for you.' At that point, the project hadn't yet reached its goals. The team hadn't stabilised or become a real promotion contender.

Next to Igor is the family's lawyer Iosu Reta, who plays a key role in the club's management, acting as a CEO figure. Their professional relationship goes back to 2003, when Unai joined Lorca as a player and needed help checking his contract. Later, Iosu helped him negotiate his first coaching contract too. Over the last twenty years, their professional bond has grown into a deep personal connection. Today, he manages Unai's finances, investments and legal matters. He is the one who pulls a face and asks Unai, upon hearing his latest idea, 'Are you sure about this?' However, lately, when Unai calls Iosu, the first thing they discuss is not the club's finances – he wants to know how his brother Igor is doing.

Igor, Alberto, Iosu, Andoni, Koldo . . . Unai may now be the centre of their lives, the one they revolve around; they may be the recipients of his personal gestures, acts of kindness, support in tough times, and both praise and pressure in moments of success; but they have been there since the very beginning. They remember the defeats, the injuries and the struggle to reach the elite levels of modern football.

Unai Emery was in fact a talented player: small, lightweight and skilful, with excellent ball control and vision. A natural left-winger, he was known for being good in one-on-one situations, with accurate crosses and a decent eye for goal, though not a prolific scorer. After a few years at Real Sociedad's academy, he spent five seasons with Sanse (Real Sociedad B). Coaches liked him because he understood the game well. On the surface he had a strong personality, there was no space for weakness. Once, while playing against Logroñés in Segunda B, he tried to dribble out of his own box in the final minutes. He lost possession, the ball rebounded and they conceded an equaliser. His coach, Mikel Etxarri, was furious: 'How could you take that risk there?'

Unai's reply was simple. 'What should I do then? Just boot it forward? You have to play!' Even at sixteen or seventeen years of age while in the academy, he had quick responses and a sense of what type of football he liked. However, mentally he did face some limitations. To perform well, he needed to feel comfortable during a match. If faced with a tough, physical defender, he struggled.

In a match at Atocha, he remembers being one-on-one with the goalkeeper and hesitating. Instead of shooting, he passed the ball to a teammate. Out of the thousands of actions that he performed during his early days in football, he remembers that one. The fear of missing had got to him.

He had the potential to reach Real Sociedad's first team, but injuries derailed his progress. At twenty, he broke a metatarsal, then tore his ACL. After surgery, he suffered an infection. He spent a year and a half sidelined. Despite this, the club renewed his contract for three years, a rare gesture at the time. He was close to making it. His LaLiga debut came in the 1995–96 season, in a 1–2 home defeat to Mérida. He came on with 15 minutes to go. That season he only played five league matches and one Copa del Rey fixture. His knee problems persisted while he was competing for a place with Javi de Pedro, who would go on to become an international player. Emery scored once in LaLiga, against Albacete. Real Sociedad were 4–1 up when he came on. Sprinting down the right, he met a cross with a powerful header. It bounced off the post and went in. The team won 8–1. That day, Gică Craioveanu, who had scored a hat-trick, gifted him the match ball. Without knowing it, it was a farewell present. Soon after, Emery left his boyhood club for good.

He often wondered what might have been, but deep down, he knew something held him back. 'When I wasn't selected, I felt relieved. I was too nervous. Fear was always in my mind, and I didn't know how to control it.' He admitted he often played better in training than in matches. 'One day, a coach shouted at us in the dressing room, "Do you have no balls?" I answered, "Yes, but they're empty!"' He made a joke, but what he really meant was that they were empty of bravery. Revealing. When Real Sociedad let him go, Mikel Etxarri, who had supported him for years, was in tears. 'He really cared about me, but I accepted it as part of life.' Maybe he did, although leaving was hard. His world had been his home town and San Sebastian, his family and the club. To his surprise, once he moved, he did not look back. 'I went on to another life. I don't think I'll even coach Real Sociedad. That train has passed.'

His next stop was the Segunda, where he played 215 matches. The first challenge was Toledo. His new residence broadened his world. He discovered nearby Madrid, a city of possibilities, a place where different lives converged, where meetings of minds sparked discoveries. At the time, he earned around 10–11 million pesetas (roughly €60,000–70,000) a year, with rent costing about €600 a month. He and Alberto Benito, both alone in Toledo, decided to share a flat. Football and cards brought them together. They were passionate about *mus*, a strategic card game. 'Unai played bravely. He wasn't predictable, sometimes he attacked, sometimes he defended. He would switch strategies suddenly,' Alberto explained. It was the same in tennis or padel, he loved attacking and playing at the net, being brave.

Leaving didn't stop him from returning home to visit his parents and the Virgin of Guadalupe, to whom he is devoted, which is located at the Sanctuary of Guadalupe, on Mount Jaizkibel, overlooking the city of Irún. Unai uses religion on his own terms. It's not religion in a traditional sense; he doesn't go to Mass, it is not so much about believing in a special entity. It's something more intimate. It is about faith in tradition. The photo of the local Virgin he carries with him in his wallet, that you can find at his home or in the office, the one that he kisses before some games is not a ritual. It is about remembering where he comes from.

He chooses which matches to take the photograph. Too much use of it and it loses its effect, he thinks. There was one, Hércules versus Sevilla, where they needed all the help he could get, including the Virgin. It came at a time when his position at Sevilla was under threat, with early eliminations from both the Copa del Rey and the Champions League, inconsistent league form, internal doubts about his methods, and pressure from fans and the board. He asked the players to trust him and the process. To have faith. The 1–3 victory allowed him to restore his authority. 'I always cross myself, before matches, every time,' Unai says. 'Out of faith.'

Unai likes to visit the Guadalupe Virgin in the shrine up the mountains above Irún. 'By car it's a 10-minute drive, but I usually walk up, with my brothers, who are used to hiking through the hills. In fact, my older brother Koldo, every time Real Unión has a match, he goes up to Guadalupe, takes a photo, and sends us a message. He does it all the time.' Unai has taken Lander with him. When he goes with company, he asks for a moment alone with the Virgin. He stays there for a while, sometimes he lights a candle or says a few quiet prayers, but it's really just about feeling at peace, at ease, comfortable. He only needs 5 minutes to connect with the place, and with himself, to feel a deep sense of both belonging and balance. A photo he took at the hermitage is now the background on his phone.

The way he lives religion has a name: cultural ritual. There is an expression of tradition and humbleness in performing these visits regularly, and it helps him reinforce identity and connection to his past. Family, friends, belonging, faith, the Virgin. It is all linked. In his village, Unai met an Italian priest named Lucio, a modern missionary and a passionate football fan. He enjoyed visiting him and their long conversations about life. Lucio eventually moved on to another assignment, but Unai kept his number and still sends him the occasional message. There's a contradiction somewhere in there, one even he might struggle to explain. A man of systems and method, guided by logic, who still finds comfort in something he can't analyse or control. He doesn't try to resolve it. It's very human to believe in an order that can't be fully explained – something that helps make sense of the inexplicable. Maybe in these small acts – kissing the photo, regular visits to the Virgin – he's acknowledging that not everything needs to make sense. Some things just are. Or maybe, like the numerous players who make the sign of the cross as they enter the pitch, it is a bit like an insurance policy.

Unai's paternal grandmother was the only practicing believer in the family. His mum was a religion teacher, even though she is an atheist. His dad recovered faith after he suffered ill health. In 2015, Unai was in Vigo about to play a game with Sevilla. He got a call from his mum and also from his brother Igor. His 'aita' did not want to get up from bed, he had to be invited to continue his day outside the bedroom. Very unlike him. Unai travelled as soon as he could, but there was not much to do. Unai had just lost his dad.

Their match against Celta Vigo is the only one Unai has ever missed in his managerial career, as he stayed for the funeral and to be with his family. His father's death left a hole. It always does. 'I didn't talk as much as I should have with my father, and that stayed with me . . . that I never really sat down to listen to him.'

When Juan passed, as with his grandad Antonio, telegrams arrived from all over the country offering their condolences.

After Toledo came Ferrol, where he spent two years. He initially struggled with the rain but grew fond of the place. He frequently stayed in the city to watch 'Super Depor' in the Champions League against AC Milan, Manchester United or Paris Saint-Germain. He admired their use of wide play. By then he had become obsessed with football. After each weekend's matches, he would memorise all the results from LaLiga, Segunda and Segunda B. He read every sports newspaper first thing in the morning before training. Once, while stretching, a teammate mentioned a match but gave the wrong score. Emery corrected him, listing every scorer and key moment.

Then came Leganés, where he met Pablo Villa and Juan Carlos Carcedo, future colleagues. There, during a match against Albacete, he had a revelation. The opponents had well-drilled set-piece routines, which his own team were clueless to stop. Their coach just shouted from the sidelines. Emery thought, *He doesn't realise they have a plan, and we don't.* They ended up losing the match, a loss that stayed with him. They weren't prepared. The coach screamed, but he never explained to the players how to handle what was happening.

'As a player, I often felt lost. No one ever told me how to deal with opponents. I had to find answers on the pitch, but sometimes I couldn't. It frustrated me. I took responsibility, but I also looked at the bench for guidance.' As a footballer he struggled more than he enjoyed his profession. In the last few years of his playing career he would not hide from debates, acting like a leader. He advised teammates on positioning and shaped discussions in the dressing room. His final stop was Lorca in the Tercera División. There, he retired as a player but received an opportunity that changed his life.

Who paid for the meal after the Real Unión game? If Unai is the one who arranges the gathering, as he often does when he comes to watch the team, he takes care of the bill. This time was no different, he even covered the meal for the two journalists sitting at a separate table. When he returns home, Unai often frequents a private culinary club which he is a member of, bringing together his childhood friends and organising a dinner for them. Known as a *txoko*, these clubs are deeply embedded in Basque culture: a place to eat, drink, sing in Basque and celebrate camaraderie through food and tradition. Historically, *txokos* were spaces of free expression and community bonding, particularly during Franco's regime. Members, mostly men, bring their own ingredients, cook their own meals and split the cost, but in the *txoko*, Unai doesn't pay a penny. That, he feels, is fair.

After lunch, the group, now joined by the two journalists, make their way to Amelia's spacious apartment in Hondarribia, overlooking the marina. It was Unai's first major investment with the money he earned from football, a home for his parents, ensuring their comfort. It's where the family gathers for meals, and Unai now joins them more often than he did as a player or in the early years of his managerial career. His mother still lives there. The visit is going to be brief; Unai and Lander have a flight to catch, and Igor is to drive them to the airport just 10 minutes away. Amelia welcomes everyone, playfully scolding Unai for being late, but lunches like today's have no set time to end. She hands out masks, explaining that she developed a slight sore throat after her morning swim in the icy sea, 10 degrees that day. 'That's why I might have a bit of a cold', she says. The masks are just a precaution. Once placed, she offers firm hugs.

Unai: 'She's the matriarch, the boss.'

Amelia: 'Boss? Not at all, I don't run anything.'

Unai: 'Sometimes you lead without seeming to.'

Amelia: 'Ah, yes, that's possible. I might do that, yes.'

Unai's head bows slightly, so subtly that if you're not paying attention, you might miss it, but it does go down. He often debates politics with his mother, always with affection. He argues because life has exposed him to different perspectives, because he now understands that there's more to life than a single way of thinking. Life has pulled him far from his home town. Had he stayed, the town of Hondarribia would have confined him.

Unai: 'You are the one who gives the orders, Ama.'

He looked around and saw three steady pillars in his life – first and foremost, his *ama*, his mother. Then his brother, Igor, who has travelled with him for years. Finally, his son, Lander. The latter two have become the public face of the Emery family. Away from football, Unai remains a deeply private person. There are aspects of his life he simply doesn't share – not with the media, and sometimes not even with those around him. It's part of how he protects his focus: by building boundaries and keeping what matters most to him intact. By keeping his personal life out of view, he defines how he wants to be seen – through his work. It reflects his belief that football is a shared adventure, the place where he offers all he has. It's where he gives his best – so the only place where judgement should take place. 'Unai always loved going out, you know,' Amelia tells the visitors with a knowing smile. She speaks with a tease, her tone firm and affectionate. 'He used to come home late, and I had to remind him where his priorities should be.' As she says this, Unai lowers his gaze even more, this time visibly embarrassed. The confident coach suddenly becomes just like a son who has been gently told off.

Around the living room, photographs of Unai in football kit adorn the walls, images of him as a young player, celebrating victories, as well as candid shots of him with his brothers and dad and mum. Unai's son, Lander, stands quietly nearby, occasionally glancing at the pictures. He has seen them many times. He likes to spend longer on the one of his great-grandad, Antonio. He, too, is following in the family footsteps, playing as a goalkeeper in Birmingham.

Amelia: 'Where are the dozens of suitcases this time?'

Unai, explaining it to the small audience: 'My mother tells me that I have too many clothes. I tell her that, because of my job, I need to have these clothes. Maybe it's more than I need, just maybe. I often bring clothes back for my brothers. Although, if I bring them a waistcoat, they won't wear it, because a vest, to them, is apparently a very right-wing piece of clothing! Only rich people wear three-piece suits, ha!'

Everyone laughs. In the Basque Country even the haircut is political.

Eventually, Unai turns to his mother, 'I have to go, Ama.' Amelia gives her son and grandson a big hug. Igor will return after he has dropped them off, so with the coffee that has been served, Amelia sits in front of the two journalists who are full of questions.

I was born in Hondarribia eighty-four years ago. I grew up in a simple home, with simple parents if I am allowed to use that expression. My father was a house painter, he was cheerful, and my mother stayed at home, which was her priority. There were four sisters and one brother, the youngest. I was the fourth daughter.

Life was creative back then, we played in the streets, always outside. There wasn't much to go around, quite the opposite. Life was tight, so we had to make do – play, imagine and discover – with whatever little we had. We were raised with a deep sense of respect. How do you teach that? Well, for one, we never gossiped about others at home. My father was welcoming. If someone was struggling, be it a friend or a neighbour, they'd come and eat with us, no questions asked.

Back then, football wasn't as popular here. Hondarribia was divided into three areas, the old town, the fishermen's quarter and the caserío, the area with big houses. I grew up in the old town, where there was a lot of immigration. The fishermen's quarter was filled with poverty. The owners of the big caseríos kept to themselves, they had large allotments and so on. Three very different worlds, even in the way people treated each other.

I went to a convent school. Later, though, we had to help out at home because my father had a business, painting and plumbing, together with a partner. The partner eventually left him with debts, and we had to carry that burden. I worked in a grocery store on the main street, the heart of the town, helping the owner serve customers. The summer people, the bathers, as we called them, the tourists, they'd order things, and I'd deliver them on my bike to their houses.

For us, France wasn't 'France'. It was just the other side. We had many relatives there. We visited family across the border, but everything still felt Basque. We had a cultural centre in the parish, went on trips, learnt to dance in Basque, and I did theatre. I was in a lot of plays, but they were performed in Spanish. I didn't live through the Spanish Civil War, but I felt it. By then, learning Basque was forbidden. That shaped everything. We couldn't fully grow in our own language. At home, I'd speak Spanish to my mother, and she'd answer in Basque. She never learnt Spanish. I did learn Basque in secret from her, though.

I had a great time doing theatre. Among my group, there were five gay boys. I must have been eighteen, in the early 1960s. We treated them just like anyone else; they were wonderful. But life wasn't easy for them. Three of them had to leave quickly for Paris. They've since passed away. I'm in a reading group now. We read a book about trans people recently, to understand them better. It was interesting, although very raw.

I then started working in a hotel during the summer. In winter, I left for Paris for five months. Took French classes every day, then came back to work in the hotel again. A couple of years later, I went to England as an au pair, to Guildford, to learn English. I spent six or seven months there before coming back to Hondarribia. And when I did, I kept studying in San Sebastián to be able to teach English.

I met my husband at a dance. He asked me to dance, and that's how it started. We knew of each other, but nothing more, Juan had been away a long time. He was eight years older than me, a professional goalkeeper, played for different clubs. He was close to retiring. After that, he coached, but just local teams. He managed Unión Palmera of Irún. Juan was a hard worker, demanding, dedicated to his family and everything he did. He worked in quality control for Decoexsa, a respected logistics company. Being near the border, transport was a big business back then. But when the customs offices closed after the creation of the European Market, Juan would say, 'What's going to happen to us now? How will we manage?' Many businesses shut down, but luckily, his survived.

We eventually bought a three-bedroom house for our four children to live in. I grew up surrounded by men – my husband, my single brother-in-law, Román, always hanging around with us, a bit of a male chauvinist if you ask me.

I gave English lessons at home, even after I was married, with four kids. I even taught Unai and, at one point, had over thirty students. I'd put him in the group, but he'd never show up. 'No, Ama, I can't go, I have training.' He must've been fifteen. He didn't really see the importance of studying. Always had an excuse. Now? Now he speaks English, French, Basque and Spanish – just like me. I didn't just teach English, I even taught religious studies! And that, coming from a leftist! But you had to contribute to the household economy.

The 1980s? It was a time of confusion, fear, violence. ETA. Heroin. A lost generation. Everyone lived it differently.

Our first three kids went to an ikastola, a Basque language school, but we sent Igor to study in France. The two oldest left school early. Koldo got into music. And Unai? He drifted in school, completely drawn to football. He wasn't motivated, didn't have much curiosity. Barely passed, convinced the trick was studying just enough to scrape by. Eventually, he dropped out to become a footballer. He left two subjects behind, one of which was Latin. I pushed him to finish them. He hated the teacher, but I'm stubborn. He went back and got it done. And later, he was grateful because he had passed a certain level of his education. After military service, he realised he needed a back-up plan. Started studying marketing and sports management while playing for Lorca Deportiva. He wasn't great at it, but he tried. That was how they were raised, seeing their parents work hard, take responsibility. In our house, effort, commitment and work always came first. I've heard Unai say, 'Responsibility means answering to people, to the fans, the owners, the players. I take that responsibility seriously, and I expect others to do the same.' I hear his father in those words. Maybe Juan didn't say it like that, but he lived it.

Unai has my energy, my fire. He got that from me. His father was calmer, more analytical. Unai, like all kids, had his rebellious phase. And here, the nights pull you in. He was one of those teenagers who stayed out late, a partygoer, just like his brothers. His father would go mad. 'If you don't come home on time, you're not getting a key.' But when Juan fell asleep, I'd sneak downstairs and let them in. That's part of growing up.

You have to go through that phase, experience things. As long as you don't lose yourself. That's the tricky part, you have to be careful not to get lost.

We argue a lot about politics with Unai. He says I'm stuck in the past. What does he know? I like fighting for what's right. Maybe I just like fighting, full stop.

At forty-seven, I had breast cancer. I found the lump myself. Checked a book for symptoms, but there are no symptoms. Went straight to the doctor. I wanted the surgery done as soon as possible. They operated. And here I am.

We're an austere family. Unai always says that when he was sixteen or seventeen, his weekly allowance was five hundred pesetas. That had to cover the bus and a doughnut, nothing more. That's why he values hard work, why he understands what things really cost. Unai is generous with others but strict with himself. He'll spend money to keep Real Unión running but for himself? Nothing material. Though, let's be honest, he has more clothes than he'll ever need! He doesn't care about brands, fancy cars or expensive things, though. Later, when he started making money as a footballer, I told him, 'Why don't you buy a place in the village? Open a sports shop or something?' Román helped him, and they bought a sports shop together. He still has it. When he started in football, players would earn maybe fifty thousand euros a year. You have ten years in the game, now they earn enough to live, sure, but then what?

Unai says he became a coach out of necessity, to stay in football, to keep earning, to take care of his family. His son hadn't been born yet, his wife was from Málaga, and as his football career was finishing, he thought, I need two homes, one in Málaga, so we can live comfortably, and another in Hondarribia, so when we come back, we have our own space, not staying with my parents. That has to be paid for somehow. He took coaching seriously. I think it was at Ferrol when he started thinking about it. Since he had finished high school, it was just three years of training. So, with the first classes and long distance travel, sometimes he'd tell me, 'Ama, you don't know how scared I've been.' When he played for Lorca, he came home for Christmas, and I could tell he was worried. He had an old car, and in winter, he had to drive through places that weren't exactly safe. 'I was scared,' he'd say. It was tough.

Unai, even as a player, kept giving suggestions to the manager. When he was at Sevilla, I visited him, and he had a room full of books, all marked up. Psychology books, mental training guides. He said, 'Look, Ama, depending on the match, I read my players this paragraph, or this one, or this one.' I was amazed at how he prepared for games.

He's intense. When he believes in a philosophy, in a methodology, he goes all in. Becomes the best at it. And when that idea no longer works, he moves on to something else. But that takes dedication. It takes time. That's why he won't fully enjoy writing this book you're planning. He wants to focus on his work. I am not sure he enjoys interviews. He doesn't see much point in them but understands they have to be done.

I can see the weight of responsibility on him. That kind of focus doesn't leave much room for enjoyment. Unai is already fifty-three. I know, at eighty-four, how fast life goes. That's why I tell all four of them: enjoy life as much as you can. Work is fine, but family, family is everything. I've always been about family. We all have. Family is what keeps us strong. It offers unconditional love. He's starting to see it more. He's realising he has old friends here, people he trusts, family. And I think he's feeling that pull again. He needs that.

People say that when someone makes it big in football, the family hierarchy shifts. It's true. Look at Andoni, Unai put him in charge of cutting the grass at the club. Unai is always looking out for his brothers. But not once, not once, has any of them called him to ask for something. Never. And yet, he's always there. If someone's sick, if something happens, he steps in. He's incredibly kind. One day, he rushed into the house while I was having breakfast with Lander. 'Ama, do you have a blanket? Give me a blanket, quick, there's a man who slept outside all night, alone.' So, I gave him a blanket. Later, he gave the man some money too.

He's at the top now. But I keep hearing people say he is more than capable of taking another step forward.

Do you think he is, do you think he wants to? Really? We'll see . . .

Ten minutes away from Amelia's flat, a flight taking Unai and Lander back to Birmingham ascends into the darkening sky, the lights of Irún and Hondarribia shimmering below. He will be back home soon. He will, once again, cram too much into too little time.

3

FINDING HIS VOICE:

LORCA DEPORTIVA & ALMERÍA

At Salto del Caballo, Toledo's modest stadium, sat a young Unai Emery, just another player on the bench, his mind buzzing with more tactical ideas than he probably should have. As the match unfolded, he couldn't help himself, he started gesturing, stretching his arms, half lifting from his seat and barking out instructions to his teammates. An orchestra conductor without a baton. It was a bit too much. Miguel Ángel Portugal, the actual manager, turned to him in bemusement.

'What are you doing, kid?'

The moment froze in Unai's mind. There he was, caught mid-gesture, half apologising with his hands before sitting back down, attempting to look inconspicuous. He wasn't trying to step on anyone's toes, he was just brimming with whatever it was that he carried inside of him that seemed impossible to contain. 'Why did I become a coach? Pure survival instinct. I had dropped out of school, and football was my only future,' Unai recalls. Coaching wasn't just an alternative, neither was just putting food on the table; it was an idea that excited him, a life plan. He could picture himself on the sideline, making decisions, shaping a team. In fact, Unai had wanted to be a coach since his days as a player, and he had already coached children in Hondarribia when he was in the Real

Sociedad B squad. In Toledo, he began his coaching courses, and by the age of twenty-five, he had earned his first coaching badge. The pull of football wasn't something he could switch off. But even then, his teammates didn't realise the depth of his ambition. He wanted to fill his head with it. 'I called Mikel Etxarri, a Real Sociedad coach who was teaching at the coaching school and told him Unai requested all the material he was using,' says his friend Alberto Benito. '"All of it?" he asked. "Yep, he wants all of it."' At the age of thirty, he finished more early coaching qualifications while in Ferrol. Twice a week, he drove an hour each way to La Coruña for classes after training, most days he would return home past midnight. Many of his peers who had started the lessons with him gave up because of the gruelling schedule.

While playing for Lorca Deportiva, his final club, in Spain's third tier, Unai also enrolled at the Johan Cruyff Institute in Madrid to study marketing and sports management. He did this alongside Juan Carlos Carcedo, a teammate from Leganés. They were kindred spirits, curious and motivated to acquire more knowledge. Very early on, Carcedo and Emery could distinguish between players who treated football as merely a profession and those, like themselves, who let the game consume every aspect of their lives. 'We knew every player in the second division, every coach, every tactic,' Carcedo recalls. 'At that time, there were maybe only three or four players as immersed in the game as we were. Even the manager sometimes asked us for insights because technical reports weren't as thorough back then, non-existent in fact. Our shared passion made us friends.' Unai's lack of interest in traditional education left a gap in his knowledge. But that void, combined with his overwhelming passion for the game, became his driving force. He transformed himself into a voracious autodidact, into a learning artisan, someone who had to plough his own furrow, step out of his comfort zone, devouring books on sports psychology, coaching, self-help and leadership. He is, in essence, a self-taught student of life and experience. Football didn't come looking for him; he sought it out.

He was also fighting other shortcomings. Despite his left foot of quality and an excellent understanding of the game, he had to accept that he was not strong enough and, on top of that, he couldn't share stories of winning Champions League titles or reaching the semi-finals of a World Cup. Those weaknesses forced him to reflect deeply on what he lacked and what made him uncomfortable in his playing days. He did not have significant mentors to guide him. His first dream was to work under Juanma Lillo, a fellow Basque and a pioneer in tactical thinking who had become the youngest coach in Spain's Segunda División at twenty-nine and later repeated the feat in LaLiga with Salamanca. Lillo, who later worked as Jorge Sampaoli's assistant at Chile and Sevilla, even became part of Pep Guardiola's coaching staff at Manchester City. Unai idealised Lillo's unique, profound approach to the game, which stood out in an era when few coaches explored football in such depth. A coffee meeting between Unai and Lillo was arranged by Roberto Olabe, a former teammate from Real Sociedad. For 2 hours, they discussed football, with Unai expressing his admiration and his desire to work and learn under him. However, nothing materialised.

Unai grew close to Pedro Reverte, a former player who retired at twenty-six and had become Lorca's director of football only a year later, the club he was playing for. 'Unai would ask me which matches I was going to watch that weekend and if I minded him joining me,' Reverte remembers. 'Unai already saw things in a game that were tricky to spot. He could see where teams were going to fail, how they could be exploited and would come up with solutions. That made me think, *This guy has something special.*' They would travel the 450 kilometres from Lorca to Madrid to watch Leganés, Rayo Vallecano, Atlético Madrid. Or they would check on local teams like Murcia, Elche, Alicante, Almería or Albacete. Back in those days, with no social media, as well as reading all the papers, he would spend hours on the phone with those that knew teams and players from the division Lorca were in.

Towards the end of 2004, a 32-year-old Emery realised his playing career was coming to an end, as his knee did not allow him to respond to the demands of even the third tier of Spanish football. As he couldn't fulfil the challenging role of a winger, he was utilised as a full-back in the five games he had played so far that season. 'If it hurts, you have to tell the coach,' Reverte told him. His teammates invited him to take a step aside. In September, he played the first half of a match in Zafra. His teammate Xavi Moro recommended him to be substituted at half-time. It was to be his last match as a professional. He went to the doctor. 'He told me that if I kept forcing the joint, I could lose mobility,' Unai remembers. '"Unai," he told me. "You will struggle to continue playing at this level."' Three months later, he was still trying to recover and rejoin the team, even though he was not fully convinced he would ever play again. There were bills to be paid, so he took more coaching exams and became a UEFA A Licence coach, which allowed him to manage teams in Lorca's division or lower.

The team, with a good squad that had the ambition of getting into the play-offs to be promoted to the Segunda División, were sitting mid-table, with a manager, Quique Yagüe, that was not impressing the director of football Pedro Reverte or the chairman Antonio Baños, who described the situation astutely: 'We had a racehorse, and Quique kept pulling on the reins and stopping him from running fast.' During the Christmas break, Reverte asked Unai to meet in a coffee shop in Lorca, 'I want to talk to you about an idea I had.' Reverte was direct with Unai. 'What do you think if I ask you to manage the team?' Unai was not expecting that and did not know how to respond. He just looked at Pedro Reverte blankly and said nothing. Pedro, who wanted to hear from Unai before approaching the chairman with the suggestion, insisted. 'I trust you, you have the coaching badges, you know the team, it is full of Basque players that know you well and we know how they would respond.' Unai's head was full of contrasting thoughts: opportunity, complications, a new step, the end of his playing career. He asked for time to think about it. 'I was relatively happy to retire, I wanted to coach, but not so soon and not under those circumstances,' Unai explains. But football dictates its own timing.

Unai did not think for long. He called Reverte. 'If you think I am ready, and you are convinced I can do this, then I will do it.' The director of football told him he was going to earn €2,800 a month, the same wage he had earned as a player, as the budget for the season had been entirely used up. Unai did not even negotiate it. The first reaction of the chairman was also one of surprise. 'Pedro ... bloody hell ... If we do this and it does not work, they are going to kill us,' were his first words. 'But if you are convinced, go ahead.'

Pedro remained convinced of Unai's potential. 'It will go well, he is ready. I will tell you something else – the results you cannot guarantee, but I know nobody will work as hard as him.' It was a very uncommon step to give the manager's position to a current player and a massive leap of faith. Unai talked to some of his teammates, the captains in particular, about it. They all agreed it was a brave move but they were supportive. 'At that point, I decided to dedicate myself fully to being a coach, without regrets. It was what I truly wanted.' Unai had played 215 games in Spain's Segunda División as a professional footballer, as well as making five appearances for Real Sociedad in LaLiga. Players called each other with a certain air of disbelief. 'Unai is going to manage us! Can you believe it?' They had left for a break, only to return and bid farewell to a teammate – someone who had shared the locker room, the showers and nights out with them – and greet their new coach.

Fans and local media could not understand the decision; there were early criticisms. 'The uproar you couldn't even begin to imagine,' explains Baños. Returning from the holidays, standing in front of his former teammates – now his players – Unai delivered his first words as a manager of a team that was eleventh in the table: 'I know the coach who has been released was a friend of yours, and another one will come at some point. For now, they've put me in charge. I have one advantage: I only want the best for you. But I do demand we have a goal. What are we doing the next five months? Are we going to fight just to avoid relegation? The position we are in now is shit. This team has the quality to aim for the play-offs. It won't be easy, but it's an opportunity for all of us.'

He was instantly recognisable as the Unai we know now: ambitious, intense in conveying his ideas and fully aware of the importance of communication. The room was quiet. The weight of his demand hung in the air. 'He touched their emotions,' Pedro Reverte admits. 'It certainly was an ambitious target, but exciting.' Had he won them over? Players exchanged glances. 'Oof, that's quite the start!' Yet, from then on, the dressing room quickly closed ranks, shutting away any doubters. They had a destination. But Unai sensed not everyone was on board.

On Saturday 8 January 2005, Emery sat on the team bus for the first time as a coach to travel over 400 kilometres to Écija, a city in the Sevilla province. 'He was looking down the whole time,' Antonio Baños says. 'He couldn't stop reading. I think he was studying the opposing players or reading something about tactics and strategy.' Unai recalls every detail of his first game as a coach. 'I remember it all perfectly – the trip, the hotel, arriving at the pitch, the line-up. We were ready.' Were they? With a sparse crowd in attendance, Unai began his new life on the touchline. Just 15 minutes into the game versus Écija, Lorca did a throw-in rehearsed in training. The full-back and the winger linked up to leave one of them free to cross the ball and the forward ran to the near post. Goal! The path was set.

Unai had started leading twenty-five players, each requiring his guidance and confidence. He had to foster harmony, design training exercises and clearly communicate his ideas, all while learning on the job, solving problems his own way. And every week he would remind them of the target: the play-offs to earn promotion to the Segunda División, to fully professional football, to better wages, to more attention. A couple of months after his appointment, despite the fact the team had been unable to put together a good run of victories, Unai and the players knew where they stood with each other. Nonconformism, respect and humility became his cornerstones. 'Respect the competition, the fans, the opponent and your players,' Unai often says. A coach also respects the fans by valuing their passion.

'I've always believed football should be enjoyable,' Unai reflects. 'When I step into a stadium, I want my players to enjoy themselves as much as the fans. And selfishly, I want to enjoy it too, I want to feel the excitement. From my time at Lorca until today, that idea and desire has always stayed with me.' A coach respects the opponent by studying them, no matter how many hours it takes and respects the players by believing in them and providing them with all the information possible. 'We must have the humility to recognise our flaws and ambition to improve,' he mentioned in one of the chats to his pupils, a sentence taken from one of the books he was reading at the time. 'I began to approach coaching differently from the coaches I had experienced,' Unai admits. 'Often, I couldn't perform at my best because I lacked information, so I made it [gaining information] a priority to incorporate that into my style.' He found someone based locally who had collected hundreds of videos of games from the Spanish third tier. He supplied them to clubs, for a price. José Antonio Paredes had been accumulating matches from all the divisions since he was nine years old and, at one point, had eleven satellite dishes attached to the top of his home. Unai and Paredes would meet in a petrol station halfway between their residences, or if the team bus was going in the direction of Paredes's home, Unai would ask the driver to stop to collect new tapes.

With Pedro Reverte's help, Unai watched the games on one VHS player and copied bits that were important for the players to see on another. One evening, at around 8 p.m., the electricity cut off and the previous two days' work was lost after they had forgotten to record them on the second VHS player. The work done with the tapes would be converted into an hour-long video for the team. Unai was not an innovator in video analysis, but he was certainly one of the first coaches to base his methodology on it.

Challenges came quickly for Unai after the initial sense of harmony. Some players were still loyal to the previous manager, Yagüe. Others were Emery's friends, but they were now questioning his decisions. To these players, every choice felt like a betrayal of trust, but Emery knew the team had to come first. Emery recalls a close friend that played with him at Lorca, Xabi Sánchez; the two shared a bond as fellow Basques. As manager, Emery had three midfielders competing for just two positions. Initially, he rotated them, but eventually, he identified who the best two were and

83

chose them for the important matches. Xabi Sánchez was the one who played less. He stopped speaking to Unai. Their friendship ended, something that has always pained him. He was never sure if the fault lay with Xabi or himself, although it taught him a very valuable lesson. One thing seemed certain – leadership required distance. 'The transition from player to coach was so fast,' Unai explains. 'But I try to relive that moment very often. *Unai, don't forget to think like a footballer*, I tell myself. As time passes, you drift further from that stage, but I don't want to forget what it feels like or how a footballer perceives a coach's decisions and behaviour, what they like and don't like. That way, I can treat players as I would have liked to have been treated myself.'

Unai kept fostering unity through shared meals and time together. But if the team went out for a few beers, he would leave after the second drink to give them some space. He no longer stayed out for four or five rounds with them. And while the run of wins necessary to jump up the table was not yet arriving, he managed to make the squad believe in his way of working. 'Believe in yourselves, in the process,' he repeated. 'Especially in the team.' During his time at Toledo in the Segunda División, Unai had learnt a valuable lesson about mindset. One weekend, before a match against promotion favourites Elche, he and a teammate filled out a *quiniela* (a football betting slip) and logically picked Elche as the winner. At Toledo, a humble team fighting to stay in the league, it was easy to accept defeat against stronger opponents. When he handed it to the Toledo supporter running the slip collection, she was shocked. 'How can you put that Elche will win? You have to believe in your team!' He never forgot that moment. Now, as coach of Lorca, he passed this lesson on to his players. When he found anyone doubting the score of their next game, he would stop the chat. 'You must always say that we are going to win.'

Players exchanged opinions with the manager, something they had not experienced before in their careers. Through the work, the way he lived his new profession and the confidence he gave them, Unai started instilling in his squad a love for football that some of them felt they had lost. He had a plan in his head on how the team had to perform: bold, aggressive football, with full-backs going up and down the wings, midfielders pushing into the box and forwards given freedom to operate as they liked. The performances were good, the results were improving but they still needed consistency. Unai sought advice from José Aurelio Gay, who'd faced a similar struggle at Pontevedra in the same division and had been sacked halfway through the season. Unai knew he was under pressure and losing the job would be a massive blow to the start of his coaching career. 'Adapt,' Gay told him. Winning wasn't just about possession or style. Scoring plenty of goals and having good performances was not enough; it was all about the result. This realisation reshaped his approach and the team's trajectory.

Without abandoning their offensive mentality, the team adapted to their opponents and to the demands of each game. Victories began to flow, which worked as a kind of magic dust sprinkled over the team, now brimming with motivation. Any lingering differences were set aside. But Unai could not stop feeling like his job was on the line during each game, even when Lorca were regularly in the top positions in the Segunda B standings, playing an attractive 4-3-3 system that was considered revolutionary for the time and the division. 'It didn't matter if we were playing away or against one of the favourites; Unai didn't care. All he wanted was to win and score goals,' recalls the Lorca player Álvaro García 'Moro', referencing the 7–1 win against Díter Zafra and the 5–0 thrashing of Marbella. With an explosive attack (sixty-one goals, making them the third-highest scorers in the league), Lorca were a team to watch. But they were also hungry to get the ball back. 'Our defensive line was pushed up high, forcing a lot of offsides,' recalls 'Moro'. 'We had four or five moves that we executed quickly to recover possession, and our pressing dominated every team.' They reached the play-offs. It was a milestone for a modestly unassuming city like Lorca, known as 'the City of the Sun' for its friendly climate, which experienced a genuine footballing revolution and captured national attention. Rarely had it been in the spotlight to such an extent. From the hilltop, the medieval stronghold of Lorca Castle stood tall and proud.

In the early days of Unai Emery's managerial career, his appearance on the sidelines did not stand out that much, a bit like Lorca itself. Passionate, yes, but with an almost teacher-like look, wearing glasses and a club shirt often paired with grey or black trousers, with a notebook always tucked into his pocket. After a while, he started wearing a tracksuit for games, but for the big matches, like the play-off semi-final against Alicante, considered the best team in Segunda B, he decided to wear a suit. The problem was that the one he owned was far too big for him, which he also paired with an oversized tie. His early attempts at dressing the part reflected his lack of interest to impress in that department.

Lorca beat Alicante. Then a rush to see potential rivals took place. Unai told Pedro Reverte to prepare a travel bag. His beloved Real Unión, in the Basque Country, were hosting Madrid-based Rayo Vallecano – one of them would be their rivals in the play-off final. But there was another match worth watching first, Unai thought. So, at 7 a.m. the next day, they began the 400-kilometre drive from Lorca to Madrid so they could be at Real Madrid B versus Conquense, a semi-final in another Segunda División B group (that tier was divided into four groups and four play-offs). From there, they flew to San Sebastián, less than 10 minutes away from Stadium Gal in Irún, where they saw Real Unión making it to the final. The club who had nurtured the talents of his grandfather, father and uncle, now stood between his Lorca Deportiva and a place in the Segunda División. 'I had many friends on the opposing team, but when I look back, I still feel proud of having been able to prioritise professionalism over personal feelings,' Unai insists. Things did not start well for Lorca Deportivo, as they lost the first leg at home, 1–2 to the visitors. Pessimism spread through the group. 'I will never forget that defeat,' Pedro Reverte recalls. 'Everyone was depressed. After the match, it seemed impossible to achieve promotion. We prepared for a few days in Águilas, an extraordinary coastal town. The coach wanted the entire team to return from that visit with the conviction that promotion was still possible – and that's exactly what happened.'

Unai rallied his players, declaring: 'This is our chance to become professionals by reaching the second division.' In small group meetings, he highlighted the positives from the first leg, the good plays and chances created, reminding them, 'We scored first. Only one goal separates us. We will score three.' In other sessions, he meticulously detailed how they could approach the second leg to secure victory. Optimism spread through the squad.

On the morning of the second leg in the Stadium Gal, Unai noticed a bus already prepared to celebrate Irún's promotion. Immediately, he knew how he would begin his pre-match talk: with this discovery. Lorca took a 0–2 lead in Irún. But the tension was unbearable. Unai's father, Juan, couldn't take it anymore. He left the stadium and walked the half hour back home to Hondarribia. Real Unión scored just before the end of regular time, forcing extra time. Unai's brother Igor was working as a journalist at the time and covering the game for local radio. He was also going through an incalculable mix of emotions that he couldn't hide from the listeners. In the 112th minute, Lorca scored their third and decisive goal that took them to the Segunda División. Unai jumped on to the pitch, running nowhere and everywhere. The rest of the bench followed him. Igor ran out of words in the commentary box, speechless, in an indescribable eruption of joy. He still doesn't know why, but he could not say a word. Perhaps it was relief. Maybe he unconsciously knew that an alternative result would have taken Unai to a very different place.

Unai turned around, and for a moment, the world seemed to stand still. Everything they had achieved in such a short time began to sink in. 'That result gave me the most intense emotion of my career,' Unai admits. He found and embraced his brother Igor. That moment seemed to last hours. 'We did it,' Unai kept saying. That evening, Juan Emery joined the Lorca coaching team for their celebratory dinner, while the players went out to celebrate their success. The next morning, the team embarked on the 918-kilometre journey back to Lorca by bus. For Unai, the trip felt short. The following day, after a tour of the city in an open-top bus, standing on the town hall balcony, with the fans gathered in the square below, Pedro Reverte and Unai reminisced. They talked about that chat over coffee and Unai's face when he was offered the job just six months before, about the games where victories were deserved but not forthcoming. About whether Unai had felt ready when given the job and the mixture of feelings he'd had about it. About where they were now. 'Look down, Unai.' They gave each other a big hug. And both cried.

The following season, Lorca became the surprise package of the Segunda División. After an extraordinary second half of the campaign, they entered the final matchday with a real shot at promotion to LaLiga. Imagine the excitement in the city, the historic district of churches and palaces transformed into a sea of blue and white. Flags waved from balconies, scarves and hats adorned supporters and shirts with the club's colours were everywhere. The bars were packed, their doors open to let the noise spill out, while the terraces on the old stone streets overflowed with locals and rival fans. Ultimately, they finished an impressive fifth.

Over that first season and a half, everyone had come to understand Unai Emery's methods and impact. It marked a turning point in Lorca's footballing history, igniting a passion for the sport. Despite the economic and sporting challenges faced by the club in the years that followed (they were relegated the campaign after Emery's departure), this golden era remains a source of pride. When players return to the city, where they go to meet each other again, they always remember that special era and the unique spirit that defined it.

Pedro Reverte was offered the job as sporting director at Almería after his excellent stint at Lorca, and he in turn offered Emery the head coach position on a two-year contract. Joining a respectable club in the Segunda División, with quality players, ambitious owners aiming for promotion to LaLiga and a healthy budget, was a step forward for both men. However, Lorca reacted quickly. To avoid losing one of the two key figures who had brought them so much success, they made a counter-offer to Reverte, convincing him to stay. Unai's friend Roberto Olabe was instead given the sporting director role at Almería, but kept the managerial offer on the table for Unai to consider.

Olabe sensed the interest from Unai and drove the 900 kilometres through the night from San Sebastián to Águilas, near Lorca. After a whole afternoon of talking, Unai was convinced to take the step. 'I thought he would be a good companion, because of a similar vision of life, because it was an adventure, an ambitious and complicated project,' recalls Olabe. 'I personally need to have a clear desire in my life for something to happen, and so does Unai. In this job we spend many hours working, enduring tough moments, learning a lot. That is why you want things to happen, you don't want to remain still.'

'Almería were relatively new,' Olabe explains, 'having come back as a different club after the original Almería club disappeared. They had just struggled to avoid relegation, and now the owner was talking about promotion.' The city of Almería was desperate to return to LaLiga after their brief first experience in the top-flight between 1979 and 1981 with the original Club de Fútbol Almería, which, after making history, had eventually disappeared due to financial struggles. The city's footballing spirit was reborn with the establishment of Unión Deportiva Almería in 1989, but it was a club that had neither proper organisation nor infrastructure. There was no youth academy, and the training facilities were not great. The objective was to achieve promotion to LaLiga within three years while also building a serious institution. It sounded like too much to do in such a short period of time. Unai, a cyclone of energy, and a determined Olabe felt capable of doing it.

They had to start by bringing in sixteen new players and letting seventeen go. A very tough challenge. The arguments about which players to sign, long and vociferous on occasion, made Olabe real- ise Unai had a particular approach to management which he had not seen before. Miguel Ángel Corona, today Valencia's sporting director, was brought in from Real Madrid's youth team as a very talented attacking midfielder. At the time, the team were search- ing for a player who could complement the strong but less creative players already on the roster. Corona's quality was undeniable, but his work ethic was questioned. For Unai Emery, this became a challenge he was eager to take on. During the season, Almería played against Míchel González's Real Madrid Castilla side, which featured players like striker Álvaro Negredo and midfielder Dani Parejo. Olabe and Emery met with Míchel, where Negredo was a topic of discussion. Everyone wanted him, the Castilla manager said, but there were also concerns about his work ethic without the ball. He seemed to put all his trust in his goalscoring talent and did not have the hunger to get the ball back. For Emery, this criticism became again an opportunity. When the meeting ended, Roberto and Unai looked at each other. Olabe knew exactly what Emery was about to say. 'We're signing him!'

'There is no other coach who would turn a player's supposed weakness into their motivation for signing them,' Roberto Olabe admits. Perhaps he saw these players as reflections of himself. It was as though he identified with their flaws and sought to coach them while harnessing their strengths. In a way, Unai seemed to be coaching himself. Juan Carlos Carcedo, who had helped Las Palmas achieve promotion to the Segunda as an assistant manager, joined Unai as his number two. His defensive focus was needed to balance Unai's attacking mindset.

In the two seasons that Unai was at Almería, 2006–08, he realised he had to fill the changing room with winners, those players prepared to step up to the plate. Whereas losers wait for others to act and remain silent, winners speak out in the crowd. The squad, although young, started gathering such footballers. In those two years, Almería featured talents like Álvaro Negredo (who eventually became an international star with Spain), José Manuel Mané, Miguel Ángel Corona, Bruno Saltor, Fernando Soriano, Albert Crusat, Juanma Ortiz. Most were in their mid-twenties, offensively skilled, hungry for success and ready to grow. Other veterans, like the goalkeeper Sander Westerveld or the Nigerian forward Kalu Uche, gave the squad some balance.

From day one, Emery's methodology was put into practice. Before each training session, he would explain what the target of the day was and why it would help the team collectively. Notebook and glasses in hand, Unai would sometimes read tactical notes, defensive and offensive actions often written five, six or seven years previously from when he was still a player. 'He had all these flip charts, sometimes with ten pages,' Sander Westerveld remembers. 'A black marker and big sheets of paper. He'd write everything down.' Before games, the team would arrive at the stadium and have meetings for at least half an hour, 45 minutes sometimes 'Right before the match! Remember, at that time nobody really knew him. At first, everyone was like "Jesus, another hour-long meeting! Bloody hell, this guy . . . !" "Un pesado" [laughs], a pain in the neck.'

What also stood out was how specific training was. Short sessions, but full of details. If footballers didn't do things properly, he would stop the drill as many times as was necessary. 'We'd spend weeks on just throw-ins or corners,' Westerveld recalls. 'Same routine, over and over – one to the ball, one behind, cross in, far-post player darts near, near-post spins far. After hours of repetition, it became automatic. And in games – bang – we scored from it. I remember one: quick throw, three touches, cross, goal. This was 2007, but he already had signals, different takers, constant variations. We scored so many corners because he was always ahead of the game.'

'I remember him once telling me about a coach no one knew, who had as many as twenty-four rehearsed set-piece plays,' the Basque coach, guru and personal friend Mikel Etxarri remembers. 'So, he started the process of having thirty.'

'Unai would go home after matches with videotapes and watch them twenty times,' Westerveld says. 'Next day he'd know exactly what we did wrong and how to fix it. And he would show us videos of the next rivals. That was his routine every new week.' There would be conversations about the video and a bunch of questions from the manager to the players.

'If you have a throw-in twenty metres from the opponent's goal, what's your first-best option? And the second? And the third?'

'How can you block the angle of a certain pass?'

'What is the ideal body position when receiving the ball?'

'Goalkeeper, why do you have to direct the ball to the player's stronger foot when initiating the counter-attack?'

'Even if just one player listens and feels inspired, that's reason enough to speak,' Unai says.

Back then, it would still take 4 or 5 hours to create 10 minutes of video footage. So, eventually, Víctor Mañas, a tech expert who joined the coaching staff and remains with Unai at Aston Villa, introduced them to new tools that slowly but surely streamlined their work.

It is fair to say the players were not used to all that intense analysis. 'In one of these meetings, we were sitting in the video room and Kalu Uche, a forward, had his chair leaning against the wall with his feet up – I don't know how he balanced it,' Westerveld recalls. 'The lights were off for the video session, and suddenly – BANG! He fell asleep, slipped off the chair and crashed to the floor! Everyone burst out laughing. This happened a few times a year with different players. I struggled as well with it once. As a goalkeeper, I don't need tactics or all that detailed information. I'm just the guy who has to save the balls, so I'd switch off sometimes.'

The budget and ambition meant they were candidates to get promoted, along with another half a dozen teams, yet at the start of the 2006–07 season their initial results didn't reflect the team's potential. Emery's side lost the first three games, including a defeat at Real Murcia where three of his players were sent off. His energy on the sidelines was now voltaic. He pulled strange faces, made inexplicable gestures, he pointed in opposite directions, he imitated the shape of a plane landing and sometimes he even appeared to be having conversations with himself. Unai wanted to live the match as if he were on the pitch, believing he could help the team that way. He was the source of electricity that he wanted everyone to plug into. 'After another defeat, I told a journalist that if we didn't change the way we played, we wouldn't turn things around in the league,' recalls Francisco Rodríguez, the club's all-time top scorer. 'The next day, during training, Unai asked me to come to his office. When I walked in, there was a newspaper open on the table. On one of the pages, my words were clearly visible: If we don't change, we won't improve. Unai gestured for me to sit down and said, "The one who needs to change is you. If you don't change your attitude, you won't remain part of this team."' The player knew the manager was right.

With Almería now in the relegation zone, Emery still had most of the players' support. However, the president, Alfonso García Gabarrón, who had taken a chance on a young and relatively unknown coach, felt the pressure mounting. He called Unai to stress how vital it was to turn the situation around, for everyone involved. Unai shared this conversation with his staff. The next game against Cádiz, at home, became a final for them all. Suspended for the game, from the stands, mobile phone in hand, Emery watched nervously as Almería took a 2–0 lead. It seemed under control until the referee awarded a dubious penalty for a foul outside the box and sent off defender Mané. Cádiz scored. Yet, 2–1 ahead and with 30 minutes to go, Almería held on for the win. From that point onwards, the team became a fortress at home, the Estadio de los Juegos Mediterráneos, winning the next five matches and not losing at home for the rest of the season, amassing a twenty-game unbeaten streak.

When you're this detailed and have long meetings, you need results. Otherwise players would turn against it. 'After a few weeks, in games, everything he predicted would happen, exactly as we trained too,' Westerveld remembers. 'It was unbelievable – like tactical witchcraft. And during the game, you'd already have solutions because we'd trained for it all week. That's when it clicks. "Wow, we need to listen to this guy, he is special, this guy knows!" I'm the type of player who needs repetition – do an exercise ten times until it's automatic. But many players just go through the motions, and get bored with repetition. Results started to arrive, and we all thought, without exception, this method works. And it became an unbelievable season. It was one of the best years of my career – not just on the pitch, but the group we had, living close together, families included. We were very close, it was special.'

That Almería side had the perfect mix of competitiveness, composure and confidence, maintaining the same composure after winning or losing. 'Mental pressure, fear, exists. I've experienced it,' Emery explains. 'The fear of knowing you weren't meeting expectations. I've had players who refused to take a penalty out of fear of failure. Coaches are, above all, generators of confidence.' It was a time of discovery. Roberto Olabe and Unai Emery were driven by an insatiable desire to explore, to never settle and to constantly ask questions. There were some players who were older than Unai and Carcedo, but their strong personalities and collaborative approach won over the squad. They imposed a style of play and a professional ethos rooted in trial and error. Instead of sticking rigidly to a single idea, Unai preferred to adapt, throwing himself into the technical details to refine whichever approach best suited the moment. 'Football evolves quickly,' Emery comments on that period. 'I've always focused on the present, taking it one day, one game at a time. I'm not one for long-term plans; I concentrate on what's in front of me and constantly look for answers to what we're doing.'

'People think the most important thing for a team is knowing who plays or doesn't play, or why someone is left out. For me, that's the least important moment,' explains Olabe. 'The most incredible part is the conversation after the match. Not immediately after the game, emotions run high – it's too heated. For collective re-flection, and to evolve to have more depth, it has to come later. Forty-eight hours after the game, it was like a battle to the death over what Unai thought and what I thought, but without conflict. Discussion is the greatest tool we've been given to grow, as long as we respect each other. After that, I would step aside because the rest was the coach's job.' Emery was there to help, but he always knew the players' talent could and should make the difference. In fact, often he believed in their quality more than the footballers themselves. Álvaro Negredo still remembers the confidence Unai had in him, which was the manager's biggest impact. 'I remember a match against Valladolid that we won 1–0. We had a free kick about twenty-five metres from the goal. Corona lifted the ball, I volleyed it. We had practised that play about fifteen times during training that week, and honestly, I didn't score a single one. Before the match, Unai came up to me and said, "If you get the chance, go for it." Another teammate looked at me and said, "You didn't score any in training. Don't do it." Unai liked taking risks. My kick flew into the top corner. Goal!'

Unai defied conventional Segunda División wisdom, which prioritised defence in a league known as a graveyard for historic clubs. 'I told myself, *Unai, you need to do something different*. If you do what everyone else does, you'll just be one of many,' the manager says. His attacking philosophy stood out. Almería played with an offensive 4-3-3 system. Full-backs provided depth and width. Negredo and Corona worked tirelessly off the ball, allowing the team to press effectively. Good results started to accompany their performances. But nobody could drop their level, that was not allowed. Once, while talking to his players about the virtues of teamwork, Unai grabbed a bucket nearby and started kicking it, representing an unwanted player in the squad. 'We'll kick him out! We'll kick him out! We don't want him with us, we don't want him on the team!'

'Every word matters,' Emery believes, 'because every fire starts with a single spark.'

'My relationship with Unai was strong,' Sander Westerveld admits. 'We were both competitive and sometimes clashed during games – shouting at each other about whether to slow the play or keep going – but we always understood each other after. He valued that. He'd hold these meetings where he'd write down: Why do you play football? He'd then start writing down: Number one: Money. Then I'd raise my hand and say, "Sorry, not me." He'd respond, "The first thing everyone thinks about when they want to be a footballer is money." And I'd insist, "No, no – not me." I told him: "I play for titles. I want to win things." When I leave a club, I want to be remembered – not personally, but I want to look back at my career and see what titles I won: Premier Leagues, European Cups. I don't want to just look at my bank account." At first, the reaction was like, "You are a strange one!". Then he'd continue writing on the board. The second point would be about titles, next personal growth. He'd make this whole list. We'd have these meetings a couple of times a year, always repeating the same concepts. Sometimes even right before a game he would bring it back! He'd say, "Let's remind ourselves again – why do you play football? To earn money? To move to a better club for more money? To secure your future?" His point was that, even in the second division, if you work hard every day and dedicate yourself completely, then you could earn enough money to provide for your family for life. That should be one of your main goals. "We want to win this championship and reach LaLiga, because you can double your wages!" Unai would say. Then he'd look around the room and add: "OK, except for Sander." [laughs] That became a running joke.'

As Almería were closing in on promotion, Unai Emery decided to experiment with his pre-match rituals. Ahead of a critical game against Xerez, matchday 35, he addressed his players with unexpected brevity. 'Today, I won't give you a motivational speech. No talk. You've heard it all before.' They lost 3–0. After the match, captain José Ortiz approached him, visibly puzzled. 'Míster, why didn't you give us a talk?' Ortiz asked.

Emery responded, 'Because I thought I'd bore you.'

Ortiz's reply struck a chord, 'I missed it, Boss. Truly.'

Almería, a close-knit and fearless group, stood on the brink of history sixteen years after their last visit to LaLiga. Promotion was within their grasp, but they still needed one final push. The entire city prepared for the showdown against Ponferradina at the Estadio de los Juegos Mediterráneos. Fans had arrived hours before kick-off, dressed in red and white, filling the stands with a sea of waving flags. They welcomed the players with chants, pats on the back, buzzing with anticipation. A counter-attack in injury time, finished by Miguel Ángel Corona, sealed a 3–1 victory. It had to be Corona, a player Emery had shaped into a fighter to complement his natural talent. The squad surged towards the goalscorer. Flags whipped through the air, fists punched the sky.

Unai Emery, dressed in a suit and red tie, walked back to the empty bench. After the final whistle, the pitch started filling with fans, players gathered in the centre circle for a collective hug. Unai couldn't escape the local television.

Reporter: 'Thrilled, aren't you?'

Unai: 'Yes, yes, absolutely thrilled.'

Reporter: 'And who comes to mind right now?'

Unai: 'The people of Almería, the lads. They're amazing.'

As soon as he could, Unai sprinted to join his players, who were hugging, crying. His smile said it had been a job well done. The first flares were lit.

Footballers who had never played in LaLiga began imagining what lay ahead. The fans wouldn't let Unai into the locker room; instead, they hoisted him into the air in celebration. Eventually, he was pulled from the crowd for more hugs in the locker room, now without his tie. Outside the stadium, an open-top bus waited to carry the team through the streets of Almería, though it quickly filled with politicians eager to be in the photo. It was a long, unforgettable day for everyone.

Lander Emery was just a baby when his father had become the manager of Lorca Deportiva. The small family moved to the city, settling into a routine that revolved around Unai's new career, but he was a man who did not check the clock when he worked. To Lander, life was simple: his world was his mother's voice, the warmth of home and the sounds of his dad coming and going, always in a hurry. By the time Lander was three, they had moved again, this time to Almería. He was starting to become more aware of his surroundings, and one thing stood out: football. 'By then, I was kicking a ball, even if I didn't know what I was doing,' Lander says now, even though he is not sure if that is a memory of his or one he has imagined to recreate a story he has told many times. For the young manager, every match continued to be a battle to prove himself. But at home, Lander just wanted his dad's attention. After long days at the training ground, Unai would come home and find Lander toddling around the house. And the kid got attention, even if often the coach's head was somewhere else.

Back at the training ground, there was one decision that had given Unai sleepless nights. 'Unai, you seem distant,' his father Juan would say when he came to visit him in Almería, noticing that his son was often lost in thought. Francisco Rodríguez, who was a symbol of Almería's growth after seventeen years at the club, was informed by Emery that he would not be part of the squad for the top-flight. It did not have to do with the doubts he had shared with a journalist at the start of the previous season. Emery simply believed he did not have enough quality for LaLiga. 'It hurt because I dreamt of playing in the first division with the team from my homeland, my roots,' Francisco admitted. He confronted Emery: 'Very well. If you have the guts, then release me.' To his surprise, Emery respectfully stood firm on his decision. However, the manager did allow him to continue training at the club but separately from the first team. During those sessions, Francisco reached the conclusion that Emery was right again, and the player moved to Granada 74, staying in the Segunda División.

What to do with Felipe Melo was another worry. The Brazilian, a talented midfielder, was offered to help the team in the First Division, but had a controversial reputation. He had played for Racing Santander and Mallorca, where his disciplinary issues had overshadowed his talent. The scouting reports were full of warnings: 'He got into a fight at a nightclub. No one wants to sign him. Be careful.' For most clubs, this would have been a red flag. 'Let's bring him in!' Unai finally declared. He felt Felipe was another player who hadn't found his place in the world. Unai was discovering one of his biggest passions: crafting players. Roberto Olabe reflects on his approach, saying, 'Performances don't flow naturally, they're built. And Unai is a daily builder of performances.'

Consequently, Emery wouldn't single out a player's weakness in front of the group. Instead, he used it as a lesson for everyone. He didn't punish players for mistakes; he saw them as part of the process. In the first few weeks of preseason, Felipe Melo didn't make many friends in the group, barely speaking to anyone unless it was to clash with his teammates and the player wasn't sure how to deal with Emery. A manager can care for all his pupils equally, but he cannot treat them all the same. 'When I was a player,' Emery admits, 'the pressure to perform, the need to do everything right, caused me huge anxiety. I didn't know how to handle it on my own. I should have got someone – a coach – to teach me to control my emotions. That is a key role of ours.'

Unai had to choose the right moment to speak to him. 'If I don't think my words will help, I'd rather wait.' But before the team's LaLiga debut, Emery pulled Felipe Melo aside. 'Relax,' he told him. 'You'll play, but trust me. Be humble. Don't show off in training that you're the best. Your time will come. Show your value in the games.' Emery also urged the rest of the team to help Melo integrate, emphasising that if he became part of the group dynamic, the entire squad would benefit. Not everyone was so sure. In that first LaLiga game against Deportivo de la Coruña, the Brazilian started on the bench. To the media, Emery explained why Melo didn't start: 'I want to honour the players who got us here.' That wasn't the whole story, of course.

Before kick-off, Emery had gathered the players for a talk. 'I'll pick the line-up by rolling dice,' he said, holding their attention with an unconventional approach. 'I'll assign a number to each of you and roll the dice eleven times. I don't care who starts because

I know we'll succeed. Whether it's you, you or you on the pitch, we'll win. I know it.' Half the starting eleven that day came from the Segunda División, players like Saltor, Santiago Acasiete, Mané, Crusat, Corona and Soriano. Almería stunned Deportivo with a 0–3 victory.

Felipe Melo made his full, starting debut in the fifth match of the season, scoring the only goal in a 0–1 win against Real Murcia. As the season progressed, his performances steadily improved under Emery's guidance, and his market value skyrocketed. By the end of the campaign, having scored seven goals, he secured a lucrative €13 million transfer to Fiorentina. From there, his career flourished further, with stints at Juventus, Galatasaray and Inter Milan. Years later, about to retire at forty-one, Melo visited Emery at Aston Villa's training ground, where he told his former manager, 'I want you as a mentor in this new coaching career I will be starting.' A fitting testament to the legacy of a coach who builds people.

That Almería, brimming with young players eager to prove themselves and fuelled by healthy competition were determined and fearless. They demanded respect wherever they went and, more often than not, they earned it. Despite having the smallest budget in the division, the team refused to bow, no matter the odds. Almería were never humiliated, not even against Barcelona at Camp Nou, where they lost 2–0 after a late goal from Leo Messi. A match against Real Madrid in Almería also stood out. Before kick-off, Madrid president Ramón Calderón addressed a gathering of fans at the stadium. One of them boldly shouted, 'Let's go, President! We have to crush Almería and score as many goals as possible!' From a window above, the Almería players José Ortiz and Carlos García overheard the exchange. Real Madrid had gone ten matches without losing, nine of which were wins, and they were approaching the game with an air of confidence. The players shared the story in the dressing room. Emery seized the opportunity. He didn't rant; he turned those words into fuel, igniting his team's resolve, before adding that 'Madrid are not invincible.'

'We stepped on to the pitch, rabid,' Ortiz remembers. Ninety minutes later, the scoreboard read: Almería 2–0 Real Madrid. That same spirit carried them to a hard-fought 2–2 draw against Barcelona at home as well as a stunning 1–4 victory away at Sevilla. The season ended with Almería in eighth place, the highest finish in the club's history, a feat they have never repeated. They even secured virtual qualification for the now-defunct UEFA Intertoto Cup, but a registration mishap handed the spot to Deportivo who sat in ninth. 'In our end-of-season meeting,' Sander Westerveld remembers, 'he told me I was one of the most important players that year and really wanted me to stay. But the president had other ideas, he refused to renew my contract.'

Emery's Almería had defied expectations, and a quiet inevitability settled over the club. The president tried to keep Emery, but deep down, everyone knew his destiny lay elsewhere. As Ortiz put it, 'He was meant to do bigger things.' Real Betis expressed interest, but it was Valencia – helmed by sporting director Juan Sánchez, Emery's former teammate – that won him over. The challenge was enormous. Valencia, haunted by its past glories of league titles and Champions League finals, was desperate to reclaim its place among Spain's elite and return to European contention. For many, Emery's youth – just thirty-six years of age – was a source of doubt. The coach, undeterred, left behind the little team that had dared to dream. For Almería, his departure marked the end of an era.

4

SURVIVING:

VALENCIA

In the summer of 2008, Alberto Benito, the new Almería director of football, called Juan Sánchez, his counterpart at Valencia and a teammate of Unai Emery's at Toledo. Benito recommended the manager to Juan Sánchez, who dutifully organised a meeting. It lasted hours. Unai couldn't stop talking about Valencia's previous season, about players, what was needed. Juan Sánchez knew he had his man, and soon after the five most important people at the club travelled to Alicante to sign him. Emery was well aware he was stepping into a club in transition, one that was steeped in recent glory yet weighed down by financial struggles and expectations. But perhaps he didn't realise the enormity of the job. Valencia would become pivotal in his career.

Fans still thought Valencia were in with a chance of winning the league against the mighty Real Madrid and Barcelona, despite the fact both clubs had three times their budget. Mestalla, once home to a team that had conquered LaLiga and Europe under Rafa Benítez, harboured doubts about whether this young coach could measure up. Part of the Valencia hierarchy also viewed Emery as an unproven outsider, they wanted a more famous name. Echoes of the dismissive comment made when Benítez first arrived – 'Who is this guy? The bullfighter El Cordobés, Manuel Benítez?' – still lingered along with a culture where nobody seemed to be good enough. Much like Rafa, Emery's response was to dive headfirst into the challenge.

'When Unai arrived at Valencia,' recalls Damià Vidagany, whose relationship with Unai started at that point, 'many people said, perhaps not without reason, that he'd taken the job too early in his career. It may have been true, but I believe it was precisely his innocence, his enthusiasm, and his sheer desire to be there that kept him in the role. That energy helped him endure situations that would have broken others. For instance, the fact that the very people who had brought him in didn't even last the summer.'

Ten days after his appointment, and a few days before the start of preseason, none of the five that travelled to Alicante remained at the club. Only the financial director, Javier Gómez, was still standing. Juan Soler, the club's majority shareholder, was forced out by banks and local politicians, hounded by the fans, discredited by his own management. The power vacuum he left behind triggered an internal war. Allies of Soler tried to block the rise of Vicente Soriano, the man expected to take over. Meanwhile, banks and regional politicians were manoeuvring to bring down both men. The city became a hornet's nest. Valencia CF sat at the centre of the hive, and Unai found himself the target of it all. In football, a weakened team creates an unsafe club – and at that moment, Valencia was vulnerable to every kind of assault. Emery had walked into an institution in total disarray, making that summer arguably the most turbulent in their modern history.

But a deal had been agreed, so Unai drove 350 kilometres from Almería to Valencia, squeezing conversations in on the road. Voro, a former player who had taken charge of Valencia for the final five games of the previous season and would stay on as a player liaison in the new regime, received a call from a fast-talking Emery.

'Tell me everything you know about the team,' Unai demanded. Later on, he added nervously, 'I've got the media presentation this afternoon and I don't even have time to eat!' Voro invited him to stop by his village near Valencia for a quick meal. Emery wouldn't entertain the idea of a pause. Then, halfway, somewhere near Murcia, it struck him. He had forgotten something essential. He pulled into a Corte Inglés, darting through the store in search of a suit.

'We will return Valencia to where it belongs,' Unai declared confidently in front of the media. After the presentation, Miguel Ángel Vara, a journalist from the sports newspaper *AS*, introduced himself. 'Vara? Vara?' Unai responded, his memory sparking. 'I know who you are! In your player ratings, you often gave me a dash when I played for Toledo, even when I thought I had played well!' In *AS*, a dash was reserved for players who had been anonymous in a match. Unai, at the time sensitive to public opinion, would soon learn in Valencia the importance of maintaining a healthy distance from external judgement. And as it turned out, his relationship with Vara would have another chapter later on.

In the middle of all the turbulence, Emery had a new CEO and president, Juan Villalonga, former boss of Telefónica, one of the largest telecom companies in the world. That ushered in significant changes. As Unai's main supporter, Juan Sánchez, was forced to leave, well-known manager Xabier Azkargorta was appointed as the new sporting director. Juan Villalonga had made contact with Luis Aragonés, the man who had just led Spain to glory that same summer at Euro 2008. On the very first day Unai walked into the training ground at Paterna, he was met with a front-page headline splashed across *Marca*: 'Aragonés to Valencia.'

Stunned but defiant, Unai rang Villalonga, not once, not twice. Twenty times. No reply. Refusing to accept the ambiguity, he chased him across the city, determined to get a straight answer. Finally, the CEO answered.

'I am busy, Unai.'

'Give me 1 minute. Wherever you want. I ask you one question, you answer and that will be it.'

Later, they met at the airport.

'Look at my eyes. Do you trust me? Do you want me here?' Unai asked.

Face to face, with no room to hide, Villalonga had to give him the truth.

'There is no problem at all with you, Unai. I'm not sacking you. You are going to be the manager.'

A baptism of chaos. Eventually, Azkargorta confirmed Emery as Valencia CF's head coach, putting to rest any rumours. Juan Viallonga's reign lasted eight days, and Vicente Soriano took over as president. In the midst of so much instability, Unai never lost his enthusiasm for managing Valencia. He never let pride get in the way, never once said, 'Pay me off and I'll leave.' No matter the chaos, he wanted to be there. Coaching the historic club was a dream, and he was determined to live it. 'That innocence,' says Damià, 'came with its own counterpart: belief and hard work.'

Unai inherited a squad that, on paper, brimmed with talent. David Villa, one of the most feared strikers in Europe, led the line. Behind him, David Silva dictated the tempo, with Juan Mata, Joaquín, and Vicente offering width, flair, and quality passes. Fernando Morientes added experience in attack, and Pablo Hernández was emerging as another wide threat. The midfield was ageing but still formidable: David Albelda and Rubén Baraja had long been the heartbeat of Valencia, leaders steeped in the club's identity. In defence, Carlos Marchena and Raúl Albiol, both international, were the most reliable pair remaining, as Roberto Ayala had just left. But beneath the surface, this was a fractured group. The 2007–08 campaign, just before Unai's arrival, had descended into full-blown crisis. The club had gone through four managers in a single season. Ronald Koeman, the most controversial of them, had won the Copa del Rey – Valencia's first trophy since the Benítez era, with Quique Sánchez Flores having maintained a decent level in between – but at a huge cost. Koeman's decision to exile club icons like Albelda, Santiago Cañizares, and Miguel Ángel Angulo caused a civil war inside and outside the dressing room. The team flirted with relegation although eventually finished tenth in LaLiga.

One of Vicente Soriano's first actions was to meet Unai and offer reassurance – finally, a gesture of calm from the club's offices. 'Forget about getting rid of Albelda, you don't need to,' he told him. Soriano would go on to build a strong relationship with Unai, backing him through a volatile and uncertain period.

The wider landscape was shifting dramatically. In 2008, as Valencia tried to stabilise, Barcelona appointed Pep Guardiola. What followed was the rise of the most dominant Barcelona side in history, one that would hoard almost every major trophy for the next several years. Not long after, José Mourinho's Real Madrid emerged, possibly the second-best team in the world during that era. The Real Madrid of Queiroz, Luxemburgo and Schuster, who had drifted through the mid-2000s without a clear identity, suddenly regained purpose. And Barcelona, who had faltered after Rijkaard's initial success, now exploded into a footballing superpower. Just as Unai arrived, Valencia found themselves caught between these two giants.

The manager, only thirty-six at the time, quickly realised that running Valencia would require more than tactics and optimism.

On his first visit to the players' dressing room, separate from the coaches' quarters, he was challenged. A player questioned his presence, to which Emery replied, 'This dressing room belongs to Valencia, and Valencia lends it to you. It's everyone's space.' It was a subtle but firm assertion of authority. More would be needed, as not all the players were convinced they were working under the right leader. Iván Helguera, a seasoned defender with an illustrious career that included two Champions League titles and three LaLiga triumphs with Real Madrid, quickly became the focal point of early tensions.

Unai had mentioned something publicly that upset Helguera, who was already frustrated about not playing regularly. The headline was then cut out and posted on the dressing room board. 'Who has done this?' Unai asked, knowing the answer full well. So, the manager went to his bosses. 'It is either him or me.' For three weeks, Emery marginalised Helguera, but the player fought back, attempting to influence the dressing room. Tensions boiled over into a full-blown confrontation in front of the entire squad. One player timidly defended Iván Helguera, but senior teammates intervened, siding with the coach.

Unai will always be the last person to give up on a player. However, there are moments when even his patience reaches its limit. When something cannot be resolved, it cannot be forced. Decisions must be made to move forward. In the changing room, Unai drew a circle on the board. 'Inside this circle are the players, the staff and everyone else involved.' And he told Helguera, looking straight into his eyes, 'You've stepped outside of it. I've come to you twice. I won't come a third time and neither will your teammates. Therefore, you're out.' Sensing the need to test the squad's loyalty and his own weight, Emery posed a stark ultimatum: 'If the majority of you don't agree with how I'm managing this, I'll leave.' The players backed him again, and Helguera's contract was terminated two days later.

Already then, he was not afraid of dressing room politics or making unpopular decisions if they were for the good of the team. That was a non-negotiable rule. David Villa, Rubén Baraja and David Albelda protected young Unai. The group expelled Helguera because they saw honesty and knowledge in their manager. They didn't defend him based on character only – players back a coach who helps them win. He had also shown he was fair: whoever is in good form, plays. In any case, Unai was very aware that he was dealing with footballers of a different calibre – those who weren't afraid to question decisions. He understood that imposing his way would require earning their respect, not just demanding it. With this in mind, he offered his players books he had learnt from. 'I've bought two for each of you. You can come by my office to pick them up.' Before long, the majority of the players showed up. Those willing to learn were identified.

If the dressing room was a battleground for control, the technical area continued being Emery's stage, never a passive observer. Some players nicknamed him 'El Transistor', for his constant flow of instructions, as if narrating the game live. Joaquín, Valencia's comedic extrovert, remarked, 'He gave us so many instructions we didn't know whether to play or listen.' His inner circle warned him that in a high-profile club like Valencia, his exaggerated emotional displays could feed into media narratives if results were negative. But Emery refused to change. 'If I change, I lose who I am,' he argued. 'I was born this way, I grew up this way, and I'll stay this way.'

As soon as the amphitheatre of the technical area was introduced, managers felt they had to do something in it. During those 90 minutes of combat, they are incredibly nervous individuals because it is exactly that – a battle – while also being confined to a small, marked technical area. Ironically, these zones are probably the least technical places imaginable: just a patch of grass, and they can't step out of it. Emery sees it differently. 'Sometimes I tell them to give the ball to someone else . . . and they do it! It is not about that. It's not about control, it's about pushing them forward. I'm with them on the pitch, driving them, supporting them. Guardiola does it, Simeone does it.'

Other situations, however, were more difficult to manage. Lander, just five years old when they arrived in Valencia, didn't quite understand why his father's work so often took him away from home. The boy was irritable, resentful towards his dad and the demands of the world around him. He didn't want Unai to leave, but when he was there, he didn't want to see him either. He refused to watch the matches, rejected the football that seemed to steal his dad away. And Unai, in the moments they spent together, devoted himself to trying to win him back.

Meanwhile, the repercussions of everything that happened inside Valencia's dressing room had multiplied a hundredfold com-pared to what Unai Emery had previously known, even as a player. In Valencia, the press is incredibly close to the team, constantly releasing information from within the club and feeling entitled not only to inform, but to demand too. If the team lost, the club suggested that an apology be made. At the dawn of social media, any outing, dinner or heated conversation, any word muted in the press conference, could quickly turn into a hotly debated topic on radio shows, TV programmes and in the newspapers. Unai once decided to celebrate his birthday with an evening dinner instead of the usual midday gathering. A few players arrived late, visibly overexcited, and it quickly became clear they had indulged in one drink too many before the meal. By the next morning, some were in no condition to train, drawing the wrath of the president. The media got wind of it. While going out was not necessarily an issue if kept under control, it became a problem when it spilled into the public eye. For Unai, it was a valuable lesson. As the saying goes, Caesar's wife must be above suspicion. Perception is everything, what the fans believe, or are led to believe, carries significant weight.

How about the style on the pitch? Unai arrived at Valencia with a romantic vision of football. In Valencia, the culture leant heavily on pragmatism. Under Rafa Benítez, for example, a 1–0 lead was nearly unassailable. Emery wanted to push beyond that, to inject excitement. 'I'd rather win 5–4 than 1–0 because football is also about spectacle,' he declared during his introductory press conference. Not everyone bought into the concept, but the team played with dynamism and an attractive brand of direct football, although the tension between attacking ambition and defensive solidity defined Emery's early years at Valencia. One early game in particular made Unai's start difficult: the second leg of the 2008 Supercopa de España, played on 24 August 2008, at the Santiago Bernabéu. Valencia had beaten Real Madrid in the first leg 3–2 and took the lead in the 32nd minute of the return fixture through David Silva. Rafael van der Vaart was then sent off 7 minutes later, but Real Madrid managed to turn the game around with four goals to secure a 5–6 aggregate victory and claim the Supercopa. A disappointing start to the campaign.

Emery's curiosity and passion drove him to push boundaries and surround himself with experts who shared his obsession with precision and detail. His staff had to be ready for an intense, all-consuming working day – anything less simply wouldn't work at Valencia. At the same time, Unai came to understand the need for a more robust, top-level coaching structure. Those around him worked hard and gave everything, but there were clear gaps and the staff lacked certain depth.

Unai also kept exploring new methods in set-pieces, individual training, explosive strength and video analysis. 'I especially remember the obsessive attention to set-pieces,' Juan Mata says. 'The sheer number of different routines we had was insane. We practically ran out of fingers to signal them all! We were often baffled because they seemed ridiculously complicated, and you needed a ton of focus just to remember them for each match, especially since they changed from one game to the next.'

'If there's one thing I learnt from Unai, it's to stop believing that details are a matter of chance or luck,' Mata explains.

Unai ensured they trained behind closed doors before trying a bold tactic: he deliberately pushed a player hard during training, knowing the player had a tendency to pick up red cards. Unai insulted and provoked him, as part of a calculated effort to teach him self-control.

'He chased a player during a session, grabbed his shirt,' recalls centre-back Adil Rami. 'He is so impulsive, so desperate to win that he sometimes goes very far! After matches, you couldn't talk to him, he was already lost in his own replay of the game.' Never the most punctual, meetings with players often started half an hour late. In them, Emery would scribble four or five key ideas on the board, a blueprint for the match. But time often slipped away from him as he delved into every point, turning the session into a long and often lively dialogue rather than a monologue. 'Emery showed so many videos that I ran out of popcorn,' winger Joaquín explains with his usual wit. 'He's obsessed with football; it's practically an illness. He's one of the best coaches I've ever had. I worked with him for three years, I couldn't have managed a fourth.'

Each player received a USB stick with personalised footage to study. But Unai knew that not all players looked at them. He handed one to Jérémy Mathieu. 'Jérémy, here's your pen drive,' he said. Mathieu nodded. Later, when asked if he'd studied the winger he'd be facing, according to Voro, he replied, 'Yes, yes.' The catch? The pen drive was empty – he hadn't checked. The squad saw Emery as fundamentally honest, natural in his manner, which gave weight to his words. And after so much work to win, defeats, twelve in total in LaLiga in that first season, were, as Unai describes them, 'a day of mourning'.

'He has a compulsive winning mentality,' says Roberto Olabe. 'It doesn't mean he can't accept defeat or that he always wins – though he almost always does. It means he never forgets a loss.' Those defeats helped Unai understand the need for a more robust, top-level coaching structure. Those around him worked hard and gave everything, but there were clear gaps and the staff lacked certain depth.

'After a defeat, I spend my time replaying the match in my head, looking for culprits everywhere,' Unai admits. 'I just want to disappear for three days, to be forgotten. But I keep it to myself because two days later, things settle into perspective.' He'd forget to eat amid the chaos of preparation. Staff had to remind him to grab a bite because he'd grown so thin. Thankfully, he'd recharge in a Basque restaurant indulging in a taste of home. Afterwards, he might wander the Valencian night, finding a moment to exhale before plunging back into the relentless rhythm by morning.

The financial crisis showed no signs of resolution, players went unpaid for two months just as the campaign reached its decisive phase, and no one at the club seemed willing or able to take control. On the pitch, after spending most of the season in Champions League positions, results began to mirror the chaos. In February and March, Valencia suffered three defeats and three draws, all against teams in the lower half of the table. At a club where managerial changes are typically swift and unforgiving, Unai could easily have been sacked. But this time, he stayed, largely because no one knew what was going to happen next. Still, amid the uncertainty, Emery guided the team to a sixth-place finish, securing qualification for the UEFA Europa League. A respectable outcome in a season where everything around him seemed to be falling apart.

Unai Emery survived the storm thanks to his resilience, but also because a few key figures chose to shield him. When Vicente Soriano became president, he appointed Damià Vidagany as head of communications and as a close adviser. It marked the beginning of a working relationship that would shape both men's futures. 'Between the president and myself, we created a protective space around Unai,' says Damià. 'There was pressure from all sides.' When Manuel Llorente arrived on Emery's second season, in June 2009, with the club still in financial and political turmoil, he asked for opinions on whether to keep the coach. 'He came to me, to Voro, to others,' says Damià. 'We all told him the same thing: Unai is a tireless worker and absolutely worth backing.'

But the attacks didn't stop. During one particularly difficult spell, a local sports paper prepared a matchday programme to be distributed in Mestalla, with Unai's face on the cover and the headline: 'What do we do with Emery?' Damià made the decision to pull it, despite pressure from both the publisher and the paper's editor, both close to the new chairman. Many asked for Damià's head but he believed undermining the coach would only deepen the club's crisis. For him, a strong manager meant a strong club. Emery had met all the targets asked of him, plus he carried himself with integrity. He deserved protection, not sabotage. Damià also worked behind the scenes to build bridges. He encouraged Unai to engage with influential voices in the Valencia ecosystem, like former goalkeeper turned pundit Santiago Cañizares, or José Luis Soler, a businessman close to the president. The idea was to let them see what Damià saw every day: a capable, honest coach giving everything for the club.

One telling moment came early on: the manager arrived one minute before the end of a one-hour live interview on Radio Marca. He hadn't meant any disrespect – he had simply lost track of time, completely immersed in football. That tendency to treat the media as a secondary accessory to the real work allowed him to isolate himself from noise. It also had consequences: it quietly multiplied his enemies at a time when competing interests dominated the landscape, the pressure was relentless, and several media outlets actively pushed for a change in regime – seeking the return of Juan Soler, the former majority shareholder with good local media contacts. In many ways, it was a rehearsal for the future for both Damià and Unai.

That summer of 2009, Valencia finally announced a recovery plan. It included measures such as reducing the wage bill and selling Raúl Albiol to Real Madrid for €15 million to avoid further immediate losses. Unai did not complain, he just wanted to know what he had to work with. Consequently, he always had the support of club president Manuel Llorente, who played a crucial role in maintaining the club's economic stability.

Their relationship was a volatile dance between fire and calculation. The passionate Llorente was demanding and didn't offer praise lightly. He pushed Emery constantly, his voice rising like a storm in meetings, demanding answers. Especially after defeats, Llorente's frustration could be overwhelming, his instinct to tear everything down and start anew, but Emery's logical but also intense responses would calm him down. At times, it seemed as though they spoke entirely different languages, but somehow, they found a way to make it work, helped by Voro and Damià, who filtered moods and words. At the end of his second campaign, Unai approached the president. 'President, I just want to say that here's your third place, your Champions League qualification. With 71 points, I'm happy, very happy. I told you everything would go well, and here you have the goal, achieved. I am very happy.'

'So am I, Unai,' the president replied in a rare show of emotion. Although his wages never increased – in fact, one season they were even reduced – Llorente demonstrated his trust in Emery by renewing his contract twice. The first time was in May 2010, after Unai's second season, when he had secured third place in LaLiga and the UEFA Champions League spot. But the following year, despite achieving third place once again, Unai had to fight to convince the president to keep him. Llorente had already reached a preliminary agreement with Luis García Plaza to take over the team. However, Unai, knowing the deal had not yet been finalised, took matters into his own hands. One night, he turned up at Llorente's house and personally persuaded him to extend his contract for another year. Llorente agreed but left Unai with a pointed remark: 'Finishing third is necessary, but it's not enough.' His words reflected the heightened expectations of the fans.

Unai's first Champions League match on 14 September 2010 was a 0–4 victory against Bursaspor and came only five and a half years after his managerial debut on 9 January 2005, in the harsh grind of the Segunda B at the San Pablo Stadium in Écija. He quickly realised that the competition, with its own anthem, sometimes seemed to have as well its own distinct smell and colour, its own way of behaving, which would undoubtedly test him against the best. To go far in the competition, he would have to find a balance that was so far elusive in his first few seasons with Valencia. In a 2011 match against José Mourinho's Real Madrid, Valencia's attacking intent left them woefully exposed again. Madrid counter-attacked with ruthless precision, going 0–4 up by half-time. Though Valencia clawed their way back in the second half, the match ended 3–6 to Real Madrid. Mourinho approached Emery afterwards: 'You've done a great job with this team. It's always tough to face you.' But this game marked a turning point. Unai realised that in order to not alienate the fans, every team must have its own DNA, and Valencia's is one of quick transitions with success built on a strong defence under managers like Héctor Cúper, Rafa Benítez and Quique Sánchez Flores. Emery and his staff began working harder to balance their attack with defensive solidity, and the results were evident: Valencia conceded fifty-four goals in his first season, but by his final campaign, that number dropped to forty-four.

The advanced PhD in football management that Emery and his coaching staff were subject to at Valencia continued for four years in total. And lessons were learnt daily. In the final match of the 2010–11 season, Valencia faced Deportivo at Riazor, a game that carried enormous weight as the historic Super Depor were desperately trying to avoid relegation. Some Valencia players, sensing the emotion of the occasion, felt tempted to ease off out of sympathy. But Unai wouldn't allow it. He had spent the entire week drilling the same message into his players, demanding intensity in training and during the match itself. For him, there was no room for sentiment. They were professionals. The schedule had dictated that this was the final game of the season, but that didn't matter. Out of respect for their work, the league and every other team, they had to approach it as if it were the first. Before kick-off, Unai gathered his squad and delivered a fiery speech. 'Gentlemen, this is how it works. We play to win. We must honour the profession. Always.' Valencia did just that. They won 0–2, sealing Deportivo's fate. The historic club was relegated that night, and they have yet to return to LaLiga.

Every summer since he had been in charge, Valencia had to get rid of key players. In 2010, David Villa was sold to Barcelona for €40 million, while David Silva joined Manchester City for €33 million. In 2011, Juan Mata departed for Chelsea in a €28 million transfer. Around the same time, Joaquín and Isco moved to Málaga for over €10 million combined. There's a common misconception that Unai Emery didn't rate Isco during their time at Valencia. In reality, Emery saw in the nineteen-year-old the potential for another David Silva and urged the club's president to keep him. Isco, like many teenagers of that era – before nutrition and conditioning became non-negotiable – needed to mature in his habits, but the talent was clear. When Málaga made an offer, Valencia were happy to sell. Isco, for his part, felt he deserved more minutes under Emery.

'Unai took the blame for Isco's departure, but this is unfair,' Damià explains. 'The club needed money. The sporting director's decision was to replace Silva with the Argentinian Chori Domínguez, and Isco felt he was no longer relevant. Plus, he got an incredible offer from Malaga CF, a rich club at the time and based in his hometown, which appealed to him and his family. Unai never said, "sell Isco". In fact he used Isco as often as he could, and even met his dad to convince him to stay at Valencia.' Many things contributed to his departure, but one of them was not Unai.

Years later, before a Real Madrid–Sevilla match, Emery approached him to talk, but Isco chose not to engage – holding on to the feeling of having been overlooked.

However, one of Emery's greatest signing success stories was Jordi Alba, who he bought from modest Cornellà as an eighteen-year-old for €6,000. Originally a left-winger, he struggled to break into the first team. 'During a training session at Mestalla, the day before a match, he told me, "Jordi, you're playing at full-back,"' the Spanish international explains. 'I was furious, and it showed. I thought, *At least play me in training in my actual position. I'm not going to play anyway.* He looked at me and said, "If you don't want to train, you can leave." I did want to train.' Jordi was stubborn, but he'd met someone even more stubborn.

The transformation was so successful that Barcelona purchased Alba, who would end up winning twenty major titles, for €14 million in the summer following Emery's departure. 'You never know when your opportunity will come. Thanks to that change in position, I was able to make a living from football and enjoy it. As an attacking midfielder or winger, I would never have reached this level with the national team and Barcelona. No chance.' Overall, under Emery, Valencia generated over €155 million in player sales and they finished third in LaLiga in 2010, 2011 and 2012, securing Champions League football. One sentence became a familiar refrain thrown at Unai: 'We're only third.' What was not acknowledged was that no team on the planet in the same situation as Valencia could realistically have aimed for anything more at that moment. Given the dominance of Guardiola's Barcelona and Mourinho's Real Madrid, third place was the ceiling.

Yet, the fans remained distant. Valencia's supporters are fiercely loyal to their team, but when they sense things are going wrong, like failing to win titles that were realistically out of their reach, the city becomes an unforgiving place. The shadow of Rafa Benítez's legacy still loomed large. This tension came to a head on 1 November 2011, during a Champions League match against

Leverkusen. Emery substituted right-winger Sofiane Feghouli for the forward Pablo Piatti, sparking a furious reaction from the crowd, who chanted 'Burro, burro, burro' ('donkey', or better translated as 'idiot') directly at their manager. Unai stood firm in the technical area. He wanted to direct their anger towards him. The move paid off: Valencia won the match 3–1.

The media also seized on his perceived shortcomings. When they privately requested pre-game line-up details, he consistently refused, which became a new source of friction. For some writers, if you don't assist them, they won't support you. Journalists accused him of overusing video analysis and favouring certain players. Each day brought fresh information leaks, forcing him to constantly extinguish fires. He faced uncomfortable questions from those who didn't think highly of him and occasionally fell into the trap of their provocative enquiries, responding with a hint of irritation. He couldn't comprehend the doubts raised in press conferences, even after regularly securing third place. Advisers suggested he soften his tone, smile more, play down the situation and avoid being drawn into debates about tactics or team decisions.

As time progressed, the dialectical battles with Manuel Llorente seemed to have a new element of tension. Some players also seemed tired of so much analysis and shared that privately. Unai insisted that, 'We have to keep making decisions. We move on, no matter what people think.' The transistor joke, the popcorn joke, the landing-like-a-plane gestures – all that stuck. People got tired of the exaggerated motion and even commented about his slicked-back hair. Fans repeated their opinion that Emery's football was boring. Often people think the grass is greener on the other side. And the coaching staff were perhaps a bit naive in dealing with it all, too. 'I always remember the good moments, but also everything else,' Juan Carlos Carcedo admits. 'The demands . . . We had never experienced anything like it before, and we never will again. It was the kind of critical period where you find yourself alone against adversity, with whistles echoing from every corner.'

The end was clearly approaching. Valencia's 2011 Champions League round of 16 exit against Schalke and their third-place finish in the Champions League group stage the following season, which dropped them into the Europa League, both felt like signs that a cycle was coming to a close. Something had shifted. The defining moment came in April 2012, after a 4–2 defeat at the Vicente Calderón in the Europa League semi-finals against Atlético Madrid. That night, he saw it in the faces of the fans, in the disappointment of the club directors on the flight back from Madrid. He felt it, his time at Valencia was over. He confided as much to those close to him. And yet, football was telling a different story. His fourth and final season was arguably his best, a third-place finish in LaLiga once again and semi-finalists in both the Europa League and the Copa del Rey. It had been a period of immense personal and professional growth, though not always filled with joy or satisfaction. Unai and his staff had achieved significant milestones that, in light of the club's continued decline, deserve far greater recognition. 'What Unai achieved at Valencia is still undervalued,' Damià reflects.

In the following four seasons they ended up fifth, eighth, fourth and twelfth. In the twenty-first century to date, no other coach has spent four years on the Valencia bench. However, both he and the club needed a fresh start. Offers came in, including one from his boyhood club Real Sociedad, an opportunity that he thought unlikely in the past, and in fact trust issues derailed the move. Instead, he took a leap into the unknown, heading to Spartak Moscow, to try to test his methods abroad. Having experienced the magic of the Champions League, he was hungry for more.

5

FIRE & SILVER:

SPARTAK MOSCOW & THE SEVILLA ADVENTURE

Unai Emery still has a home in Valencia, a place full of light, of walking paths, restaurants where meals never finish and where he returns to rest as often as his demanding schedule allows. But in the summer of 2012, it was time to fly again.

AS Roma had expressed interest in Emery shortly before he signed with Spartak Moscow. Unai agreed a three-year deal with the Russian team, lured by the promise of a strong squad and the ambition and resources of its owner, Leonid Fedun, a businessman with significant investments in the oil industry (Lukoil) and finance. Spartak, the most popular club in Russia and known for its attacking philosophy that aligned perfectly with Unai's ideas, had finished second in the league and secured a spot in the Champions League qualifiers for the 2012–13 season. But the journey to Moscow became a detour. For a man who thrives on meticulous communication and building connections, Moscow was less a footballing opportunity and more an alien landscape – cold, vast and linguistically impenetrable. This challenge was unlike any other. At Spartak, he found himself not just in a new club but in a culture with codes he could not decipher. Every instruction, every motivational word was diluted by a triple-layered process of interpretation in Spanish, English and Russian. Emery met with a teacher, Evgeniya, several times a week to learn a language he knew nothing about or at least to pick up enough football-related vocabulary to ensure he could do his job. However, with his meticulous preparation, he barely had time to fully immerse himself in Russian. Meanwhile, he leant on his improving English. The lack of a shared language was not just a logistical problem; it was a chasm that swallowed the essence of his coaching. Emery's hallmark video analysis quickly became a challenge at Spartak. 'Imagine analysing matches with three languages in play. We had to learn to be shorter and sharper, or the message would get lost,' Juan Carlos Carcedo explains.

Football, for Emery, is about harmony. 'The player must be happy but working at the required level. It's a pact, a kind of meeting point,' he often says. In Moscow, however, that balance eluded him. The process was meticulous: clips of opponents were broken down into defensive, offensive, strategic and individual analyses. After assembling the footage, Unai added final touches and presented his ideas to the players. For a single match, they would study six or seven games of the opposing team, showing, for example, the ten to twelve most common reactions to crosses or to a counter-attack. Yet, this painstaking preparation didn't fit Spartak's unique environment. The players could not concentrate long enough. Discipline posed another challenge. During one training camp, two foreign players were spotted with women at the hotel in the early hours of the morning. Everyone knew. Unai spoke to them but chose not to punish them, granting forgiveness. However, as Carcedo observed, 'When a player gets away with something like that, it changes how they start to behave.'

Emery always conveyed a positive message to the press, a stark contrast to Russian football culture, where a coach is expected to embody suffering and authority. To add salt to the wound, his arrival at Spartak had not been universally welcomed. Valery Karpin, who had just finished his stint as head coach but remained as general manager, seemed to harbour resentment. Many believed Karpin had always dreamt of managing Spartak long term. From the very start, he distanced himself from Emery and displayed open jealousy, unable to understand why the club had chosen Unai. What was more, it was clear from the outset that Spartak lacked the quality to challenge for the league title, yet the expectation from the club was nothing less than first place. Emery tried to divide his players into smaller groups to maximise focus, but the disconnect grew. The players remained sceptical, the environment frosty. As Jamie Carragher once said, 'A manager never truly has the dressing room; he just hopes to hold on to it for as long as possible.' In Moscow, Emery lost it very soon after arriving.

'It was my absolute failure,' Emery would later admit. 'There was no direct communication, and the lifestyle in Russia was so different. I never felt at home there.' Without connection it wasn't possible to lead. For all his energy and drive, Moscow drained Unai Emery. He likes to impose his ideas. Wherever he is, he has to be the clear, unique leader. In Moscow, he couldn't do that. He did not belong there and felt adrift, as if his compass had lost its true north.

One of the few things that was consistent was communication with his son Lander. 'From a young age, I had a phone so we could stay in touch,' Lander explains. 'We did video calls, which is better than just hearing someone's voice. Seeing them makes a difference. Almost every day before bed, we'd talk, it was our routine,' he recalls, at that point still annoyed about what football was doing to his family. The kid, nine at the time, required some stability, hence him staying in Valencia. It is the kind of story that football tends to hide but it sharpens and creates personalities. 'My mum is from Málaga, very affectionate and positive,' Lander says. 'I missed Dad, but she covered a lot of ground.'

With Champions League commitments, Spartak played twice a week, and damaging defeats quickly snowballed: 2–1 against Lokomotiv, 0–2 against CSKA, 2–1 against Anzhi Makhachkala at the end of October. 'There was a player I believed in – the best in the team,' Unai recalls. 'A Scotsman, Aiden McGeady. He wanted to leave because he was fed up, but I convinced him to stay. Then came injuries, suspensions . . . it just didn't go our way.' By November, despite three wins in a row and a draw, things still weren't fully working. They faced Barcelona at home in the second leg of a Champions League group tie, and McGeady had just re-covered from an injury. He asked to play.

'I told him no, because he had only trained for two days, but I insisted he should be ready for the matches after that.' Spartak lost 0–3 to Barcelona. That Saturday, in a top-of-the-table clash against Dynamo Moscow, Unai left him out again. McGeady came to complain.

'You told me you were going to call me up.'

'No, I told you to get ready. That's it. Now stop busting my balls.'

Unai explains that he said it like that because he was fed up too. 'I felt not all the players were doing what they had to.'

The emotional roller coaster had its highs too. There were mo-ments of joy, mostly with his coaching staff and the few players who understood what he wanted, including Andrei Moj, who had played for Leganés and spoke Spanish. Some dinners were memorable, expats and wanderers in an unfamiliar world. But Emery knows how to read dressing rooms, and he quickly real-ised he was losing this one. By then, Spartak were fourth in the league, a position that might have been celebrated elsewhere but was unacceptable in Moscow. Unai had benched Artyom Dzyuba, an international striker, a few times which led to clashes. Dzyuba, influential in the media, didn't hesitate to use his connections to criticise Emery. He wasn't the only one, others also exploited their direct lines to the press.

'I started to feel alone. Very alone,' Unai admits.

Then came the breaking point. Valery Karpin convened a meeting where he harshly criticised the players. Unai defended them, questioning Karpin's approach. The argument turned into a heated confrontation. The direction was clear. On 25 November, after a crushing 1–5 defeat to Dynamo Moscow at home, Emery was sacked just six months into his tenure. Karpin personally announced the news to the press. They applauded.

Due to bureaucratic issues, Unai had to stay in Moscow until 20 December, living in a hotel. The financial pay-off was significant, he earned more in six months than he had in four years at Valencia. But the emotional toll was heavier. 'It was the only time I didn't truly give myself to the project, because I couldn't,' Unai admitted, his self-belief momentarily shaken. 'The truth is, I never should have gone there. I was sold on a project that didn't exist, and I ended up at a club where no one helped me. When I left, I explained that the biggest issue had been the language barrier.' There was no need to elaborate further.

Emery emerged from the experience with a deeper understanding of adaptation, cultural sensitivity and the importance of the right environment. Spartak had been barren ground. But somewhere in that failure, Emery found the seeds of his next triumph. Espanyol called him first, but seven weeks later, he ended up taking over at Sevilla FC.

*

In the aftermath of their dismissal, Emery's team reached a unanimous conclusion: as well as the importance of communication, the experience had taught them the value of understanding players on a psychological level. He needed to know what drove them, what blocked them, what annoyed them. From that point on, discussions about how to approach and interact with players, and how to adapt behaviour to unlock their best performance, became an integral part of the coaching staff's daily work.

After turning down Espanyol in early 2013, Unai Emery found himself waiting in a private lounge at the discreet Meliá Hotel in Valencia. He had agreed to meet Monchi, Sevilla's director of football and the mastermind behind the club's successful recruitment, who wanted to find a replacement on the bench. Sevilla had lost five of their last seven LaLiga matches. The club was drifting. 'We had just lost to Valencia 2–0, with Míchel as our coach,' Monchi recalls. 'After the game, we had an emergency meeting at [the president] José María del Nido's house. There were two options: take a gamble on an untested coach, Diego Martínez, who was leading Sevilla Atlético, our reserve team, or go for Unai Emery. We spoke to Diego, but he admitted he wasn't ready. So, we called Unai's agent, Iñaki Ibáñez, and arranged a meeting at the Meliá Hotel in Valencia that Monday morning.'

Monchi wasn't interested in interviewing multiple candidates. He didn't want to waste time. He wanted to fall in love with one – fast. From the moment Monchi arrived at the hotel, he knew Emery was different. Unai had already requested a whiteboard from the hotel. It was waiting for them when they sat down. Before Monchi could start, Emery took control of the conversation. 'Why have you thought of me? What are you looking for in a coach?'

The question caught Monchi off-guard. Usually, clubs interrogated managers, not the other way around. But Emery wanted to understand Sevilla's vision before committing himself. Monchi explained the club's turmoil. After years of success, Sevilla had lost stability. They had burnt through managers – Antonio Álvarez, Marcelino, Míchel – and needed someone who could get the best out of an underperforming squad and embrace the club's philosophy. Emery spoke endlessly, bouncing from one topic to another. He was restless. Both men were looking for the same things: stability, redemption, a fresh start. Sevilla, Monchi explained, was not like other clubs. José María del Nido, the president, was passionate and hands-on. He was demanding. A man who valued hard work but expected results. Could Unai handle that?

They spoke for 6 hours – a marathon session of tactics, ideas, philosophy. Time flew by. 'We spent the entire morning exchanging opinions, drinking coffee and water, while Unai scribbled notes, drew on the board and mapped out his ideas. Slowly, we started to fall for each other – not just as professionals, but as believers in what Sevilla could become.' Not a single word about money.

As the meeting came to a close Monchi, already convinced to sign Unai, asked one final question: 'If we work together for two years, where will Sevilla be?'

'We will be champions,' Emery replied without hesitation. It was classic Unai – ambitious, all-in. In reality, he had not yet won anything, he did not know the way to ultimate success.

After the meeting, Monchi went to lunch with agent Iñaki Ibáñez. A photo was taken. News leaked. Míchel had not been sacked yet and people in Valencia knew Monchi was in town. Action had to be taken.

The financial deal was agreed swiftly and Emery signed for six months, with an option for another year. 'I hadn't planned to stay the night,' Monchi explains, 'but I did. The next morning, I bought some clothes and flew back to Seville on Ryanair, sitting next to Unai.' A new era had begun. The immediate transition was anything but smooth. That same afternoon, as Míchel arrived at the training ground to say goodbye to his squad, he unexpectedly crossed paths with Unai in the dressing room area. The outgoing manager and his replacement, face to face. An uncomfortable moment. Monchi later admitted it was a mistake to have let that happen.

On 14 January 2013, Unai Emery and Juan Carlos Carcedo were announced as the head coaches at Sevilla FC. The squad was fractured, divided across at least eleven nationalities. The captains weren't even on speaking terms. Stéphane Mbia, a gifted but inconsistent midfielder, was underperforming. José Antonio Reyes, a club legend, was on the verge of fading out. Off the pitch, the institution itself was on shaky ground. President José María del Nido was facing serious legal trouble, with his time at the club nearing an unceremonious end. So, Emery focused on what he could control: the football.

Del Nido started organising regular meetings with Unai at a restaurant inside the stadium, where everything was discussed in brutal detail. One by one, he asked Emery for assessments on each player. In one of those early meetings, Unai made a bold declaration to the chairman: 'Do you know what I want to achieve with Sevilla? We're going to finish in the top four. We're going to the Champions League.'

At that moment, Sevilla had won nine major titles. Del Nido smiled and leant forward. 'Unai, have you ever lifted a trophy?'

'No,' Emery admitted.

'Well then, you're about to find out what that feels like.' For Unai, this was the first time a president had told him that competing was not good enough, winning was the goal. Del Nido spoke passionately about what it meant to play in a final – the mobilisation of fans, the sense of belonging, the hunger for glory. He drilled into Emery that success wasn't just about qualifying for Europe, it was about touching silver. In Andalucía, they call it *'tocar plata'* or 'touching silver'. At Sevilla, he was about to experience it. And not just once. Three times. Between 2014 and 2016, Unai Emery led Sevilla to three consecutive Europa League titles – turning a team in crisis into a dynasty.

From day one, it all began: work, video analysis, obsession and psychology to improve confidence and team spirit, all recurring themes of Unai's management style. He continued diversifying his coaching staff, always seeking people that made him think. 'Unai likes to consult on everything, to know at every moment what you think, although of course, the final decision is his,' says Pablo Villanueva, former Córdoba manager who joined Unai at Sevilla and remains with him. His new assistant had known Unai for fifteen years. The dressing rooms at Racing de Ferrol and Leganés (where they also crossed paths with Juan Carlos Carcedo, still Emery's first assistant at the time) forged an unbreakable ca-maraderie. 'It's hard to remember a conversation where football didn't come up,' says Pablo, whose football career derailed while he was at Real Madrid because of injuries. 'Even if you thought differently, we always started from shared principles. The most important part of our job was to reinforce his work. When you have an idea, you must back it up with data, always staying aligned with his approach and avoiding creating doubts.'

Unai was disciplined, demanding, hyperactive, bold. After a recent derby against Betis, where Sevilla squandered a 0–3 lead to draw 3–3 after midfielder Gary Medel got a red card, the team gathered in a hotel room for a video analysis session. Emery stood silently, locking eyes with each player in turn, creating an unset-tling tension. Finally, Gary Medel, who everyone called Pitbull, broke the silence: 'What's going on? Eh! What's going on?' Straight away, Unai spoke to him. 'What has just happened is what happened in the Betis match. You were defensive, reactive, unable to control your emotions,' Unai said. 'We need to work on this, Pitbull.'

Despite a few months of inconsistent results, a highlight of which was former Almería striker Álvaro Negredo's best-ever season with thirty-one goals, which earned him a move to Manchester City, Sevilla found themselves in with a chance of qualifying for Europe. Compared to the previous seasons, there was a renewed energy. Goalkeeper Andrés Palop reflects on Unai Emery's early impact. 'He recovered my enthusiasm. His passion was evident.' In the season's final game, they faced Valencia, who were battling for fourth place and a Champions League spot. Another ending of a season against a club Unai was emotionally close to. Sevilla triumphed in a thrilling 4–3 victory, with Negredo scoring all four goals. Despite finishing ninth in the league, they secured a Europa League place due to fair play sanctions against Málaga and Rayo Vallecano. But something had changed.

The 2013–14 season began with uncertainty. Sevilla were still searching for an identity under Unai Emery, and off the pitch, turbulence surrounded the club. On top of that, it wasn't just a few transfers that were needed. The squad had to be rebuilt from the ground up. 'During preseason, I called Unai to tell him we'd signed Raul Rusescu, a Romanian striker from Steaua Bucharest,' Monchi remembers. 'I only told him once the deal was done because I knew he wouldn't like it. And I was right. He completely lost it on the phone. It didn't go down well.'

Monchi and Unai argued constantly during that transfer window, sometimes escalating into intense shouting matches, but always out of passion. They were both demanding, strong-willed, hard to convince. One of the biggest disagreements was over the attack. Unai wanted Jonas, the experienced Brazilian striker from Valencia. He was proven, already accustomed to LaLiga. Monchi refused. Jonas, he felt, was too old. Sevilla needed players they could develop and sell later, not short-term fixes. Instead, Monchi pushed for Carlos Bacca and Kevin Gameiro. Unai barely knew them, but he had to trust his sporting director's vision. That summer, they brought in players like Vicente Iborra, Daniel Carriço, Nico Pareja, Vitolo, Jairo Samperio and Sebastián Cristóforo. It was almost a brand-new team, an experiment that could either collapse under the weight of change or lay the foundation for a competitive future. Jonas, meanwhile, kept scoring every weekend for Valencia. And every Monday, Unai would confront Monchi with the same words: 'Did you see? I told you so.'

The team struggled early on. At one stage, they were second from bottom, with just 2 points from their first 15. October then brought another painful lesson. Unai chose to take the game to Real Madrid at the Santiago Bernabéu. It was an ambitious approach, but Madrid made them pay. 7–3. Cristiano Ronaldo hat-trick. Bale and Benzema with two goals each. Against the very best, something was missing. This was followed by a 0–1 loss at home to Celta Vigo. The club was on edge and whispers of Unai's dismissal grew louder. 'I reassured him,' Monchi recalls. 'If you trust someone, you have to show it. People don't believe me when I say this, but it's true, Unai was never in doubt. Never.' A turning point came with a 1–3 win against Espanyol in Cornellà. There were rumours that if Sevilla had lost, Unai would have been sacked, but Monchi dismisses that theory. 'We made sure Unai felt our trust,' he explains. 'Sometimes the best way to show confidence is to step back. It is what we did.' From that moment, Sevilla started climbing. Carlos Bacca had scored the third goal. As the season was unfolding, it became clear. Unai had to admit it. Monchi was right about the strikers.

Then came a seismic moment off the pitch. On 5 March 2014, José María del Nido, the architect of Sevilla's rise, was sent to prison, sentenced to seven and a half years for embezzlement and bribery. His replacement, Pepe Castro, had a very different style. Unlike Del Nido, he was less involved in footballing matters. With a leadership vacuum, Monchi and Unai had to pull closer together. Despite everything, Sevilla steadied themselves. Monchi had planned a six-month stay in London to improve his English and study the Premier League's structures. Sevilla kept progressing in Europe, so he found himself constantly flying back and forth. One day, while in London, he called Unai. 'We're really happy with your work. We want to renew your contract.' Unai appreciated the vote of confidence, but time couldn't be found to finalise details.

Meanwhile, the Europa League became both an escape from the off-the-pitch struggles and a place where Sevilla could prove themselves. 'Of the three titles we won with Sevilla, the first in 2014 was the most special because of what we overcame,' Unai recalls. 'We had to navigate two knockout rounds in preseason while managing constant squad turnover.'

The bond with the fans deepened. 'That season ended up being the most beautiful in terms of connection with the supporters,' Unai remembers. 'And in Seville, when things go well, it's absolutely marvellous. Football is everywhere.'

One memory stands out: Estoril, Portugal. 'We played there, and more than four thousand of our fans travelled with us.'

And then, a Sevilla derby like no other. It was the first-ever European knockout match between Sevilla and Real Betis, who were struggling at the bottom of LaLiga. The first leg of the round of 16 match at home at Sánchez-Pizjuán was a disaster. A 0–2 defeat. A gut punch. Dinner with Monchi had been arranged for after the Betis match, a meeting meant to finalise Unai's contract renewal. But as they sat down, neither spoke about it. Other irrelevant issues were raised. Eventually, the inevitable topic surfaced. Monchi sighed. 'After losing to Betis . . . if we get knocked out, we'll all have to leave.' Preparation for the return leg began the very next day. 'Forget the first match,' Unai told the squad. 'We're going to turn this around.' It was a message echoed by his coaching staff, as Unai insisted they would have their chance to win at the Benito Villamarín – provided they played to their strengths, believed in themselves and were clinical in front of goal. Training sessions in the days leading up to the match reflected this belief. Unai and his staff adjusted the intensity, focusing on pressing more aggressively, executing quick transitions and being resolute in set-piece situations. That brave approach was going to be mirrored in the line-up.

At the Benito Villamarín, Sevilla took the field with fire in their veins. Two wingers. Two strikers. All or nothing. Reyes scored. So did Bacca. 0–2. Extra time. No more goals, so penalties were necessary. Sevilla winger Vitolo stepped up first – missed. But Sevilla's goalkeeper Beto, playing through excruciating pain, became the night's hero, saving two spot kicks. Sevilla survived. Coke, who won all three Europa Leagues under Unai, reflects: 'That game changed our mentality. In training, Unai always reminded us to "fight until the last minute".' They had done that and had been rewarded. In football, nothing happens by coincidence.

Sevilla beat a Porto side featuring Ricardo Quaresma and Jackson Martínez in the Europa League quarter-finals. After losing the first leg in Portugal, they produced a whirlwind first half at the Sánchez Pizjuán, a fearless display of attacking football that saw them score three goals. Porto were swept aside, losing 4–2 on aggregate.

Unai and Monchi agreed his renewal would be announced after the semi-finals against Valencia. Sevilla won 2–0 at home in the first leg – a crucial first goal from Sevilla midfielder Stéphane Mbia. But at the Mestalla, it all fell apart. Valencia stormed back. 1–0. 2–0. 3–0. Monchi, watching from the stands with Damià Vidagany, wondered if they should announce Unai's renewal the next day, as planned. And then . . .

A Sevilla goal would send them to the final on the away goal rule, but it was the 94th minute, the game about to finish. There was one last chance. Rakitić, corner. Mbia, near post. A glancing header. The ball looped over the penalty area . . . and dropped into the far corner. Silence at the Mestalla. Then pandemonium. Unai Emery exploded on the touchline, just as he had years before when Lorca secured promotion. A celebration Valencia fans have never forgotten, a reminder of what could have been. The next day, Monchi and Unai sat side by side in a press conference to publicly announce his renewal.

The Europa League final in Turin in May 2014 felt like the culmination of a season that had constantly pushed Sevilla to the edge. It was the first final for 80 per cent of the squad, an untested group thrown together just months earlier. 'Perhaps the fact that Benfica were favourites gave us the freedom to focus on our strengths,' Unai reflects. 'If we were going to beat them, it had to be by playing our own game.'

Monchi remembers it just as clearly. 'We weren't favourites, but we arrived with incredible energy after overcoming so many obstacles. It was an incredibly tough match, but that momentum, that belief, carried us to Sevilla's third European title – and Unai's first.'

The game was tense, physically draining, emotionally exhausting, decided on penalties. When Kevin Gameiro scored the last one, and Sevilla were crowned champions, Unai turned to his staff, hugging them tightly. It was like a sudden flash of light. His first title. No screenwriter could have written it better. They had faced elimination multiple times. The president had gone to prison. The sporting director had been in and out of the country. It had been chaotic, unpredictable, at times even surreal. Unai finally understood what José María del Nido had meant in that conversation months earlier. This was what touching silver felt like.

Soon after beating Benfica, Unai received a message that made him smile. 'Do you still coach for money or for titles now?'

'Ah, Sander,' Unai answered straight away, 'for title, for titles!'

After winning the Europa League and finishing fifth in the table, the summer of 2014 started with a surprise and another crisis. Monchi and Unai had arranged to meet in Turin to plan the new season, but when the director of football arrived, Unai shut the conversation down immediately. He had no intention of planning anything because he was leaving for AC Milan. It was a shock. Monchi hadn't expected it, and the argument that followed was intense. While the team left for a preseason tour in Indonesia, Monchi worked behind the scenes to find a solution. When Unai returned, he went to the director's house with his lawyer, Iosu Reta, and after long discussions, they settled everything. To seal the moment, they took a photo together and Monchi posted it on Instagram.

What ultimately convinced Unai to stay? It wasn't just an improved contract. It was the project, the chance to defend their Europa League title, to play in the Super Cup against Real Madrid, to build something bigger. It was not the time to leave, despite the need to rebuild the squad again. Just weeks after lifting the Europa League trophy, the team was picked apart. Success had come at a cost as bigger clubs came calling and Sevilla's key players left. Rakitić, Negredo, Navas, Kondogbia, Medel – all gone. The squad saw key arrivals including Grzegorz Krychowiak, the Polish defensive midfielder who would become instrumental to their success, along with Aleix Vidal, Iago Aspas and Denis Suárez.

In the 2014–15 season in LaLiga they achieved a historic 76 points – the highest in Sevilla's history – though it only secured them fifth place again. In the Europa League, however, they were unstoppable. 'During my second title, we didn't experience such extreme situations as the year before, but we faced great opponents: Borussia Mönchengladbach, Villarreal, Fiorentina . . .' Unai recalls. 'Unlike in the 2014 final, this time we were the favourites. Not many people knew who Dnipro were, but they eliminated the competition favourites, Napoli, in the semis.'

'That Europa League campaign wasn't a walk in the park,' Monchi remembers, 'but we were far superior. If the first Europa League win was madness, the second was complete dominance. The 2014–15 squad was one of the best in Sevilla's history. In the final in Warsaw, Unai left players like Gerard Deulofeu and Denis Suárez on the bench. That's how strong we were. We had an incredible team – Banega, Vitolo, Reyes, Bacca . . . We suffered a bit in the semi-finals against Zenit, but overall, we competed with authority. I think that was the year we played our best football.'

The 2015 Europa League final in Warsaw was pulsating. Despite falling behind early to a Dnipro goal, the Andalusians rallied with goals from Grzegorz Krychowiak and Carlos Bacca, who was the hero of the night with a decisive brace, sealing a 2–3 victory. Unai had claimed the club's fourth European title, his second and he qualified the team for the Champions League.

'At the end of that season, we were playing a friendly in Morocco, in Tétouan, and I noticed that Unai was unusually focused on Napoli,' Monchi recalls. 'I couldn't understand why. When we arrived back in Seville, I saw I had a ton of messages from Italian numbers. Right away, I knew something was up. Then, news broke that De Laurentiis had travelled to Madrid to meet with Unai. He didn't return my calls until later that afternoon. When he finally did, he said, "Monchi, I couldn't tell you before, but Napoli wanted me. I'm not going, I'm staying, but I had to hear them out." At least let me know! I told him. In the end, he stayed.'

On the pitch, to reach the heights Sevilla wanted to keep to, Unai had to master the delicate balance of coaching, knowing when to push, when to pull back and how to manage different personalities. José Antonio Reyes was one of those personalities. A player of instinct and raw talent, he often thrived on freedom rather than structure. After one of Unai's notoriously long tactical sessions, he joked, 'Now I even know where the left-back lives.' Reyes was special. He had to be handled with patience. One day, there was an issue. It started when Unai saw him eating sweets on the team bus. The manager called him out on it, and the situation quickly escalated. Realising it needed to be addressed properly, he called Reyes into the manager's office the next day. Monchi took on the role of bad cop. He let Reyes have it, holding nothing back. Unai watched in disbelief, wondering how Reyes didn't just get up and punch Monchi in the face. But Monchi knew him well, almost since childhood, and understood exactly how far he could push him.

That balance defined their working relationship. Unai managed certain players, Monchi handled others. Together, they became an exceptionally effective duo. Through moments like these heated confrontations, carefully designed training drills and the meticulous use of video analysis, Unai was building an unshakable foundation in his work. It became his safety net, a structure so strong that it gave him the freedom to take risks, to step beyond what was expected and to explore new ideas with confidence.

'Before matches, I always prepare thoroughly. I create a clear line of action, though adjustments often arise with injuries or other circumstances. I'm meticulous about sticking to what I've worked on, it's where I feel most comfortable. But sometimes, during a game, I had gone off script. *Unai, take a risk*, I told myself, *do something now that shakes things up, even if it goes against your initial plan.* I remember a match between Sevilla and Real Sociedad. We were struggling; it was 0–0, and things weren't going our way. Real Sociedad were creating chances, and the match was slipping away. In the beginning, I used to ask for input from the bench quite often, listening to every suggestion. But over time, I've grown to trust my own instincts more and ask less. If someone tells me something, I still listen, but I don't seek as much advice as I once did. In that particular game I made the bold decision to throw on three forwards, not what was planned, I did not ask anyone about it, and we ended up winning 1–0 with a goal from Gameiro.'

The tough competition between the two strikers Carlos Bacca and Kevin Gameiro mirrors what he would later encounter at Aston Villa with Jhon Durán and Ollie Watkins. Both strikers were performing well and capable of starting, but Bacca was a disaster if he didn't start, lacking energy coming off the bench. Gameiro, on the other hand, would come on for 20 minutes, score and accept his role without complaint. The players had to be managed carefully.

Other players simply weren't on the same wavelength. Fernando Llorente didn't play much under Emery at Sevilla. When one of his children was born, he spent three days in the hospital, sleeping in a cot. Sevilla was scheduled to play Athletic Club de Bilbao, and Llorente told Emery he wasn't ready to play, he hadn't slept well or trained properly. But Unai insisted he be part of the team. Llorente, who had formerly played for Athletic Club, believed the manager wanted to use him against his old team out of superstition. A similar situation had occurred when Sevilla played Juventus, another of Llorente's former clubs, and Emery included him by surprise in the line-up. After the Athletic Club match, Emery didn't use him much, or so Llorente recalls, though in reality, he played thirty-seven matches that season. Essentially, and Unai would likely remind him of this if their paths crossed again, Llorente played whenever the team needed him, regardless of the opponent. 'Superstition is a weakness we all turn to from time to time for reassurance. But I don't believe in it,' Unai admits.

A couple of days before a big match in the advanced stages of the Europa League, Llorente had been caught on camera out partying at the Sevilla Feria, a week-long spring festival, known for its flamenco, horse parades, traditional Andalusian attire, all-night celebrations in *casetas* (tents) – and distracting players. The manager was once angry with Llorente. But Unai doesn't hold grudges. 'If I get angry with someone, it passes quickly. I argue with players, but I let it go. In the end, I even laughed with him about his little slip-up.'

Unai kept revitalising those players that were willing to change, even if they were considered lost causes. Bacca, Aleix Vidal, Federico Fazio and Adil Rami are some of the most notable examples in both categories. The Argentinian Éver Banega is another. 'What's the first thing that comes to mind when I think about Unai?' Éver says now. 'That's easy, he's like a father to me.' He grew up in a humble, working-class family in Rosario, a city deeply passionate about football. His upbringing, marked by financial struggles and limited education, shaped his fiery temperament; football became his escape. Banega, signed by Valencia as a nineteen-year-old, is a kind, lovely, incredibly sensitive guy. He was, though, different from the rest. 'I learnt so much from Unai,' he says. 'On the pitch, he changed the way I played. He taught me how to press in different ways, how to handle pressure, how to try to score more often – something he often repeated – but most importantly, he taught me how to always help my teammates in every possible way. I've never been a selfish player, but before, I didn't work as hard for the team. Off the pitch, I learnt even more. Especially, on the human side.'

During Emery's second season at Valencia, a 21-year-old Banega returned to the club after a season on loan at Atlético Madrid. 'I don't count on you, I don't know you. But let's see how preseason goes,' Unai told him. Banega performed brilliantly. 'You're staying,' Emery confirmed. He believed in Éver, thinking *I'll create the right environment for him, manage the person and let the player emerge*. At first, Banega didn't play much. Emery reassured him, using the same plan as with Felipe Melo at Almería: be patient, train well and your time will come. When it did, Banega stood out. But he was temperamental, prone to difficult moments. 'At Valencia he was immature,' Unai explains. 'In our conversations, I had to make it clear I was the authority. But, eventually, he was endearing and receptive. When you give to Éver, he gives back.' Most coaches would simply say, 'I'm the boss, and it's my way or no way.' But Unai adapted to Banega's personality. The result? He won the player over. Unai adds, 'Many times, I had to act like a father to him, tell him things he needed to change. We had some big arguments, but he always responded well.'

'Big arguments? We had some massive arguments,' Banega confirms.

At Sevilla, during the summer of 2014, Unai, fresh off his first

Europa League title, repeated the same request to Monchi: 'I want a player like Banega.' Eventually, Monchi had had enough. 'If you want someone like Banega . . . why don't we just sign Banega?' It wasn't an obvious move. Banega was frozen out at Valencia, barely training with the squad, his career at a crossroads. But Unai saw an opportunity and both he and Monchi personally called the player to convince him. While the deal between the clubs was being finalised, Banega trained alone, waiting. Emery stayed in touch, sending him messages, checking in on his progress and jokingly reminding him to lay off the McDonald's. 'He had incredible ability,' Monchi recalls. 'But he needed someone to push him.'

Unai was confident about the move. 'If you bring him to Sevilla, he will make people get out of their seats,' he told Monchi. 'I know how to handle him.'

Sevilla signed him in the summer of 2014 for just €1.5 million, an absolute bargain for someone of his talent. He had to replace Ivan Rakitić, who had just left for Barcelona. Unai gave him freedom to play behind Carlos Bacca and Kevin Gameiro, but with clear defensive duties.

At twenty-six, Banega still needed discipline. And care. During his first months in Sevilla, Banega struggled. He had personal problems and found it difficult to adapt. Every morning, the same ritual between coach and player: 'How's your wife? What's your weight?' Unai treated him like a son, sometimes caring, sometimes scolding, but generally he played the good cop, with Monchi as the bad cop. 'Ah, Banega,' Monchi says. 'There were days when he would show up in a terrible mood – his family had left, he was alone in Seville, and you could tell he just didn't want to train. Unai is excellent at dealing with players face-to-face, but one day he wanted to kill Banega. My role then was to say, "Relax, don't kill him – he's too good."' Arguments in training were constant, heated, explosive at times. But they always ended in reconciliation. After some of these clashes, Banega would retreat to the showers or locker room to cry, hiding so no one would see. 'Yes, there were tears,' he admits. One day, a discussion boiled over, and Unai kicked him out of training. Banega was furious. He came to Emery after the session and said he wanted to leave. Unai's response was, 'Take three days. Think about it.'

The days passed, Unai sat him down and asked, 'So, what do you want to do?' Banega didn't hesitate. 'I'll stay.' That moment changed everything.

'Of course. When I realised he was right in our arguments he helped me become a better person, a better player. I still don't know how to thank him for everything he did.' Banega showed his gratitude on the pitch. As Monchi says, 'He did things others couldn't.' Banega was the engine of Sevilla, the man who set the pace for when to pause and when to attack.

This relentless focus on turning rough stones into diamonds made Emery a perfect fit for Sevilla's philosophy. 'As a player, I didn't behave like a professional,' Emery insists. 'I didn't eat what the team nutritionists told us to, I didn't seek proper medical care … But the tools are meaningless if the player doesn't apply himself with the intention to learn and improve. Your entire life has to centre around football. If a player understands that, he'll perform at his best. I didn't, and didn't go far.'

Meanwhile, the Sevilla players adapted to his brutal work ethic. That's why, in every match, you saw a team that never gave up, one full of pride, competitiveness and generosity in its effort. These values, combined with the victorious DNA of the club's past shaped the beautiful story of this team and the Europa League. 'Unai is a true company man, the kind of dedicated worker any employer would dream of having in their team,' the former president of

Sevilla, José María del Nido, says. 'In Sevilla, I was very loved, though perhaps also hated at times. In Valencia, I was hated more often than loved. In Almería, even when we won, I felt like I wasn't fully recognised because I was still young. Some coaches achieve success very quickly but don't sustain it over time. Recognition comes when you can demonstrate consistency,' Emery reflects. The misunderstandings, the players who resisted his methods, the boos from the stands, the memes, the caricatures, even the universal love, 'It's all part of my journey as a coach,' Emery accepts. 'I learnt to live with criticism and whistles, but also with the praise, without betraying myself.'

With a huge amount of information, Unai created a team with layers, capable of adapting to various scenarios. At Sevilla, his offensive model was primarily built around quick transitional attacks but also included players capable of dominating possession when required. Emery's teams were known for employing high defensive lines, aiming to keep play far from their goal. They focused on aggressive pressing and minimising the spaces between lines. But finally, balance was becoming his signature style. The coaches he admired, such as Pep Guardiola and Diego Simeone, were vastly different, but were good at controlling both phases of play, with and without the ball and, most importantly, they very often won. Unai had faced Guardiola several times before, with little success. After losing so often to the young Barcelona manager, first at Valencia and later at Sevilla, he decided to show his players two days' worth of video sessions analysing Barcelona, with each session lasting an hour.

'Bloody hell, Unai,' the players said to him. 'You've gone overboard with the videos.'

'I just love how Barcelona plays, it is historic what they are doing, and I wanted to share it with you,' he replied.

'Simeone, for example, started with a purely competitive mind-set, winning against stronger teams,' Unai notes with admiration. 'From there, his team progressed significantly in its footballing style, with a proactive approach when necessary. Associating Simeone solely with unattractive football is a simplistic and mistaken conclusion. I've followed Atlético closely, so I know what I'm talking about. When you analyse others so much, you start asking why do they do this? I see a coach whose team plays well, and it excites me. Teams that bring something new to football always challenge me. And I want to be challenged.'

But not all the time. During working hours, to decompress he found a hobby: chess. He would go on his iPad and play anonymously against rivals in other parts of the world. He did not do it to learn, though, he played to win. And when he had a longer break, he would travel to Valencia to meet up with ten-year-old Lander, who realised his dad was making the effort to stop the relentless world he inhabited to spend time with him. The kid started playing with a football again.

During the 2014–15 season, Banega was instrumental in Unai's second Europa League success, earning himself the man of the match trophy in the final against FC Dnipro. The trophy was rewarded with a presence in the Champions League which returned to Nervión in 2015–16 but that European journey did not come with a leap in quality. The departure of essential players like Bacca – and failing to replace him effectively – became an insurmountable burden. Even so, despite a disastrous start, Unai worked tirelessly with each of the ten new signings who had arrived. Sevilla finished third in the Champions League group stage behind Manchester City and Juventus (beaten by a single goal from Fernando Llorente in their most memorable result), and moved into the Europa

League. After knocking out Molde and Basel, they met Bilbao's Athletic Club in the quarter-finals.

'We had won 2–1 in Bilbao, and everything seemed to be in our favour,' Emery remembers. "But at the Sánchez-Pizjuán, we sat back, and Athletic staged a comeback, forcing the game to extra time. There was a moment when Athletic Club's Susaeta found himself one-on-one with our keeper. It felt like the tie was slipping away. If he scored, it would have been over for us. Yet, as I watched, I kept telling myself, *Stay calm, stay calm, stay calm* . . . because in football, anything can happen. Susaeta didn't score, and I realised how difficult it is to convert in such high-pressure situations. That moment taught me to approach these situations with composure, to accept both the chances that go for you and those that go against you and the outcome of them. Whether it's a moment of brilliance from my players or a missed opportunity, I've learnt to stay grounded, these things are simply part of the game.' The match ended in a penalty shoot-out, and Kevin Gameiro, cramping and barely able to walk, was still chosen by Unai Emery for the crucial fifth penalty. 'You'll be the one to send us through,' Emery told him. Gameiro delivered, smashing it into the top corner.

As Sevilla progressed to the semi-finals against Shakhtar Donetsk, Éver Banega signed a contract to join Inter Milan in the summer once his deal at Sevilla expired. Emery, determined to keep his focus on Sevilla, visited Banega's home to talk. They spent hours discussing their shared goals, ultimately vowing to give everything to secure another European triumph. That was their joint promise over a few cups of coffee. It would prove fateful as Banega faced a pivotal moment during the second leg of the semi-final. One minute before the end of the first half, and after a lacklustre performance, Sevilla had conceded a goal, making it 1–1. Éver returned to the dressing room visibly angry and disheartened. Emery immediately intervened. 'Juan Carlos, take care of the team,' he instructed his assistant. Emery pulled Banega aside for a private talk. 'What's wrong? Tell me,' Unai demanded in his office located within the changing room. 'What do you need? Do you want me to replace anyone? Who do you want on or off the pitch? I'll give you the support you need. Just tell me. You either change or we will not win.' It was Emery's way of empowering his player, giving him responsibility and belief. Banega returned to the pitch and dominated the second half. With the player's leadership, Sevilla stormed into the final after a 3–1 victory.

The final was going to be played in Basel, against Jürgen Klopp's Liverpool. 'Like us, they had to win to secure Champions League qualification for the following season,' Unai remembers. 'But the Europa League was our competition.' In the build-up, Emery repeated the same routines he had used before the finals in 2014 against Benfica and 2015 against Dnipro; the huddle with the players, his speeches emphasising the importance of their journey. But this time, he surprised the team with a touching gesture: by giving a special mention to their teammate Krohn-Dehli. The Danish player had suffered a serious injury, dislocating his kneecap in the semi-final against Shakhtar.

'It's one of the most epic matches in Sevilla's history,' Monchi recalls. 'We were outmatched in every way. In the stands, there were six thousand of us against more than twenty thousand English fans. Liverpool's squad was superior, and we suffered a lot in the first half. But everything changed after Unai's famous half-time talk in the Basel dressing room.' Sevilla needed to rally after a 1–0 half-time deficit against a Liverpool side that had so far dominated and should have scored more goals. 'Unai, we are losing by one goal, bloody hell, it is fantastic news,' Gameiro told the manager on the way to the changing rooms. The team seemed scared. Throughout 2016, Sevilla hadn't managed to win an away game in LaLiga. 'But I remembered where we were strong, where we won most matches, where we were supported and loved,' Unai recalls. The manager spoke to a very quiet changing room: 'We have rarely lost at home this season. We have beaten Barcelona, Real Madrid and Juventus. There we feel powerful, indestructible. Guys, we're not in Basel; this is the Sánchez-Pizjuán, we are at home, and our fans are outside.' Some tactical changes were introduced. Emery instructed the full-backs to push higher, and he emphasised quick attacks after regaining possession.

In the first half Sevilla had created just one chance on goal. But players now came back out on to the pitch free of pressure, willing to show their fans what they were made of. They were in Sevilla now. Kevin Gameiro's equaliser in the 1st minute of the second half, initiated by a driving run from full-back Mariano, was a psychological blow to Liverpool. Emery urged his team to maintain their intensity and press higher, leading to Liverpool's defensive collapse. Sevilla produced some of their best football during Unai's reign and won 3–1. The three Europa League titles, achieved by the time Emery was forty-four years old, made him the most decorated manager in the competition's history, tied with Italy's Giovanni Trapattoni, who had won two with Juventus in 1977 and 1993, and one with Inter Milan in 1991. There was still a Copa del Rey final to be played against Barcelona, but it had already been an extraordinary season for the manager and Andalusian club – the undisputed kings of the Europa League with five wins.

Meanwhile, Éver Banega's Sevilla journey ended on a bitter-sweet note. A few days after the European triumph, Banega was sent off in the Copa del Rey final. His late foul on Neymar in the

90th minute earned him a red card. The match, which went to extra time, ended in a 2–0 defeat for Sevilla. Later that night, after what turned out to be Unai Emery's last game with Sevilla as well, the team gathered at a hotel in Madrid to celebrate their Europa League victory and the season's achievements. Banega, holding a beer, knew it was also his farewell. Quietly, he approached Igor Emery and whispered, 'You need to convince your brother to join me at Inter Milan.'

In 2015, West Ham had pursued Unai Emery. Napoli had also shown interest, but after his experience with Spartak Moscow, he rejected the offer as he felt it lacked stability. Adriano Galliani of AC Milan also tried again to secure him with a number of personal calls, but Emery remained patient.

Preparations for the next season had begun before the cup final. Sevilla were in the process of signing the forward Pablo Sarabia. While Monchi was in Madrid finalising the deal, he picked up a copy of the *Marca* sport newspaper and saw the headline: Unai Emery, PSG's top target. Confused, he called Unai directly. Unai admitted it was true. He hadn't been allowed to say anything before, but now he could confirm not only that they were interested, but actually that he was leaving. 'I wasn't upset that he left,' Monchi recalls, 'but I would have liked to have known earlier. I already had a couple of signings done and now had to find a new coach too. That was early June, more or less. I had to move fast, and in the end, we brought in Jorge Sampaoli.'

Unai felt his cycle at Sevilla had finished, and it had ended with a title. He knew there were higher levels and he wanted to be tested by them. In fact, he started to dream that one day his work might allow him to manage Real Madrid or Barcelona, or at least a club that could challenge for and win the Champions League. His ultimate target. In May 2016, PSG's interim sporting director

Olivier Létang had approached Emery. At the beginning of June, representatives from PSG had met with him in Valencia, offering a two-year deal with an optional third season to replace Laurent Blanc. After two weeks of talks, Emery agreed to terminate his Sevilla contract, with PSG paying €2 million in compensation and allowing the coach to bring his staff with him to Paris.

Paris beckoned. Yes, the moment felt right to move on to a club that needed to win everything.

6

TOP OF THE TREE:

PARIS SAINT-GERMAIN

Unai Emery has always preferred living in the heart of a city, surrounded by its rhythm and energy. Paris was no exception. At first, he settled in Neuilly-sur-Seine, a prestigious neighbourhood where many footballers live. It was a strategic choice, offering a quick commute. From there, he could take the Avenue Charles de Gaulle, passing through the tunnel where Princess Diana had her fatal accident. Later, he moved closer to the stadium, settling into a penthouse.

The decision to live in the city was deliberate. In Moscow, he had done the opposite, choosing to stay near the training ground, a decision he regretted. The Russian capital felt too chaotic, but being isolated left him feeling alone. His coaching staff had also lived nearby, but even then, the experience was tough. In Sevilla, he had made a different choice, also opting for a penthouse close to the stadium, where he lived comfortably for three years. Not quite in the centre, but still connected to the city. 'I don't like living far away from things,' he explains. 'In Paris, I liked being able to go out for a coffee, to have dinner somewhere.'

In Paris, as soon as Unai learnt about a motorway pass that granted access to a special fast lane, he got one immediately. The 25-minute drive from his home to the training ground, Camp des

Loges, often began before dawn, taking advantage of the quiet streets before the city's infamous traffic took over. The journey became a time for reflection. 'I think a lot . . . I also make calls. I call my brother [Igor] a lot, just to check in, see how he's doing. Sometimes I call people in football too, just to ask things.'

Camp des Loges, about 20 kilometres west of the capital, lies in the middle of a lush forest, a place of calm and seclusion. The narrow streets are lined with charming houses and greenery, worlds away from the chaos of the city. By starting his day early, Unai also avoided the clusters of teenage fans who gathered outside the training ground, desperate for a glimpse of PSG's galaxy of stars. Once the doors opened, the modest nature of the facility became apparent. Long, low-lying buildings flanked the entrance, unassuming in appearance and in stark contrast to the club's glamorous reputation. Opposite stood container boxes, converted into temporary offices and facilities, that resembled makeshift set-ups found on construction sites rather than a world-class training complex. At the far end, the pitches and gym awaited, functional but lacking the sophistication of elite European clubs' training grounds. When Emery reached his office, on the first floor of the main building, which overlooked the training grounds, he often found himself reflecting on what was needed to make the outdated facility more practical. Though PSG's ambitious new training centre was already in development, it remained years away from completion. Emery knew he wouldn't reap the benefits of it. Paris doesn't wait for anyone.

When Unai first stepped into the Parc des Princes stadium, he found himself at the helm of a club filled with contradictions. In 2016, PSG were a team considered top of the pile by the best managers in the world but at the same time weighed down by the expectations and impatience of their Qatari owners. While they had established the club as the undisputed force in French domestic football, Champions League success remained an elusive dream. And for the club, there was no middle ground: it was either lifting the biggest European trophy or disaster. The dismissal of Laurent Blanc, despite his domestic success and composed leadership, was a stark reminder that good wasn't good enough. PSG showed impeccable timing when they approached Unai Emery. The coach felt he had reached a natural conclusion of his Sevilla era and, determined to secure him, PSG's president Nasser Al-Khelaifi personally took charge of the matter. A meeting was arranged in Valencia, where Al-Khelaifi, PSG's sporting director Olivier Létang and Emery sat down to discuss the future. 'As always, I asked Nasser, "Why are you hiring me? What are you looking for in me?"' Emery recalls.

'Because your career is on an upward trajectory; you've won three consecutive Europa Leagues. It's not the Champions League, but with a team like Sevilla, that's a tremendous achievement. You already have a winning mentality. We are a winning team, but we need to improve the finer details,' Al-Khelaifi explained. Unai signed a two-year contract, but there was still the matter of resolving the agreement between Paris, Sevilla and Emery, whose contract with the Spanish club ran until 2017. Negotiating with Monchi was no simple task. However, their relationship, built over three and a half years of debates, lessons and disagreements, ultimately paved the way for Emery's move to Paris.

This was not Sevilla, with its modest budgets and overachieving squads. PSG, in the City of Light, sought global stars – a strategy that could dazzle but also confuse. The departure of Zlatan Ibrahimović left a void that the club hoped to fill with the improvement of the Uruguayan striker Edinson Cavani, who had been overshadowed by the Swedish forward as he generally only played when Zlatan did not. There was also hope in the flair and potential of the new arrivals that summer. Tricky forward Jesé Rodríguez was signed from Real Madrid, while Hatem Ben Arfa joined after a sensational season at Nice, bringing creativity and unpredictability. Emery convinced the board to bring in the midfielder Grzegorz Krychowiak, a player he deeply trusted from their successful time together at Sevilla. Additionally, he began working with Giovani Lo Celso, a talented and promising young midfielder who was eager to make his mark.

But Paris does not welcome just anyone. The media were not about to simply analyse Unai Emery's tactics or judge him based on PSG's results; their intention was to scrutinise every aspect of his persona – his demeanour, his French, even his choice of ties. Yet Emery remained unfazed, focusing little on appearances or his functional French, a language he first learnt as a child and was now determined to master. 'I don't watch myself in press conferences,' Emery admits. At that point in his career, his meticulous attention to detail didn't extend to himself, even though he was beginning to consider how expressive he needed to be on the technical area. He concluded the trajectory of the season, and the unique pressures of PSG's environment, would likely make that decision for him. His obsessive focus on every footballing detail that could yield results left little room for personal balance. Unai was already living on the edge of a perpetual storm, juggling football and life with no shelter. That conflict only grew fiercer in Paris where dominance was the minimum requirement. All his efforts were put into making PSG a winning machine and, in particular, giving Cavani full attacking responsibilities and getting him to respond. It was a key to immediate success.

Edinson Cavani's start to the 2016–17 season was anything but smooth. In the second Ligue 1 match against Metz, the striker squandered a string of clear chances, frustrating the Parc des Princes faithful. In PSG's Champions League opener against Arsenal, he repeated the pattern, despite scoring an early goal. Unai Emery, however, stood by him. After the Arsenal match, Emery spoke to Edinson: 'For me, the most important thing is that you're creating these chances. I'm happy with that, but we need to work on converting them.' It was a pivotal conversation. Emery squashed doubts in Cavani's head about his capacity to fill Zlatan's shoes. But the manager did not leave it there. 'You don't need to score thirty-five goals this season, you need to score fifty. You have the talent to do it.' Cavani left the room thinking his boss was crazy, but he also started wondering how he could achieve those stats. Cavani responded spectacularly. He became the focal point of PSG's attack, delivering one of the best seasons of his career. In a match against Caen, Emery substituted him at half-time after he had already scored four goals. By the end of the season, Cavani had scored an astonishing forty-nine goals in fifty matches across all competitions, a personal best. He was named Ligue 1 player of the year and firmly established himself as one of the best strikers in the world. Over time, Cavani would cement his legacy at PSG by becoming the club's all-time leading scorer, surpassing Zlatan Ibrahimović.

Despite Cavani's brilliance and after four consecutive league titles, PSG finished second in Ligue 1 that season behind an extraordinary AS Monaco side featuring Kylian Mbappé, Radamel Falcao, Bernardo Silva, Fabinho, Thomas Lemar and Benjamin Mendy. However, the European stage was going to be the yardstick by which everyone's worth would be measured. In Unai's first season at the club, PSG would meet Luis Enrique's FC Barcelona, featuring the likes of Messi, Neymar and Luis Suárez, in the last 16 of the Champions League.

The route from the Reina Isás Hotel, where the squad rests, to the Parc des Princes stadium, winds past the Roland Garros tennis courts. For Unai Emery, this journey always held a certain charm. Though it doesn't pass iconic landmarks like the Seine or the Arc de Triomphe, the route has a quiet allure and offers the opportunity for a reflective moment before a match, with most of the work already done and only a few key words left to be said in the dressing room. For a tennis enthusiast like Unai, it is also an iconic route. He deeply admires the sport, particularly Rafael Nadal, frequently praising his work ethic and mental strength while drawing parallels to football. Perhaps that could be it? The message for the day: a reminder to the players to stay strong, this was a *carpe diem* moment, to recognise the opportunity before them. In the home changing room of the Parc des Princes, Unai Emery delivered an emotional pre-match talk before the first leg. He ended it with a declaration that resonated deeply: 'I've faced Barcelona sixteen, seventeen, maybe eighteen times, and I've beaten them only once. Every time, I saw it as an opportunity but mostly I did not succeed. But do you know something? I've never had a team like this. I know, with this team, I will beat Barcelona.'

And beat them, they did. On that February night in 2017, PSG delivered one of the most memorable performances in their European history. It was a collective masterpiece, both offensively and defensively. Emery's tactical plan was clinical. His assistant, Juan Carlos Carcedo, summarised it: 'Stop Barcelona's flow. Force them to play differently.' The execution was flawless. Ángel Di María opened the scoring in the 18th minute with a stunning free kick, and Julian Draxler doubled the lead after Marco Verratti's brilliant run. In the second half, Di María struck again and Cavani sealed the 4–0 rout. PSG had destroyed Barcelona. One thing that Unai will never forget is the look of pure joy on the president's face after their victory. Al-Khelaifi wasn't one to impose, though he might occasionally visit a training session to say hello, always with great respect. Emery held him in high regard, describing Al-Khelaifi as polite, respectful and kind, someone who always looked you in the eye when speaking. On matchdays, the president would sometimes stop by the hotel while the players were having their pre-match snack to shake hands with everyone. That evening Al-Khelaifi entered the dressing room to congratulate the team, and he could not hide the grin.

Happiness was acceptable, but too much of it, not so much. It worried Unai. 'After the first leg, it felt like we had won the World Cup. I had never seen such euphoria,' Emery recalls. The celebrations spilled on to social media, with some players posting photos of the 4–0 scoreline. Within the staff, however, there were murmurs of caution. *Better not wake the beast*, they thought. Emery himself warned his squad repeatedly against overconfidence. 'Do you think Barcelona will just sit back? Respect them, or we could hurt their pride. A wounded animal is always dangerous.' Yet, the seeds of complacency were already sown. Emery observed how success could fracture a team, a club even, more than a defeat could. When results falter, solidarity often prevails as players and staff band together with a siege mentality. But after victory, particularly in moments of euphoria, the illusion of individual triumph can take hold. Flattered by those around them, some players begin to believe the success is solely theirs, putting the team's cohesion at risk.

As the days passed, the optimism continued. PSG crushed Marseille 1–5 in Ligue 1, feeding the belief that the 4–0 was the start of something historic. Club executives began scouting hotels in Cardiff, the host city for the Champions League final. Emery insisted: the job isn't done. He repeated it like a mantra. At the same time, the French press, particularly *L'Équipe*, relentlessly propagated the idea of *la remontada* – the comeback. This was repeated to the point of exhaustion, becoming the dominant narrative surrounding the second leg. However, *la remontada* was a term that reflected Barcelona's mindset, not the one PSG needed to adopt. It emphasised the risk of losing something precious rather than the opportunity to secure their triumph, casting them as the team with everything at stake.

But things began to shift, at least in the changing room. Unai's warnings started to resonate with some of the players. If you looked closely at the words of the veterans as they prepared for the return leg, you could detect an uneasy undercurrent beneath the optimism of those outside the group. A famous video from a dinner featuring Draxler, Matuidi, Meunier and Verratti in the days leading up to the match at Camp Nou revealed as much. In their expressions, their hesitant laughter, it was clear: fear was creeping in. Thiago Silva even voiced it aloud, admitting that the only way Messi could be stopped was 'by praying'. Emery, who had been searching for respect for their rival, not fear, often reflects on what was missing for PSG in that moment, repeating a phrase he holds close: 'In the important games, our team lacked a step in the process. It still lacked its Bakero's goal, its Iniesta's goal.' Emery borrowed the sentiment from Pep Guardiola, who once told him that to win the Champions League, Barcelona needed those two defining moments in the club's history. The first was José Mari Bakero's legendary header in the dying moments against Kaiserslautern in the 1991 European Cup's last sixteen, a goal that kept Barcelona alive in the competition that they ended up winning. The second was Andrés Iniesta's iconic strike in stoppage time against Chelsea in the 2009 Champions League semi-final, a goal that sent Barcelona to the final and solidified their destiny.

These actions were not just lifelines, they were moments that turned potential failure into belief, forging the backbone of a team's identity. Founded in 1970, PSG had no history of miraculous resilience to draw from. They did not have enough football heritage. They were unprepared for any potential upheaval. Thiago Motta was sidelined with a calf injury, leaving Unai Emery to plan for Adrien Rabiot to step in, but Rabiot had missed training the week before the match, having lost over 3 kilos in just a few days due to a stomach virus. Ángel Di María was still recovering from an injury too, and Javier Pastore left training with discomfort in his calf. With few options remaining, both Rabiot and Di María were declared fit enough to play, though it was more in hope than certainty.

As the footballers left the hotel, they were met by an overwhelming crowd outside the Camp Nou, intimidating in its sheer noise. As one Barcelona official put it, 'Our only chance was to make them live through hell.' The players watched silently, headphones on, no one uttering a word. However, two PSG officials debated which champagne bottle they would open that night. Everything that could have gone wrong in the lead-up to the match did, and the game itself began no differently. The warm-up felt off, with players complaining the balls were too new, particularly goalkeeper Kevin Trapp. As the team walked down the tunnel and on to the pitch, they were met with an earth-shaking roar, deafening and violent.

'We weren't facing eleven players,' Emery later reflected, 'we were facing a hundred thousand people.' PSG had reached the gates of hell, and Barcelona had just thrown them open. The players' faces drained of colour. From the first whistle, PSG looked rattled, missing simple passes and falling back nervously. Emery, pacing the touchline, waved frantically at his defenders to push forward, but his gestures were met with no response. Three min-utes in, Luis Suárez struck, igniting the Camp Nou. The second goal came just before half-time, and moments into the second half, Leo Messi scored a penalty, making it 3–0. Panic set in, but then Edinson Cavani, with a powerful finish, clawed back hope for PSG in the 62nd minute, bringing the score to 3–1.

'I was in the stands with my nephew, Lander,' recalls Igor Emery. 'Cavani's goal was a relief.' But it was fleeting. Neymar was in the middle of orchestrating one of the most decisive performances of his career. In the 88th minute, he curled a stunning free kick into the top corner to make it 4–1.

Minutes later, Neymar converted a penalty with unnerving composure, levelling the tie at 5–1. 'With that penalty, I was overwhelmed,' Igor remembers. 'I couldn't stay where I was sit-ting. I went to the back of the stands, covered my ears. Lander did the same. When we heard the roar after the last goal ...' The final blow had come in the 95th minute. Neymar lofted a perfect cross into the box, where Sergi Roberto lunged forward to score the decisive sixth goal. At that moment, PSG's hopes disintegrated. On the bench, Unai Emery lowered his head and covered his eyes with his hands. He felt numb. Something had cracked inside. The Camp Nou roared, and he could barely hear his own thoughts. Staring at the grass, he wondered, *How did this happen?*

'That,' Igor Emery later reflected, 'is the image that stays with me from that match. Lander and I both broke down in tears. Lander said it was the saddest match of Unai's footballing life.'

At the Camp Nou, the game's aftermath was immortalised in a single photo. As chaos erupted around him, with fans roaring and players piling on top of each other, Lionel Messi stood atop an advertising board, arms outstretched, gaze steady. He wasn't celebrating wildly but instead exuded the calm of a conqueror, leading his team to a victory that seemed impossible. That night was also transformative for Neymar, who had been Barcelona's best player. He decided that the Catalan club, even with its glory, would never propel him to the pinnacle of football. To win the Ballon d'Or, to step out of Messi's shadow, he needed to leave. In fact, he asked to leave on the back of that fixture. He wanted to be the superstar of another team.

For PSG, the loss was devastating. Thiago Motta captured the team's turmoil: 'Do we lower our heads or hold them high?'

Emery, determined to rebuild, told his players, 'If we survive this, we will grow from this wound. There is no middle ground. We either overcome it, or we collapse.' Lander Emery remembers waiting under the stands after the match. 'I was shattered, and so was my dad. He was trying to be strong for me, but you could see that it was a cruel, brutal moment. He was trying not to cry.' In fact, nobody ever remembers seeing Unai crying, maybe during one celebration with Lorca, but he managed not to that night. The 6–1 defeat became one of football's most unforgettable tragedies, leaving a scar that would follow PSG for years to come.

'Knowing I had the president's support was all I needed at that moment,' Unai Emery recalls. The coach and the club's leadership reviewed the match and the season in detail. Together, they created a meticulous list of changes, restructuring both the team and its organisation, blocking the group from exterior influences, including prohibiting player entourages from accessing the locker room. 'I accept my place, my moments,' Unai reflects. 'I know I can be on top one day and at the bottom the next, but I keep working the same. And learn from everything. Even from that terrible night.' Emery's assistant, Juan Carlos Carcedo, remembers, 'It was a brutal moment for us. We've shared this with players since: never believe you've already won something. Until you do.' That match became a turning point in Emery's understanding of the game. Despite dominating possession, Barcelona had torn them apart on the counter, so he shared this thought with his coaching staff: 'If you attack recklessly, with overly offensive full-backs and no structure, truly great teams will bleed you dry. We need to adapt.'

Years later, Unai decided to rewatch that painful night at the Camp Nou. He couldn't bring himself to sit through the entire match – just a 30-minute stretch in the second half – but it was enough. In that short window, what struck him wasn't the goals, but the absence of leadership from key players. At the time, he had rationalised the defeat as a freak event, a perspective reinforced by a phone call he never forgot. It was Juan Ramón López Muñiz, the former Sporting Gijón manager. 'You played a good game,' he told Unai. 'You defended well. Nothing really happened except a few isolated chances. The referee could have made different decisions. Everything was under control.' And yet . . . something was still missing.

That summer, Antero Henrique, formerly Porto's strongman, arrived as the new sporting director. The club was reinforced with players suited for big occasions, like Dani Alves, a seasoned winner. Then came Neymar, the most expensive player in football history at €222 million and both a sporting and media icon. But Emery and PSG's focus was on another priority: Kylian Mbappé, the revelation of the previous season at Monaco. Determined to sign him, Emery visited the Mbappé family home in Bondy, a modest Paris suburb. At just eighteen years old, Mbappé already knew what he wanted. Despite interest from Real Madrid, he was drawn to the vision of leading PSG, his boyhood club, alongside Neymar, Cavani and Verratti. But his ambition was clear: he told Emery he wanted to play every single game.

*

With the help of their new stars, PSG set out to overcome the scars of *la remontada* and rebuild their European ambitions, all while navigating the relentless pressure and global media spotlight that accompanied their high-profile arrivals. Managing a squad filled with superstars meant adapting training methods and handling the team differently. 'I wonder,' Unai asks himself, 'would you act the same way at PSG as you did before? I don't think so. Why? Because I arrived there as the Sevilla coach. I thought, *I'm going to do what I've always done, what has brought me success.* But then I realised that not everything would work the same way.' For a start, the coaching staff was enormous, with twenty-five to thirty members compared to the seven or eight Unai was used to working with at his previous clubs. Many players had personal trainers and physiotherapists, and managing these layers while keeping the squad united and performing was a delicate balancing act.

Unai prioritised building close relationships with his players, speaking to them individually to convey his ideas and gain their trust. But it wasn't always easy, it required the ability to connect at the right moment. 'In big teams, players expect the coach to always be right,' Unai says. 'There's no margin for error. Every decision, whether in training, planning or even the words you use, must align perfectly to help you win. It may look easier from the outside, but it's the opposite: every detail matters because winning is the norm.' He added: 'People talk about managing egos, but egos exist at every level. In the Segunda B, I've dealt with players being upset about not playing. The difference at the top is those egos have more impact.'

Emery realised he had to approach training with a certain distance. 'At first, he was meticulous,' recalls right-back Thomas

Meunier. 'He stopped drills over the smallest mistake. There were also endless videos, we had to sit through them all! But he adapted to the players, shortening sessions to focus on the essentials.' It was not exactly as Meunier explains it, but there was a fascinating evolution in training that did not have to do only with the body, but also the mind. Before PSG, Unai Emery had been obsessive about training and the intensity of it. He liked, as do most coaches, training the day after a match. They are the start of the so-called micro-cycles, a short-term training plan that typically lasts a week, until matchday, or even until the day after a game, with the intention of giving players who didn't play the same workload as those that did.

But there's also another aspect to consider. Normally the day after a match, players were divided into two groups: those who played, who focused on recovery work, and those who didn't, who took on a heavier workload. A divided group. Not ideal. The day after a match is often the hardest for players, whether they didn't play or whether they underperformed or were substituted and felt the need to prove themselves. Navigating that whirlwind of emotions was something Unai began to understand. He realised that, at times, giving his players a day off after a match and resuming training two days later could be beneficial. It allowed them time to reflect, reset and return to training refreshed. Footballers rarely experience the luxury of a Sunday off, a simple pleasure millions take for granted, a day to rest while the world around them slows down. When PSG played on a Saturday, Unai made it a point, whenever possible, to give his players the Sunday off. It was a chance to reconnect with their families, children or partners, offering a brief escape from the relentless cycle of elite football. His new approach had another intention: injecting a sense of normality into their highly controlled environments.

In any case, no two weeks were ever the same. The thing Unai dislikes most is routine, doing the same thing over and over. As a player, that kind of monotony bored him to death. That's why he constantly rethinks and refines his plans. Even his gestures on the touchline evolved. 'I toned down my gestures at PSG because I realised it was the most convenient thing to do,' Emery admitted. 'At PSG, scoring goals and winning are much more likely than in other places, so you naturally feel more relaxed.' As a coach, Unai always sought to guide his players, much like controlling movements with a joystick. However, at PSG, he realised that many players, particularly someone like Neymar, instinctively found the most effective solutions on the pitch for themselves.

'I have three rules for set-pieces: do them fast before the rival team can organise themselves, keep them short to force the opponent to move and lose shape, or attack directly the goal depending on your position and the rival's. With Neymar, very early in the season, there wasn't time to teach all of this. In a game against Toulouse, he took a quick corner, and Kurzawa scored. I told him, "All my work narrowed down to your genius."' What complex organisms teams are, driven by emotion and that elusive element that is collective energy, even at this elite, meticulously prepared level. Yet, there is a human behind every decision on the pitch; even the most towering tree depends on its roots to stand tall.

'I spoke with Neymar about this,' Unai explains. 'With a player like him, sometimes he is the strategy. As Marcelo Bielsa says, some players have natural talent for certain movements, while others need repetition to make those plays automatic.' While Unai learnt by looking at the reaction of certain players to his demands, he kept asking those whom he admired, like Bielsa, the Argentinian coach, for advice. Unai Emery had once spent three days in

Valencia with Marcelo Bielsa, alongside Mauricio Pochettino. At the time, Pochettino was preparing to begin his coaching career, and Bielsa, then the coach of Chile, took the side to Spain for a training camp. For three days, Unai and Mauricio both attended Bielsa's training sessions, held meetings and immersed themselves in his meticulous approach. Bielsa's obsession with detail extended beyond the field. He held countless meetings with his players at the hotel, reviewing recent games on video and telling them exactly what needed to improve. It was familiar work for Unai.

'I admire him,' Emery admits, having taken note of the way his colleague worked. 'He works analytically. If it's dribbling, he practises dribbling constantly, repeating exercises. If it's defensive cover, he drills cover. Every offensive and defensive principle, he breaks it down and works on it individually. He says players should imitate those with talent, then repeat, repeat and repeat.' While at PSG, Unai vividly recalls waiting for a scheduled call from Marcelo Bielsa, one that he had personally requested. Bielsa, true to his meticulous nature, had set the time himself: Tuesday night, at 10 p.m. precisely. Emery had also been warned that Bielsa would ring only once. So, in his home in Paris, Unai sat on the sofa, eyes fixed on the phone. When it finally rang, Bielsa's words took him by surprise.

'I admire you all a lot, but I could never coach a player like Neymar or Messi, they play while walking,' Bielsa remarked. Emery chuckled inwardly. *That's no compliment*, he thought. If that's all you're going to say, better not say anything at all. It was classic Bielsa: blunt, honest and unintentionally humorous. But Emery understood the underlying message. Bielsa was alluding to the challenge of managing players who, with a single moment of brilliance, could decide a game without needing to exert themselves relentlessly. At PSG, Emery wrestled with this very issue:

how to maintain intensity in a team that often found Ligue 1 matches too easy.

To counter this, he constantly pushed his players, sparking discussions, creating tension and trying to unsettle the dressing room, anything to keep them engaged and ensure their hunger for competition never dulled. Emery sought to ensure that matches were dynamic and driven by a collective effort, rather than relying solely on the individual brilliance of his superstars. However, he would admit that his efforts, coming from someone who had not won the Champions League, sometimes backfired. Every training session was an exercise in balance. So, eventually, training became less tactical, less detailed, except for those key moments in the Champions League. With top players, it was harder to enforce the tactical work that Unai had valued at Sevilla.

'A coach's relationship with players is like that of a parent with a child,' Unai explains. 'When necessary, you must confront them, even if it risks upsetting them, but handle it delicately to avoid breaking their trust. With a child, the bond remains, but with a player, the relationship can falter, or even end. In smaller teams, the coach is the unquestioned leader, but at top clubs, leadership varies. Jorge Valdano's reflection captures this, "At Barcelona, the leader is Messi; at Real Madrid, it's Florentino Pérez; and at Atlético, it's Simeone."' At PSG, the leadership was meant for Neymar, that's why he was brought in. But the question remained: did Neymar truly want it? After Neymar's record-breaking €222 million arrival and Mbappé's €180 million transfer, it was clear the team would revolve around these two superstars. By all accounts, Neymar is a good person, but like many star players, his schedule is dominated by marketing commitments, sponsorship events, photoshoots, sometimes even taking precedence over time on the pitch. A new challenge for the coach.

And what about Cavani? He had earned star status after his outstanding season, but now, he had to accept that the hierarchy had shifted once again. Harmony between the three players was key for success that season. Not easy. Tensions quickly arose, especially between Neymar and Cavani. One of the earliest flashpoints came during a Ligue 1 match against Lyon in September 2017, when the two clashed on the pitch over a penalty. Cavani insisted on taking it and missed. Both Neymar and Cavani had a penalty conversion rate in the eighties – impressive numbers. But Neymar thought, *At Barcelona, with Messi, the best player in the world, they let me take penalties. And now I come here, and I can't?* When Neymar signed for PSG, the club told him he would be the centrepiece, the face of everything. And if he was everything, that included taking penalties. What the club promised him mattered, and the coach had to respect that. So, when Neymar demanded something, Unai understood. Neymar also had the feeling that Cavani wasn't willing to share. But Neymar had shared before with Messi and Luis Suárez no less. And this wasn't just any version of Neymar; this was Neymar at his absolute peak. He had it all: acceleration, movement off the ball, dribbling, hold-up play, free kicks, headers. He was unstoppable. Unai explained this to Cavani, adding that in the previous season, he had been the team's third most active defensive player, but with the arrival of Neymar and Mbappé, his defensive workload had decreased. Unai asked him to work harder, to accept the changes brought by the two superstars. If not, the club might need to consider moving him on. As for Mbappé, only a teenager at the time, it was clear he had immense potential. But his game still needed refinement, especially in areas like hold-up play and physical duels. His body wasn't yet fully developed. If you compare a photo of him during his first season at PSG to when he left, the transformation is striking. Unai had promised Mbappé he would start on the wing and, over time, transition to playing as a number 9, out of respect for Cavani's established role. These were the politics the PSG manager had to navigate. Many would think Neymar and Mbappé might struggle to coexist, given their overlapping roles and preference for starting on the left. At first glance, it seemed like a potential conflict. But that year, they demonstrated a special connection on the pitch. They passed to each other, sought each other out, exchanged one-twos and gifted each other goals. It was an era when Mbappé wasn't yet taking penalties, and Neymar adored him.

In the end, PSG had three offensive players who were a joy to watch. Sometimes, there was even a fourth: Ángel Di María. But when Di María joined the trio, defensive balance became an issue. The manager demanded more from the midfielders, who had to cover significantly more ground. There were more fascinating headaches. Unai quickly realised that while Mbappé had a clear sense of direction and patience to find his moment, Neymar needed encouragement and emotional support to stay on track.

'The first thing I did that season,' Unai remembers, 'was to establish my priorities. I had to keep Neymar happy, that was the first thing. I have had many conversations with him about this subject, some successful, some not. Once, we had an honest chat for forty-five minutes, with our hearts on our sleeves. It was great. Neymar is like a child at heart. I told him, "You're someone who has everything. Who's ever going to tell you no? But sometimes, you need to hear no." I had to tell him no a couple of times, and, of course, he got upset. Hopefully he understood why I did it.' The manager took the time to ask Neymar about his family, his roots and his goals. Unai sensed that Neymar wanted to open up, and eventually it came: 'Míster, I know I have a lot of responsibility,' he said, with a hint of worry, acknowledging the immense weight of expectation on his shoulders and the many people who relied on him. That moment helped Unai understand him on a deeper level.

Since his early days at Santos, the Brazilian frequently travelled with two key members of his entourage: a physiotherapist and a fitness trainer. One of them once said, 'I adore Neymar, but the Neymar from Santos listened to me more than the Neymar at PSG.'

Understandably. The Neymar at PSG held significant influence, which included the choice not to play in away games in order to disappear from the group in certain parts of the season, as well as the power to push for a coaching change, if he desired. Neymar went through an adjustment period to adapt to Emery's methods and vice versa. He was generally positive, but he occasionally expressed minor dissatisfaction within his circle. These comments often snowballed and were amplified by the press, creating a false narrative of serious conflict between them. They were misinterpreting and misunderstanding their relationship.

'There was an international break, around October or November, and the media kept trying to create this idea of tension between Neymar and me. I told Antero Henrique, "I'm in Neymar's hands. How could I have a problem with him? If there's an issue, he has to tell me." Then, during a friendly Brazil played in Japan, Neymar told the press, "They're trying to pit me against the coach, but I have no problem with him." I remember flying from Paris to Valencia, and when I landed, I saw a message from Antero, "Wow, Neymar's statement was fantastic!" From that point until the end of the season, things went very well.'

But the line between discipline and stardom was very thin. Neymar once approached Unai the day after a game, during a recovery session. 'Boss, I want to train today.'

The manager, calm but firm, replied, 'No, it's not scheduled, you have done different work today and you won't train with the group.' Neymar's face darkened with frustration, but Unai reinforced his point. 'Ney,' he said, 'we have a plan for you this week. Remember. Someone has to tell you no.'

It wasn't the end of it. Kylian Mbappé, young and eager, joined the scene. 'Boss, if we both want to train . . .'

'Kylian,' he said, unwavering, 'hit the showers. I've already told Neymar no, and I'm not about to tell you, yes.' It was a matter of principle. Unai knew where the temptation to train came from. That day, the famous NBA player Kobe Bryant had visited, and the players wanted the legend to see them in action. But the manager did not bend.

Unai was not aware, always focused on football, of what it would mean to the young superstars to interact with a sports legend like Kobe.

Yet, there had been moments of encouragement to balance the demands from the players. During a Champions League match at the Parc des Princes, as the second half was about to begin, Neymar was nowhere to be seen. The rest of the team were already on the pitch, waiting for the restart, but the Brazilian was deep in conversation with Unai Emery. For a brief moment, Emery felt as if time had frozen. Then, realising Neymar was late, he made a spontaneous gesture, one of trust and understanding. He embraced him, kissed him on the forehead and sent him back out to join his teammates.

Driven by the players' instincts and mixing it with the organisation and control proposed by Emery, PSG evolved into a team with a devastating counter-attack. The trio up front delivered outstanding performances, with PSG reclaiming the Ligue 1 title in 2017–18 and dominating domestically. Cavani, finally proving he could coexist with the new stars, scored forty goals that season. However, the team once again fell short in the Champions League, losing in the round of 16 to Real Madrid, one of the era's dominant forces in Europe alongside Barcelona. Neymar's injury during the crucial February knockout round – a recurring issue for him – further weakened PSG's chances, and they never managed to replicate the heights of their first-leg performance against the Catalans from the previous year.

'That year, at the Santiago Bernabéu in the first leg, Madrid were suffering, and I told my players, "For them to lose, they have to suffer." At 1–1, I was calm. We had discussed the need to strike when Madrid were vulnerable and to be careful at the start and end of each half. But we didn't capitalise. They scored late in the first half, missed chances followed and Madrid scored twice at the end. We didn't know how to close the match out.' The second leg needed the chaos of the Barcelona match, a counter-attacking, box-to-box approach to make Madrid fearful. It didn't happen. 'At the Parc des Princes, I had started players meant to handle tense key moments, but by the 15th minute, I knew it wasn't working. From that minute, I'm frowning on the bench. We didn't have the answers we needed for that match. My greatest achievement is that, even after our defeats to Barcelona and Real Madrid, the team's morale didn't collapse or fall apart. We continued performing at a very high level. I know it's something deeply internal that won't be appreciated from the outside.'

Even in those dark moments of the Champions League knock-outs, Emery had found a way to reframe them. *Unai, you still have wonderful opportunities ahead as a coach*, he told himself. The losses hurt, undeniably, and they lingered. Yet, after a few days, the pain began to fade. 'I've learnt that at massive clubs, even when you win 80 per cent of the time, the remaining 20 per cent can carry more weight than the victories. That's the reality of football, and I accept it. I came to realise how difficult it is to manage every key aspect of running a big team.'

A few weeks after the Real Madrid defeat, PSG played AS Saint-Étienne. After a horrible first half, which saw the Parisians go down to ten men after Presnel Kimpembe received a second yellow card, the team reacted and stood up, scoring a 92nd-minute equaliser to make it 1–1. A staff member told the manager after the whistle, 'Unai, today the players have shown they are on your side. If they weren't on your side today, we would have lost.' Unai Emery cemented PSG's reputation as France's footballing power-house, winning seven trophies during his tenure. These included a Ligue 1 title achieved with the third-highest points tally in the club's history, highlighted by a stunning 7–1 victory over reigning champions Monaco to secure the title with five games to spare. Additionally, Emery guided the team to two Coupe de France and two Coupe de la Ligue trophies. During the league title celebrations, Unai Emery publicly embraced Neymar again, a gesture that was warmly reciprocated by the player.

Despite the achievements, he was often mocked as a provincial man trying to adapt to a city that devours outsiders and resists change. In France, football can sometimes feel insular, locked into its traditions and suspicious of novelty. The scepticism towards Emery wasn't limited to whispers; some television producers and sports editors actively encouraged journalists to find voices willing to say on camera that Emery wasn't capable of managing elite players. Such criticism was questionable, especially when Emery had previously dealt with stars like David Villa, David Silva, Jordi Alba and Juan Mata. The same arguments resurfaced constantly: the Europa League isn't the Champions League. Sevilla isn't PSG. Emery, aware of the scrutiny, tried to communicate his vision in any way he could. Emery, limited by his imperfect French, relied on gestures to convey his point. Once, during a press conference, he used water bottles to explain his ideas, as he had done successfully at Sevilla. A journalist from *L'Équipe* later called him to ask if the demonstration was premeditated, perhaps a gimmick to go viral or gain attention. In truth, it was spontaneous.

Some gestures, like pretending to put a gun to his head when a player didn't understand his instructions, a joke he often used at Valencia, were seen in Paris as eccentric or even unhinged. Yet, for Emery, these were simply tools to connect, to break barriers with humour. Despite the media storm, Emery rarely took the criticism personally. On weekends, he joked with his brother Igor, who often stayed in Paris and managed his press relations, 'Find me something nice they've written this week,' knowing full well that the headlines were usually far from kind. One week he was called a 'weirdo', a 'pyromaniac' and accused by an influential daily newspaper of managing his team like 'an eight-year-old child'. He understood the impact of the media narrative, especially given PSG's failure to progress far in the Champions League. Unai now admits that his communication didn't fully resonate with the Parisian press, something had been lost along the way. However, the real obstacle wasn't the language; it was the challenge of facing Barcelona and Real Madrid too early in the competition. Disaster had struck.

If asked whether he believed he could have continued to grow PSG, his answer would be an unequivocal yes. And if asked whether he felt he left something valuable behind, he would also answer yes. Young players arrived and improved. Established players maintained their level or grew in new ways. He contributed to PSG's future. Still, he reflects, 'Maybe I could have been more flexible. I was rigid at times, insisting the one performing best would play. But then you have Neymar . . .' And if they had knocked out Barcelona . . . a sliding doors moment. So, Unai had navigated the stormy peaks of football's elite. More than that, perhaps. But he left with the sense that the next time he set foot in that rarefied air, he wouldn't just cling to the rock, he would build something lasting. It all ended with a mature, professional dinner between Emery, Nasser Al-Khelaifi, and Antero Henrique. Over the meal, they agreed to part ways after two seasons.

The decision was mutual and so was the respect for one another.

7

THE HURT, THE REINVENTION, THE REWARD:

ARSENAL & VILLARREAL

Taking over at Arsenal was a monumental task. Unai Emery, arriving as 'head coach' rather than 'manager', faced the challenge of stepping into the void left by Arsène Wenger, who had shaped every facet of the club for over two decades. Wenger's departure not only marked the end of an era but also revealed the cracks in Arsenal's structure, necessitating a shift from a single-authority model to a more collaborative framework. It wasn't just about hiring a new coach, it was about redefining the way the club operated, both on and off the pitch.

At the time, Unai Emery did not have an agent. When it became clear that Arsène Wenger's successor needed to be identified, renowned Spanish representative Arturo Canales met with Raúl Sanllehí, Arsenal's head of football operations and a former FC Barcelona director with an extensive network. Canales was surprised to learn that Unai Emery wasn't on the list of candidates. Several other names were being considered, including Mikel Arteta, Massimiliano Allegri and Julen Lopetegui. Enter Miguel Ángel Vara, the same journalist from *AS* who once assigned Unai a dash in his player ratings at Toledo. By then, Vara was working alongside Canales, and when the topic of Emery came up, he delivered a glowing recommendation of his qualities. Canales seized on this and used it to persuade Sanllehí to take a closer look.

After Arsenal suffered a defeat in Europe, Unai Emery received an unexpected call from the club's management, expressing their interest in meeting with him. Sensing their urgency, Unai questioned whether their interest was solely due to the recent loss. He emphasised to the club he would only consider travelling to London if they were genuinely interested in him, not merely interviewing multiple candidates. Agreeing to these terms, Arsenal facilitated his journey.

Before departing, Unai meticulously prepared but remained cautious. He enlisted his staff to compile a comprehensive report on Arsenal. In many ways, these types of interviews become an exercise in telling the club exactly what they want to hear. The high-stakes interview process is a curious phenomenon in the eyes of someone that comes from the Spanish football culture. Instead of sitting down for a simple chat with a coach, it might be more effective to conduct thorough research, analysing their career, studying their methods or observing them in action. After all, how can the passion or true essence of anybody be captured in a conversation? But if that was the game, Unai was willing to play it.

Accompanied by his goalkeeper coach Javi García, who assisted with translation, Unai attended the meeting held at Raúl Sanllehí's residence. Also present was Josh Kroenke, the son of Arsenal's owner, Stan Kroenke. While Josh, with a key role in Arsenal operations, was amiable, he lacked a deep understanding of football intricacies but was impressed by the Spanish coach from the start.

'We talked for many hours,' Emery recalls. 'It was very intense.' Arsenal's DNA demanded excellence and results on the pitch. Emery's track record demonstrated his ability to build competitive squads, often capable of delivering the type of high-quality performances that Arsenal desired. His expertise in balancing sporting success with financial prudence, developing players who could later be sold for profit, was another added value. He was also a proven winner, having won ten out of the thirteen finals he had participated in. Arsenal, without a European trophy in over twenty years, saw him as the man to change that.

Emery asked as always what they knew of him and why he was wanted by them. He heard all the above. Next, Unai didn't hesitate to challenge the room. Looking at Raúl Sanllehí and Josh Kroenke, he offered a blunt suggestion. 'You should get Luis Enrique.' The response was silence. They didn't know how to answer. Finally, they dismissed the idea. 'No, no, he's not a club man.' That answer didn't sit right with Unai. What does it mean to be a 'club man'? Does it mean always agreeing with the owner and sporting director? Never pushing back? Never challenging decisions?

Unai was the manager chosen for the new phase of the club. After hours of discussions with agents, journalists, managers and players who knew the Premier League inside out, Unai Emery had finally achieved another dream of his: coaching in the most prestigious and demanding league in the world. He was about to face the best managers, from Pep Guardiola to Jürgen Klopp, and he was doing so with a club that, he hoped, would give him the opportunity to compete for every trophy. At that time, Roberto Olabe, newly appointed as Real Sociedad's director of football, was trying to persuade Unai to return to Spain. But that idea would have to be put on hold. His hesitation to go back to the club he had supported since childhood remained. In May 2018, after the Arsenal board made the decision to appoint Unai Emery, they requested that he travel to Atlanta to meet with the club's owner, Stan Kroenke. Upon arrival, Emery was taken directly to his home, where his son Josh was also present. The conversation was brief due to Stan's tight schedule, but the meeting served as an important personal introduction. Then Emery immediately returned to the airport for his flight back to London. Just a few hours later, he was to be officially presented to the press as Arsenal's new head coach. Exhausted from the journey, he quickly showered, changed and made his way to the Emirates Stadium. There had been little time to prepare for the event, and the fatigue made the experience a blur, but he knew there were a couple of things he wanted to say.

'Good afternoon. Thank you, Kroenke family, for me it was a very good meeting, a very good conversation. Thank you, Arsène Wenger, for your legacy.'

The club's new framework featured Sven Mislintat as head of recruitment, known for his excellent work at Borussia Dortmund. Initially, Mislintat operated under chief executive Ivan Gazidis, a key figure in the development of Major League Soccer, but he left soon after Emery's arrival. Mislintat now found himself answering to Vinai Venkatesham, whose expertise lay primarily in the commercial and sponsorship sectors. Raúl Sanllehí was also part of the decision-making process. While these figures had significant business acumen, their footballing experience paled in comparison to Emery's.

Unai was hired as a club man, tasked with aligning Arsenal's policies and guiding them back to the Champions League. One of his primary responsibilities was to oversee a generational transition, phasing out key players like Petr Čech, Aaron Ramsey, Nacho Monreal and Laurent Koscielny at the right time, while integrating young talent to secure the club's future. In his first weeks at Arsenal, Unai Emery held one-on-one meetings with each of his pupils. He asked them why they played football, their aspirations at the club and their personal goals. He was building early connections within the squad.

However, Emery also faced some initial challenges, such as financial constraints that hindered key signings. Additionally, long-term contracts had been awarded to players whose best years were behind them. Mesut Özil, for instance, had been given a lucrative deal under Wenger despite his declining performances. While his talent was undeniable, Özil often displayed his best in home games or against less demanding opponents. His massive social media following and illustrious past with Schalke, Werder Bremen and Real Madrid granted him significant influence, helping him maintain his status. Emery was warned by some of his new players that he had to tread carefully around him, navigating a locker room with a dormant fault line, capable of shaking the stability of the entire team at any moment. Despite this, Unai was open to working with the player. Challenge accepted.

Another situation arose with Jack Wilshere. At a time when top Premier League midfielders were shaped differently, more energetic and physical, the English international had been offered a three-year contract but sought clarity from Emery regarding his role. While it wasn't Unai's place to address pre-arranged contracts, he was honest, explaining that he respected him as a footballer, especially having come through the ranks at Arsenal, but he saw Wilshere as a squad player rather than a regular starter. So, Wilshere chose to join West Ham.

The 2018–19 season began promisingly. Emery's Arsenal set a record with the most successful start to a campaign in the club's history, going twenty-two games unbeaten, and holding a top four position for most of the year. Having learnt how to manage players with exceptional individual talent at PSG, Unai now faced the hurdle of adapting Mesut Özil, Pierre-Emerick Aubameyang and Alexandre Lacazette to the team's new structure. It was no easy task, as the three most individually skilled players in the squad were two number 9s and a 10. The solution came in the form of a 3-4-1-2 formation, which proved to be the most effective in that first campaign.

Unai Emery quickly discovered what many before him had learnt – in the Premier League, every match is a battle and no opponent is easy. As Arsenal's league form wavered in the final stretch, securing a top four finish became an uphill struggle, especially in a tight race with a strong Tottenham side. With a Champions League place on offer for the Europa League winners, the competition became the club's clear priority, and in April 2019, Arsenal reached the quarter-finals after eliminating Rennes. They then had to beat Napoli and Valencia to reach the final.

A pivotal moment in this priority shift came when Emery heavily rotated his squad against Crystal Palace in a Premier League match played between the Europa League quarter-final second leg against Napoli (Arsenal won 0–1 on the night, 0–3 on aggregate) and the semi-final first leg against Valencia. Several players were carrying minor injuries, while others were at risk of more serious issues. Emery made significant changes to keep players fresh for the European competition. Roy Hodgson, Crystal Palace's manager, initially didn't expect much from the game at the Emirates. But when he saw the Arsenal line-up, his confidence grew. *We have a chance*, he thought. And he was right, Palace won 2–3. After the match, Hodgson and Emery shared a glass of wine – a tradition among managers that has practically disappeared from the game – and Hodgson told Unai that his selection had given Palace hope.

That defeat was costly, but it was followed by two more losses, to Wolves and Leicester, and a damaging draw with Brighton. Arsenal only won two of their last ten games, losing six, and had let Champions League qualification through the league slip away. Arsenal finished fifth. There was still one last chance.

Arsenal had reached their first European final in thirteen years after overcoming Valencia 3–7 on aggregate in the semi-finals. Now they had seventeen days after their last Premier League match until a Europa League final against Chelsea. Chelsea, managed by Maurizio Sarri, had already secured Champions League qualification through their league position, in addition they had something Arsenal lacked in that era: a winning culture, a team that felt comfortable on the big stage. For Arsenal, this was an opportunity to cause an upset and start a new wave of success.

The final was scheduled for 29 May 2019 in Baku, Azerbaijan, a location that quickly became one of the most criticised in UEFA history. Due to political tensions between Armenia and Azerbaijan, the talented Armenian Henrikh Mkhitaryan, crucial in the creation department in Unai's team, opted not to travel. His safety could not be guaranteed. Both clubs had been allocated just six thousand tickets each, but due to the cost and difficulty of travelling to Azerbaijan, many supporters couldn't make the trip. Arsenal and Chelsea had raised concerns about the venue, suggesting a change of location, but UEFA refused.

Arsenal chose to fly to Baku four days before the final, while Chelsea arrived just two days prior. The long journey, coupled with an extended stay, proved physically and mentally draining. Time moved slowly. There were training sessions, of course, but endless hours in the hotel made the days feel even longer. The team felt disconnected, isolated in a city that lacked the buzz and anticipation expected. Preparation followed the usual process of video analysis, tactical meetings and team talks. But, when matchday arrived, something felt different. Of all the finals Emery had been part of, this one lacked energy, excitement. The Olympic Stadium in Baku, with a capacity of over 68,000, was far from full. In the end, only around 3,500 Arsenal fans were present. The stands were mostly filled with UEFA guests and local attendees. The long journey also made it difficult for families to attend, and many of Emery's staff were alone. He brought Igor, Iosu and Lander, but it wasn't the same as having everyone together. For Unai, the contrast with Sevilla was clear. The Spanish club would organise a plane for 240 people, players in the front and their closest family members and the coaching staff's families behind them. It created unity, an emotional connection, that was not present in Baku. 'In a final, you need to feel your supporters, even your families,' Emery later reflected. 'Fans remind you what you're playing for, they connect you to the history of the club. Families make the moment even more of a collective memory.' In Baku, it just didn't feel like a European final was about to take place.

The first half went exactly as Emery wanted. Sarri's Chelsea were a strong side, led by Eden Hazard at his peak, supported by Willian and Pedro. Arsenal knew Chelsea were the better team. The key was to defend well, keep the game tight and strike when the moment came. The teams went to the changing rooms at half-time with a hopeful 0–0 for Arsenal. But within minutes of the restart, everything collapsed. Giroud struck first, a diving header past Čech. 1–0 Chelsea. Unai knew, and he'd mentioned it at half-time, that the important thing if you concede first was not to be pushed away from the final. However, 11 minutes later, Pedro doubled the lead. 2–0. Arsenal's bench felt it. That was the moment the match slipped away. Chelsea smelt blood. Hazard's penalty made it 3–0. Iwobi's stunning half-volley briefly sparked hope, 3–1, but 3 minutes later, Hazard struck again. 4–1. In 23 ruthless minutes, the final was gone.

For Emery, this was more than just a loss, it was a missed opportunity. 'We couldn't secure a title that would have been crucial in strengthening Unai's position,' assistant Juan Carlos Carcedo admits. At times during that first season, Arsenal had shown flashes of the brilliance and competitiveness Emery had been brought in to restore. But expectations were still shaped by the best years of Arsène Wenger, a standard that was no longer easy to replicate. Inconsistency became a recurring issue, frustrating sections of the fanbase. Some players struggled with fluctuating commitment, with effort levels varying from one game to the next. That lack of focus proved costly in crucial matches, making it clear that further changes within the squad were needed.

Returning empty-handed from Baku and having slept just 3 hours, Emery arrived at the training ground intending to meet individually with his players before they departed for their holidays. Özil was conspicuous by his absence. Unai's son Lander, who was sixteen at the time, returned with him to London from Baku. He visited the capital once a month, whenever he had a break from school or a long weekend. Football once again was becoming a familiar and cherished ground for the teenager. He would spend hours at the Arsenal training ground, watching people move in and out of meeting rooms, some pacing the corridors, others glued to their screens. Lander noticed that, when his dad crossed paths with all of them, there was a sense of tension in the air, like students straightening up when the headteacher walks in. Every now and then, in his office, Unai, lost in thought while looking at family photos on his phone, shared with his son the few treasured images of Lander's great-grandfather, Antonio *Pajarito* Emery, along with those of his grandfather and great-uncle, all goalkeepers. But especially Pajarito.

There aren't many photos of Antonio. But in one from 1924, he stands out. Dressed in a white jersey with a black V stretching from shoulder to shoulder, he looks effortlessly cool, composed, almost aloof. He stands alongside his teammates, all upright, their expressions a little fastidious, as if the camera was an unwelcome distraction from the task at hand. When the neighbourhood team Lander played for back in Valencia found itself without a goalie, Lander figured he wouldn't do too badly in the role. It fit naturally with the family history, and once he put on the gloves, he never gave them up. Eventually, Lander found himself playing for CD Roda, a club that operates as an unofficial feeder team for Villarreal, and Unai would often come to watch him. From time to time, a thought would creep into the boy's mind – one that had been in his head for years but that he never dared to say out loud: 'What if one day my dad ends up coaching me?' Whenever it crossed his mind, he would momentarily drift away from the session, glance at his father in the stands who would give him a thumbs-up, and have to shake his head slightly to snap himself back into training.

Meanwhile, the honeymoon period at Arsenal was over for his dad; it was now time to continue with the restructuring of the decision-making team. Sven Mislintat had departed, leaving a gap in the club's recruitment strategy. Emery advocated for Edu Gaspar to fill the role. A member of Arsenal's legendary Invincibles squad and the general co-ordinator for Brazil's national team, Edu had spent hours talking football with Emery and was someone he felt was very much on the same wavelength as him. His arrival in July 2019 was seen as a step towards creating a strong foundation.

That summer, Arsenal invested £130 million to bring in Nicolas Pépé, Kieran Tierney, David Luiz, Gabriel Martinelli and four other players to replace departures. Soon, the leadership void became apparent as the last four captains – Petr Čech, Aaron Ramsey, Nacho Monreal and Laurent Koscielny – had now left the club. Ramsey, in particular, was a significant loss. His energy, commitment and winning mentality could have provided stability.

The leadership mantle, which might have naturally fallen to Özil due to his seniority, instead went to Granit Xhaka following a squad vote initiated by Emery. Xhaka, embodying the values the team needed, was the natural choice. Özil, however, lobbied for the role but lacked the trust of his teammates. While he retained allies within the dressing room and clearly among fans, his influence was divisive. Managing Özil required a delicate balance, a slow phasing-out rather than a dramatic exit. Emery made Özil dispensable, even though he knew any defeat could become fuel for fans' discontent, potentially leading to his own dismissal. So, he used him selectively, often favouring him in home games where his creativity could shine. The player understood he was being gradually sidelined and was not pleased about it. This cautious approach angered fans, who questioned Özil's limited involvement especially when the team dropped points. But the manager knew it had to be done, no matter what.

Amid these challenges, Emery turned to youth. Players like Bukayo Saka, Gabriel Martinelli, Reiss Nelson, Eddie Nketiah and Emile Smith Rowe became central to his vision for the rebuilding. For a brief moment, there was hope. Arsenal climbed to third in the Premier League after the October international break in 2019. Yet, the cracks in the team were already evident. A 1–0 defeat in the league against modest Sheffield United was followed by a 2–2 draw with Crystal Palace at the Emirates, the start of a seven-match winless streak in all competitions: Arsenal's worst in thirty years. Xhaka was substituted in the second half of the Palace game and reacted angrily to jeers from the crowd, removing his shirt and storming straight down the tunnel, escalating tensions. The incident led to Xhaka being stripped of the captaincy, further destabilising the squad. From that point on, the little optimism that was left faded rapidly.

Around that time, when Unai spoke with his mother over FaceTime, often drained in the 24 hours after a match, she showed her concern and would say to him, 'Unai, enjoy yourself,' to which he would reply, 'No, but I do enjoy it, I love my profession.' It was true; he loved and still loves it deeply. But he was in the eye of a storm. However, sometimes there wasn't a metaphorical suitcase big enough to carry all of the solutions or bear the weight of all the problems. There also weren't enough people around, particularly in high-level decision-making roles, to help him carry it. Or at least, that's how Unai felt.

The controversial and noisy draw against Crystal Palace followed by the chaotic 5–5 draw with Liverpool in the EFL Cup three days later epitomised Arsenal under Emery. The defeat on penalties might have delighted fans with its attacking spectacle, but it highlighted the imbalance within the squad. As confidence drained, divisions within the team deepened. Attacking players felt unsupported by the defence, while defenders struggled with the way they were exposed. Poor results amplified these frustrations. Emery worked tirelessly, engaging players individually and experimenting with defensive set-ups, but he struggled to establish a balanced identity on the pitch. Over the years, both as a player and a coach, Unai Emery has learnt that a poor run of form often stems from shared stress. Good stress generates excitement and leads to satisfaction. Bad stress, caused by overstimulation, leads to frustration and brings out the worst in people. Managing stress is a matter of balance. Balance is a concept he considers fundamental. It's about stepping out of the comfort zone, the calm, the inertia that can lead to complacency, without entering the panic zone, which causes paralysis.

'I try to be very mindful of the language I use. If we feed ourselves with negative thoughts through communication, the bad run will continue.' Such a difficult thing to achieve, balance. Fluidity. Harmony.

Fans are important in helping you achieve it. Emery's approach to building a link with the supporters was not rooted in grand gestures. Managing a group still under construction, he felt the need to be more present in the technical area than he had been during his time at PSG. His focus was on developing a team with energy, solid defensive principles and effective attacking play. However, even Emery acknowledged that the team's foundations were too fragile at that stage, and the connection with the fans lacked stability. The vast Arsenal fanbase, already disillusioned by the team's inconsistent performances, began to redirect their frustration towards the coach.

Language barriers compounded these obstacles. Emery insisted on speaking English from day one, both in training and during press conferences. His expressive body language did help convey his ideas on the training ground. 'How did I do?' he would ask an English member of the coaching team after every tactical chat. 'Getting there, but the main message reached the players,' would be the regular answer. Lander pushed his father to improve his English, but press conferences proved to be a greater challenge, especially as negative results brought harsher scrutiny. After matches, Emery would typically prepare for the first two or three questions, ensuring he could clearly explain what had happened and outline areas for improvement. However, by the fourth, fifth or sixth question, fatigue would set in and the words wouldn't flow as easily.

Emery recalled how the former Welsh manager of Real Sociedad and Real Madrid, John Toshack, had once been celebrated for his charming but broken Spanish during successful times, only to be mocked when results turned sour. Similarly, Emery believed his own English would have been seen as charming if victories had come more consistently. He accepted criticisms, even though some hurt as they questioned his capability to run the team. And, he kept working.

But he could sense that the mood had shifted dramatically. Just seven months earlier, the Emirates had roared with chants of 'Unai Emery's red and white army' during a commanding performance against Napoli. The energy had been electric, the belief tangible. Now, that felt like a distant memory. The negativity within the club had grown too deep-rooted to be overturned by even his relentless work ethic. This wasn't just about tactics, training sessions or matchday performances. It was something bigger, uncontrollable. Even systemic.

The breaking point arrived on 28 November 2019. Despite Pierre-Emerick Aubameyang giving Arsenal an early lead, the team crumbled in the second half, succumbing to a painful 1–2 Europa League group stage defeat against Eintracht Frankfurt at home. The toxic atmosphere in the stadium hit its boiling point, with fans vocally venting their frustrations, chanting, 'You're getting sacked in the morning.'

Which is what happened. The following morning, at 9 a.m., Raúl Sanllehí delivered the decision to dismiss Emery, visibly pained by the outcome given their strong working relationship. But, when the moment came, Unai wasn't surprised. He had felt it in the air, the way the club had begun to move around him rather than with him. Yet that didn't make it any easier. Emery requested that the players individually bid farewell to the coaching staff, who remained together in a single room throughout the process. One by one, they came, expressing their gratitude. These public gestures of respect were later followed by private messages of support from many of his footballers, some of whom struggled to understand the rationale behind the dismissal. As he packed up his office, he looked at the tactics board one last time. *I was always fighting the tide*, he thought.

For Emery, the outcome had seemed inevitable yet unfair, a conclusion to a month-long downward spiral that he felt could have been reversed. He accepted it with composure, returning to Valencia and the Basque Country to spend time with his family, friends and assistants. There, he began a period of deep reflection on what had gone wrong. This was not how his time in the Premier League was supposed to have gone, and he felt he belonged in that small, privileged club of elite coaches who were lucky to manage in the English league. Or did he?

Although, for some mysterious reason, it is not always typically done, Emery spent an hour on the phone with his replacement, Mikel Arteta, after his appointment, offering his insights and even the house he had rented in North London, an offer that was eventually not taken. Arsenal did not fully leave his thoughts for months. The period following his dismissal was difficult and Emery even admitted later on that he regretted some of his public comments during that time, recognising that holding grudges was unproductive. He learnt another vital lesson: the importance of separating the personal from the professional. Football is inherently competitive but allowing that intensity to spill over into personal relationships is a sign of poor character. Today there is not a single ounce of resentment towards Arsenal.

In fact, Unai's stay at the Emirates eventually became fuel for him.

Unai left Arsenal in November 2019, and the next eight months would prove to be another turning point in his career. 'In Paris,' Unai recalls, 'after two years of achieving most of our objectives, the biggest one still eluded us, elevating PSG to the next level in Europe. At Arsenal, even after reaching the Europa League final and finishing fifth in the league, I still felt there were things missing. At that point, I didn't know how my career would realign. I was fully aware of that.' He also knew that he had yet to consistently compete with those teams right at the very top. At the time, football was being shaped by dominant forces: Pep Guardiola's transformative Manchester City, the tactical benchmark for countless coaches; Hansi Flick's Bayern Munich, a finely tuned machine built on positional play and attacking power; Jürgen Klopp's Liverpool, a relentless force fuelled by high-energy, rock-and-roll football; and Zinedine Zidane's Real Madrid, an outlier that thrived on instinct, big moments and its own set of rules.

How could Unai Emery reach that level?

For most of his career, he had barely paused for breath. After weeks of dissatisfaction and reflection, he channelled his energy into having new conversations, meetings and travelling, discussing with those closest to him which way to go next with his career. Unai couldn't stand being still. He was willing to adapt, to learn – not just about tactics but about the emotional side of the game, man-management and leadership too. He read, he studied basketball, even five-a-side football, searching for new ideas. That kind of humility – accepting that you are never a finished product – is rare in football, a world where showing weakness is often seen as fatal. But those who don't move forward get swallowed up by the system. The complacent ones never see it coming.

'I had come this far, but I asked myself, *What more can I do?*' Unai reflects. Before making fundamental changes, there was something that had to be done first. Change always comes with impact. For sixteen years, all the way back to their time at Lorca together, Juan Carlos Carcedo and Unai Emery had worked side by side, Carcedo the only assistant who had been with Unai from the very start. 'When you've been that close for so long, you end up seeing football the same way,' Unai says. 'But, over time, there's professional and personal wear and tear.' It was time for new energy, new ideas. So, the inevitable conversation had to happen.

Carcedo knew the moment was coming and, deep down, he also wanted to test himself as a head coach. Meanwhile, Unai was looking to return to Spanish football and had heard that Villarreal might be interested in hiring him.

The chat happened over the phone. With movement restricted by the Covid-19 pandemic, Emery called Carcedo, who had decided to remain in London to improve his English, explaining that it was time to go their separate ways. Carcedo did not fight Unai. They also exchanged words that had long been on the tip of their tongues, but ultimately they agreed their professional journey had reached its final stop. Today, Juan Carlos Carcedo is the head coach of Pafos in the Cypriot First Division, and in 2023–24 won the club's first-ever trophy, the Cypriot Cup.

In March 2020, as football came to a standstill due to the pandemic, Unai Emery found himself in an unusual position – with time on his hands. He spent much of it in Madrid, engaging in new encounters that shaped his thinking, before later moving to Valencia to be closer to his son. 'It was a good time for me,' Unai remembers. 'My relationship with my son was good, but I had spent so much time away, in Seville, Moscow, Paris. He would visit me, and I would visit him whenever I had a free day or two. But I needed to go deeper, to really be present with him.'

That period of forced pause not only became a time of accelerated learning, it also allowed him to reconnect with familiar faces, like Imanol Idiakez. Idiakez is a Basque coach Unai had known since their time together at Real Sociedad's reserve side, Sanse. Both had made the leap to the first team, but neither had ever truly felt like they belonged to that elite group. Their coaching careers started at similar times and had taken different paths but now both were out of work. Idiakez had spent years studying modern tactical trends, working closely under Juanma Lillo, the coach Unai had once tried to work with and a key mentor to Pep Guardiola. Meanwhile, his own managerial career had taken him through Real Unión, Lleida Esportiu, Toledo and then to AEK Larnaca in Cyprus, where he had replaced Andoni Iraola. Unai saw an opportunity. He called Imanol and offered a simple invitation: 'Come to Madrid for the weekend. Let's watch some football.'

They started with a Getafe match. The team was coached by José Bordalás, whose football philosophy was the complete opposite of Unai's. Bordalás's Getafe was built on defensive solidity, constant pressing, tactical fouling to disrupt rhythm and a brutally direct attacking style. Everything about it contrasted sharply with Unai's more fluid, attacking-based approach. But Unai wasn't there to dismiss it.

'Let's see what we can learn from this Getafe side,' he suggested. Watching closely, something clicked.

'I really liked how Bordalás organised his defensive line, how they compressed space, how they pressed, how they held a high line,' Unai recalls. 'Back in my Lorca days, I also trained with a very high defensive line. Watching Bordalás, I thought, *This is something I needed to reinforce.*'

Through their conversations, ideas clashed, debates flared, but Unai found what he was looking for. He asked Idiakez to join him as his assistant. They struck a simple deal: 'I'll take things from you, you'll take things from me. If it works, we continue.'

Unai thrives in environments that challenge him. 'Surrounding myself with people who know more than me isn't a threat, it's another tool to make us stronger.' With Idiakez, he saw an opportunity to take another step forward, to better understand positional play, the tactical approach that Guardiola used to revolutionise football, one that offered more stability, and one that Idiakez had studied and implemented throughout his own career. Until then, positional play had never been part of Unai Emery's coaching DNA. His style had always been built on controlled chaos, a mix of structured aggression, rapid transitions and adaptability. At first, he neither understood nor fully embraced the positional play movement. But through conversations with Imanol Idiakez and his own evolving tactical thinking, Unai began to see the game differently. *This could be the key to reaching a new level*, he thought.

Unai met with Real Betis representatives in Madrid, discussing the possibility of taking over. The conversations continued via Zoom, as the club tried to persuade him to return to Sevilla. But something didn't feel right. His son was against it – going back to the city where he had already made his mark with Sevilla FC didn't sit well. It wasn't just an emotional decision; it was also a less convenient personal option than Villarreal, the other club that kept pursuing him. But, was Villarreal the right place to grow? Rescued from the lower divisions by local businessman and millionaire Fernando Roig in 1997, the Spanish club had experienced exceptional peaks since then, including a Champions League semi-final in 2006. Yet, at that moment, Villarreal were a club in transition, boasting strong individual talent but struggling with instability in the dugout and a lack of results to truly establish themselves among Europe's elite. They had also never won a major title in their history.

Unai turned to Javi García for guidance, who is not only his long-time goalkeeping coach but also a trusted voice of reason. 'I asked him, "What do you think about Villarreal? Is it worth it?" And he told me, "It's the best place for you, Unai. They'll let you work, they have great facilities, a demanding culture and enough resources to compete with the big clubs."' On top of that, there was the other key factor. 'My son was in Valencia, just 45 minutes away,' Unai explains. With his mind made up, the manager took charge of the negotiations himself. He made one principle clear: his contract had to provide balance and security for both sides. A €6 million release clause ensured exactly that, protecting Villarreal while keeping the door open for future opportunities. Agreed months earlier, the three-year deal was officially announced in late July 2020.

Unai never forgot the gesture the club made just before the news broke and that confirmed earlier impressions: Villarreal was a club with the right values. Despite finishing fifth in LaLiga, the Roigs did not renege on the difficult decision to part ways with the manager Javier Calleja, a coach who had been a former player, deeply respected by the family. 'They had already started talking to Unai when Calleja's Villarreal wasn't doing so well,' says Damià. 'But even though the team finished strongly the club stuck to its word. Even Unai would have understood if they had changed their mind. But they didn't. That loyalty meant a lot to him. That is why working for the Roig family was a great thing for Unai. They demand a lot, but they are good people, competitive. It was the perfect match.' At his unveiling press conference, Unai was keen to set the pace for the project, like a captain charting a bold course in his new vessel: 'My dream is to win the first trophy for Villarreal.'

Pau Torres, born in Villarreal in 1997, is a composed, left-footed centre-back whose rise from local academy talent to international defender reflects his intelligence on the pitch, bravery to pass out from the back, technical elegance and ambition. After a formative loan at Málaga, he became a cornerstone of Villarreal's defence, especially under managers Javier Calleja and Luis García Plaza. He has been a regular for Spain since 2019, including appearances at Euro 2020, the 2022 World Cup and the Tokyo Olympics. For Pau Torres, Unai Emery's arrival was a statement of intent. 'It felt like a clear message, we were doing things well, but now we wanted to take it to another level. From the very first moment, you could tell he was a different kind of coach.' Unai arrived as a winner. At Sevilla, he had learnt the art of relentlessly pursuing trophies. At PSG, he became accustomed to lifting silverware and competing in the Champions League every season. In fact, by the time Emery arrived at Villarreal, he had spent over a decade in European competition, year after year. Now his task was clear: to lead and elevate the team, showing them the path to success. From his very first talk with the squad, Emery made his objective crystal clear: unlike his predecessors, he didn't shy away from the ambition of a title, he embraced it. In that same meeting, he highlighted something crucial: the squad had the right balance of experienced leaders, players at their peak and young talents with great potential. He made success feel within reach.

Gradually, Unai Emery began to explore ways to apply some of the ideas he had discussed with Imanol Idiakez or at least he started thinking about how best to integrate them. For now, though, the style was going to resemble what he had implemented at Sevilla and Arsenal, built around players comfortable on the ball, allowing both coach and squad to settle into a familiar middle ground. In football, change is the hardest thing to achieve and getting players to accept it is even harder. 'We trusted in our approach because it had worked for us before,' Pau Torres recalls.

'As players, we also wanted to test ourselves with our own ideas, to see how they worked. It was still early in the season, we had time to adjust if things didn't go as planned.'

Villarreal's season under Unai Emery began with a disappointing 1–1 draw against Míchel's Huesca, a newly promoted side. The performance was poor. The full-backs, Mario Gaspar and Alfonso Pedraza, were still playing high up the pitch, closer to the system Unai had used before. The following game, a narrow 2–1 win against modest Eibar, did little to inspire confidence. Again, the team played poorly. Next up was a far bigger challenge: Ronald Koeman's Barcelona, making their LaLiga debut at an empty Camp Nou due to the pandemic. By half-time, Villarreal were 4–0 down. In the dressing room, Emery didn't hold back: 'For fuck's sake, it's 4–0, play dead if you have to. Go down to the floor, play dead! The game is over. I've only conceded six goals once in my life, and I don't want that happening again. Now we play, we stay compact. If we put one in, fine. If we do it again, great. But we cannot concede more.'

Pau Torres, who scored the own goal to make it 4–0, recalls their miscalculated approach: 'We thought we could go toe-to-toe with Barcelona, stretching the play. But in the first half, we allowed them too many transitions.' Pau could not remember if it finished 4–0 or if they managed to score at least one goal. It was 4–0. Emery voiced real doubt to his coaches: 'Something isn't working. I got sacked at Arsenal, and now I come to the Camp Nou and concede four in forty-five minutes. My structure against Barça was awful.'

But something else stood out to Pau Torres, something he had never heard a coach do before: 'From the very first moment, Unai took full responsibility. He said the biggest mistake had been the game plan. He owned it.'

It was time to move from theory to practice. The change he had been talking about with Imanol Idiakez had to happen now. This was when Unai Emery began integrating elements of Idiakez's positional play philosophy. His assistant introduced him to a structured approach, one rooted in clear positions and roles. The principle was simple: players had to hold their positions, no wandering or improvising beyond the system. The aim was to create superiority in every area of the pitch, ensuring that, wherever the ball was, Villarreal always had one extra player. The full-backs no longer had to be purely attacking outlets, instead they needed to be comfortable on the ball and contribute as auxiliary midfielders. The goalkeeper had to become an outfield player at times. The team's attacks also needed to be organised. If they were well placed when attacking, they would automatically be in the right positions to defend. Pressing high was now essential, not just to regain possession quickly but to maintain control over the game, Emery's new obsession.

They beat Alavés 3–1 in their following match, just before they faced Atlético Madrid. Those games introduced the first tactical adjustments. Against Atlético, the bigger test of the two, two natural midfielders, Manu Trigueros and Moi Gómez, were placed theoretically on the wings. Neither was a traditional winger, but that was the point. Their presence coming inside helped Villarreal control the midfield. It wasn't a spectacular game, ending 0–0 and without any big moments, but the foundation had been laid in those two matches. From the Alavés match onwards, Villarreal went on a nineteen-game unbeaten run in all competitions.

To fully develop these new positional structures, the collective had to be trained as a unit. But Emery also added something else: a dedicated individual tactical coaching department. This wasn't just about technical work, though that played a part. It was about tactical understanding, teaching each player their exact role with their obligations and responsibilities. To lead this work, recommended by his collaborator Alberto Benito, Emery brought in Rodri, a former lower-division footballer in Catalonia, later a third-tier coach, who had most recently worked at a player agency. Players responded well to this approach. Over time, this one-on-one focus became engaging, they felt they were being coached not just as part of a team but as individuals. One of the immediate beneficiaries of this personalised approach was Pau Torres. Already a high-quality player, Emery immediately identified areas for improvement, particularly in his physical assertiveness. After regular training sessions, Pau stayed behind to work with Rodri, focusing specifically on duels, positioning and anticipation. With Rodri's background as a striker, he provided unique insights, highlighting the movements and tricks attackers used, helping Pau adjust his positioning and use his body more effectively in challenges.

Football was evolving towards positional play and specialised individual training, and Unai Emery wanted to be at the forefront of that movement. 'What stood out most,' Pau Torres explains, 'is that some coaches surround themselves with friends, but Unai prioritises professionalism. He maintains good relationships, but no one is anyone's best friend. And while past coaches often left early, Unai stays at the training ground until 8 or 9 p.m. at night, fully committed.'

With greater ambition came more work and more work meant increased delegation. For the first time, Emery felt ready to hand over more responsibilities. His staff were well prepared, and this allowed him to step back, not to relax but to dedicate himself to the things he valued most. One of which was spending 8 hours meticulously crafting the hour-long video he showed his players before matches, as he had done ever since Lorca, which he has never stopped doing and is part of the control he is not willing to surrender. His assistants had to step up. During that first season of internal revolution, some of his staff struggled with the intensity of his demands. Unai set the bar extremely high, determined not to repeat the mistakes of Arsenal. He often held those closest to him to an even higher standard, sometimes without fully realising it. If frustration boiled over, his communication could be sharp. But, just as quickly, his human side would take over, he would seek people out, make things right and remind them that conflict was just part of the job.

'Tensions happen, but I value you.' That was the message he wanted to get across. Delegating wasn't just about his staff; it was also about managing the players. To keep the squad engaged, he had to avoid becoming overexposed. Villarreal's club delegate, Xisco Nadal, acted as a player liaison, constantly in tune with the squad's mood. Unai relied on him.

'How are they, Xisco?'

'They're fine, Unai.'

'Even after a defeat?'

'Yes, Unai.'

'Any doubts?'

'None.'

'What about the video?'

'No complaints.'

That was after an hour and a half of talk and video analysis, but Unai liked to test the waters, just in case. If a player ever voiced a concern, Unai would read between the lines. Was it just one player speaking out or did he actually represent the other twenty-five as well? Sometimes, people just complain about what bothers them personally, it's not necessarily an issue for the wider group. Knowing the difference is crucial.

On the rare occasions Unai did leave the training ground early, it was to drive to Valencia to see his son, Lander. Lander had school in the morning and trained as a goalkeeper during the evenings. Unai would watch him train, they then had dinner together. Even then, his mind was often still on football. He could be distant. Lander sometimes struggled to pull him out of that state, but at least he had him there, sitting next to him.

Much of Unai's focus was on the club because now, like Simeone at Atlético Madrid and Guardiola at Man City, he wasn't just a part of it, he was its driving force. Villarreal had invested everything to create the perfect synergy between his leadership and their vision, ensuring the team could progress. 'I saw Villarreal as an opportunity. I built a very strong and honest relationship with my boss, Fernando Roig Jr [Villarreal's CEO and the son of the owner], and he shaped the team closely to what I asked for, he really understood me. We were both demanding. When expectations push you to the absolute limit of your capabilities, and you thrive in that space, the feeling is incredible. That's where I feel most comfortable now.'

Villarreal's road to the 2021 Europa League final was nothing short of flawless. They navigated the entire tournament without losing a single match, showcasing defensive solidity, tactical discipline and a well-balanced squad. They dominated their group stage, finishing top against Sivasspor, Qarabağ, and Maccabi Tel Aviv, before eliminating Red Bull Salzburg (round of 32), Dynamo Kyiv (round of 16) and Dinamo Zagreb (quarter-finals), winning every leg along the way. The night before every big game, a new routine began. After everything had been prepared, Unai would go to the bar area and sit down with Damià Vidagany and occasionally his lawyer Iosu, his brother Igor and Lander. There was some talk about the game ahead, but nobody recalls the details of those conversations with great clarity, only the feeling that the game belonged to tomorrow, not to now. That meeting of friends also took place the night before the biggest test: the semi-final first leg against Arsenal.

'To compete, we had to deliver a complete performance but one that remained true to our identity and the journey we had taken to get there,' Unai reflects. 'I felt the team had matured, and that game was the confirmation of that feeling. The process had been just as beautiful as the victory itself, not just winning, but everything that led up to it.' Before the match, Emery made a point to his players: 'This time, they are the favourites.' He didn't say it to add pressure but to shift the focus. Football always provides ways to challenge a superior opponent, to chip away at their advantage.

The first leg at home was spectacular. In the first 45 minutes, Villarreal played with intensity, going 2–0 up by half-time. Arsenal hadn't expected it but Emery had. 'I knew we could surprise them.' Even though they conceded to make it 2–1, there was no sense of disappointment, only satisfaction at how they had executed their plan. For the second leg, the pressure was now on the opponent. The team remained disciplined, focusing on control rather than opening the game up. They allowed only two clear chances, neither of which were enough. 'We played a highly effective game, practical, complete and without unnecessary risks.'

Villarreal were in their first-ever European final.

The final league game of that season was supposed to be almost meaningless for Unai's team. With the Europa League final against Manchester United just days away, their trip to Valdebebas to face Real Madrid – the Bernabeu was being renovated – seemed to some an unnecessary distraction. Their European spot for the following season was already secured but only for the UEFA Conference League. To qualify for the Europa League, they needed an almost impossible combination of results: Villarreal had to beat

Real Madrid, who were fighting for the league title, and Betis had to lose at home. The scenario was so far-fetched that not many had even considered it a possibility. Apart from Unai. European football has been a measure of his talent, so he wanted the biggest stage possible for Villarreal.

In the build-up to the game, there had been speculation that he would field a second-string squad, saving his key players for the biggest match in the club's history. But when the team sheet came out, it was full strength. From the stands, the Villarreal directors watched in shock. No one had expected this. They sat there, frozen, just hoping for no injuries. Every clash was received with an apprehensive grimace. Villarreal stormed into a 0–1 lead. Suddenly, they were on the brink of pulling off the unthinkable. But Madrid fought back, scoring two late goals. In the end, the result didn't change their standing, but it raised another, far more pressing question. Had Unai risked too much?

Once the match ended, they headed back to Villarreal by train, a Covid-era journey, carefully co-ordinated with players and staff packed into separate vans before making their way to the station. Hernán Sanz, the club's head of media, had already built a good relationship with Unai by that point, and the moment seemed too big to ignore. Sitting in one of the vans together, he turned to the coach. 'Bloody hell, you really took a risk today!'

Unai snapped his head around. 'What did you just say?!'

Hernán hesitated. 'Well . . . with the final in three days, I mean, you took a risk . . .'

'Risk? What does risk even mean? A player can get injured in training. A flight can be delayed. This van can crash. Anything can happen at any moment. What is risk? Explain it to me!' Unai wasn't letting this go. He launched into a full speech on the nature of risk, on preparation, on controlling what can be controlled.

Hernán had touched a nerve. Maybe Unai had in mind that Crystal Palace defeat with Arsenal and Roy Hodgson's words ('I saw the weakened line-up and I thought: we have a chance'). By the time they reached the station, he was still going.

In preparation for the final in Gdańsk, Emery meticulously analysed seventeen different Manchester United matches, looking at every detail, every tendency. He knew this game was a test of control, discipline and mental endurance. United's pressing and attacking waves were relentless, and it was unclear whether Villarreal could impose their usual rhythm. His task was to neutralise their strengths and find the right moments to strike. Expecting a tight, tactical battle where every decision mattered, Emery prepared his team to frustrate United.

The Europa League final between Villarreal and Manchester United was the first major final after the pandemic, the first time fans were allowed back into the stands, and even at training sessions there was a buzz, a sense that something special was coming. The atmosphere was charged with belief. The popular club delegate Xisco Nadal, usually measured, was adamant: 'We're going to win, for sure.' That confidence, quiet and unshakeable, emanated from Emery. But it needed to be balanced, not overflow. His first message to the squad was grounded in humility: 'We beat Arsenal in the semi-final even though we weren't the better side. To beat United, the first thing we must accept is that they're better than us.' From there, the plan took shape – organisation, strategic patience, and resilience. They drilled set-pieces over and over again, knowing a single moment could decide the game. And above all, they prepared to suffer.

'Unai is a perfectionist and mentally, he transformed us,' forward Gerard Moreno says. 'It was the club's first final and for most of us, the first of our careers. Yet, it felt as if we had been there before. His experience, having lived these moments so many times, gave me confidence.'

Pau Torres recalls a light-hearted moment from that week. 'The day before the final, during the team talk, Carlos Bacca raised his hand and said, "Míster, just a heads-up . . . in the two Europa League finals we've played together at Sevilla, I've always started. Just in case you're thinking about tomorrow . . ."' Everyone was stunned. Unai just laughed.

'Carlos had not played much that season,' Pau says. 'In our last league game against Sevilla, we won 4–0, and Bacca, if I remember correctly, scored a hat-trick.'

In the team huddle at the Polish stadium the evening before the big day, Unai Emery delivered a message of pride and identity. He reminded his players that they were about to represent a city of just 55,000 people. He made it personal, speaking about Pau Torres, the only player in the squad born in the city they were fighting for. Later, circumstances out of Emery's control would shape the final line-up. Striker Paco Alcácer felt some discomfort following a recurring hamstring injury. The next day, a few hours before the final, Bacca learnt he was going to start.

In the changing rooms, Unai Emery stepped back and allowed Vicente Iborra, one of Villarreal's captains, to lead the final pre-game speech. Iborra was sidelined with injury, but his presence carried weight; he had been part of Emery's Sevilla side that won three consecutive Europa League titles. Unai delivered one last message. Finals aren't played; they are won. And they start with a plan but things can go in so many unexpected directions. You have to be ready.

From the start, Emery sensed that United's confidence could work against them. 'I knew they felt like winners, and we used that to our advantage.' Villarreal had to stay patient, dragging

United into a slow, controlled tempo. United wanted a high-speed duel, with Mason Greenwood and Marcus Rashford in full flight. Villarreal craved control, Parejo and Trigueros dictating the tempo. But neither got their way. Pressing high proved difficult, and United's intensity made it hard to keep possession. But Emery had planned for this. 'We had to make sure very little happened in the game, they had to feel uncomfortable. And when possible, we had to find our opening.' Ole Gunnar Solskjaer's team were forced to play against their nature, prodding at a Villarreal side that refused to open up. Emery's men, meanwhile, were pushed back, battling on the fringes of goalkeeper Gerónimo Rulli's box. United, physically superior, won every clash, every duel, every collision. Pogba thrived. McTominay bulldozed forward.

Then, Parejo broke the deadlock. Edinson Cavani had lunged in, late. Parejo absorbed the hit. Free kick. Parejo and everyone else remembered the work put in during the week's training. He cradled the ball and carved a perfect pass forward. Gerard Moreno took off. Shaw was left behind. Lindelöf grabbed at his shirt – too late. The Catalan striker struck. De Gea beaten. Villarreal ahead.

Cavani equalised after the break. Then, nothing. Just tension. With the match level, they headed into extra time. Unai Emery brought the team together and delivered a crucial message. 'Look at them, they've made their substitutions and now they have players on the pitch who haven't played much this season,' he told them. With fresh but less experienced footballers, maintaining structure, style and intensity becomes harder. This was Villarreal's moment.

'He reminded us that all the pressure was on Manchester United,' Pau Torres explains. 'We had come into the final with nothing to lose, they were the giants, the favourites. They weren't used to a so-called smaller team standing toe-to-toe with them, pushing them this far. Emery was convinced we could win it in extra time. He saw the momentum shifting.' But the final twist was yet to come; they had to go all the way to penalties.

'The team was so mentally prepared that even players I wasn't entirely confident in ended up scoring,' said Fernando Roig Jr. 'I think some of them had never even taken a penalty in their lives.' Everyone scored their penalties. Twenty-two had to be taken! The last two fell to the goalkeepers. Rulli stepped up first – and scored. Now, it was David de Gea's turn. Rulli dived. And saved it.

After 3 hours of a tough contest Villarreal had just won the first major title in their history. No city so small had ever conquered Europe before. Villarreal had now joined the pantheon of Spanish clubs that had won European titles, which included Real Madrid, Barcelona, Atlético Madrid, Sevilla, Valencia and Zaragoza.

The embrace between Unai Emery and his coaching staff was electric, emotional, a release of pure adrenaline. Shouts filled the air, words lost in the chaos. The Villarreal players hoisted their coach into the air. Those closest to him – Lander, Igor, Damià and Iosu – felt that on that night, Unai shed the weight of his darkest days, the ghosts of that night in Barcelona with PSG, the fall at Arsenal. This was his redemption, his reward. Winning the first major trophy in Villarreal's history, against such a giant of the game, restored him to a place of prestige. Years from now, children will whisper the names of those who made history – Gerard Moreno, Manu Trigueros, Pau Torres, Raúl Albiol, Dani Parejo, Paco Alcácer, Gerónimo Rulli ... Unai Emery – like a sacred verse. 'It was May 2021,' people will say, 'the year of the pandemic.' The elders will recount every detail, remembering how they too were standing by the penalty spot. Villarreal wasn't the strongest, the richest or the biggest club. They became champions, not by overpowering their rivals but by outlasting them, outthinking them, refusing to break. That's the Emery way. The power of persistence. The strength in weakness.

After the final, Emery made a point of breaking the illusion: 'I admitted we hadn't practised penalties.' It would have been easy to say otherwise, to claim meticulous preparation and take the credit, but that wasn't his way. For him, penalties are about more than repetition – they are about moments, pressure and instinct. 'In Sevilla, penalties won me two titles, but the journey mattered just as much.' He sees them as decisive moments that can't be fully controlled. A player who takes them flawlessly in training might crumble under the weight of a final. 'You can't train for the emotional moment.' That, he believes, is what makes penalties so unpredictable. No simulation can replicate the stakes, the tension and the silence before the run-up. What the coach can do, however, is firstly ask his goalkeeper coach to prepare his goalie, to study the opposition's habits and secondly trust his most reliable takers, those with a statistical edge. This time it just about worked.

For Unai, there was relief as well after winning another Europa League title. He had refused to entertain the thought of losing the final, it simply wasn't an option. At Valencia, Emery placed less emphasis on knockout ties because the goal was to finish third and qualify for the Champions League. Commentators even claimed he was a coach built for consistency but not suited to knockout competitions. How foreign all that sounded then.

Since April 2012, when his Valencia side fell to Atlético Madrid in the Europa League semi-finals, Emery had gone on to win twenty-one consecutive knockout ties in the competition, a record unmatched. Only two active Spanish managers – Pep Guardiola (thirty-one titles at the time, forty now) and Rafael Benítez (thirteen) – have won more trophies than Unai (eleven). Four Europa League titles. The master of the competition. Unrivalled.

'When the trophy was handed over,' Pau Torres recalls, 'I

grabbed Unai and Bacca and told the manager, "In the end, you listened to him.""

Unai just smiled and replied, 'Who wouldn't? Otherwise, I'd have to deal with him afterwards.'

After the first hugs in celebration, Emery continued, overjoyed, but remained composed. In every post-match interview on the pitch, he dedicated the victory to the Roig family – both Fernando Roig Sr and Jr. – and vice president José Manuel Llaneza. He didn't want to forget those who had built Villarreal into a great club, after hours, days and years of commitment. His most vivid memory of that night wasn't lifting the trophy or the roar of the crowd but watching them walk around the pitch, smiling, hugging everyone in their path, their embrace with him lasting just a little longer. Unai knew he had cemented his place in the club's history. He had done something nobody else had done.

But it was also time to admit the truth, to himself and those around him. Being sacked by Arsenal had hurt. He felt like the elite had slipped away, that his career was tilting downward. Doubts crept in. At forty-nine, was this the start of a slow decline? Taking over at Villarreal felt like one of the calculated risks he sometimes took on the pitch with his team, a coin tossed into the air. Certainly, there was logic behind it: a return to LaLiga, familiar ground, a club with ambition but without immediate pressure, close to home. But more than that, it was perhaps his last chance to cling to the elite, to prove he still belonged at the highest level. Like a climber who had once conquered the tallest peaks but now found himself slipping, he needed one last foothold to pull himself back up. Europe had become a stage where he had defied the odds, where he had brought down giants. And the same had happened again. But it was a different Emery. He had evolved tactically, refined his ideas, pushed himself in a new direction. And the gamble had paid off. He had heard the whispers, that his name was no longer in the conversation for the biggest jobs in football. Let's see if they dare to ignore him now.

The celebrations lasted for two whole days. The team flew from Gdańsk to Villarreal. 'Some of us didn't sleep on the plane,' Pau Torres recalls. 'We landed and went straight to a local bar for breakfast with whoever was there.' A team lunch followed, then the victory parade, a moment for the whole community. 'With Covid restrictions, few fans made it to the final,' Pau remembers. 'But that day, the whole town came out. Being from Villarreal, I saw friends, family, everyone. Unforgettable.' Unai preferred to stay quietly in the background during the parade. He had done his job. But he could sense the pride of a city that, hardly present in history books, had a moment to call its own.

Having won the title, they were given the gift of facing Champions League winners Chelsea in the UEFA Super Cup that summer. After a 1–1 draw in normal time, they fell in a penalty shoot-out. Unai Emery reflects on the match: 'We took them to penalties, that earns you respect and recognition. And that always feels good. But you can't dwell on it.' In November 2021, during the middle of the next season, Newcastle United came calling with a lucrative offer. Their ambitious project intrigued Unai Emery. It was a blank slate, a chance to build from the ground up, unlike his time at Arsenal, where he had first needed to dismantle before rebuilding. But the timing was brutal. Villarreal, sitting on just 4 points after three Champions League games in a group that included Manchester United and Atalanta, had a must-win match against Young Boys. With speculation swirling, Emery had to focus. His team won 2–0, but the post-match interview on Spanish TV was tense and awkward. He seemed genuinely undecided. Ultimately, he chose to reject Newcastle.

The real test for Villarreal and Unai Emery came in the knock-out rounds. Facing Juventus, a European giant, Unai Emery had a personal hurdle to overcome: despite his vast experience, he had never taken a team past the Champions League round of 16. That streak ended in Turin. After a 1–1 draw in Spain, Villarreal shocked the Italian giants with a stunning 0–3 away win, sealing a 1–4 aggregate victory. A new barrier broken.

Then came Bayern Munich. 'We looked at the draw and thought, *Wow. It doesn't get tougher than this,*' Unai remembers. 'But you could feel the team believed. The players said, "It's tough, but it's not impossible."' At La Cerámica, Villarreal dominated the first leg, securing a 1–0 win that could have easily been 3–0. The German giants looked stunned, unprepared for the intensity and structure of Emery's side. The second leg was different. This time, Bayern pushed Villarreal to the limit, dominating possession and putting them under continuous pressure. Villarreal struggled, barely holding on, and when Lewandowski scored, it felt like the inevitable comeback was on. But the belief was present. 'At half-time, we looked at each other on the way to the changing room,' Unai recalls and thought, *Damn, we might actually make the semi-finals.*

Villarreal weathered the storm and then, with just minutes left, Samuel Chukwueze struck a goal that sent shockwaves through the Allianz Arena. Bayern were out. Villarreal had done the impossible. That night, it felt like the entire Villarreal fanbase that had travelled to Munich was at the hotel, celebrating with the team. In his room, Unai embraced Lander, a long, noisy hug, filled with spoken words as well as those that didn't need saying.

'So, when Liverpool came next, we just thought, *Well, why not?*' A defining moment: the change of style and the resilience being built into the side made him realise he had found a way to beat the biggest clubs. Villarreal's Champions League dream came frustratingly close. After a 0–2 defeat at Anfield, they stunned Liverpool in the second leg, levelling the tie by half-time. The stadium believed. Then, three quick Liverpool goals ended the fairy tale. His players had shown their limits. The season was extraordinary but the next level up was an agonising step too far.

'Reaching the semi-finals? It's not enough,' Emery admitted. 'We could have made the final. I'm left unsatisfied.' For Unai, European football isn't just a challenge, it's a necessity. 'Fourteen straight years I have played European competition, it defines me,' he said that night. 'It pushes me, forces me to adapt. Without it, I wouldn't know how to operate.' It's a constant test, balancing analysis, long trips and league consistency while fighting against Europe's elite. 'It's exhausting, but professionally, it's everything.'

With Imanol Idiakez, Unai Emery embraced shared learning, always seeking to evolve. After two years together, Idiakez moved on and Emery's focus sharpened. There was one trophy that had eluded him so far: 'When I started in Segunda, my dream was reaching LaLiga, I made it. At Valencia, it was qualifying for the Champions League, we got there. At Sevilla, it was the Europa League, we won it. In Paris, I dreamt of the Champions League, but fell short. At Arsenal, I aimed for a trophy, we reached the Europa League final. At Villarreal, I wanted silverware, we lifted the Europa League. And I still dream. My goal remains the same, to one day win the Champions League.'

Football never waits. It moves, it evolves and so must you. Two months into his third season at Villarreal, after two remarkable campaigns accumulating new experiences and reinventing himself, after filling his bag with defeats, wisdom and victories, Emery made his move. He returned to the Premier League with Aston Villa.

PART II:

THE PRIDE

People talk about winning. They ask: Can we achieve something? Can we lift a trophy? *I understand that. I have lived it before. At Villarreal, the players said to me, 'Boss, you have won three Europa Leagues, maybe with you, we can win it too.' And I told them the truth, what really matters is the experience of competing, the process of growing. Trophies? They bring joy, yes. We all want them, no doubt whatsoever, it makes the story more relevant for you and for the audience, it gets you better jobs. But they fade. What stays with you is the experience, the work, the fight. That, for me, is football.*

That is why I am here. Aston Villa has ambition, a desire to push further. When I arrived, I felt that same hunger I saw at Villarreal or at Sevilla. That belief that we can go higher, that there are no limits. But the beauty of football is its difficulty. If we only measure success in silverware, we set ourselves up for frustration. No. Success is in competing, in improving, in being better today than we were yesterday. That is a winning mentality. Not lifting a cup but never giving up on the idea of lifting one. The desire to improve is what I want to bring here.

I have changed as a coach. Now I have a clear idea of the direction we are all going. A team must have identity. In football, I work 70 per cent on who we are, on our strengths, on building something unique. The remaining 30 per cent? That is adaptation – adjusting to each opponent, each competition. But identity comes first. I want a team that enjoys having the ball, that feels comfortable in possession. And when we lose it? We fight to win it back immediately. When players trust the style, when they feel comfortable in their roles, that is when they give their best.

I have always believed in my players. When a substitute comes on, I tell him: 'You will score.' Maybe he tries ten times and doesn't, but when he does on the eleventh, he remembers. Confidence matters. Belief matters. But belief alone is not enough. We have to focus on football for 75 per cent of our life. You have to go to sleep thinking about football. I know every dressing room is different. Some players arrive with strong values – discipline, respect, a drive to work. Others need to learn them. Some players, you guide with words. Others, you say very little to. And some, you must challenge, even if they don't like it in the moment. Because being an elite athlete is not easy. Nobody tells you 'No'. But the ones who listen, the ones who reflect, the ones that have football as the axis of their lives, they grow.

Clearly football is more than tactics and trophies. It is about what you create for people. I think about my uncle, he was ninety years old and did not follow the details of different competitions, did not separate one tournament from another. But when at Villarreal we won the Europa League final, he was happy, because we had reached our target. But it became even better for him. The next day, when he walked through his town and everyone congratulated him, he felt it fully. That is what matters – the way football reaches people, the way it lifts them. *That is what I want to create here. A team that makes its people proud.*

And for me, this is not just about what we build at Aston Villa. It is about my life. I want to be happy every day. To feel enjoyment in my work, in the relationships we build, in the process of improving a team. I have been fortunate – I have worked in places where I have felt that happiness, where I have been comfortable. That is what I yearn for.

If you win titles, if you coach bigger players, of course, that fills you. But once you reach a certain point, ambition changes. I have already taken big steps – in Sevilla and Paris, in London, in Villarreal. Now I want to push as far as we can go, to find stability in the team, to improve, to be in Europe, to entertain, to fight to get titles. To enjoy football, to enjoy my profession.

In short, what do I seek at Aston Villa? Fulfilment. Memories.

8

THE DISRUPTORS:

NASSEF & WES

Unai Emery has always had a clear sense of his place in the world. Agents and friends can distort reality. But he understands where he stands. There were moments in his career when he was punching above his weight, like, for instance, at Valencia. Nobody needed to tell him this. He knew that, at thirty-six years old, you don't usually get handed the reins of such a historic club. So, he woke up each morning with two aims: to survive and compete. Over the years, he learnt to manage players better, to find new tactical solutions, to handle expectations. Equipping himself with answers. But when the two biggest jobs of his career came – PSG and Arsenal – achieving new heights were just beyond reach. He was aware something was missing.

After winning the Europa League with Villarreal, beating Arsenal and Manchester United along the way, and taking the club to a Champions League semi-final, he re-established himself among Europe's elite. So now he felt ready for anything. The Premier League remained the dream, but the agent that was advising him, Jorge Mendes, told him what Unai didn't want to hear – although he knew it was true.

'What happened at Arsenal still shapes how people see you, Unai.'

Mendes had played a key role in Aston Villa's transition following the turbulent tenure of Tony Xia. The new ownership, Nassef Sawiris and Wes Edens, were fully aware of the toxic atmosphere that had taken hold, as the supporters had turned on Steven Gerrard, and the sense of drift was palpable. They were determined to take Aston Villa to a different level. Other names had been suggested to Nassef Sawiris, among them Mauricio Pochettino, recently departed from PSG, and Thomas Tuchel. But Unai Emery ticked many boxes, or so Nassef thought. Once it became clear Unai was open to listening, a meeting had to happen. Still at Villarreal, Emery made one thing clear: he wasn't going to Birmingham or London. If it was going to happen, Sawiris would have to come to him or at least meet on neutral ground.

Emery believes that meetings which change lives – and careers – should be face to face. He needs to feel truly wanted. From time to time, he reflects on the places where that feeling was real. Not at Lorca, his first job, where doubts surrounded the young manager and recognition outside the club – among fans and in the press – never quite came. It didn't stop him working, but he remembers it. At Almería, by contrast, the connection was immediate and enduring, from the first day to the last. At Valencia, even after three consecutive Champions League qualifications – the club's stated goal – respect was never unanimous. Perhaps the absence of trophies weighed too heavily. Moscow was a disaster. Sevilla brought him back into people's hearts. At PSG, the owner valued his dedication and the staff liked him, but the fans and press never embraced him. At Arsenal, he received little warmth, with Mesut Özil doing little to ease his path. Villarreal was different. There, he felt fully appreciated. At half the clubs he's worked at, Unai hasn't felt loved, even when the objectives were met. That's why he longed for a place where love didn't melt away at the first sign of heat, like chocolate in the sun.

Nassef, one of the richest men in the world – so pretty busy himself – sensed all of that and agreed to travel to Jorge Mendes's house in Madrid. Wes was happy to let Sawiris lead the search for the new manager. The trust and synergy between the owners are absolute. In fact, that was the case from very early on in their professional relationship. Their purchase of Aston Villa wasn't planned, at least not in the meticulous way takeovers are usually orchestrated, with teams of analysts, layers of due diligence and years of strategic foresight. Aston Villa appeared suddenly, unexpectedly for Nassef Sawiris and Wes Edens. A door left ajar that they chose to walk through. 'The opportunity was too big to pass up,' one associate would later say.

In July 2018, Aston Villa stood on the brink. Cash flow had evaporated and debts loomed, as the club failed to pay a post-season tax bill. Villa had to take out a loan secured against the sale of a staff car park valued at £4 million just to stay afloat. Administration was a whisper away. Then, from opposite corners of the world, two men stepped forward. Nassef Sawiris from Cairo. Wes Edens from Montana. Two billionaires bound by ambition, instinct and one urgent cause: to rescue Aston Villa, imagining what it could become.

Their paths first crossed many years ago at an investors' and entrepreneurs' convention in Idaho. They discovered they had mutual acquaintances and kept running into each other at various conferences across the United States. Neither was actively seeking to invest in a football club at the time, but when the opportunity presented itself, they were both attracted by the idea and moved quickly, completing a deal that rescued Aston Villa from financial crisis. NSWE (later V Sports) was founded in July 2018 with a single purpose: to invest in Aston Villa.

For Sawiris, football was never just business. Born into one of Egypt's most powerful dynasties, he grew up in a household where the game was a constant presence, with weekends spent dissecting matches alongside his two football-mad brothers, discussions in coffee shops, hundreds of games watched. He didn't play seriously, but he did live the game. As Egypt's wealthiest man, he was no stranger to scale. His family's conglomerate Orascom Construction Industries (OCI) had shaped skylines across continents. But football was something else entirely. Could the principles he'd honed in business be applied to a football club? Was it wise – or even possible – to turn passion into a project? His approach was always grounded in his Christian faith and a deep sense of responsibility. He realised quickly that Aston Villa was a civic institution, a cultural force in Birmingham, and he soon converted that understanding into tangible actions, including his support for the city's homeless through the Villa Foundation. From the start, Sawiris took an active role, especially when problems arose. One example was the decision to end the club's deal with kit manufacturer Castore, whose products had been publicly criticised by fans and players. Although the commercial team handled the negotiations, Sawiris offered decisive guidance, drawing on his knowledge of the global market and his connections with Adidas, where he holds a minority stake, to convert Adidas into the new kit manufacturer.

Wes Edens, by contrast, is a self-made billionaire from rural Montana. He has his main office in Manhattan, but his sanctuary is back home, in one of the finest hotels in the United States. Once a top-level skier with Olympic potential, he studied finance and began his career as a broker before becoming a serial entrepreneur. He co-founded Fortress Investment Group, a global powerhouse in asset management, and built a business empire spanning more than four hundred companies. His portfolio is vast and diverse, stretching from petrochemical plants and energy infrastructure to sports franchises and transportation megaprojects, including a new high-speed rail line connecting Las Vegas and Los Angeles. In sport, Edens is best known for his transformation of the NBA's Milwaukee Bucks. Under his stewardship, the team evolved from perennial underachievers to league champions. He brought that same competitive vision to Aston Villa. Some of the people that helped grow the NBA franchise were employed to oversee back-room staff operations and mastermind the design of Aston Villa's new performance centre.

Like Villa, the Bucks of 2013 were also an underperforming outfit. Without a play-off series win since 2001, fans were frustrated and wanted more than a middling team. Recruitment had been poor. Time and patience were needed to get the franchise moving. Edens, alongside fellow investor Marc Lasry, secured a contract to build a new stadium, Fiserv Forum, which officially opened in August 2018, a month after the Villa takeover had been completed. By then, Giannis Antetokounmpo, much like Jack Grealish at Villa, was a superstar. His transformation into the NBA's Most Valuable Player in both 2019 and 2020 coincided with the Bucks compiling the Eastern Conference's best regular-season record in both years. Edens saw first-hand how a singular talent like Antetokounmpo could lift an entire organisation, such success without individual brilliance would have been impossible, but he also learnt that sustainable growth came from something deeper: structure, clarity and detail. He recognised the power of a superstar and initially fought hard to keep Jack Grealish at the club. Although he also understood that the shine of a star can sometimes obscure more fundamental flaws. Eventually, when Grealish was sold for £100 million, it reinforced a lesson he already knew: stars can accelerate a project but only structure sustains it.

Although he's less involved in the day-to-day running of the club due to his commitments in the United States, Wes knows the club inside out. Not just the first team but also the youth squads, the reserves, he follows everything that goes on.

It's a wild ride that could have been so different. Villa made it into the Premier League via the Championship play-off final at Wembley Stadium in May 2019, less than a year after the take-over. Few matches in football carry more pressure than the Championship play-off final, with around £170 million at stake. In the jubilant dressing room, Sawiris offered to pay for a group holiday to celebrate the promotion. Most players had already made plans with family or friends and politely declined, but the gesture – along with pay rises, promotion bonuses and personalised commemorative watches – left a lasting impression. That win over Derby signalled the beginning of a new era. 'The sky is the limit,' said Sawiris. For the losing side, Derby County, defeat marked the start of a steep decline, one that nearly brought down a club that have twice been champions of England. By August 2019, NSWE had assumed full ownership and began reshaping the club. They did not issue grand public statements but offered steady, strategic action. They invested in both the squad and infrastructure, including the development of a £6 million High Performance Centre at Bodymoor Heath. They also initiated plans to expand Villa Park's capacity.

Despite their different backgrounds, Sawiris and Edens share more than ownership. Both are deeply attentive, thoughtful. For all their success and the scale of their responsibilities, they move through the club with care, listening closely, building trust. They've brought patience, ambition and discipline to a club that needed all three. As supporters, they live the highs and lows like anyone else.

Financially, the club saw significant progress. A minority stake sale to US firm Atairos in 2023 valued the club at over £500 million. In the 2021–22 season, Villa's revenue totalled £178 million, generating a net profit of around £336,000. In 2024, the club's revenue soared to £275.7 million, marking a 27 per cent year-on-year growth. This financial upswing kept Aston Villa on the Forbes list of most valuable football clubs globally. Throughout their tenure, Sawiris and Edens have insisted their involvement in Villa is driven by purpose rather than profit. 'Anybody who does football and says this is a pure investment, in 95 per cent of the cases, he's a liar,' Sawiris told the *Financial Times*. 'It's a passion. It's addictive. And it can ruin your weekend and go into the following week.' They just needed someone in charge of the team that matched their aspirations.

The meeting to convince Unai Emery took place in Jorge Mendes's elegant Madrid home, in a highly gated district where players and managers live. Nassef, coming from London, arrived first. He flew in that morning, battling gastroenteritis, pale, dehydrated. His wife had urged him to cancel the trip. He refused. 'Even if I'm dying, I have to go,' he told her. 'This is a massive opportunity for Aston Villa.' He was greeted by Mendes, along with members of his staff: João Camacho, Valdir Cardoso and Paulo, Mendes's sharp, marketing-savvy nephew. Nassef took his place on the sofa and waited.

Then the door opened, and Unai Emery walked in with Damià Vidagany. There were no presentations, no PowerPoints, no laptops. Everything was verbal. Nassef watched closely, listening for more than just words. Unai and Damià spoke not just of tactics but of culture. Success would take time, they said. The real problem at Villa, they argued, was years of confused ambition. Nassef understood. He'd seen it up close. Villa had hoped Steven Gerrard would be the figure to lead them forward. They'd backed him heavily with £90 million in new signings, a level of investment they haven't repeated since. It hadn't worked. Gerrard never imposed a culture bought into by everyone at the club, and the dressing room never stabilised.

Nassef looked across at Unai. 'I don't know when,' he said, 'but I want you at Aston Villa.' Nassef offered Unai a blank piece of paper. Unai listened. He didn't commit, but he was intrigued. Nassef felt Unai wasn't ready to walk away from Villarreal. Not just yet, but a seed had been planted.

After the meeting, Sawiris returned to London. Even if Unai had not promised anything, he was the one. The club would wait. Then, after a draw at home to Nottingham Forest, a loss to Chelsea and, the low point, a 3–0 defeat at Fulham, Villa dropped to seventeenth. Nassef didn't need more evidence. It was time. He moved quickly. Sawiris asked Jorge Mendes to call Unai. 'We will pay the release clause straight away.' While Nassef waited, the pieces moved quickly in Spain. Two days later, he got the call with the answer he wanted. Unai had taken the step to become Aston Villa's leader. With everything agreed, Nassef invited Emery to his home in London. He reiterated to Unai that he would back him, not just with words, but with structure, resources, time. The scale of this project is rare in modern football. With that came pressure but also opportunity. Unai knew it, so in return he took on the responsibility the role demanded. He was going to give everything to the club. Those were the promises they exchanged. From London, Unai and Damià, not wanting to waste a second, drove to Birmingham.

Emery's appointment in October 2022 marked a major turning point. It felt as though Villa had secured a name above their station but what was truly sealed was the hope of a cultural shift.

Emery's meticulous, hard-working nature mirrored the values already embedded in the V Sports project. Recognising the need for specialised leadership, Sawiris and Edens restructured the club's management, looking to bring in someone to run the sporting department (president of football operations, eventually Monchi) and a president of business operations (Chris Heck from May 2023). But Emery was going to be the engine.

Unai would be given full authority within a clearly defined structure. Across much of Europe, the sporting director model is the norm – long-term planning is led from above, and the head coach is seen as part of a broader system. In the UK, that approach is becoming increasingly common too, though the culture still clings to the perception of the manager as the beginning and end of a club's identity. There are deep, cultural reasons for this. British football has long idolised the figure of the all-powerful manager – Shankly, Clough, Ferguson, Wenger – leaders who weren't just tacticians but institution builders. In times of crisis, the solution is often to appoint a 'fixer', a strong personality who imposes discipline and reshapes the environment through sheer force of character. The media plays a decisive role in sustaining this narrative. Managers are portrayed as singular heroes or villains, and press coverage tends to amplify personal authority over collective planning. Tactical nuance or club-wide vision is often secondary to the character and charisma of the individual in charge. Success is credited to the manager's leadership; failure, to their loss of control. The headlines demand strong men, not strong systems.

What was being built at Aston Villa, however, was a deliberate hybrid: a structure with modern governance, one where the manager retained central influence, designed around Unai Emery, but built to outlast him. It's about having elite professionals managing every layer of the organisation, creating the conditions for sustained success. Whether this becomes a model for other clubs remains to be seen, but there are echoes of it in other successful projects, like the executive structure at Manchester City built around Pep Guardiola, Txiki Begiristain and Ferran Soriano, an inspiration for the Villa hierarchy. Unai knew what he needed after his time at Arsenal. He wanted control, as well as a strong, supportive environment that allowed him to focus entirely on football without the distractions of boardroom politics or internal power struggles. At Villa, everything Emery had envisioned to progress the team could be actioned almost immediately. For a coach, this is fertile ground.

The owners and Unai all knew that to take Villa to new levels, glass ceilings had to be broken. They wanted to survive at the top under rules that were not written for clubs like theirs. So, everyone at the club had to be disruptors, the situation required it to overcome the structural limitations of modern football governance. The financial controls now in place, particularly the Premier League's Profit and Sustainability Rules (PSR), make it almost impossible for clubs outside the historical elite to bridge the gap. The aim was to establish Villa as a serious contender with a permanent presence in the top six, just as European and domestic football became more regulated than ever.

This wasn't the case in previous decades. The likes of Manchester United, Chelsea, Liverpool and Manchester City built their modern identities in an era of financial freedom. During the 1990s and 2000s, there were no meaningful restrictions on spending. Owners could inject funds, clubs could borrow aggressively and financial risk-taking was often the route to competitive transformation. These same clubs ran up substantial debts that, ironically, helped them grow. Those investments enabled them to scale, globalise and ultimately lock in vast commercial advantages that continue to compound today. Aston Villa, by contrast, entered this landscape after the gates had closed. The club cannot spend beyond its means. It cannot carry significant debt. Every move must be justified against its existing revenue base. And that base, though growing, remains far smaller than those of the clubs Villa are now expected to compete with. While those clubs benefit from legacy income streams – decades of global brand-building, Champions League access and entrenched commercial relationships – Villa are forced to operate at maximum efficiency just to keep pace.

The rules governing financial conduct don't reward ambition; they entrench status. The need to comply with PSR and UEFA's squad cost ratios has in many ways made things even harder. Clubs are now required to keep total football expenditure – wages, amortised transfer fees and agent commissions – within a fixed percentage of their income. Whether that's 85 per cent, 80 per cent or 70 per cent, the logic is the same: your spending power is determined entirely by your existing revenue. And that, in effect, makes it structurally impossible for clubs like Villa to build squads of comparable value to the established elite.

Unlike the traditional top six, Villa cannot absorb failure in the same way. If Manchester United or Chelsea miss out on Champions League football, their revenue base remains vast. Their commercial deals continue. Their fanbases are global. They have built-in insulation from short-term sporting setbacks. Villa do not. A single misstep – missing out on Europe, a bad season in the league – can force immediate, painful correction. The club must comply while maintaining performance, adjusting the wage bill and, crucially, generating profits from player transfers. There is no safety net. Internally, the club is acutely aware of this tension. The challenge of remaining competitive while reducing the squad cost is like threading a needle in the dark.

Unai sees the flaw in the current logic. Football needs stars. It needs competition. If capital is available to raise the level of the sport, so long as it's done responsibly, why block it? Sawiris has openly criticised the Premier League's PSR, calling them anti-competitive. For him, it's not just frustration, it's principle. In every other industry he's worked in, growth comes from investment, but in football, the rules punish ambition. 'Managing a sports team has become more like being a treasurer or a bean counter,' he's said. 'If you can't invest to grow your business, that's counter-intuitive. It becomes a financial game, not a sporting one.' This is where Villa's project becomes political. It's not just about winning. It's about challenging a system that claims to protect football but, in practice, preserves inequality. Sawiris and his team have proposed reforms: temporary exemptions for clubs qualifying for European competition for the first time, adjusted thresholds that reflect a club's growth trajectory, more nuance in how revenue and investment are measured. UEFA, they say, is more open to discussion. The Premier League, far less so. Legal action was discussed at one point. For now, Villa remains focused on compliance, but all options remain on the table. If Aston Villa succeeds, it won't just be a sporting triumph. It will be a rebuke to the system itself, a demonstration that intelligence, structure and conviction can overcome a model designed to prevent new challengers. If they fail – not through mismanagement but because the system makes progress unsustainable – then the lesson will be just as stark: modern football is no longer about merit. So, something had to be done to get Villa to eat at the table of the entrenched elite.

In the world of football, the label 'disruptor' is often applied too lightly. In the case of Nassef Sawiris, it fits. In business, disruption has been his method and often his advantage. He built his empire by doing what others wouldn't: investing where markets were unstable, pushing into sectors before the crowd, dismantling companies to create value. Across sectors such as pharmaceuticals, construction and fertilisers, he's challenged the status quo. In the construction industry, he has built a portfolio in regions others avoided, operating in countries like Egypt, Iraq, North Korea, Nigeria and Algeria. That bold strategy forced a global bidding war and ended with Lafarge, who Sawiris was the largest shareholder of, becoming a market leader in several countries. In fertilisers, OCI built the first major US plant in forty years, pioneering decarbonisation before it was the standard. Controlled disruption, long-term plans that defied conventional risk profiles, paid off. Even his recent comments about OCI – exploring the idea of transforming it into a cash-shell company for future acquisitions – suggest a man constantly prepared to rebuild while still on top. Not all football owners use their broader business acumen to club operations. Sawiris does. Long before Unai Emery arrived, he and Wes Edens took their time to learn about the club, from the inside out. What followed was a quiet, deliberate shift: the gradual implementation of business principles Nassef and Edens have honed over decades. Clear hierarchies. Empowered decision-makers. Recruiting elite people to execute a long-term plan. Massive immediate benefits are not the target; the intention is to create a legacy. And disrupt established norms.

At Villa, this has meant pushing the limits with higher wage expenditure than is usually demanded and even logical at Villa's level, betting on successive appearances in European competitions, while also trying to change the rules, putting their case across publicly to the fans, negotiating for manageable deals and gaining a better understanding of the Aston Villas of the footballing world. This mindset is what sets Villa apart. Perhaps that's why

Unai Emery and Nassef Sawiris connected so seamlessly from the start, both are disruptors in their fields. They don't wait for progress to occur but build the structure to make it happen.

Unai's entire career has been about breaking through barriers, 'otherwise you die,' he says. At every club, he has refused to settle for the limits imposed by history, status or expectation. At Lorca, in the depths of Segunda B, he told his players they had to think like professionals, push harder, demand more, because staying still meant sinking. At Almería, when the owner gave him two years to reach promotion, Unai replied he needed just one 'because I don't know where I will be in the second year.' And so on and so forth. He looks around and sees the difference that that approach makes. Many of his peers from two decades ago have faded, some brilliant but unlucky, some incapable of adapting. But Emery is still here, still competing with Simeone, still facing Guardiola. 'Some people used to say to me, "You never beat Guardiola's Barcelona," and I'd tell them, "No . . . but if I'm still facing him ten or twenty years later, it means I'm still in the elite."'

For a club like Aston Villa to break free from mid-table obscurity, two things were essential: investment and good management. One without the other doesn't work. Spend without a plan and it ends in ruin. Manage well without resources and you might overachieve but not consistently. A foundation had to be built at Villa. If sporting success followed, it could drive financial growth but only if matched by commercial development. On its own, success doesn't bring in revenue. You have to turn it into something lasting, into loyalty, sponsorship, ticket sales, better commercial deals, new fans. That takes time because revenue growth lags behind performance. You can't convert a great season into sustained income overnight. Consistent success is what changes the curve. That was the owners' belief. If Villa could eventually reach an income level comparable to Tottenham's, the long-term picture might shift. In 2024, the contrast was stark: Villa earned £275.7 million, whereas Spurs earned £528.2 million.

Geography also matters. Tottenham benefits from being in London: a global city of nearly ten million, with endless footfall and international reach. Villa is rooted in Birmingham: passionate, but with a much smaller population, lower average income and far less global pull. Birmingham poses a unique challenge. It doesn't yet attract the kind of tourism or extended stays that support football-as-experience. Unlike Barcelona, Valencia, Liverpool, Manchester or Seville – where football is embedded in broader cultural and hospitality ecosystems – Birmingham's transformation is still evolving. Infrastructure projects like high-speed rail, hotel capacity and urban renewal are ongoing. The potential is there but not yet realised. Local government support has also been limited. In Spain, the state often plays an active role in football infrastructure. In England, it's the opposite. When asked about Manchester United's new stadium project, one UK official famously said the government cared 'less than zero.' That's the environment Villa operate in. To close the gap, a major step would be needed. A new stadium, most likely. The Atlético Madrid model offers a reference: regular Champions League qualification, financial stability, reinvestment in infrastructure. That consistency has turned Atlético into a sustainable, international club. If Villa wants to make that leap they'll need to follow a similar path, but in a harder, more competitive league.

For now, the focus is on expanding Villa Park. Add ten thousand seats at £1,000 per season ticket, and you bring in an extra £10 million a year. Not insignificant, but the expansion might cost £50 million. A new stadium entirely? That's at least a £800 million project. To make that viable, you don't just need more fans, you need higher-spending fans. Those are easier to find in London than Birmingham. Expansion is also about more than just capacity, it's about profile. Villa may have twenty thousand or more fans on a waiting list but what transforms a commercial model is having fans from around the UK and abroad, each willing to spend upwards of £500 per matchday. That's what moves the dial. Tottenham, again, is the benchmark. Its stadium alone generates around £400 million a year. Villa Park doesn't come close to £50 million. It's not just the number of seats, it's what each seat earns: through ticket prices, hospitality, events, retail. Tottenham's prices are among the highest in Europe and their location supports it. Villa doesn't yet have that economic ecosystem.

That said, the work of Villa's commercial and business departments – accelerated after Unai's arrival – has been good. The stadium experience has improved, operations have strengthened and the club is thinking strategically. Still, neither Emery nor the leadership is fixated on redeveloping Villa Park or building a new stadium. A two- or three-year construction project, with all the disruption it brings? It's not the priority. The focus is on proving staying power. When Villa can point to consistent success – when they're no longer an exception but a fixture among Europe's elite – then the stadium conversation becomes real. That's when transformation becomes viable.

From the outside, the instinct is simple: spend more, sign better players. But it's not that simple. Injecting capital without generating revenue now risks point deductions and long-term consequences. You can't just buy progress. That's why the focus remains where it always has been: the results on the pitch and best utilisation of the current squad. Maybe that's the most endearing part of the story. For all the regulations, the financial frameworks, the long-term strategy, Aston Villa are still chasing something beautifully simple: excellence. One season at a time. One match at a time. With a manager who knows what limits are and how to break them.

To do it the club is finding new allies. The investment fund Atairos, led by Michael Angelakis, formally joined Aston Villa's ownership structure in 2024, becoming the third strategic partner alongside Nassef Sawiris and Wes Edens. Their arrival marked a new phase in the club's off-field growth, rooted in capital but also in expertise and long-term vision. Atairos invested approximately £150 million to acquire a significant minority stake in the club and two seats on the board, even though Nassef and Wes will continue to own 100 per cent of the club. Upon their entry, Angelakis emphasised their commitment to the club's values and ambitions: 'Aston Villa is a club with tradition, potential and a clear strategy.'

Angelakis, a former CFO of Comcast, a highly respected figure in media and finance and friends with both owners, is not involved in the day-to-day running of the club but plays a key role at board level. He and Chester Hall, Atairos's day-to-day liaison for the club, typically visit three or four times a year. While less present than Nassef, Angelakis is deeply engaged during board meetings, where his focus is clear: financial strength and long-term sustainability. He asks the right questions, seeks clarity on strategic plans and, once aligned, is consistently constructive. With Atairos now in place, the club has effectively added a third pillar to its leadership structure. Their arrival coincided with the club's success in qualifying for the UEFA Champions League – a moment that marked Villa's re-entry into the top table of European conversation.

Funnily enough, among the disruptors reshaping Aston Villa stands an unlikely ally: a future king. Prince William, the Prince of Wales, is the club's most famous supporter. Isn't that just the most Aston Villa thing imaginable? Villa is not the safe choice.

Not a global powerhouse picked for its silverware but a club defined by its contradictions – historic, yet often overlooked; ambitious, yet perennially underestimated. A club that stubbornly writes its own story. The fact that a royal chose them is exactly the kind of twist that fits. As a teenager at school, surrounded by friends supporting Manchester United or Chelsea, William chose differently. He wanted a team that came with risk, story, pride and struggle, he wanted the emotional roller coaster. And in typically dry Villa fashion, nodding to the club's unpredictability, he later joked: 'Looking back, maybe not the best idea.' He ended up discovering a club that is perceived as a beautiful, traditional beacon of hope for the locals.

His first real encounter came at the 2000 FA Cup semi-final between Villa and Bolton. He was in the crowd, wearing a red beanie, sitting among the Brummie faithful. Villa won on penalties, before losing the final to Chelsea. His first visit to Villa Park didn't come until 2013, hosted in Randy Lerner's private box. Since then, he's become a regular presence when his royal schedule allows. He watches games religiously, appears both home and away and is known to the players and staff. He has visited Bodymoor Heath to watch training sessions and on several occasions entered the dressing room to wish the squad luck before kick-off. He once asked for Jack Grealish's number 10 shirt. On another occasion, he received Christian Benteke's boots. When former captain Stiliyan Petrov battled leukaemia, William offered his support. Though the details of these meetings are private, insiders confirm he and Nassif Sawiris have spent significant time together on matchdays. As soon as William heard about Unai Emery and the exciting journey ahead, he looked forward to crossing paths. He now brings his son, Prince George, to games too. George is a Villa fan in his own right, although William has admitted he won't impose football allegiances on his other children. With one exception: anyone-but-Chelsea.

Once the vision was set and the main characters were in place, there was plenty of work to be done at Aston Villa. Between the high-level strategy of ownership and the day-to-day intensity of coaching, things have to be held together. That's where the supporting cast becomes indispensable. Few roles are more vital to Aston Villa's structure than those played by Damiá Vidagany and board member Bashir Lebada. In a high-performance, high-stakes environment, success often hinges on the relationships between strong, immovable personalities. Unai Emery is intensely focused, immersed in training and match preparation. Nassef Sawiris, meanwhile, is a clear thinker with a sharp strategic mind and little appetite for unnecessary friction. To function, the relationship between Unai and Nassef needs trust and clarity. Maintaining that is a subtle but critical task. That's where Bashir and Damià come in.

Bashir Lebada is a Canadian business executive who plays a pivotal role in the strategic and operational management of Aston Villa Football Club. Increasingly involved at the club over the past few years, Lebada holds directorships across multiple entities within the club's ownership structure, including NSWE Sports Limited, NSWE UK Limited and Aston Villa Women's Football Club Limited. His involvement extends to overseeing various aspects of the club's operations and growth initiatives. His role also includes facilitating communication between the club's ownership and management, ensuring that strategic decisions are effectively implemented.

From the beginning, Unai made it clear: Damià would be his voice in dealings with ownership. What Damià tells Nassef is not his interpretation, it's what Unai thinks. Damià works constantly in the background, shaping the dialogue, preparing the groundwork and making sure both sides understand the full context before any major decision takes place. Damià's role isn't new. He performed a similar function at Valencia, helping manage the sometimes combustible relationship between Unai and club president Manolo Llorente. It worked because the conflict wasn't avoided, it was channelled.

Bashir and Damià are in near-constant contact, the two 'lubricants' as Bashir calls them, who keep the system moving smoothly. Both know when to shield and when to expose, building bonds strong enough to weather the occasional heated discussion that inevitably takes place. They both know that football clubs are built on relationships.

Finally, as Emery approached his first match in charge, the questions turned tactical. It was time to start turning the ideas exchanged in Madrid and London dining rooms into decisions that would shape what happened on the pitch. When Emery arrived, he inherited an underperforming but heavily invested-in squad. Since Aston Villa's promotion back to the Premier League in 2019, owners Sawiris and Edens had spent around £500 million on the team. Key players like John McGinn, Tyrone Mings and Ollie Watkins had stalled under Gerrard's rigid 4-3-2-1 system, which clogged the midfield and over-relied on wing-backs for width. Unai's coaching staff studied footage of Aston Villa before arriving in Birmingham and what they saw was chaos. The goalkeeper hit long balls upfield, second balls flew everywhere, passes were played blindly into the channels and players collided constantly, then just ran and ran. There was talent, yes, but no structure, no clear pattern of play. Everyone seemed to be in everyone else's way.

Changing it felt impossible to do quickly. One week they could win 4–0, as they did against Brentford; the next, lose 0–4, like they did against Newcastle. When Emery was appointed, Villa were seventeenth in the table, just a point above the drop. He had to bring the shackles off. But first, he had to make them believe. The preparations for the first match against Manchester United, with less than a week to prepare, had to be mostly carried out by his assistants, as Unai's work permit had delayed his formal arrival and he could only join a session. 'I believe around 60 per cent of a manager's success depends on whether the players are emotionally open and willing to respond,' Emery would reflect. 'In this case, they were.'

With little time and even less tactical complexity, he focused on the essentials. He began with the defensive structure. A medium block. A back four that continually adjusted. Some elements from Villarreal were introduced, such as triggers for pressing, how to shift across the pitch, how and when to form a back five. Clear roles were implemented. 'I wanted us to defend in a very specific, structured way,' he said. 'There would soon be time to change the focus, but at that point it was a priority.'

The result was emphatic, but misleading: Aston Villa 3, Manchester United 1. Before the game he had held two video sessions with the players – one defensive, one attacking – but the team were still playing largely on instinct. Unai was not happy. 'We had won by following the players' principles rather than mine,' he admits. 'There was some structure and order, but not enough control.'

The next match, away at Brighton, was a very different test. Emery didn't know Roberto De Zerbi well then but that afternoon left a mark. 'I've come to greatly admire his bold, courageous approach,' Emery says. 'Brighton's man-to-man pressing high up the pitch forced us to defend deep with discipline.' Villa conceded inside the opening minute. A build-up error, punished. Douglas

Luiz lost the ball in midfield. Brighton scored. But Emery wasn't agitated. 'A mistake? OK. We will use it to refine,' he says. 'These moments, especially the errors, offer clarity. They reveal our limits and strengths, and from there we adapt.'

The same player who gave the ball away won it back later with a high press, and Villa scored their second. Danny Ings, starting in place of an ill Ollie Watkins, scored both goals. Leon Bailey, also unwell, managed just 20 minutes. Villa won 1–2. It was messy, reactive football, but it carried a trace of something else: adaptability.

Unai Emery's first two league wins gave him a cushion. They allowed him to feel he had passed his first test and – most importantly – to earn the players' respect and authority. Then, the break. The league paused for the Qatar World Cup. For Emery, it came at the perfect time. He had ideas to shape, but he needed space to breathe. 'We tried to turn that time into something positive,' he says. 'A chance to let ideas breathe, to allow concepts to settle.' The squad had ten days off. After that, there were still four weeks before the Premier League resumed, so the staff organised a mini training camp in Dubai, nine days of concentrated work with almost the entire squad. Only Emiliano Martínez (Argentina), Matty Cash and Jan Bednarek (Poland), as well as Leander Dendoncker (Belgium) were at the World Cup. 'It's funny,' Emery reflects now. 'Back then we only had four away. Two and a half years later, when we were in another Dubai camp during the international break, we had only nine first-team players available and two of them were injured!'

'Aston Villa was the first club where, from the moment I arrived, I said, "I want players who can help me maintain the structure, formation and the style I had at Villarreal."' He believed in the positional game he had built in Spain. So, he began to adapt the players he had to fit that style of play. Douglas Luiz and Boubacar

Kamara formed the base. Jacob Ramsey shifted slightly inside from the left. On the right, Matty Cash and Ashley Young were trained to step inside during build-up. Leon Bailey gave width, while John McGinn pushed forward into more advanced areas, closer to the striker. Lucas Digne offered width and delivery, but Emery wanted more depth and variety, so Àlex Moreno arrived in January from Betis and swiftly claimed the left-back spot. Emery could not conduct a major overhaul of the squad to ignite Villa's rise, but someone else was added to the team. Jhon Durán, signed from Chicago Fire. He added depth but featured sparingly at first. Unai hadn't known Durán beforehand and, with the deal already well under way, he only gave it the green light after watching footage and spotting a raw potential he believed he could shape.

In those first weeks, Unai focused on something the team lacked entirely: how to manage possession. It wasn't just about changing how they played, it was about changing how they thought. Some players, like Ashley Young, genuinely believed that playing at full speed was the right approach. Emery introduced something different: long periods of possession, precise positioning and patience. Day after day, relentlessly, he repeated the same messages. 'Ashley, not there. You, stay here. Don't move from this spot. Do this. Now that.' The ball became his obsession. After introducing basic defensive concepts to protect themselves in those first games, Emery then focused on building the team through its attack, refining the structure of the team when they had the ball and from there, letting the rest of the defensive shape fall into place. Defensive discipline (the height of the line, players covering gaps, when and how to press) would follow, but everything had to begin with possession of the ball. This applied to individuals as well. Every new player had to learn to wait, to pass only when the timing was right, to create traps for the opposition to fall into. To develop relationships on the pitch, between full-back and centre-back, striker and second striker. Previously, the instinct was to arrive and cross. Now, it was arrive, wait, see who is around, choose the right decision and the right moment.

Dubai was providing an ideal working environment. They played a friendly against Roberto De Zerbi's Brighton, which ended 2–2. Another match followed against Chelsea in Abu Dhabi, a 1–0 win on 11 December. Back in England came more work in Bodymoor Heath and another friendly against Villarreal on 15 December. The coldest day some could remember in England, the pitch was frozen and they lost 0–1.

Everything was done with full respect for what had come before. Unai did not criticise Steven Gerrard once, but the difference between the team he inherited and the one it was beginning to turn into became clear almost immediately. Some players were not going to survive the process, not because the manager discarded them but because the demands were simply too high.

9

THE START OF EVERYTHING:

FROM DAY ONE

Unai doesn't want to move on just yet. What is coming next is a bit of exercise in an empty gym, but he doesn't want to start with the taste of defeat – this time in an anonymous online chess match. Ten-minute games to sharpen his mental agility. At least, that's what he tells himself. The truth is, he is hooked on winning. He has just lost this last one . . . and the second-to-last one as well. He needs to change his strategy. Too defensive today. Next time, he'll go on the attack.

He has spent the entire day at Bodymoor, arriving at 8 a.m. Now, nearly 12 hours later, the place is practically deserted. Unai Emery works out of an office that hasn't changed much since the previous manager left. There's even a framed picture on the wall that still belongs to that era. He hasn't felt the need to personalise the space. He has his routines, his comforts and a clear sense of what matters. One of those comforts is practicality: the office has its own bathroom and shower. Soon the training ground will have more. A project has already been approved to build private rooms at Bodymoor Heath, spaces for players and staff to stay overnight.

There's a sense of calm at Bodymoor Heath, even in busy times. Unai describes it as equilibrium. At Sevilla, during renovations in the coaching areas, they struggled to maintain that calm. At

244

Villarreal, the training ground is an oasis. Unai remembers a very different time during his playing days. Back then, the atmosphere was chaotic. People came and went – journalists, girlfriends, outsiders. Madness.

For most people, heading to the gym at this hour, finally wearing a generous smile after a win in their last chess game, would feel like a chore. Walking down the hallway for the twentieth time that day, taking the stairs down to the spacious workout area, turning on his iPad, sitting on the bike, rewatching a match – it would all feel like an effort. But for Unai, this is a source of energy. And, at the same time, a form of rest. He struggles to separate the two. Every moment has to be used, but energy is limited. As he makes his way downstairs, he feels the weight of fatigue creeping in. 'Come on, Unai. Keep going. Don't stop. Move forward,' he whispers to himself, words that could be the soundtrack to his life.

Sport is never far away. At Almería, he used to join in on the odd football match in between training sessions and more video work. At Sevilla, there were long, competitive games of padel. When the weather was good, he played tennis, which he wasn't bad at, but he hated losing, so he pushed himself too hard and his knee paid the price. Now, he has to settle for the cross-trainer or the treadmill three times a week. After the cardio he improvises a few exercises, his own version of a workout, instinctive, doing what feels right to keep shaping a body that has now crossed into its fifties. Transformation in football doesn't always announce itself. Sometimes it slips in through the side door in the form of quiet routines, long days and evening rituals in an empty gym.

Sweating, after 20 minutes of watching the football match on his iPad, he gets lost in thought looking at the darkness outside. He walks briskly out of the gym, showers quickly, slicks back his hair with gel, grabs his things, including kit to wear tomorrow, and hurries to the exit. He nods to a coach still wrapping up his work, to a cleaner finishing up for the night, to a couple of other people too. Those who cross paths with him straighten their backs slightly, moving aside just a little to give him space and offer a subtle, unconscious nod. 'See you tomorrow, boss,' they say. For many, that is the only interaction they will have with him for days. The few people who can slow him down, such as Damià, Monchi or Alberto Benito, aren't there. In fact, he needs to call Benito from the car.

The night is certainly pitch black, like most nights in the Midlands. The security guard at the gate raises a hand in greeting, possibly relieved that the day has finally finished. Unai has a 30-minute drive back to Birmingham city centre, where he lives. He dials Lander first. His son has trained with the Under 21s in the afternoon and is already at his flat, in the same building where father and son both live. Just a quick call to say they'll see each other tomorrow and have dinner together, that today he is exhausted. Lander has noticed a change in his father over the last few years. Basques aren't usually known for being warm and expressive, but lately, Unai has been creating small, meaningful moments. They are still in the process of making up for lost time. Having been a November where results were not going Aston Villa's way, Unai has been retreating into himself again, his mind endlessly replaying situations. Like today, he doesn't always make it up to his son's apartment.

After speaking to Lander, the next call is to Benito. While patience defines a lot of his decision-making, behind the wheel, a bit like the way he moves around Bodymoor Heath, it is a different story. He drives with urgency, overtaking where possible, accelerating, scanning for shortcuts. Just as he pulls out to pass a van, Benito picks up. His friend had been over a few days ago, and they had caught up on family, mutual friends and, of course, the last match. Liverpool. A 2–0 defeat at Anfield. Villa had played well, but they were still far from breaking out of their inconsistent run, unable to string together two wins in a row.

The team had ended the previous season on a high, securing an extraordinary fourth-place finish in the Premier League that took them to the Champions League, but the early months of the new campaign exposed their struggle to keep that momentum. They lacked the consistency needed to stay in the top four and were finding it difficult to adapt to the dual demands of the Premier League and the newly formatted Champions League, with two more games than the previous group stage. The loss to Liverpool left them ninth in the table, which came hot on the heels of a defeat to Club Brugge in Europe, which meant they had got just one win, two draws and a defeat in each of the Premier League games after each of the Champions League fixtures so far that season. Unai can see a pattern emerging, and he is relentlessly searching for solutions to halt the slide.

Chatting to Benito – brought in for his wide-ranging experience, sharp eye for talent and global web of football contacts – offers more than just a way to reflect on the day. It opens a window beyond Bodymoor: the latest odd move by Donald Trump or some other headline-grabbing politician, the scoreline from Toledo's match, or news of a former player changing clubs somewhere far off. For the next game, at home against Crystal Palace a group of friends are coming along, and Benito is organising a dinner afterward. He runs through the guest list: Lander, Iosu, Igor, Damià, Pablo Rodríguez, a close associate of Unai's who works with Benito.

Traffic is all of a sudden annoyingly slow but that allows for one more call to his lawyer, Iosu. He needs some information about one of the restaurants he owns, La Casita de Sabino in Valencia, a place specialising in Basque cuisine. Just talking about it makes him hungry. He has taken food – some fish, vegetables, fruit – from the training ground and will heat it up at home. Unai has been to a few of Birmingham's Michelin-starred restaurants, he goes regularly to a couple of eateries that know what he likes, he certainly appreciates good food but prefers something simpler as long as the ingredients are top quality.

In life too, Unai has never been one for excessive ambitions. If asked about moments of pure happiness, his mind always travels back to childhood, his mum's food, spending time with his friends, his brothers, his family, playing football. He needs to recreate that feeling, so that is why he returns to Hondarribia and Irún whenever he can. The last time, a few weeks ago, before the season had taken any kind of shape, he had a morning coffee with Roberto Olabe, his close friend as well as Real Sociedad's sporting director. What was supposed to be a quick chat turned into 3 hours. He then went for lunch with his brother Igor and Iosu, alongside some members of the Real Sociedad board. In the evening, he went to a concert in Hondarribia with his brother Koldo. That, for Unai, is contentment and a busy rest.

Finally, home. It is too late for a walk along the Birmingham Canal – his escape, an exercise in clearing his mind, hidden beneath a cap. He doesn't do it often, only when the weather is gentler or the day's demands loosen their grip. Tonight, neither has. After dinner in his flat, he picks up his iPad and scrolls through a streaming platform. He has already watched *All or Nothing* on Manchester City and the documentary on Luis Enrique. He is tempted to watch a six-part series on Real Sociedad, but he stops to listen to Xavier Marcel, a university professor specialising in leadership and innovation, discussing humanistic leadership. Then he finds the highlights of Almería's latest match in the Segunda

División. One particular dead-ball situation catches his eye, something he will mention to his set-piece specialist Austin MacPhee tomorrow. 'Oh, look,' he has just discovered a match from his own playing days with Toledo. 'We were terrible,' he mutters to himself.

It is getting late, 2 a.m. You'd think that after three or four strong coffees during the day, he'd struggle to fall asleep. But tonight, like always, he will be out the moment his head hits the pillow, slipping easily into his usual 4 or 5 hours of rest. Still, the weight of the team's struggles creeps into his thoughts. When things aren't going well, he reaches for the book that is always within arm's reach: *Searching for and Maintaining Peace* by Father Jacques Philippe.

There was a time when Unai used to give books to his players. He would hand over ones that had taught him something, telling them to read it. He believes in the power of a good book and how much it can help. But things have changed. At Aston Villa, he no longer does this. A book doesn't hold the same place it did a generation or two ago. Instead, he might show them a short clip – 2 minutes, perhaps – of someone like Kobe Bryant on YouTube.

He switches off all the lights except for the small lamp by his bed and reads a couple of chapters. One phrase stands out:

> The spiritual battle is not about winning every time, but rather about maintaining peace in the heart in any circumstance, even in defeat.

When the words stop sinking in, he turns off the light. Sleep comes easily.

The next morning, with his first coffee of the day, he skims through the newspapers: *Diario Vasco*, *Las Provincias*, *El Mundo*, *El País*, *Marca*, *AS* on his iPad. It is a training day. That makes dressing easy, the tracksuit he brought from Bodymoor. If it had been a matchday, he would have taken more time. Unlike in his early years, when comfort was his priority, he now likes dressing well. As a player, he had worn whatever kit the club provided, even in the afternoons out in town. Now, if there is a match, he picks a tie that represents the club, its colours or crest. His style is casual but elegant, with classic shoes. He always wants to look right in public, fit in, almost anonymous, not flashy, not out of place. Never jeans, never trainers with smart clothes, never too casual. Matchday is like going to church on Sunday, you have to step out looking right. The official suit, though, he rarely wears. In England, no one does. And besides, it is too easy to get dirty.

Anyway, today, tracksuit.

He runs gel through his hair, slicking it back again. He thinks of his mother. She always says that the wet, combed-back look makes him seem like 'a conservative' – one of those right-wing Spanish politicians with hair as rigid as a sculpture. He should leave it loose, she keeps saying to him. But no, this is how he feels most comfortable. There is always gel in his toiletry bag. Once, he had to ask the club delegate to buy some because he had run out. Can't do without it.

Then, the usual half an hour's drive to Bodymoor. He heads north from Birmingham city centre, past the Victorian terraces of Aston, then out beyond the industrial scars of Erdington. The red brick gives way to warehouse grey and eventually to hedgerows and silence. He puts the radio on. He happens to hear a quote from himself in a recent press conference. He hates hearing himself speak. A friend had once told him, 'You speak faster than you think.' He rushes when he speaks, but in English, he makes an effort to slow down, to pick the right words. It doesn't always work, especially if he is affected by something that did not go as planned. But the more he speaks, the better his English will become. Although he doesn't really have time to improve his English right now.

The final stretch of Unai's drive takes him through Kingsbury, a village that feels like a place bypassed by time, and then down a narrow lane flanked by fields and low trees. There's no fanfare, just a discreet turning. Bodymoor Heath doesn't so much rise as emerge: first the spacious training pitches on the left and a slight turn to the gate. It is close to 8 a.m. and he gives a quick wave to Matt Lambert – the gentle giant always at the entrance, who for years has stood just outside the threshold of the first-team building, never once stepping inside. On a few occasions, when Unai is waiting for a taxi, they will exchange a few words – not about football, not about work. It is how Matt found out where Unai comes from and his plans for the summer. That sort of thing. He is genuinely curious about everyone who spends so many hours behind these walls. If he has the chance, Matt might tell Unai that he's beaten cancer. Not because he wants sympathy but because he doesn't mind sharing the thing that has changed his life. It explains why he always seems so relaxed, so content, and why he counts himself lucky just to be there, on the edge of an elite world he has never been part of but is grateful to witness up close. He admires them all.

After parking, Unai walks briskly towards the long, two-storey, curved building with large windows – the first team's sanctuary – its entrance marked by a reception area staffed by Danielle Fulford. She always seems half-hidden behind a counter that is either too high or her chair is too low, surrounded by a cluttered mountain of shirts waiting to be signed, spilling across the desk. She hasn't been in the role for long, but knowingly or not, she has the presence of someone who, with a big smile, makes you feel truly welcome in the building, like the keeper of a secret garden, quietly proud of what lies beyond.

251

Sometimes, if Unai arrives in a rush, like that morning, he grabs a quick breakfast from the canteen upstairs – just a banana or a juice – and heads straight to his office, walking past a few doors and empty rooms. He says a warm 'good morning' to the assistants already in front of their computers. Normally, Unai would begin with analysis of the Liverpool defeat. There were issues to address. But focusing too much on mistakes could cloud the players' minds. Today, he takes an alternative approach – identifying that Crystal Palace will pose a different challenge – and uses analysis to rebuild confidence. Training will focus on solutions. He will then spend the rest of the day assembling a 50-minute video on Palace, preparing the plan for tomorrow's session. Around 12 hours of work lay ahead, at least 10 of them intense.

This isn't the kind of place where anyone can drop into his office to chat about what's on at the cinema. Unai often speaks to Damià about it. Unai knows his own strengths, and he knows his own weaknesses. As he did not play at the highest level, he sometimes wonders if he works so hard to cover perceived gaps. He had recently heard of impostor syndrome. Sometimes Unai feels that if he does not work such long hours, he is deceiving people. Who? Who knows? All of this work, the constant, necessary pursuit of a new and better place, has been there from day one in Birmingham.

'For me, change is not a threat, but a fascinating challenge. The unknown doesn't create panic, it excites me, it's an adventure,' Unai admits. At Villa, that process began the moment his appointment was confirmed. As with every club he'd joined, his first task was always the same: conduct a deep analysis. The club's structure, its players, even its ownership, everything was scrutinised to understand how best to adapt his methods.

And then he got to work.

Even after the work permit arrived, the first week was re-lentless. The team had so far played thirteen games that season and had just 13 points. Unai watched every single one of those matches. So did Pako Ayestarán. The goalkeeping coach, Francisco Javier (Javi) García, went even further, studying footage of every goalkeeper in the academy. Damià looked into all of the people that ran things within the club and inside Bodymoor Heath.

Aston Villa had been growing as a club, but inconsistency on the pitch had led to managerial changes. The arrival of Unai Emery was seen inside the changing room as a turning point, as Emiliano Buendía admits. 'Bringing in a manager with Unai's track record, mid-season, showed real ambition. His arrival excited me even more than the day I signed for the club.' Born in Mar del Plata, Argentina, Emiliano Buendía was raised within a footballing culture that prized flair and street-smart intelligence. But it was his move to Real Madrid youth academy at age eleven that truly moulded him. There, and at Getafe where he moved next, he was immersed in the detail-orientated, high-level tactical thinking that defines top-level European football. He began to understand the game and this laid the groundwork for his success at Norwich City. Before Unai Emery's arrival, Emiliano Buendía, Villa's record signing when Dean Smith bought him, had had a mixed spell at the Midlands club. He showed flashes of creativity but struggled for consistency even with the new manager, Steven Gerrard. Buendía, who had even been linked with Villarreal during Unai's time there, kept explaining to his teammates how the new Spanish manager worked. And told them to get excited.

Unai made a few key calls before heading to Birmingham, so by the time he finally set foot in Bodymoor Heath, he already knew exactly who his team was. His coaching staff were already familiar with Austin MacPhee, the set-piece coach with a degree in psychology who had worked across multiple countries and continents under sixteen different managers. He had been part of international coaching staffs for Mexico, Northern Ireland and Scotland, and when Villarreal faced Liverpool in the Champions League semi-finals, one of Unai's assistants, Víctor Mañas, reached out to MacPhee's analyst, the Spaniard José Rodríguez Calvo. Víctor wanted insights into how Villa had troubled Liverpool and, more broadly, how Villarreal could improve on a glaring weakness – their lack of offensive productivity from set-pieces, at a time when Aston Villa had become one of the best in Europe. So, Unai picked up the phone to call Austin. 'I love set-pieces, and for years, I've been thinking about bringing in a specialist. I've analysed your work, it's impressive. I don't know if we'll be a good fit, but let's try it for six months.' Prior to Unai's arrival, MacPhee had been at Villa for two seasons and became the only member of Gerrard's coaching staff who stayed at the club. He saw this as a chance to earn his place alongside the most accomplished manager he had had the chance to work with.

Four days before the Manchester United match, the first of a new era and a chance to end twenty-seven years without a home win against them, the new Spanish contingent touched down at Bodymoor Heath. Austin was allowed to remain in his usual spot, and watched the meticulous transformation unfold. It felt clinical, precise, methodical. Something between professional and corporate. They moved swiftly into their offices, assembling desks, setting up laptops and oversized monitors. Within days, there were six big new screens installed. Everyone had a clear role. They knew they were going to work – a lot. There was banter but not often. And then, once everything was in place, silence. This wasn't the traditional British coach's room.

The first meeting Emery had was with the staff, held in the video analysis room. The chat with the players had to wait as Unai didn't yet have his work permit. In fact, for the first training session, only Javi, the goalkeeping coach, and his assistant Pablo were allowed on the pitch; no one else had clearance. Unai joined them a couple of days later, and on that occasion the manager started the day with a meeting in the gym to address the players for the first time.

Walking into the area, he suddenly realised the gym had glass walls that overlooked the training pitch, so he imagined it had been purposely designed so that players inside – particularly those recovering from injury – could still feel connected to the rest of the squad. He was still discovering the impressive facilities. Another thought crossed his mind. He had a history of success but also knew there were more levels to reach. *Here, you could reach them, but from the very first moment, you have to demand it*, he thought to himself before turning to the group. 'You all know why I'm here. But I'm not happy. Do you know why I'm not happy?'

Nobody spoke.

'I'm not happy because they sacked another manager to bring me in.'

And then he explained, simply and clearly, that he was there to win. Just as he had said years before at Lorca, and later at Sevilla, Paris Saint-Germain and Villarreal.

Unai was going to make a conscious effort not to implement drastic changes right away. His message to the group was clear: focus on the stitches, not on the whole tapestry. Put your effort into the intense training sessions, on the corrections suggested by the individual coaches, or into the video analysis sessions. Don't look beyond that. So, before Aston Villa became a team reborn under Unai Emery, Bodymoor Heath started changing, one habit at a time.

Then came his first session. In England, training traditionally emphasises quick ball movement, a fast-paced rhythm that reflects the intensity of the game, with players limited to one or two touches, everything done at a high tempo. It began with rondos, a piggy in the middle, but in these rondos players weren't allowed to pass in just one or two touches. They had to take their time. Many weren't sure why. For Emiliano Buendía, those first few days under Unai were highly enjoyable. 'From the very first training sessions, you could feel the difference. His approach was simple and clear. The hardest thing in football is to make things look easy.'

Then things evolved. New training routines were introduced, as were daily habits. Steven Gerrard lived in Liverpool and would leave training early, sometimes around 12 noon or 1 p.m. Players would finish lunch by 1.30, the chefs would be gone by 2 p.m. and the cleaners would be tidying up staff areas by 2.30. Under the new regime, mornings at Bodymoor Heath begin early. When Unai Emery arrives, Javi García, the goalkeeping coach, is often already there. Unai powers up his computer, reflects on the day's training or match preparation and starts shaping the plan. Between 8 and 11 a.m., he often moves back and forth between his office and the adjoining staff room, sharing ideas, adjusting exercises and refining focus. He doesn't like to repeat sessions and is always looking to improve, even at the last minute. His assistants are nearby, always on hand, sometimes to execute specific tasks, sometimes simply to listen. Conversations rarely stray from football. Everyone is tuned into the same frequency.

Training typically starts at 11 a.m., often following a team meeting. Once the session ends, there's a brief pause for lunch around 1.30 p.m. – or pushed later to match the extended working day. The canteen offers the only real pause in the day. It's where the staff gather to eat, decompress and briefly step outside the relentless focus of their work. Even then, football is generally the main topic. Then staff head straight back into meetings, planning or analysis. There are always people moving around, coming out of rooms, walking up and down the corridor. Casual chats happen standing up in the canteen, in the hallways, across floors, from upstairs to reception downstairs.

Players usually leave by 3 p.m. but that habit is about to change as Bodymoor Heath enters the new phase of development with the construction of on-site accommodation: a new building with around thirty-eight to forty rooms, designed for players and key staff to stay overnight when needed, particularly before matches or after late returns from away games, or even ahead of early training and treatment sessions. For a player scheduled for double sessions – or treatment in the morning, training in the afternoon – being able to rest properly in between can make all the difference.

Several players, like Lucas Digne and Ezri Konsa, live in London. Others on the operational side, such as kit men or the team manager, also live far from the training ground. While there are currently a handful of small rooms available to staff and some have used nearby hotels like The Belfry or even small flats near the facility, the new building will provide a far more integrated and permanent solution. Ideally, players would live closer, but Birmingham isn't always the most attractive option for families. London offers more, and many choose to base themselves there. The result is long commutes, some taking over 90 minutes each way, even with a driver. This new residential model is already standard across many top clubs in Europe: Real Madrid, Sevilla, Villarreal and a growing number of Premier League teams. At Villarreal, for instance, staff speak fondly of the simplicity it brought, you could skip hotel stays entirely and focus the group in a familiar, controlled environment.

Unai Emery sees the value too, on a personal level. Sometimes he'll go home for a quick nap and a coffee and return by 6 or 7 p.m. but having a space on-site will make it easier. As he says with a smile, 'The rooms might be for the siesta.' In truth, they're much more than that. Unai has spoken increasingly about the importance of finding the right balance. He calls it a 70/30 split: 70 per cent football, 30 per cent for life. 'If I'm here for 10 hours and working for 8,' Unai says, 'the other 2, you will find me in the gym or the canteen.'

Among the staff, that ratio feels idealistic. Passion blurs the lines. They love what they do. And that, perhaps, is both the reason and the excuse. Most evenings, staff don't leave before 8 p.m., and on some nights, it stretches to as late as 10 p.m. Then they pick up their kit, cleaned and ironed, go home and return in the morning fresh and fully kitted, ready for more. For many, it's not just about necessity, it's about setting a standard, or maybe about not being the one who leaves early. Walking out at 5 p.m. can feel like submitting an exam before everyone else: it draws looks, raises eyebrows. Unai takes pride in that ethos. He's fostered it. 'It's a bit like Jesus and the apostles,' he has been heard to say as a joke, instilled with admiration. The commitment is near-religious. 'Whatever else they say about us, they'll never be able to say we didn't work.'

These things might seem small, but they build a culture of high standards. The moment the team started winning, people began to associate these meticulous details with success.

If you ask Unai what part of his job he enjoys the most, whether it's analysing the opponent, or his team's performance, training or matchday itself, he wouldn't hesitate: post-match analysis of his own team. Very early on at Aston Villa, Unai shared stories about his early days at Toledo, how he would pause VCR tapes, meticulously breaking down games. 'Luis Enrique, at PSG, spoke about spending the day before an important Dortmund match out with his wife, going for a bike ride. I could never do that. For me, the process is all-consuming. Preparing for a match feels almost spiritual, like a pilgrimage to Mecca.' Unai prioritises data and analysis most as he genuinely believes that his own personal analysis can be the difference between winning and losing. In fact, his success proves that approach works.

His early analytical work at the club started improving the area he felt needed the most attention upon his arrival: the defending. He introduced a 4-4-2 system, emphasising the importance of a compact shape and the specific roles each player needed to respect. 'It reminded me of the way I was coached growing up,' Buendía admits. 'It was football in a language I understood.'

The first video analysis meeting took place the day before the Manchester United match. It was a long one. After the win, there was a second review, an in-depth breakdown of the game. It lasted about 90 minutes. Previously, at Villa, meetings rarely went beyond 20 minutes. After the first two under Unai, some players quietly shared their thoughts with teammates that 'This won't last.' The squad was clearly divided. Some players were naturally more analytical, able to stay engaged in extended meetings, while others struggled to focus. However, they all soon realised, with varying levels of enthusiasm, that detailed analysis was central to Unai's methodology. Many were not used to that level of tactical precision, everyone came from different footballing backgrounds. 'What I liked most was that he didn't just correct mistakes, he also showed you what you did well,' Buendía remembers. 'That stays with you. When you're on the pitch, you remember.'

The fans celebrated the win against Manchester United, but Unai knew the way his players understood the game needed to evolve. It was chaotic box-to-box football, lacking control. So, the analysis started straight away and meetings became more frequent, and longer. The first thing Unai Emery does after a match is watch it back – immediately. Whether it's on the plane, the bus or back at Bodymoor Heath, the review process begins straight away. He codes the game while watching it four or five times, clipping key moments times, extracting every detail he needs. 'You can't just focus on the final image,' Unai says. 'Say we concede a goal, there's always more than a mistake that everyone might be able to see. Many things lead up to that last action. Eventually I know what really happened.' Spectators might label a player 'terrible' after an error or call a conceded goal 'a howler', but Unai digs deeper. 'Why is he terrible? Because he gave the ball away to the keeper? I look at whether his teammates were in position, whether the decision was right, whether the pass he received was good, or whether the two passes before should have been different.'

He doesn't miss anything. 'Not a delayed recovery run. Not a missed pressing trigger. Not a one-v-one. Not a lost duel. Not a failed cover. Not a late track back. Not a lapse in defensive support. Not a run off the ball. People can criticise me all they want, but when it comes to analysis, this is my field. No one beats me there.'

Some ask him why he bothers rewatching matches when the result can't be changed. His answer is simple: 'It's the opposite. Everything I am as a coach comes from what I've learnt watching our matches and creating videos for the players.'

Once the key clips are selected, Unai overlays them with di-agrams, arrows and notes to highlight movements, mistakes or decisions. He combines his own findings with the analysis team's reports. The objective of the video process is clear: 'To reinforce what we do well, correct what we don't and help players understand their role – individually and collectively. It's not about praise or blame. It's reinforcement. A way to make learning visual and habitual.' Preparation is structured around three key meetings. The first focuses on the previous match, what went well, what needs improvement. 'I stop the video and point things out. I'll tell someone not to dive in there, or that a one-metre shift in the line makes all the difference. I don't just show it, we train it after.' The second meeting is devoted to the opposition. The final meeting is about mindset. It's the emotional briefing before the match, a reminder of who they are, what they're capable of and what's required. 'It's about helping them go out there focused and confident,' Unai says.

Not every player processes information in the same way. 'Some want everything. Others just want to know if their opponent is right- or left-footed.' But video analysis has become an indispensable part of learning. 'We show footage from almost every game, maybe forty-five out of fifty-five each season.'

At Sevilla, this kind of analysis became foundational. At PSG, he had to adjust. 'In France, some players only switch on for the Champions League or big domestic games. Against smaller teams, they think they can win without the coach. At Villa, it's more like Sevilla. They're hungry to learn.'

Sometimes, these deep dives lead to recruitment opportunities. 'We spotted Morgan Rogers while analysing a Championship team in the FA Cup. His touches, acceleration and decision-making stood out. What started as an incidental clip became a proper scouting case.'

Unai often draws inspiration from fellow coaches. He likes to reference Juanma Lillo, whom he admires deeply. 'He once said the real task isn't analysing the match afterwards, anyone can do that. It's anticipating it. But football isn't linear. You can prepare for everything and still lose. The key is to understand why and to make fewer mistakes next time.' He recalls a Luis Enrique documentary, where the PSG manager, after losing a first leg match to Dortmund, told his team: 'We're going to win the second.' Unai has a variation of that approach. 'I always say: we must work hard and prepare well to give ourselves the best chance of winning. That's the mantra.'

How do you explain what was happening inside Bodymoor Heath? There's a popular Spanish TV series on Netflix called *Money Heist*. It's about a genius professor who devises an elaborate plan not to steal money, but to print it. He recruits ten people, not friends, but experts in explosives, printing presses, logistics. They come from different backgrounds, each obsessed with their craft, each a little eccentric. That's the closest comparison to Unai's coaching team. His data-driven coaching – training sessions, individual meetings, casual chats driven by analysis – needs specialists. So he hires those who can deliver. Pure pragmatism. Like building a Formula 1 team: every role has to be precise, every piece engineered to perform, there's no room for sentiment in the pit lane. Over time, some may become part of his inner circle, but that's never a given. What truly matters is that they share his obsession with detail and match his work ethic. 'I rely heavily on the experience and knowledge of those around me. The more people I bring in, the more eyes I have to see the game – and that helps a lot. It's a collective effort. After twenty years in this job, I feel in a good place, both professionally and personally. And a lot of it is down to the people I work with.'

Pablo Villanueva, who dissects opposition players with forensic precision, is more than just an assistant; he is a pillar in Unai Emery's professional and personal life. He interprets what Unai thinks and finds out what he needs, something that is becoming more common lately as managers cannot be everywhere at once. Their bond dates back to their playing days at Ferrol and Leganés, and over the years, their relationship has only deepened. Unai called him to join his coaching staff after Pablo's stint as a head coach at Córdoba, in the third tier of Spanish football. Loyal, noble and highly professional, Pablo knows when he or anybody else should step in, when to challenge and even when to absorb Unai's frustration after a tough result. His ability to read both the game and Emery himself makes him indispensable.

Víctor Mañas is one of the longest-serving members of Unai Emery's staff, alongside Pablo. His journey with Unai began at Almería during their season in LaLiga, where he started as the fitness coach for the reserve team while also assisting with video analysis. Over time, Víctor's role has expanded, particularly in the digitalisation of video analysis. When he first joined, Unai was still working with VHS tapes, and Víctor played a key role in modernising the process. His growing expertise and commitment saw him earn a place in the first team set-up when Unai's fitness coach at the time left for Real Madrid. From then on, he took on a dual role, combining analysis with physical preparation. Although he wasn't able to follow Unai to Valencia, when the manager took charge at Sevilla, he wasted no time in bringing Víctor back into his team. Since then, he has been a permanent fixture in his staff.

Rodri fixates on the smallest individual details and how they slot into the tactical model. He is so obsessed with football, he will forget to eat lunch and dinner, but seemingly survives on a mixture of chocolate, popcorn and orange juice.

They all collaborate with the clips that Unai prepares. With Víctor's help, Unai's video sessions no longer solely focus on the opponent but on how Villa must respond. Rodri prepares detailed individual images. Pablo provides dossiers on every opponent, their tendencies, position, international caps, even age and nationality. 'It's about tactical awareness, but also respect for the opposition,' Unai says.

Javi García, whose intense focus on goalkeeping leaves nothing to chance, realised at age fourteen that he wasn't a very good goalkeeper himself, so he started to train his little brother Alberto, who ended up playing in LaLiga. Javi arrived at Sevilla a year before Unai and worked alongside him for a season and a half. After a brief spell away, he returned to Sevilla and they spent another year collaborating. When Unai moved to Paris, Javi remained at the Spanish club, but their connection was never lost. In Unai's second year at PSG, Javi rejoined his coaching staff, and they have been working together ever since. He has an obsessive eye for detail, conducting in-depth analyses of every action related to the goalkeepers, both opponents and their own team, producing extensive post-match reports that are ready by the following morning – no matter how late the match ends. He also studies opponents' signals for corners, looking for any pattern that might give his players an edge. Teams are not always particularly structured and their signals can be inconsistent. Still, Javi refuses to let it go. Maybe a player adjusts their sock before a delivery. To most, it's nothing. To Javi, it's a potential clue. And so, he'll watch another ninety-seven corners, convinced there's a pattern hidden somewhere. Meanwhile, quite likely that guy just had an itchy sock.

Jaime Arias is a young, highly promising coach with an impressive academic background, including a Fulbright Scholarship from Berkeley. The son of a former Oviedo player, he always knew he wanted to be a coach, despite holding a degree in telecommunications. Jaime's dedication was evident from the start. He initially contributed at Villarreal in any way he could, spending long hours helping out, often working in the background without expecting anything in return. His commitment and hard work gradually caught the right attention, earning him a place on Unai's staff. Now, after three and a half years with Emery, the manager holds him in high regard, not just for his talent but also for his loyalty and work ethic. He often jokes that when he retires and Jaime is managing in the top flight, he'll happily return the favour and serve as his assistant.

Moisés de Hoyo is a seasoned strength and conditioning coach whose journey with Unai Emery has been both eventful and integral to the teams they've served. When Emery took charge at Sevilla, he aimed to bring in a new group of fitness coaches, leading to the departure of the existing staff, including Moisés. However, when the new appointments fell through at the last moment, the turn of events led to Moisés being rehired to support the team's fitness needs. When Emery went to Paris Saint-Germain, Moisés remained at Sevilla under manager Jorge Sampaoli. After a year, he decided to seek new challenges, leading him to roles at Levante, Deportivo La Coruña, Badajoz, Leganés and Watford, where he contributed during their promotion campaign. The Covid-19 pandemic presented personal challenges, as his family remained in Spain while he worked in England. Despite being offered a three-year contract extension at Watford, he chose to prioritise his family and planned to return to his academic role as a university professor. However, fate had other plans. Through conversations with Víctor and Pablo, who were aware of his departure from Watford, Moisés learnt of an opening for a strength and conditioning coach at Villarreal. This opportunity led to his reunion with Unai Emery's coaching staff, where he has been a valuable addition ever since.

Additionally, Pablo Rodríguez serves as an external consultant, offering his expertise in a role similar to that of Alberto Benito. A former teammate of Unai's at Ferrol, Rodríguez was part of the technical analysis team at Villarreal during their 2021 Europa League triumph. His insight feeds into Villa's increasingly global recruitment model, helping identify talent beyond traditional markets.

On day one, ten Spanish staff members joined Unai at Bodymoor Heath: coaches, analysts, physios, performance experts. Over time, that number would more than double, eventually encompassing every major area of the club, from medical to recruitment. Monchi joined too as president of football operations, an Americanised name equivalent to director of football – his son also works in his department. Generally, meetings include twenty-five players and twenty-six assistants. All of Unai's backroom staff are obsessed about a specific part of the game, each have their quirks, none of them are your average coaches.

For any club, that level of change risked division with two groups, two cultures, pulling in different directions. But that didn't happen. One of the key reasons it didn't was Damià Vidagany. Socially aware, emotionally intelligent and fluent in the rhythm and nuance of both Spanish and English football environments, Damià played a pivotal role in managing the transition. In those early weeks, he quietly became the bridge between the incoming Spanish staff and the existing British framework, between the manager and departments that had never worked under such intensity before, between old assumptions and new standards. He understood that integration didn't just happen; it needed attention, empathy and structure. For Damià Vidagany, Bodymoor Heath has become more than just a workplace, it feels like a family he's helped build. He sees himself almost like a meticulous father, needing to listen, to sense the mood, to make sure everything is in order. Even when he's away, he finds his mind drifting back. In the supermarket, buying school uniforms, running errands, he's always thinking about the training ground, about the meetings to have, about Unai, about the people there, the details waiting for him. Time is tight, so he blends his two worlds. He brings his children to Bodymoor when he can. His youngest, still in his early teens, likes to hold his hand tightly, as if trying to anchor him. After training, they'll shoot hoops together back home, catching up on the moments they've missed. There have been times where, because of travel and the requests of the job, he has not seen them for a week. He loves his family deeply but to give everything to both worlds, he knows he has to stretch himself every single day.

At first, when the Spanish crew arrived in Birmingham, they were alone, no families, no distractions. They all knew they had to survive Unai's demands, the sheer level of details. For Austin, it was about discovering what was normal in this environment. After a few months, and confirmation he was going to stay put, Víctor turned to Austin: 'Ah, you've done well to survive here.' The set-piece specialist laughed and replied, 'Challenging can also be good.'

'Ah, Austin, you have to remember,' Víctor added, 'our job, the long hours and all that, is to normalise the abnormal.'

Unai remains supportive when things go wrong but demanding when they go well, always pushing for improvement, maintaining accountability while fostering trust. He rarely offers direct praise, yet he also avoids harsh criticism for mistakes. Instead, he takes responsibility, using setbacks as opportunities for growth. A clear example of this came after a Liverpool match when issues with set-pieces arose and were blamed by many commentators for conceding two goals. Rather than assigning blame, he addressed the problem constructively, focusing on solutions.

Of the ten Spanish staff who joined Unai on day one, nine arrived from Villarreal – his *Money Heist* band – but he felt he needed one more. Someone with strong social skills, someone who could connect with the security team, the cleaners, the kitchen staff. Someone who would challenge him tactically and who could help him understand even further the nuances of the Premier League, and could help, like Damià, build bridges. That was Pako Ayestarán.

Pako is probably the one staff member with a hand in everything. He's the most experienced in England, having been part of Rafa Benítez's Champions League-winning staff at Liverpool. At this stage of his career, he is calmer, having already navigated the challenges of establishing himself. Unlike a specialist brought in for a defined role, he had to take on multiple responsibilities, discovering his place within the set-up. His intelligence, both socially and professionally, along with his fluency in English, made this integration smooth. Unai's call to Pako came as a surprise. It had been years since they had worked together at Valencia, their relationship fractured by time and circumstance.

Their history stretched back to 2009, to a meeting in a Sevilla hotel. Back then, Unai had driven down from Valencia, Pako from Extremadura, both of them armed with ideas, papers covered in diagrams and structures. Unai was looking for the best fitness coach for Valencia, and Pako was at a crossroads, hoping to eventually become a manager himself. They spent 4 hours sketching out what their work together might look like. And yet, despite the effort, despite the time, something had never quite fitted. Their season together had been difficult, an awkward dance of two minds who struggled to meet in the middle. A newspaper interview, where Ayestarán expressed his desire to be a head coach, had raised eyebrows. It had marked him. By the end, Pako left. Unai felt it was for the best. There had been the occasional check-in, a phone call here, a passing conversation there, but nothing substantial. Life has a way of circling back, and Unai does not bear grudges. Now, he wanted to meet Pako again. At first, it seemed casual, but something was in the air. Unai was on the verge of something new, weighing options, considering paths. One of them led to Newcastle. Another, still unclear at the time, to Aston Villa.

Weeks passed, then another call. This time, there was urgency. 'Let's meet,' Unai said. Pako agreed, thinking it would be the usual talk of tactics, training and philosophies. But then Unai clarified: 'Tonight. In Villarreal. After our match.' So, late into the night, Pako found himself walking into Unai's hotel, the air thick with unspoken history. Emery got straight to the point. He had thought about this moment, had considered what people would say. 'There were those who asked why I would call you again, knowing how things were before. But I told them, I want the best, so I need to talk to Pako.'

Then, a moment of raw honesty from Ayestarán. 'I know I made mistakes. You're catching me at a different stage in my career. I think now, I can serve you better.' Pako had certainly changed. He had learnt that a head coach doesn't need problems but solutions. He had been too rigid back then, too determined to carve his own path, and it had cost him opportunities.

Unai made his case: 'We were different people then, in different moments. Now, I want you with me.'

Football has changed since they both started their coaching careers. At Liverpool, in 2004, five staff members handled everything. The role of the manager has also shifted, it is no longer about controlling everything but about structuring the right team. Unai knew this. Pako understood it, too. Sitting in another hotel thirteen years after their first encounter, Pako listened to Unai lay out his vision. He needed someone who could reach where he couldn't, whether that was on the pitch, in training or in general communications. 'I don't want to repeat my mistakes at Arsenal. I was too alone. I need someone who is there, everywhere. Even when I go to the bathroom, I need someone who sees what I don't.'

So, their paths converged once again. And Pako, like Damià, needed to apply his charm to make sure things worked from day one as there was no hiding from the fact that the cultural shift at Bodymoor Heath was real. That transformation wasn't cosmetic – it touched every corner of the club. What had previously been casual, even improvised, became methodical. Communication improved, systems were introduced, responsibilities became clearer. Support staff – chefs, physios, kit-room staff – could feel the transformation. For many, this was disorientating at first. Some British employees quietly questioned their place in this new model, but what eventually won everyone over wasn't the language or the nationality of the staff, it was the consistency. Unai's team didn't speak about revolution, they lived it in the routine. The sheer volume of work, the relentless attention to detail, the results. It became impossible not to respect it. Their commitment extended well beyond matchdays. Everyone around them saw it, and over time, began to mirror it. The common goal – winning – became the glue.

Phil Roscoe, who joined the club in May 2022 after seventeen years at Liverpool, also played a crucial role in aligning this off-pitch transformation. In charge of player care, he arrived to find a club that hadn't yet built the support systems needed to match its ambitions. Everything was fragmented. This person does that little bit, this person does this other bit. Mostly the flashy stuff, like perks. The culture around player care was not based around what can be done for the player to perform to his highest level possible. Communication was uneven, practical help for players and their families was inconsistent, and the processes that should have been standard were either missing or met with resistance. Roscoe sat down with one of the first players he visited at their home and quickly understood why things hadn't been working. They felt isolated. Their family lacked visas, there were unresolved medical issues and they hadn't been properly connected to the club's infrastructure. The player was scathing, not out of bitterness but because he'd been left unsupported. Roscoe left that meeting with a clear sense of what needed to change. And under Emery, it did. Now, when a player arrives – like Pau Torres, for example – everything is ready. He gets asked, 'Who are you? What is your family like? What do you need?' Immediately, housing is sorted. Medical appointments scheduled. Schooling arranged. The player's partner and children are looked after just as carefully as the player himself. The club builds a circle around them, making the transition seamless. That's not a luxury. It's the foundation of performance.

Depending on the kick-off time, players often stay in a hotel the night before, and it's Phil who stands at the door with the clipboard in hand. 'Where are they? What's going on?' If someone is late, it's on Phil. It's not a case of 'Oh, the player didn't sort his booking.' No, Phil takes responsibility. That is his job. There's a system in place for tracking arrivals, but it's not about punishment. Phil doesn't go to the manager to report a player for being late. He only brings it up if Unai asks. 'Why is he late?' the manager might say. Then the next questions would be: 'How can we help him? How can we educate him so it doesn't happen again?' There are no fines imposed from above. The players handle that themselves.

Roscoe feels trusted. He has the freedom to do his job. If the manager were to walk into his office right now and say, *Phil, I need 10 per cent more from you*, it would hit him hard. He'd think, *Am I not doing enough?* But then, just as quickly, he'd be up and ready: *Alright, come on then.* That's the feeling around the building. Whatever Unai needs, everyone is in.

A bit like Liverpudlian Phil Roscoe, the Scotsman Austin MacPhee found himself in a unique position. Not fully part of an 'English group', not part of the 'Spanish group', he and Phil had become a kind of informal bridge between both. They helped create a real sense of togetherness. And building a culture like that? It's hard. It can fall apart in 5 minutes. The real challenge is keeping it together. Winning helps, of course, as well as clarity in the direction they are moving. Austin's proximity to the coaching team has given him insight into the way Emery operates. In those early weeks, Unai asked him constant questions: about the squad, about personalities, about the mood in the dressing room. Why did Tyrone Mings lose the captaincy? What were the internal dynamics? Austin, having seen the team struggle before, was the only one who could offer that context.

Emery returned to those questions only once – when the team hit a difficult patch. Winning would become the norm quite quickly, but when results dipped, he wanted to know: what happens to this group when things go wrong? Once Unai felt he understood where he was – and who the people were that he crossed paths with daily at the training ground – he chose to deliver a speech. It was before the 2023–24 season, shortly after signing his new five-year contract. He wanted to clearly set out his vision from within. 'The 1980s belonged to Liverpool. The 1990s to Manchester United. The 2000s to United and Chelsea. The 2010s and 2020s to Manchester City.' Then he added: he was here because he believed Aston Villa could dominate the 2030s. That moment, spoken with conviction, crystallised the project for many. Staff who had once felt uncertain about their place in a Spanish-led structure now felt included in something far bigger. Because the message was about purpose.

Outside the formal environment, bonds were forming too. In the early months, before families had relocated, staff met regularly at a local pub. They'd go every Thursday and talk football, plug laptops into the pub's TV, share food, argue over systems and roles. Over time, the Spanish staff's families moved over. Children started school. Wives settled. The club, once in flux, began to feel anchored. Competitive. Stable. Logically much was made of the tactical overhaul and the influx of Spanish staff. But quieter changes – such as in the kitchen – spoke just as loudly. In March 2024, Michael Bache joined as executive performance chef, tasked with aligning food with the club's high-performance demands.

With fifteen years of experience in elite sport, Michael understood the brief. But Bodymoor Heath operated differently. Standards were very high, and everyone – chefs included – was expected to match them. The kitchen evolved into another cultural crossover, blending British ingredients with the Mediterranean habits of the growing Spanish contingent. Fresh, seasonal food became the norm: vegetables, olive oil, fish, shellfish, high-quality proteins. He adapted quickly, though not without learning the hard way. One of his first paellas included chorizo. The Spanish coaches were merciless. The next attempt was textbook: fish, shellfish, no chorizo. This time, he earned praise and a pat on the back from Unai. The kitchen has since become a quiet symbol of the club's rising standards.

That culture showed its value during a preseason trip to the USA. A last-minute flight issue forced the squad back to a hotel with limited facilities. Michael sprang into action. He called the kitchen staff he'd already built relationships with, knew what ingredients were left and had food cooking before the team arrived. Within 30 minutes of their return, dinner was on the table. Unai Emery thanked the staff personally. For him it was another example of how, across every corner of the club, people have raised their level.

The Spanish-speaking group continued to grow. Language classes expanded, with British staff now learning Spanish, just as the Spanish arrivals took English lessons. Among the new recruits were physiotherapists Igor Saavedra and Carmen Márquez Sánchez, along with fitness coach Hugo Sánchez, who works closely with the goalkeepers and also supports on the pitch and in the gym. Added to that was Mexican nutritionist Elisa Ceñal, the club's lead in her area, whose role goes far beyond menus and meal plans. She works at the heart of performance, overseeing every detail of what players consume, how they recover and how they're physically prepared for the relentless demands of the Premier League. With a PhD in sports nutrition and over a decade of elite experience, she brings both scientific rigour and cultural awareness to a job that is becoming more sophisticated by the day. Her work rests on four pillars: body composition analysis (tracking muscle mass and fat levels, crucial in such a physical league), supplementation, blood work and diagnostics, and innovation – using tools like DNA or microbiome studies to personalise every plan. From what a player eats 24 hours before kick-off to how they recover the night after, her remit is total. Team sport but personalised support.

Elisa's journey to Birmingham started far from the Premier League. Born and trained in Mexico, she began working unpaid in the women's team at Pachuca, while still juggling commitments with Olympic sports and making regular trips to Mexico City to work with triathletes and divers. Over time, she rose through the ranks – from women's football to the academy, then the first team and eventually overseeing the club's entire nutrition pro-gramme. She later joined the Mexican national team set-up before the Premier League opportunity came calling. Recommended by Pako Ayestarán, who knew her work though they'd never worked together directly, she relocated to the UK with her husband and began a new chapter. At Villa, she brings more than expertise. She represents a shift – still slow, still challenging – in the gender make-up of technical staff. There are still very few women in foot-ball environments like this. Elisa shares a lot of time with Carmen Márquez, the team physiotherapist. The women's changing room has had to be expanded recently. 'What a nice problem to have,' she says. They are still a minority, but for Elisa, that's part of the point. 'It's difficult,' she says, 'but it's also beautiful. Because open-ing doors always is.'

She speaks about the responsibility of representation with a quiet confidence. 'This isn't just our fight,' she explains. 'It has to be a shared one. If the men on these staffs don't believe in it, then it doesn't move forward.' That's why Unai Emery's leadership has meant so much. He's curious, attentive, open. He doesn't just work with people, he wants to know where they're from, what they've lived. Elisa has worked with many coaches but few who take the time to ask what's happening in your country or to engage with who you are beyond your title. 'That kind of connection,' she says, 'makes the day-to-day different. It makes the work deeper.'

In England, the 'banter' of football still shapes much of the dressing-room language. Elisa notices how often someone makes a joke, then turns to her and quickly says: 'Sorry, sorry.' Sometimes she doesn't even catch it. 'I'm on airplane mode,' she laughs, but the self-awareness is clear. She's worked in Mexico, where double meanings and off-colour humour were more common. Here, people pause. They adjust. It's not perfect, but it's progress. That's been her experience at Villa, too: a high-performance environment that respects quality above everything. She's here not because she's a woman, but because she's exceptional at what she does. However, the visibility of her role, alongside Carmen's, also matters. Her presence is a revolution in its own right.

Unai's leadership is direct and decisive. Training is not a collaborative debate, he dictates most of the sessions with clarity and authority. While staff members can offer inputs about the session, the overall vision remains his. Remarkably, he operates without conventional coaching materials; there is no structured session plan, no pre-printed templates with football diagrams. Instead, he works from blank paper, jotting down ideas in a free-flowing manner. This is where Pako and Pablo become essential. They translate Unai's vision into structure. Every detail, from dimensions to drills, is precisely executed. They ensure that every session is documented. They maintain a video diary of all their work, allowing for refinement.

In fact, one of the biggest changes in Unai's evolution as a coach has been in his approach to training design. In his early years, he personally shaped each training plan on a day-to-day basis rather than following a rigid weekly schedule. For his staff, this

Pajarito Emery was the first goalkeeper to concede a goal in LaLiga, but he was much more than that, of course. He was the first in the Emery family to play as a goalkeeper for Real Unión, a tradition that was carried on by Unai's father, Antonio, and Unai's son, Lander.

Left Unai played 5 games for Real Sociedad in the first division and even scored one goal. Whilst there, he made many friends that would become crucial in his future coaching career, such as Roberto Olabe and Mikel Etxarri.

Right His son Lander is, of course, a constant presence in the life of Unai but the evolution of their relationship shows the difficulties football managers go through to balance life with the profession.

'En las fiestas' is how Unai calls this image in his photo album. Going to his annual village festival is a way to reconnect with friends and family, but also with himself. He needs his roots so that he may stand tall.

Unai's uncle Román (right) became a father figure to Unai. Román used to take Unai and Igor (left), Unai's brother and now president of Real Unión, to training as kids.

Unai (right) and his brother Koldo (left) as children. Football was ever present in the Unai family. All four kids played it, but only Unai became a professional. Koldo was part of well-known music bands in the Basque country.

Unai's mother, Amelia, is a force of nature. Now in her 80s, she swims in the sea each day. The pair often have heated political discussions, but Unai goes back to being a son (not the leader of a football club) when he is in her presence.

Unai wishes now he had spoken more with his dad Juan. But he learnt from him the need for responsibility (to have respect for your rivals, for your job, for your pupils, for the fans, for the owners, and your obligation to give absolutely everything all the time) in everything he does in football.

Unai likes to visit the Virgin of Guadalupe, near his village. He practices religion on his own terms, more cultural faith than religious devotion. He is a symbolic believer, someone who values the meaning of religious practice more than its doctrine.

At Lorca, Unai's first managerial job, he didn't pay much attention to his appearance. He had to work hard to earn the respect that came with authority. As usual with him, the targets were met ahead of schedule. (Getty Images)

The suit appears with a tie linked to the club he is managing. Almería was the perfect platform to confirm that Unai was a hard-working manager and a winner. (Getty Images)

Unai was 36 years old when he signed for Valencia, a club that had exaggerated expectations due to a brilliant recent past, but the expectations did not reflect the context of a club in disarray. The recognition for his work there – three consecutive third-place finishes in LaLiga – came long after he had moved on. (Getty Images)

UEFA CHAMPIONS LEAGUE

Above The short spell at Spartak Moscow is reflected in this photograph. It was difficult, Unai felt abandoned by the club and realised the powerful need for direct communication with players, not through a translator. (Getty Images)

Sevilla changed Unai's understanding of what truly matters in football. It was there that he won his first major title and cemented his place in European football history with three consecutive Europa League trophies. (Getty Images)

At every club, Unai had to adjust and rethink his approach to implementing his methods. At PSG he had to deal with Neymar and Mbappé, and superstars like that do not accept long video sessions easily. (Getty Images)

At Arsenal Unai fulfilled a dream: managing in the Premier League. He also learnt what he was never going to do again — he could not manage a club of that stature without holding enough authority and being isolated. (Getty Images)

Villarreal was a huge turning point. Unai knew that it might have been the last chance to be recognised as an elite manager. He was backed by the owners and transformed his football style, winning the club's first title and beating Manchester United in the Europa League final. (Getty Images)

At Aston Villa, everything revolves around a central trio: Unai Emery, Damià Vidagany, and Monchi. Their shared past is rich and fascinating, their relationship forms one of the strongest synergies you'll find in football. They are the engines driving the club forward.

Even holidays become working meetings. The bond between Nassef Sawiris and the club's three pillars is seamless — a relationship built on trust, open dialogue, and shared ambition.

In the USA, Wes Edens has always welcomed the trio with warmth and generosity. Beyond hospitality, Edens openly acknowledges how much he has learned from Unai and his team's work ethic and methods.

Above The Money Heist crew. Unai has learnt to delegate, but also to expand his circle of trusted assistants, each one an expert in a specific area of the game. This group operates at the cutting edge of modern football. Walking into Bodymoor Heath feels like stepping into NASA headquarters.

Left Unai has immense respect for the fans, but more than that, he needs them to generate the right kind of energy. For that to happen, he first makes sure they understand what he's trying to build. One of his greatest achievements at the club may be how he transformed the way Villa Park thinks about football. (Getty Images)

Jhon Durán was a challenge for Unai. The manager was the one who never lost faith in him, but Durán felt his path was a different one. There is a touch of sadness when Unai talks about the Colombian. (Getty Images)

Marcus Rashford arrived at Bodymoor Heath having been warned that Unai Emery wasn't like most managers. What Emery encountered, however, was a young man eager to impress, polite, shy, and someone who had slightly lost his way. 'You will be an international again,' Unai told him. (Getty Images)

Unai is genuinely struck by Prince William's humility and deep passion for Aston Villa. The Prince listens attentively, yet offers thoughtful remarks and questions that reveal a true fan's insight. For Unai and his staff, his presence feels less like royalty, and more like a devoted supporter stepping into their usually hermetic world.

could be challenging. At times, even 10 minutes before training, there was no clear outline of what was coming. During his time at Valencia, for instance, he operated in a constant state of urgency, focused solely on winning the next match at any cost. Challenges were met head-on. He would identify a problem in a match and immediately design a solution for it, often creating drills on the spot in the final minutes before training. His idea was clear: each session was a standalone event. 'I have to give the training session the importance it deserves today. Tomorrow, I'll see what life brings.'

But, as Emery recently learnt from the Marseille chairman Pablo Longoria in a discussion about manager Roberto De Zerbi, one of the key challenges for modern managers is organising the club's information flow to protect the mental and physical sharpness of the head coach. So now, at the highest level of management, he still directs operations, but he has learnt to pace himself, recognising the importance of managing energy and delegation to sustain his intensity, ensuring he remains at peak performance, not just for individual games but across the entire season. So he has started to assign training sessions to his assistants that follow his instructions, while he focuses on other aspects of the team's strategy. This shift reflects a broader trend among elite managers. Pep Guardiola recently acknowledged that while he used to watch five full opposition videos, he now relies on just one carefully curated edit from his staff. On that though, Unai is not there just yet.

Generally, Unai's decision-making process is dynamic. When it comes to scouting and analysing players, he is open to discussions, actively seeking input from his staff before making a final call. However, his decision-making becomes more streamlined and less open to debate when it is related to team selection and substitutions in games. While he occasionally consults his staff, he largely keeps his choices to himself, and as the season progresses and the stakes rise, the trend intensifies. During matches, Unai is selective in receiving feedback. His staff know when he is receptive to input and when he prefers to process the game independently. He once explained that he avoids asking too many opinions because he doesn't want to be distracted or influenced away from his conviction. In any case, Emery's staff play a crucial role in his success. Their job is not just to analyse and suggest, but also to create an environment of trust and high performance, where Unai can focus on decision-making. The assistants' contributions also ensure that the players aren't always hearing the same voice.

Unai Emery's methodology is not simply a coaching style but a surgical strategy for imposing clarity in a world defined by chaos. Like Pep Guardiola, Emery obsesses over control, but where Guardiola leans into aesthetics and philosophy, Emery focuses on functionality and survival. He is a craftsman closer in nature to Marcelo Bielsa, who famously lives in a modest flat near club training grounds and watches matches alone with a stopwatch, or, outside of football, akin to Jeff Bezos in his Amazon years: precise, data-obsessed, demanding and absolutely committed to the process over the personality. For Emery, the authority doesn't come from force of presence but from the consistency of thought and the credibility of action. In this way, Emery resembles what psychologists call a 'system-builder' – someone who leads not through charisma or emotion, like a José Mourinho or a Steve Jobs, or through relationships, like Carlo Ancelotti, but through systems, detail and long-term coherence.

But Emery also knows his own limitations. He fears his own ego. He worries about selfishness creeping in, about losing sight of the collective. He fights it in the only way he knows how: total immersion. Football is a test of conviction, and Emery's is forged from the certainty that no one will outthink or outwork him.

A never-ending chess game.

10

THE FIRST KEY GAMES:

IN UNAI'S WORDS

SEASON 2022-23

After the World Cup break, Aston Villa returned to the league with a 1–3 defeat to Liverpool on 26 December. Then came a 0–2 away win against Tottenham, followed by a 1–1 draw with Wolves in early January, and then wins against Leeds (2–1) and Southampton (0–1). The team was still inconsistent, still finding its feet. Then came three shocking defeats and Unai's ultimatum to the squad.

Aston Villa 2–4 Leicester, 4 February 2023; Manchester City 3–1 Aston Villa, 12 February 2023; Aston Villa 2–4 Arsenal, 18 February 2023

After the World Cup, it became clear that the team still lacked a solid, reliable structure. The matches against Leicester and Arsenal taught us a lot. They were a turning point. We conceded eight goals at Villa Park, and in between that, City put three past us away from home. It was a difficult stretch.

When we lose, I suffer a lot, especially that same day. At that point I need to be around my people, the staff, those closest to me. I need to talk, debate, reflect. Sometimes we argue, sometimes we laugh. We spend hours after games dissecting everything – what we did, what we didn't, what we could've done better. But when we lose, they know they have to let me get it all out. I need that process. It's how I reset. But usually, by the next morning, I come back. I have to. I get up, face the group and take the bull by the horns.

That first defeat against Leicester, though, left a bitter taste that didn't fade so easily. There was something deeper beneath it, something unsettling. At that time, the team was often swept up by the energy of the crowd, who wants everything to happen quickly, right away. I told the players, 'We need to educate the fans.' Not in a negative way, just to help them understand that our tempo, fast or slow, has to be ours, not dictated by anxiety or impulse. They had to understand that patience and passing create real chances. In England, at Villa Park, the crowd often wanted you to run and shoot from anywhere, but we had to change that mindset. Especially at home, I kept telling the players, 'We need to play in an organised way, to control the rhythm of the match.' We can speed up or slow down, but we have to be comfortable with those changes.

Arsenal were the next team that came to our ground, a team that would finish runners-up in the league. Another 2–4 defeat. At 2–2 we had a huge chance, and then in the final moments, they scored two more. One of those goals came after our goalkeeper went up for a corner. I'll be honest, I don't like that. Not in a league match at home. I said so publicly, and I spoke to Emiliano [Martínez] about it. I understand the emotion, but when the keeper goes up and you don't score, you lose all structure. Whether you lose 2–3 or 2–4 might not matter much on paper, but to me, that detail does matter. I want order. After *that, I told the players very clearly, 'That's it. From now on, we play with organisation and with our heads more than our hearts.'*

I said, 'If I can't implement my way of playing, then I have no reason to be here. The buzz of the new coach has passed. Now it's time to work with a method, with a clear idea and a style we can build on.' From that point onwards, we had to look for players who matched that style, who could thrive in the Premier League, bringing those qualities of structure and intelligence. We went to play Everton knowing we needed a shift. We won 0–2, and it was a match we controlled. That was the beginning.

At home, we began to slow the game down, to bring calm into our play. We moved the ball through passes, progressed when we could. And when we couldn't, we didn't panic. We stayed composed. The crowd whistled sometimes. Emiliano stayed calm, starting from the back, waiting for the right moment to move forward. It was a process, not just with the players but with the fans as well. I said it in press conferences, with respect but also clarity: this would only work if we all understood the direction we were going in. And fans eventually did.

We started a good run: Crystal Palace (1–0), West Ham (1–1), Bournemouth (3–0), Chelsea (0–2, which took us into the European spots and sadly cost Graham Potter his job), Leicester (1–2 with a goal in the last few minutes from Bertrand Traoré), Nottingham Forest (2–0), Newcastle (our rivals for the European places, 3–0, two goals from Watkins). Little by little, we climbed the table.

That change in mentality and style led to a run of ten games unbeaten and then something even more powerful: fifteen straight home wins in the league, across two seasons. For me, it was one of the most brilliant experiences I've had here, to feel that connection with the fans, to see them understand what we were trying to do. The key is about reducing risk. If a team usually takes eight corners, limit them to two. If they cross fifteen times, keep it to six. And how do you do that? Generally, by having the ball. By dictating the tempo. When the opponent gives you space to run, we run. If they don't, then we make the game ours. That balance, that sense of control, it became our identity. Against teams like City, yes, they will have their moments, where we'll have to suffer, where we won't have the ball. But even then, I want us to try to impose our idea. If we can't do so, then we adapt, but we're always looking for the moment to hurt them.

One of Emery's smartest tactical shifts was pushing Villa's defensive line higher, turning the offside trap into a weapon. By May 2023, they'd caught opponents offside 163 times – far ahead of Liverpool's 93, second in that table – and averaged a European-best 4.8 offsides per game. Meanwhile, they were caught offside themselves just twelve times, the second-lowest in the league. The small details made the team more effective. At home, Villa Park was turning into a fortress, starting with a 1–0 win over Crystal Palace in March, making their fifteen straight Premier League home victories their best run since 1983. Edens and Sawiris rarely attended Villa matches. That changed as their admiration for Emery grew and as they began to see a team that was not only improving but winning.

Liverpool 1–1 Aston Villa, 20 May 2023

What makes me proudest here is the way we're building a strong mentality. I'm very demanding when it comes to work.

My players joke about how strict I am. Sometimes they tease me, saying I'm always serious, always focused. I've seen other coaches – Marco Silva at Fulham, for example, who I like a lot and have a good relationship with – who always looks angry. I get the feeling that sometimes I come across in the same way [laughs]. But I think the players understand that while I can be light-hearted in the right moment, when it's time to work, I don't compromise.

The players were becoming really competitive in training, and I liked that, it showed they were engaged. But I also wanted them to control their emotions. There was one session where Emi Buendía asked for a foul, play continued, but he kept complaining. He was close to me, so I said, 'Come on, you can see the ref is not giving it, keep playing!' I gave him a proper telling-off right there on the pitch in front of everyone. You have to maintain focus at all times. I had a few of those with Buendía, a kid I really like but who sometimes gets on my nerves! He is intense, and sometimes that came out in training, but I understood it came from a place of frustration. He could see the value in what we were trying to build, though not everyone embraced it in the same way at first. I told him to trust me, to stay calm. That it was my job to bring everyone on to the same page. And that's exactly what happened.

Some players did struggle with the changes at the beginning, but once we started winning regularly, everything began to fall into place. With Emi Buendía, like everyone else, it was about refining his instincts. He used to feel that he had to be everywhere on the pitch, constantly on the ball to feel involved. I helped him to understand something different, that staying in his zone, trusting the structure, would connect him to the game in a better way. In defence too, he learnt to be more efficient.

Not chasing everything but staying where he could actually make an impact. These are habits you build over time. And once a player sees they work, sees the result of something they've been told and shown, it reinforces the whole idea. He began to realise that maybe he wouldn't touch the ball ten times, but if he touched it three times in the right position, he'd create more.

I remember one assist he provided for Ollie Watkins that led to an equaliser. We had shown him in video sessions, 'If you reach the byline, deliver the ball to the penalty spot.' We repeated it so many times that when that exact moment came, he crossed without thinking, without even looking. That's how deep the idea had settled. He told me after the game, 'I knew if I put the ball there, the striker would be there, because that's what we'd been taught repeatedly. If he's not, that's on him. I did what was asked.' When you influence his instinct, that's when you know a player has fully understood.

I believe more and more in the collective contribution of coaches and the multi-directional nature of football when it comes to performance. You have to work on the pitch, of course, but also with the group dynamic. Then there's the individual: sometimes you speak to a player during the week, sometimes it's just before the match, when you know the right moment to reach him emotionally, to find his motivation. Sometimes you shout at him, other times you let him go. Then there's everything outside the pitch, managing what comes from above: the sporting director, the owners. Football moves in many directions at once. To keep a high standard across all those areas, I think today's managers are living with their minds constantly switched on 24 hours a day, searching for answers to everything. I am learning to delegate in order to reach everywhere.

At the end of that first season at the club, there was one match that really stuck with me, not because of the scoreline but because of what it meant: the 1–1 draw against Liverpool at Anfield, the second-to-last game of the league campaign. That match demanded everything from us. Focus, discipline, belief. Liverpool were still fighting for a place in the Champions League. They needed the points. It was Roberto Firmino's farewell at Anfield, a very emotional night for them. We had just beaten Tottenham at Villa Park, and we knew that getting a result at Anfield could be decisive in our push for a place in the Europa Conference League . . . only seven months after the team were close to the bottom three! And we played well.

Sometimes, other coaches joke about my ability to 'predict' what will happen in a game. But it's not prediction. Klopp had just started using Trent Alexander-Arnold in a hybrid midfield role, stepping into central areas when Liverpool had the ball. I saw an opportunity. I gave the players two clear scenarios. First: if we win the ball on the right and Trent is committed to attack, we find a midfielder quickly and then Ollie runs into the space left by Trent – we'll find Watkins. Second: if we go back to Emi Martínez and Mings drops very deep, we can draw the Liverpool press to the left side. [Mo] Salah will press hard, but if he's had to run 50 metres forward and Trent isn't following him, there will be plenty of space to exploit.

On the day, we recovered the ball, Salah had gone, Trent was still high and McGinn played the ball into the channel for Watkins. He went one-on-one with Konaté and won a penalty. We missed it – but we had created a moment of danger. We then lost both our left-backs – Àlex Moreno and Lucas Digne – to injury. In the end, Ashley Young, with all his experience, stepped in at left-back and gave us everything. It was a real *battle. Jacob Ramsey, in his hundredth appearance for the team, scored first. Then Firmino equalised in the 89th minute – football does that sometimes, it gives little gifts to the storyline, even if you're on the wrong side of it. But that point meant everything. It was a serious performance, and it showed exactly what this team had become in a relatively short amount of time. Competitive.*

That makes me proud.

Aston Villa 2–1 Brighton, 28 May 2023

In the dressing room, we pushed the message through the captains. Emiliano Martínez was key in that process, he supported me from the beginning. At first, finishing in the top ten was considered ambitious, but for me, it wasn't enough. I wanted more. I spoke openly about qualifying for Europe. When I joined Aston Villa, I told the club's owners: 'Look, I've spent thirteen consecutive seasons playing in European competitions. So, it's hard to accept not being in Europe now.'

Europe has given me so much – knowledge, experience, perspective. I love what it represents: a chance to face new football cultures, new countries. Yes, the Premier League is the most demanding domestic league, but I believe it's possible to build the mentality and strength to compete in both.

Emiliano helped carry that message into the group. Even when we were far from the European spots, we set clear targets. I looked at Brentford, Fulham and especially Brighton. Brighton felt like a real benchmark – a club clearly on its way to Europe. So that became our target: catch Brighton. If we could do that, we could get close to Europe. I remember Emiliano saying to the dressing room, 'If we can win two or three matches in a row, we'll have a real chance at Europe.' Some teammates were sceptical, but he kept repeating it. It was about raising the bar of expectations, even if we fell short.

For me, that was the biggest shift in mentality I brought here: we have to set high goals, even if they feel out of reach. And if we fail, so what? We fail trying. I'd rather feel frustration in the effort than settle into comfort without ambition. That's the kind of frustration I can live with.

And there was something else very pleasing for me. I really enjoy working with the defensive line – shaping it, adjusting it, watching it grow. I remember when we started pushing the line higher, and suddenly I saw the centre-backs, especially Mings and Konsa, fully believing in the idea. They stopped dropping too deep, they no longer collapsed into the box. Some of my assistants would say, 'Unai, this is too risky.' But I'd reply, 'How can I change it now? Look at them, they're not just doing it, they're enjoying it.' Because they understand that holding that line means we can win the ball higher and from there, build further up the pitch.

It's a strange feeling, like you've created a kind of automaton and we were Doctor Frankenstein. You build something, shape it carefully . . . and then, suddenly, it walks on its own. In the end, we climbed from eighth to seventh. And we did it by beating Brighton on the final day at Villa Park. We didn't finish above them, but we beat them – and that win secured our place in the Conference League. There were celebrations all round. The group, the coaches, the owners, loved the fact that next season we were going to compete in Europe, ending a twelve-year wait.

SEASON 2023–24

Ahead of the 2023–24 season, Emery was given more freedom in the market and made key additions. Pau Torres arrived from Villarreal for £47 million, bringing composure and passing quality to the back line, while, when it became clear Villa could not get Nico Williams from Athletic Bilbao, Moussa Diaby joined from Bayer Leverkusen for £51.9 million with add-ons, quickly forming a sharp understanding with Watkins in attack. Nicolò Zaniolo and Clément Lenglet came in on loan, adding valuable European experience. Youri Tielemans joined on a free from Leicester City. Aston Villa offset part of their summer 2023 spending by generating around £40 million in player sales, including £18 million from Cameron Archer and £12 million from Aaron Ramsey.

Emery's first preseason was intense, packed with travel, including a US tour, and a heavy match schedule that pushed players harder than under previous regimes. Despite the fatigue and knocks from the final friendly against Valencia, the commitment from footballers and staff never wavered. Emery kept Aston Villa on course, as key players suffered major injuries. Tyrone Mings, who had once been criticised by Steven Gerrard, had regained both form and authority at the heart of defence, only to suffer a season-ending ACL tear in the opening match against Newcastle. Emi Buendía also sustained a serious knee injury just days before the campaign began. Jacob Ramsey injured his foot while on duty with England's Under 21s, returning briefly to score in a 6–1 win over Brighton, before suffering a setback that sidelined him for seventeen matches. Alex Moreno spent months out with a hamstring problem, leaving Lucas Digne as the only senior left-back available.

And yet, the team thrived. Ollie Watkins, freed from rotating with Danny Ings who had left, became Emery's trusted striker, involved in thirty goals across the manager's first thirty-seven Premier League games, behind only Erling Haaland and Mo Salah in that span. Perhaps most impressive, though, was how Emery transformed a modestly assembled midfield – costing just £26 million – into one of the league's most effective. McGinn (£4 million), Douglas Luiz (£22 million), Kamara (free) and academy product Jacob Ramsey were all integrated seamlessly. Luiz, now the heartbeat of Villa's midfield, matched his total Premier League goal tally from the previous 118 games in just 27 under Emery. Tielemans initially took time to adapt but became another key piece. In contrast to clubs like Chelsea, who spent over £330 million on midfielders like Enzo Fernández and Moisés Caicedo without breaking into the top four in their first season, Emery's approach proved efficient.

One defining moment came in December 2023, when Villa hosted Manchester City at Villa Park. In a break from routine, Emery called a low-intensity training session that morning. He walked the players through tactical patterns and team shape, drilling the specific spaces where City could be exposed. A rotating midfield four created overloads and passing lanes, controlling the game from the start. The 1–0 scoreline didn't tell the full story as Villa dominated in possession, intensity and chances. They weren't punching above their weight anymore. They were competing on equal ground with the elite.

Then, three days later, they beat Arsenal at Villa Park by the same score. Back-to-back wins over the previous season's top two and the two teams fighting for the title again. What Emery called 'the most difficult week' became a statement of intent. Villa were establishing themselves as one of Europe's best-run clubs.

Parallel to the advances on the pitch, on 28 November 2023, V Sports – Nassef Sawiris and Wes Edens' holding company – announced a strategic partnership with lower-league Spanish club Real Unión, the historic Basque club Unai's grandfather and father had once played for, and that was barely surviving in the third tier of Spanish football. It provided full backing to what is a personal initiative for Unai: to take and establish the club in professional football. Just months earlier, in June, Emery and his brother Igor had also acquired a controlling stake in Real Unión. Strengthening ties between Villa and Real Unión meant enhancing the club's footballing structure, allowing the two to share methodologies, particularly in coaching, scouting and data.

Close to the end of the season, Villa travelled to London to meet Arsenal once again.

Arsenal 0–2 Aston Villa, 14 April 2024

For the 2023–24 season I wanted us to control the ball more, that's why we brought in Pau Torres. Actually, when I joined Aston Villa, I spoke with Pau. I wanted to bring him in sooner, ideally in January 2023, because I knew how well he understood my ideas. But Pau told me Villarreal was his home, his lifelong club, and he wanted to finish the season there, to leave properly, not walk away mid-campaign. I respected that completely. It said a lot about his character, and that's the kind of player I wanted with me at Villa.

We also looked for a number ten who could offer depth more than just feet to the ball, Diaby attacked the space well. Then, in the winter transfer window, Morgan Rogers arrived. As well as Diaby, I was looking for a number ten or second striker who could come inside, combine and connect with others, and that's exactly what Morgan brought.

We've come a long way but adapting to what I want isn't easy, even for new signings. Someone like Pau Torres already knew the demands, he understands where I want the passes, the pace, the positioning. But others come from completely different systems and need months to grasp what we ask of them, in both attack and defence. It's a long, demanding process and not everyone gets there.

When I arrived at Aston Villa, my objective was clear: I wanted us to reach Europe. And once we achieved that earlier than expected, the next question was, what now? Next was to establish ourselves consistently among the top teams that qualify for Europe regularly. Once you're in that position, then yes, the next step is to compete in the Champions League, not just be present.

And how to do that? By building a structure that gives us identity and stability to be able to compete against any rival in the world. The players have to understand where they need to be – positionally, tactically – and we work on specific patterns, both in attack and defence. That repetition gives us a base, something we can rely on. I am not trying to be invincible, but I want the team to have a clear idea of our style of play, one that gives the players confidence. We give the team both freedom and discipline, they know the system and within that, they can express themselves. At the end of the 2023–24 season we were certainly getting there.

That season, we'd already beaten Arsenal at home, and Chelsea and Tottenham away, teams fighting for the same places we were. But the match that truly opened the door to the Champions League was the one at the Emirates. Arsenal were in great form. They had just drawn against Bayern at home in the Champions League, while we had beaten Lille at Villa Park in the first leg of the Conference League quarter-finals. I knew that to win in London we had to adapt, we had to make the game as long and uneventful as possible. That was the strategy: few chances, little chaos. If the game was slow paced, with little flow, we could feel comfortable in that kind of discomfort. And we hoped they wouldn't. Especially with their minds partly on the second leg in Munich.

Before every match, I tend to write a message on the dressing room whiteboard. It's something I've always done, a ritual. Sometimes it's simple: the league table, the target, the 3 points. Sometimes I'll ask a question or get the players involved. I like them to think. To understand not just the what but the why behind our decisions. For instance, to shift the players' mentality, I write things like 'We must win.' It's about instilling the mindset that winning is the only option. For Arsenal, I wrote one word: 'Crucial'. I meant it. I knew that if we won, it would give us the push we needed to reach the end. There were five Premier League matches left. I also knew if we needed points at the end of the season we wouldn't make it. I could sense the effort to participate in different competitions was taking its toll.

Before kick-off, Damià likes to spend fifteen or twenty minutes with me, just to get a sense of how I'm feeling, to see if I need anything, or if there's a player who might need a word. It's part of our connection before the tension of the match begins. I also appreciate when Nassef Sawiris, the co-owner, is present. I like him to be there, in the tunnel, greeting the players. For me, that adds a sense of responsibility, not just for me but for the squad. It sends a message: this matters. It raises the level *of expectation. I remember how he started coming to even EFL Cup fixtures.*

That day against Arsenal, I started Zaniolo and Diaby, and left Leon Bailey on the bench, even though he'd played almost every game and had been very good all season. In the 61st minute, I brought him on and said to him, 'Leon, now is the time to win the game.' And he did, stepping up in the 84th minute to break the deadlock. Three minutes later, Watkins sealed it.

It was a match won not just with talent but with maturity, patience and intelligence. That's something I talk about constantly with the players, building a team that is mature, responsible, one that respects the plan, respects one another and knows how to manage the game. Not to be dragged by emotion but to own each moment. That night showed we could do exactly that. Under pressure, we had a clear head. These moments are not easy, especially for young players. But that day was about clarity, experience and especially trust in the plan.

Aston Villa were outliers that season. Statistically, they covered the least distance in the Premier League, pressed with the lowest intensity and ranked near the bottom for tackles and interceptions, yet were just behind Manchester City in some metrics. Confusing data when you see how well the season went for them. Not only were they fighting to be in the Champions League for the first time in forty-two years, they reached the semi-finals of the Europa Conference League.

Emery's structure was built not around constant use of energy but efficiency and control. Actually, Villa conserved energy with a deep build-up, drawing teams in before exploiting the space behind. This approach was aimed at balancing European and domestic demands. Even after a gruelling penalty shoot-out win in Lille, they outlasted Bournemouth a week later, drawing praise for their composure and durability. After that game, Bournemouth's Andoni Iraola remarked to Emery, in admiration: 'Even after extra time, not a single cramp!'

Still, when teams pressed high and turned matches chaotic, Villa struggled. The semi-final against Olympiacos was going to offer that type of challenge. Villa had conceded in almost 80 per cent of league games and let in sixty-one goals in fifty-one games, a record that needed improving. Emery had consistently downplayed talk of a top-four finish, reminding everyone that Villa were 'not contenders yet' and that 'seven teams were more likely' to finish ahead of them. But quietly, the team kept climbing. They were on course but also ahead of schedule.

Then came the final push for Champions League qualification, one last step to try to get a historic achievement.

Aston Villa 3–3 Liverpool, 13 May 2024

We reached the final stretch of the season with a small, exhausted squad. Competing on multiple fronts became impossible. We made it to the semi-finals against Olympiacos – a dynamic, well-oiled team that were difficult to stop with their direct physical football – and were close to qualifying for the Champions League. Reaching the European final would've been fantastic, but what if we'd made the Champions League instead? Which one matters more? That question stayed with me. Ideally, you do both. But sometimes you simply can't. A point comes where you have to choose. In the end, I prioritised the Premier League. That's what gives you everything. Reaching the Champions League changes your career and a club status.

We had four games in twelve days. Against Chelsea at Villa Park [2–2], we got an important point. Then on 2 May, in the Conference League semi-final first leg at home we lost 2–4, with only four changes from the previous game. There wasn't much more to choose from; that was the core of the team. Brighton away [lost 1–0], I rotated three players. In the return leg in Greece [lost 2–0], just two changes. There was no time to breathe, no chance to recover. Every decision counted. Two games left.

Next came Liverpool. The final push.

I knew very clearly that if we arrived at the Crystal Palace match, the last one of the season, without having taken anything from Liverpool, we would most likely lose in London. We were already at our limit – physically, mentally, even I felt it. That match at Villa Park was a last act of strength. Our last chance to qualify for the Champions League.

Liverpool is a club I respect deeply. I have a good relationship with Jürgen Klopp. We've faced each other before – when I was at Sevilla, we beat his Liverpool in the Europa League final, and even though that defeat meant they missed out on European football the following season, they still went out and celebrated as they had planned. That's Klopp, he's charismatic, different.

In this match, they had already secured third place and a return to the Champions League. We started with Emi Martínez making an error, and they went ahead in the first minute. Soon it was 1–3 to them. With 11 minutes left, I replaced Zaniolo, injured only 15 minutes after coming on for Tielemans.

Sometimes I make three changes at half-time. Or four in one go in the second half. Or like this one, a bit of a throw of the dice. You know, when the game is moving, when it's alive and shifting in front of you, you don't always have time to discuss. You feel things. That's something I've learnt over the years. There's no time for committees. No time to open up a laptop, check numbers, ask three people. Sometimes, you just know. It's about intuition, yes, but built on thousands of hours, on years of watching, managing, failing, learning. When I see something on the pitch, I react. I trust what I see. If it's minute 45, or minute 85, it doesn't matter. If the change is needed, it has to be done now, not after another 5 minutes of thinking.

Bam, we're changing. Bam, three subs, or four, or one. The decision's made. And the players have to be ready for that. It's not arrogance. It's not impulse. It's the clarity that comes from having seen it so many times before. From knowing that if I start doubting, if I ask too many questions, I'll miss the moment. And players, they feel that. They see when a coach is certain and when they feel that certainty, they follow. So, I sent on Jhon Durán, hoping he might give us a moment of quality. Or two.

I was on the bench, focused, pushing, encouraging. Klopp looked over and smiled. He asked me, 'What do you need to qualify?'

I told him, 'Winning. That's what we always have to do.'

Jhon scored. That gave us hope. Fans pushed us.

And then, 5 minutes from time, it happened again. A moment of pure instinct and talent. That's what Jhon has, the ability to appear in a difficult moment and make something happen. He saw where Diaby's pass might go, stretched a foot instinctively, took the ball in a different direction . . . and 3–3! He had produced something special, two goals in 3 minutes with only a couple for the game to finish!

I have seen my celebrations after that goal. I don't like seeing myself on television but I caught it some days later. I had turned to the fans and jumped and jumped. My face twisted, shouting something. Pablo was asking for people to be calmed, to think, what was left was to control the emotions and see the game through. That is also football, isn't it? Emotions, shared, that take you to a new planet. The philosopher Plato might have called it a kind of 'divine madness', those rare moments when collective feeling transcends the rational and touches something purer, almost metaphysical. In football, like in art, we are briefly lifted out of ourselves. The game finished 3-3. Our qualification no longer depended on us. We had to wait. Tottenham needed to lose to Manchester City the next day in London. All we could do was hope. What we had done so far was massive. It kept alive the dream of being in the most attractive competition of all.

After matches, I usually go straight into the tunnel. Here, there's a tradition of going out to the fans at the final whistle, but I don't do that. If you win, they'll applaud; if you lose, they'll insult you. And I'm not going to go out only when we win, so I don't go at all. But that night, I broke my own rules. It was the last home game of the season, and we were so close to reaching our goal. I walked around the stadium and applauded the fans, not just to thank them but to share the emotion that overwhelmed me in that moment.

Relief. Happiness for the job done. So many afternoons and evenings together, and we were celebrating that we had reached the target of being in Europe. Perhaps the Champions League. The stadium announcer handed me the mic and asked me to say a few words to the fans. Both owners were in the stands, players were doing the typical end-of-season lap of honour.

I don't even remember exactly what I said, probably something about how proud I was of the season, regardless of what happened with Spurs the next day.

When I finished, Damià nudged me and said, 'Don't forget to shout a big "Up the Villa."' And actually, I liked the idea. I really felt it. So, I grabbed the mic from the announcer and I shouted it to the crowd.

'UP THE VILLAAAA!'

It felt good. Maybe I should share those moments more often, but would I lose the mystique that a leader needs?

Tottenham Hotspur 0–2 Manchester City, 14 May 2024

I still follow the path where it all began. I relate a lot to what happened to Luis Aragonés when he moved from player to coach. Something similar happened to me at Lorca. I was given the chance to go from player to manager midway through the season, and it all happened so fast that I still try to hold on to that moment. But I often remind myself: 'Unai, don't forget how it feels to be a player.' With time, you naturally drift away from that stage, but I don't want to fully lose it. I want to remember how players feel about decisions, about behaviour, about what they like and don't like. Even as I grow older, I try to stay close to that mindset, to treat players the way I would've liked to be treated.

I say everything to the players face to face. That's how I work. And I don't like bothering them when they're with their national teams. I want to respect that space, they're with their people, a different coach, a different style, a different environment. The players know we're watching, that we're following everything, but I prefer not to be present in a way that feels intrusive. I don't mind if the players see me as a teacher or a demanding coach. I'm not trying to be their friend, that's not my role, and it's not possible. But you have to put yourself in their shoes.

Back in my days at Lorca and Almería, I used to train mornings and afternoons on Wednesdays and Thursdays – double sessions, every week. I always tell that story. But over time, I've learnt. I've understood that rest matters, not just for the players but also for the staff. Now, for example, when there's an international break and the game was on a Sunday, I give them two days off. I have been thinking more about managing the workload of the growing list of internationals we have. For those who head to South America, it's incredibly tough – long flights, days spent in hotel camps, constant travel. When they come back jet-lagged and drained, I try to give them space to recover, not just physically but mentally too. Recovery isn't rest – it's part of performance.

It frustrated me when I saw players like Morgan Rogers being called up to the Under 21s. What's the point? He was already a regular starter with us, performing at the highest level, what more is he going to learn there? Look what happened to Jacob [Ramsey], when he picked up a metatarsal fracture while on international duty with England Under 21s in July 2023. I'm glad that now Morgan is with Tuchel, a fully fledged international. He deserves it.

I like to vary what I do with the players, not always do the same thing. I'm not someone who sticks to routines. Sometimes I work with the starting eleven before a game, sometimes I don't. Some days I make things clear early, other times I leave it open – either because I haven't decided yet or because I want to keep the players sharp. But some players reach a limit they can't go beyond. And when that moment comes, it's time for them to move on. In the first two years, we changed half the squad, and those who have come in are growing and helping us grow with this level of demand. Those who were already here, we've improved their contracts. And those who arrived, they're evolving. This is the environment we've built – clear, demanding and focused on progress.

There are all kinds of ways to be a coach, but you still need to tick a few key boxes. A coach has to have knowledge, a strong work ethic, leadership, empathy and, above all, humility. And that one – I always carry with me. Always. These are values I consider essential. And there are more: responsibility, commitment, passion and respect. Passion is the one I bring, it's what I transmit naturally, but I don't name it. Responsibility, though, I use that word a lot. Responsibility means showing up, doing what's asked of you and owning your role. Respect for the badge, for the dressing room, for the institution. It's not about being strict with clocks and timetables. I'm not interested in that kind of discipline. What matters is discipline on the pitch.

Back in the day, there were coaches obsessed with punctuality, watching the door to see who came in late. Me? I haven't handed out fines in years. I don't believe in them. If someone messes up, I might go to them and say, 'Hey, don't do that again.' And I think about how to stop that happening again. But what's the point in fining a player a thousand euros? They earn so much it means nothing. It's like saying, 'Can I be late every day for a thousand euros? Fine, here's your money.' That's not discipline. That's just a transaction.

Then there's commitment to the club, to your teammates. César Luis Menotti once told me: 'Players buy into knowledge, into what the coach knows. And that knowledge has to help them become better, individually and as a group.' But I'd add

301

this: players also buy into how hard you work, your commitment. You can have the best ideas in the world, but if they don't see you putting the hours in, going beyond the basics, they'll stop listening. The idea alone isn't enough. It needs to be developed, tested, lived and that takes time and dedication.

The end-of-season awards is a chance for players to enjoy, relax, even have a couple of drinks if they want to, it is very much their moment. The day after the Liverpool game I was sitting at one of the tables at the Lower Grounds at Villa Park for the event. Everyone was in their place – players, the staff, some of the people who have been with us from the beginning – about to celebrate the 2023–24 campaign. It was meant to be a night to hand out awards, everyone in their expensive suits, lots of smiles. But our eyes kept drifting to the big screens. Spurs were losing. City were doing their part. Are we going to be a Champions League team?

I tried not to let myself go there too early. But you could feel it building. The room was shifting. The talking was converted into loud chatter. All heads turned. And then the noise began to grow, a slow, rising wave. The result was going to hold. Every pass, every clearance from City was greeted with cheers. It was impossible to stay still. I looked around, players on their feet, staff leaning forward, fans with phones in their hands filming the moment. Eyes on the screens.

Then the whistle.

And everything burst.

It hit me all at once.

We had done it. Aston Villa were in the Champions League!

I stood up. I couldn't stop smiling. I looked at Monchi, at Damià, we didn't even need to say anything. We embraced. Because we knew what it had taken. Not just tactics, not just matches won but time, patience. So many things that don't show up on a stat sheet. I took the mic. I had to say something, even if the moment said it all. I had nothing prepared. I said it was a special night. Because it was. But not only for what we achieved, it was special because of how we got there. From the first day, we spoke about being ambitious, about daring to set high standards, but we knew what that meant. It meant long days. Hard conversations. Real commitment.

When I heard John McGinn speak, it moved me more than anything. He talked about being in the Championship. About the handful of them still here from those days. Tyrone Mings, Jacob Ramsey, Kortney Hause, John himself, were the only ones remaining. All four of them, part of that Championship journey and then surviving in the Premier League. That matters. That history is part of this. You can't build something meaningful without roots. We talk a lot about dreams in football. Maybe too much. But this qualification, this moment – it belonged to everyone, we all dreamt it. It belonged to the players. To the staff. To the people in the offices. To the fans who tried to understand what we were doing even when they weren't sure where it was going.

We were about to play in the Champions League. A competition for the best, yes, but also for the ones who understand what it takes to get there. Now that we were there, we wouldn't just take part. We said it clearly: we were going to compete. The aim would be to win it one day like in 1982. In the end, prioritising the league was justified when we qualified for the Champions League and especially when, a few months later, we played the quarter-finals against PSG!

By the way, as expected, we lost at Crystal Palace. 5–0.

On 27 May 2024, Aston Villa announced a new five-year contract for Unai Emery, no longer described as head coach but as manager. A significant shift in stature, but a reflection of what was happening behind the scenes 'I share the owners' vision,' Unai told the club's official media. 'We have to keep working hard, making smart decisions and staying united.' Chairman Nassef Sawiris added: 'We're building the club around Unai, with the aim of returning Aston Villa to where it belongs, among football's elite.' Privately, the owners were overjoyed. They made it clear to those around them: Emery was taking the club to a place it hadn't reached in decades. What they were seeing was transformational.

The longest I stayed anywhere was Valencia, four years. By the end, the players were worn down. I was worn down. And the fans were already feeling it before us. But we carried on – and that fourth year was our best. We finished third in the league, reached the semi-finals of the Europa League and the Copa del Rey.

I know I'm the kind of coach who wears people down, and I wear myself down too. So, at Villa I need to break through that barrier. Can I sustain it? It's tough. I'm very demanding with myself, because I believe that's the only way to reach our goals. And I'm convinced it's worth it. I ask the players all the time: is the sacrifice we're making worth it as a group? The day I feel it isn't, I won't stay. And the day they feel it isn't, they'll have to go. No one is indispensable – not me, not the staff, not the players.

At Villa, I originally signed for three and a half years, with an option for one more. When the owners wanted to renew, they came with improved terms and more years to consolidate the project. I said yes. I'd only been at the club one season and a half. We'd just qualified for the Champions League. Everything still felt fresh. But I warned him: 'Now everything depends on how persistent and sustainable we can be in our growth. If we sit down and try to forecast where we'll be in three years – will I still have the same motivation I have today? I don't know.' The goal is to have it, of course.

What I need most is constant motivation and to manage fatigue.

From a club adrift to a Champions League contender in under seven years, Aston Villa's transformation under NSWE is a case study in how clarity of vision – and the courage to change direction when needed – can reshape a football institution. Unai Emery had sharpened the intentions and vision of the owners, and he had maximised the potential of the squad. The owners would even say they have learnt from him. After seeing the day-to-day reality at Bodymoor Heath, Nassef Sawiris offered an honest reflection: 'Owning the club changed my perspective on what it takes to be successful, both in business and in sport. You really come to the conclusion that attitude and work ethic beat talent any day.'

The most profound change had been cultural. For the first time in decades, Aston Villa are competing at the highest level with a coherent identity. Like an architect, Unai was handed both the blueprint and the freedom to shape the structure from the ground up, one precise angle, one correction, one player, at a time.

11

THE ENGINE ROOM:

HOW TO SHAPE A PLAYER

Even those who question Unai's methods rarely doubt his ability. Emery can coach. For him, the essence of coaching is taking a group of people and shaping them into a team, person by person, using this philosophy: 'I believe excellence is a habit, and mentality is the key. It's not about what a player is today, but how he builds himself. Mentality changes everything.'

But Unai is fighting on difficult terrain. He's up against a generation with a shrinking attention span, in an era where truth does not hold sway. We no longer describe facts or defend ideas; instead, the goal is to construct emotional landscapes. Meanwhile, Unai insists on grounding his work in facts – statistics, video, positional detail – and in ideas: improvement, collective purpose, a future built on impact and success. To get all this right, Unai and his coaching staff must maintain regular, meaningful contact with the player. They have to bring him fully into the process, invite him into the inner circle and find ways where understanding and commitment can take root.

He has different solutions to the conundrum, but one is key: moulding the squad to his idea by signing those players that *get it*. Another one is to create a space that allows for improvisation, such as last-minute changes and the freedom to do some work away from Bodymoor Heath, giving ownership to the players. But, above anything, he applies a constant routine.

After the first coaches – Pablo, Javi and Rodri – arrive around 8 a.m., they spend a few minutes at their desks reviewing the last match, checking the schedule or venting any stress. Unai usually joins briefly, with the piece of fruit or juice collected from the canteen in hand, before heading to his office next door.

By 9.15 a.m., the assistants and manager meet. Unai sets the day's focus, *Right, we need to reinforce this or that.* The coaches break down responsibilities, distribute drills, and Rodri highlights which players need extra attention based on recent workloads. Players trickle in between 8.45 and 9.30 a.m. A downstairs tablet tracks arrivals, though the odd latecomer might cheekily ask a teammate to sign them in. Coaches, of course, always know who's late. Traffic is forgivable. Repeated lateness? That gets noticed.

The players walk in relaxed, each with a different idea in their head. Some go straight for breakfast, others have a shower and get changed, or have a massage before training, treatment, weights. A few sit quietly with a coach, with the doctor or slip into a side room to speak with the manager, who normally is in the office working on videos till it is time to start. When the coaches head down to the gym or the dressing room about an hour and a half before training, everyone's already there, with their resistance bands on and doing their pre-activation routines.

Training times, generally starting at 11 a.m., are co-ordinated through Teamworks, the club's internal app managed by first-team support staff. Each Monday, Unai sets the week's plan – sessions, rest days, travel – and it's uploaded in real time for players to follow. After the collective work, routines splinter again: some join Rodri and the individual coaches, some head to the gym, others to do recovery plans or massage. Some might meet with the support staff, others with the media team. Meanwhile, the assistants head back to the office to review the session, while Unai keeps working on his video analysis. Just before lunch, he'll come out and share two or three key points with them.

Everyone meets in the canteen around lunchtime and stays for about an hour. They eat there, unwind, look at their phones, go over the day. A few players – not many – grab their meals to go but most stick around. Food for breakfast and after training is compulsory. It is fuel but control too – chefs and the nutritionists make sure players consume what they need to. This is one of the battles with the footballers.

When Unai arrived at PSG, one of the surprises came on the very first flight, where attendants were handing out sweets. Little things like that stood out. One of the first decisions at the club was to remove sugary snacks. The kitchen actually worked quite well at PSG but at Arsenal, things were not great. Nacho Monreal once said, 'I'd love to stay and eat here, but the food is just terrible.'

At Aston Villa, the approach is very different. The team travels with its own chef but some eating habits have been hard to change – like ketchup, sauces, butter, grilled cheese sandwiches . . . It was madness at first. Still, you have to be careful when limiting these things. It's a long fight and diet is just one front. Players can get upset over small changes, so the strategy has to be gradual, phasing things out until they become normal. Take butter, for example. You don't make a big announcement, you just stop putting it out. If someone asks for it, you give it. If four ask, eventually it'll go down to two and then to none.

The club uses a DEXA machine every six weeks to measure body fat. Players lie down, and the scan gives a complete picture. Putting on weight isn't necessarily a problem if it's muscle mass; losing weight isn't always good if it means muscle loss. So weight alone doesn't say much anymore. Some players are at 8–9 per cent body fat, others at 13 per cent and the goal might be to bring them down to 12, but that's often easier said than done. Each player gets individual reports and tailored plans. Take John McGinn, for instance. He may give the impression of carrying extra weight, but he's built like a tank. His body fat percentage is unusual for a footballer, but it works for him. Others, like Tyrone Mings, are natural athletes and don't require the same interventions. Clearly, every player is a unique individual. Some players such as Youri Tielemans and Lucas Digne treat their body like a Formula 1 car – carefully monitored, properly fuelled, finely tuned. They listen to their bodies and manage every detail. Others need convincing. They have to be shown why these things matter – why recovery, nutrition and preparation aren't just add-ons but essential tools if they want a long career. There have to be standards, even if not everyone sticks to them. Players get corrected, and they fall in line for a while, then drift again. Some wonder if they've made it this far, why keep pushing themselves to eat exactly what they're told? They train well and that's enough, their genetics allow them to get further with less. They don't place as much importance on the extras, and they approach it all with less rigour.

How a player absorbs what the coaches ask also depends on a wide range of factors: current form, minutes on the pitch, recent results. It often feels less like coaching and more like teaching – chasing after pupils to make sure at least some of what was taught actually sticks. So, Unai needs people around willing to confront players when needed. That takes courage. Assistants often hold back, they're aware they don't command the same authority as him. Nutritionists have to earn the players' respect before they can truly change habits.

It's all a carefully orchestrated balancing act.

If training has taken place at 11 a.m., the footballers go home between 2 and 3 p.m., having spent enough hours under the supervision of the coaches. In the afternoon, after lunch, that's when 'the show starts' as one assistant puts it. From around 3.30 p.m. to 7.30 p.m., the pace intensifies. Unai comes in and out of his office repeatedly, sharing comments, disappearing, then returning again. No one leaves before 5.00 p.m. The coaches try to hold on to that amateur spirit, the feeling that they're there because they love it. It's true for many of them. Yes, they're earning good money, but they're also coaching Watkins, Rogers, Durán, Emi Martínez . . . There's still a real sense of excitement in the work. Eventually, around 7.30 or 8.00 p.m., they all head home.

Day after day, the same routine.

When Unai, Pablo and Rodri were players, every Thursday the footballers would meet for a long lunch outside the training ground, often without the coaches. That has gone. Players hardly do things together outside the training centre. So when they are at home, what do they do? Some have gyms, some have their own physios and sports scientists. Some even a chef. Some are club-aligned, others independent. Another struggle for the manager. Any work done away from the club should be shared and complement what is being done in the training ground, but it doesn't always happen.

At PSG, Thiago Silva had his own personal trainer and his own warm-up routines. When Unai's staff arrived in Paris, he kept telling them, 'I don't want that, I don't like doing this.' It caught them off-guard. Unai changed that habit. There are a lot of physios and fitness coaches who end up siding more with the player than with the club. They build such a strong connection that they carve out their own path. You find a lot of external physios and osteopaths with big reputations, but when you ask around, that reputation doesn't hold up – they've just gained the players' trust.

Those were experiences mostly at Arsenal and PSG. But Villa has not got that size or stature, players do not think they own the place. So it has been easier to create more of a familial culture, a sense of unity. In every area Unai and Damià have brought in people they can trust. At first, you'd see some of the existing staff a bit unsure about, say, a new physio coming in from outside. But over time, the work speaks for itself. And the feeling Unai has is that everything is under control, even the work done away from Bodymoor Heath.

And if a player does not fit in for whatever reason, he has to find another team. Douglas Luiz is a good example of what Unai does to players and vice versa. A very talented Brazilian player, a good guy who is deeply appreciative of Unai, Luiz often says Unai was the coach he learnt the most from. Douglas wanted to engage with Unai, to understand more. But he also had moments of homesickness, and Unai's staff had to constantly stay on top of him – managing schedules, keeping him sharp in training, making sure he didn't switch off. Eventually, it started to feel like they had already drawn everything they could from him. For Douglas, keeping up with Unai's demands was exhausting – those were his own words. When a player reaches a point where he's only following along like a zombie, just going through the motions, it's often time to start planning for his exit.

When Unai joins a club, he likes to bring in players he knows, ones he trusts or who have worked well with him in the past. They are his 'soldiers'. The players Emery has handpicked from clubs he managed previously – such as Nico Pareja, Giovani Lo Celso, Éver Banega and Pau Torres – have all responded when called upon. That trust comes with a sense of shared responsibility. With them, Unai feels confident enough to push harder, to demand more. If that player begins to stray from the path they agreed on, Unai won't hesitate to let them know. Take Giovani Lo Celso at PSG, for instance, someone he would have liked to bring to Aston Villa. Unai considered him one of *his* players. There was a moment before a PSG game against Bayern Munich when the team were preparing a tactical move in training. Lo Celso lost focus for a moment, and Unai immediately came down on him, harshly. In that kind of session, if you forget to close down or seem distracted, you get an earful. He's not aggressive or confrontational in a physical sense, but he doesn't let things slide. Lo Celso put his head down and corrected himself.

At PSG, though, Unai sensed that most players didn't respond well to that level of criticism. They didn't like being called out, even when it was warranted. But every team has its own dynamic, and every squad requires a different kind of management. If a player shows frustration in public – pulling a face, reacting negatively – Unai will sometimes speak through an assistant, to avoid direct confrontation. Whereas in private, he will be direct if he has seen something he doesn't like. It's important to distinguish between isolated flashes of frustration and a recurring attitude problem.

That said, Unai is not the kind of manager who calls players in the middle of the night to keep tabs on everything. When the team is in camp at a hotel before games, he focuses to use the time effectively. He often holds one-on-one meetings in the evening or the following morning. He'll explain how he wants to approach the game and make the player feel a real sense of responsibility for what's to come. Moulding a footballer, their habits, their brain, requires all the time you can get. But not in the middle of the night.

Also key is the help from those around you. At Villarreal, Unai made a deliberate decision to begin building an individual development department. He brought in Rodri and that unit has since become an essential part of how he works, fully embracing football's growing emphasis on tailoring preparation to each player. Rodri's journey to this role was anything but conventional. He was a forward that started as a Barcelona youth player in a strong generation – alongside names like Guardiola and Lluís Carreras – but he lacked the natural talent to go far. He became a regular in the lower leagues, playing in Segunda B and eventually joining Lleida under manager Mané during their promotion to LaLiga, though he rarely featured. He moved through historic Catalan clubs like Nàstic and Palamós, and it was at Palamós, playing with Eduardo Vílchez, that something clicked.

Until then, coaches had simply told him he was playing and given him three general defensive and attacking guidelines but never really taught him how to read the game. No one showed him how to gain an advantage in specific situations, how to connect with a midfielder or how to attack a centre-back depending on the flow of the match. Vílchez told him one day: 'Look, when I was in Madrid with Hugo Sánchez, he always made this movement inside the box. I think it could work for you.' In his first league match, from a corner, he tried that exact movement and scored. That was the moment he fell in love with individualised coaching.

After retiring, he started training youth players. His methods caught the attention of Raúl Agné, who invited him to work with his senior team at Peralada. That opened the door to Girona, then Zaragoza, then Cádiz. At each step, Rodri applied the same principles he used with young players to professionals. To his surprise, many of them still lacked basic tactical understanding. They played on instinct and chemistry but not always with a grasp of the game's structure. A key turning point came when the company Regenera invited him to provide tactical support alongside their psychological and nutritional work with players. Working privately with professionals like Atlético Madrid's Spanish international Marcos

Llorente, Rodri carefully shaped their decision-making based on their club's requirements, never positioning himself against the head coach, always complementing the system. Llorente improved significantly and word spread. More players and agencies began to seek him out. Rodri used video analysis, travelled to meet players and tailored feedback to their game. With Benfica's Álex Grimaldo, for instance, he broke down why defending the outside channel was a losing battle due to his physical profile and gave him a more effective alternative. It worked.

At Cypriot club Anorthosis, sporting director Alberto Benito brought Rodri to the club and was impressed by his methods. He later recommended him to his friend Unai Emery. Unai had already been thinking about formalising this kind of work, having done something similar in the past with Juan Carlos Carcedo. Back then, Pablo was involved too, but the work was less exhaustive, focused more on video analysis and correcting situations on screen, without a consistent practical application on the pitch. It wasn't yet a structured, systematic process. Arriving at Villarreal mid-season wasn't easy for Rodri. Players were naturally wary, why was this new guy suddenly telling them how to play? But gradually, Rodri earned their trust and found ways to integrate his work seamlessly into the group.

Rodri continued working privately with top-level players like Real Madrid's Marco Asensio. He recalls how his wife would say, 'Tomorrow I've got something planned,' and he'd reply, 'I can't. I have to go to Madrid.' Marco wasn't training with the team at the time, and Rodri would drive the 311 kilometres from Villarreal to Madrid, sometimes in the freezing cold, to meet him on a random pitch. Asensio, seeing the progression and the effort, would say to him, 'I'm with you all the way.'

Yerry Mina, then at Everton, is another admirer of Rodri's work.

At the elite level, everything becomes easier. Players understand faster, they engage more and, often, they come up with solutions themselves. The Colombian once told Davide Ancelotti, Carlo's son and his assistant at the English club, 'There's someone who's helping me.' That prompted a call from Davide. Rodri explained to him, 'I know how your father defends, how your system uses zonal defence, influenced by Sacchi. All I need is for him to focus on a few key details.' Carlo and Davide let him do as Rodri instructed.

Over time, it became clear that maintaining high-quality work at Villarreal required more hands. Jaime Arias was the first to join, followed by Albert Carbó and later on, at Aston Villa, both Pablo Villanueva and Pako Ayestarán also became part of the individual development set-up. The group functions like a pit crew: Unai is the driver, setting the direction and giving the in-structions. Pako changes the tyres by taking group sessions, Pablo handles the oil helping with whatever is required and Rodri and his assistants take care of the fine-tuning. Rodri's role involves constant co-ordination with the coaching staff, understanding what Unai wants to do each day, aligning types of physical effort, pitch dimensions and even whether individual work is needed at all. It also includes working closely with the medical department to manage player recovery when injuries occur. The plan for gym sessions, set up by performance coaches, also defines Rodri's focus and how it fits into the broader schedule. Nutritionists are also part of this co-ordination: what the players eat, how meals are prepared and gradually adjusting culinary habits. On top of all that, match analysis feeds into tailored video clips, which are then used in one-on-one sessions with players before or after training.

That is the scope of Rodri's and his team's work. For Rodri, this is all about knowledge transfer. Unai has full confidence in his work, the manager doesn't need to know in advance what Rodri is going to say to the players or what exercises he's going to propose. Unai often asks him to focus not just on individual attackers but on broader attacking combinations. The training sessions simulate different defensive behaviours from their rivals – deep blocks, high presses, mid-blocks – and players are given tactical solutions for each. It all starts with the basics and gradually moves towards more complex concepts. The aim of Rodri's work is to remove hesitation from the players' decisions. It's about creating habits so that their reactions on the pitch become automatic. Once those habits are in place, he adds fine adjustments: changes in body shape, specific angles to receive, subtle timing cues. He often compares it to training a muscle. At first, there may be raw strength but precision is lacking. The process involves layering in detail until the player gains a deep understanding. That way, during a match, they only need to focus on a few key cues, rather than processing everything from scratch.

Rodri studies defenders in detail. Some try to lead the attacker into their comfort zone, that's where deception comes in. With someone like Van Dijk, who appears to offer space but is actually luring attackers into a trap, Rodri teaches players to fake acceptance, then suddenly switch direction and attack from the blind side. Rodri uses metaphors to communicate with players. One of his go-to ideas is to tell them: imagine you're going into battle against a dragon. Study its weaknesses. If it breathes fire, position yourself here. If it's too powerful to face head-on, use another approach. Over time, players begin to think that way, stepping on to the pitch already armed with solutions before the problems arise.

How long this process takes depends on the player, but Rodri estimates that three to four weeks of focused work is usually enough to internalise these concepts until they become second nature. Take Ollie Watkins as an example. Rodri points to the way he now positions his feet like a sprinter ready to launch. That posture, refined over time, allows him to break quickly in any direction. Previously, his movements were flatter, less reactive. Leon Bailey is another case in point. Before playing Newcastle, Rodri worked with him on a specific move: receive on the inside, then explode outside. They had identified that Bailey's marker would commit heavily if challenged inside. In training, Bailey practised turning at the right moment and, when he executed it in the game, the defender had no answers. Once doubt is created in a defender's mind, everything changes. The pressure eases, and that's when players start to dominate.

For Rodri, the real joy isn't just a goal, it's seeing the things prepared the day before come alive in a match. Not isolated set-piece routines, but patterns, combinations, behaviours and understanding. The more players know, the more they control time and space, both so limited at the highest level. That coaching is like cutting, sanding and shaping the best wood.

Morgan Rogers's early steps in the Premier League were a baptism of fire. Signed from Middlesbrough in February 2024 at twenty-one years of age, he was thrown into the action much earlier than expected against Luton, a month after his Villa debut. Jacob Ramsey limped off after just 29 minutes at Villa Park and suddenly Rogers was in. The first half went well enough. But the second half was something else entirely, a flurry of transitions, tactical expectations and defensive duties he wasn't yet equipped to meet. 'It just hit me. I didn't know where to be, didn't know what to do,' Rogers remembers. As Villa lost control of the game's structure, Emery made a decision to protect both the result and the player.

Rogers came off in the 79th minute. Seeing his number come up was a difficult moment. 'It's not nice. You never want to come off, especially if you've come on,' he says. But the lesson was valuable. The team won, and he saw the bigger picture. 'It was the right decision.' Unai explained it to him after: it was about positioning and defensive obligations. Rogers understood. 'At the time, I hadn't learnt how to get away with it and get through the rest of the game.'

His signing had been a rare throwback in a modern game shaped by algorithms and metrics. Villa's pursuit of Rogers was pure instinct, a decision born from footballing brains – and above all, from Unai Emery. When Unai watches matches, if a player catches his eye, he says so. While preparing for the away FA Cup meeting with Middlesbrough in January 2024, Víctor and Pablo had already flagged Morgan as a possible option. Pablo puts together 2 or 3-minute summaries for each opposition player, which Unai reviews individually. Víctor, who analyses the opposition and prepares the tactical visuals, had also seen Morgan's potential while reviewing Middlesbrough. Unai decided to watch full Boro matches. 'He wasn't performing at that level yet,' Emery says now. But the manager was struck by a player whose raw ability revealed itself in flashes. In particular, one moment stood out: a League Cup tie against Chelsea, in which Middlesbrough were hammered 6–1. Rogers scored in the dying minutes, finishing a 70-metre run with a dribble and a good finish. 'I asked myself, *Can he really do that in the ninetieth minute?*'

He asked around for references. 'Other coaches we asked had doubts.' He wasn't a regular starter for Boro, his stats were modest. But Rogers had something. He understood the game. His frame, his attitude, his intelligence – they all pointed to a player worth investing in, even with the added risk of a shoulder issue that required medical attention. Also, he was from the West Midlands, from the market town of Halesowen, a local boy with a lot of potential. A good combination. When Damià asked what to do, Unai said: 'Let's go for him.'

Had Aston Villa not drawn Middlesbrough, who knows where Rogers might be today. But they did, and after Villa edged it 0–1, several first-team players approached Morgan to relay Emery's enthusiasm: 'He keeps mentioning you.' That personal nod helped seal the deal, and by 1 February, Rogers had joined Villa for £8.5 million. A bargain.

Rodri and the assistants sat with Emery to weigh the options: should Rogers play as a second striker or inside left? 'We were going to get mixed up if he did both at the beginning,' Rodri recalled. Unai made the call – Rogers would be developed to play off the left. Emery allowed him to ease into training, observing him carefully before gradually introducing tactical instructions. Rogers needed to understand more than just how Villa played. With Unai, everything begins with intention. That means defining exactly how the team wants to attack and defend and structuring each player's role to serve that goal. For attacking phases, it starts with what they call the 'first square' – the two centre-backs and two midfielders. The objective is to get the ball into this central unit and from there, progress. Rogers had to grasp that when the ball reached midfield, it was meant to arrive to him in specific areas. His role was to interpret the defensive line's movements and break it, ideally by turning and releasing the striker through on goal. If that wasn't possible, he was expected to link with the next option or drive forward with the ball. The entire team shape was designed to give him the best chance to operate in that zone. He was also coached on how to handle different types of marking: what to do when facing zonal pressure, how to deal with tight man-marking, how to find space. To help him adapt, Villa's staff used match clips and visual modelling. They showed him footage of Jacob Ramsey, not in order to mimic the player but to understand the demands of the position. Ramsey himself had previously studied Manu Trigueros at Villarreal in the same way.

And then, the disastrous Luton game happened. At first, he didn't fully grasp how to respond. 'I didn't know what to do,' he admits now. 'It was all that was in my head for the next few days ... just thinking about what I did wrong, how I can get better. I want to be the best version of me every time I step on the pitch, and when I'm not, I want to know why and fix it.' What helped him keep perspective was learning that an important player like Leon Bailey had gone through a similar experience earlier in the season against Liverpool. He had come on and played 46 minutes before being replaced. Unai Emery had spent the following entire international break reflecting on how Bailey might have felt, eventually sitting down with him and explaining it wasn't meant to humiliate. He apologised for how it might have come across and clarified that it was a tactical decision made in a tough match. Unai handled Rogers in a similar way. 'That made me feel a bit better,' Morgan says. 'Leon played every game after that, so I knew there was a way back into the team.'

When he first arrived, Rogers was quiet and reserved but open and eager to learn. And the talent was clear for all the coaches to see. He possesses a rare mix of power and finesse. With his 6-foot-3-inch frame and strong build, he can glide past opponents while absorbing contact, often drawing comparisons to a rugby league player in full flow. He has a natural ability to interpret the spaces between the lines, especially close to the rival box. He knows how to receive in a way that lets him drive forward, and once he beats a man, he has the power to leave defenders behind. These are the fundamental attributes you need at the top level and that needed to be refined with regular work with Rodri.

Unai Emery considers versatility the most important trait in a modern attacker, and he valued Rogers for his ability to play effectively on both wings, as a number 10 and even as a centre forward, as well as for his intelligence to adapt to each position. From the very start, Unai had made it clear: until Morgan proved himself as a Premier League player, he was a Championship one. Not something a young player wants to hear, but Rogers later admitted it brought the fire out of him. 'You don't want to be called that,' he said. 'You want to be on the same level as them. So, it made me want to learn.'

Morgan Rogers talks of his relationship with Unai Emery as one of love and hate. Emery began pushing him hard in training. He told him he had to be demanding of himself in front of goal, with his final pass. Because six missed goals, six missed assists, those are the margins between finishing sixth and finishing in the Champions League spots. The player had to adjust quickly to a new level of tactical education. He'd sat through meetings before but never like this. At Villa, the sheer length and intensity of Unai Emery's video sessions caught him off-guard. Staying laser-focused for such a long stretch took effort. At the beginning, he would naturally concentrate more when it touched on his position, or when something piqued his interest directly. But soon he realised he had to be locked in from the first minute to the last. Emery expected his players to know not only what they had to do individually, but also to understand how every teammate's role fitted into the bigger picture.

He quickly grew comfortable within the environment, warming to the staff and showing his personality. He became affectionate, even playful, handing out hugs, bonding easily. Over time, as he earned status in the squad, the dynamics evolved. He became more serious, more demanding of himself and others. The coaches reminded him: 'Stay humble. Keep what makes you special.' Rogers was one of the few players who got on well with Jhon Durán, at least on the surface. But there were limits. During a team meeting, Rogers happened to sit in a chair Durán considered his. When Durán told him it was his seat, Rogers calmly told him to sit elsewhere. When Durán insisted, Rogers stood up and, without drama, told him he was being immature. A small exchange that revealed Rogers's increasing coming-of-age.

He would stay after training with Rodri, working on the basics – receiving and passing, repetition of runs and combinations with Ollie Watkins. 'It might look boring or simple,' Rogers says, 'but when you see it play out in a match, when that one thing you worked on two days ago creates a chance or a goal, you realise that's why we do it.' For Rogers, much of what he does on the pitch now feels second nature. He explains that the steady rhythm of training routines, paired with the precision of each player's responsibilities, makes the team hard to break down – even for opponents who know exactly what to expect.

When Morgan Rogers relaxed, and it happens with young players, Unai didn't need to call it out directly. Instead, he used subtle reminders: showing clips of missed chances, drawing lines between training habits and match outcomes. Rogers had begun to take more shots that flew off-target, and Emery would quietly point it out: 'Three wild ones in training, three more in the match.' It was a nudge. In Europe, against Ajax, a first-half yellow card gave Unai a useful excuse to pull him early, it helped him manage minutes and expectations, without risking damage to the player's confidence. This is where Unai excels. He gives space but always maintains control. 'What would I say now to that version of me that played against Luton?' That version of Morgan needed to hear one thing: trust the process. The last time Unai called Morgan Rogers a Championship player came towards the end of the 2023–24 season. Rogers's evolution reached a new level against Brentford the season after, when he played in five different positions in a single match. The achievement spoke volumes, never once complaining when moved out of position. He has accepted each role with humility. That's rare. Like John McGinn before him, he's shown a willingness to put the team before himself. It's one of the qualities the staff admire most about arguably the best player in Aston Villa's squad.

In November 2024, he was handed a new contract with a significant pay rise, less than twelve months after arriving from Middlesbrough. Another improvement is likely on the horizon, especially with interest growing from Europe's elite. In the same month, Rogers earned his first start for England under Thomas Tuchel. He had come through West Brom's and then Manchester City's academies but never played under Pep Guardiola. Around Villa's home match against Manchester City on 21 December 2024, eleven months after his arrival, Pep Guardiola praised Morgan Rogers, calling him 'an exceptional player', explaining that he had been blocked at City by stars like Silva, Mahrez and Sterling. By then Rogers was more established in the team, and the expectations around him had shifted. Early on, any positive contribution he made was encouraging. But with progress comes greater responsibility. The coaching staff, led by Unai Emery, now demand more. It's a message applied not just to Rogers but to others like Cash, Kamara, Amadou Onana, Konsa, Mings – players who need to break through their current ceiling. For Emery, Aston Villa must not settle as a mid-table team. The aim is Europe and with that comes the need for players to raise their level consistently, not occasionally.

After another great display from Morgan and a win, Unai told staff: 'Tomorrow I'll show Morgan two clips from the Brighton game. He did everything, played everywhere without complaining, but there are still two defensive moments he can improve. And if he does that too ... wow.' His maturity is taking him far, on and off the pitch he has the perfect context to develop. Rogers has contracted his own chef, his brother Daniel is a qualified psychotherapist who has worked with Chelsea and Tottenham, while another brother, Ash, takes charge of Morgan's individual training over the summer.

The next step in his evolution may be the most difficult yet. The signs of a new challenge are starting to appear. Rogers has shown flashes of frustration, raising his arms when a pass doesn't come, reacting more visibly when he loses the ball or doesn't get a foul. That didn't used to happen. He's entering the stage where being the exciting young talent is no longer enough. Now the expectation is consistency, finessing his end product, showing leadership. That's what separates a great run of form from a great career. Internally, no one doubts him. 'This is the moment,' one coach said, 'where he has to keep his feet on the ground.' Even when he rejected a handshake from Unai after being substituted against Manchester City – something he wouldn't have done a few months ago – the coaching staff weren't worried. They saw a competitor, not a diva. 'He has an elite mentality,' Unai says. 'He knows he can win us games.'

Rogers, for his part, tries to soak up every lesson. 'I want to play in the big games. That's why I look up to people like Unai.' He's even joked he'll never speak ill of Emery unless the coach 'cuts off his ear', but Emery doesn't want blind loyalty. He wants growth. Losing Rogers would hurt, but the club's stance is clear: if someone offers a world-class sum, they'll find a replacement. That is the game Villa is in. Still, even for a pragmatic outfit, some players are just that much harder to replace. No matter how long he stays at Villa, one thing is certain: there is more to come. If Unai's world is about refining potential, Rogers is his ideal student.

Jhon Durán, on the other hand . . .

At Villa, many players arrive without ever having seen the training ground. To prepare them, an induction video is sent out, ideally watched on the drive in. It introduces the first team support staff: first team player care manager Phil Roscoe, club secretary Sharon Barnhurst, Monchi, the nutritionists and sports scientists. Phil becomes a regular presence for the players from the very start, even at the medicals, where he gets straight into it. Where do you want to live? What kind of car? Do you have children? How many? Is your partner pregnant? How far along? (The club had six births in the past year alone!) From that moment on, Villa walks with them every step, so they can focus on football.

In those first 24 to 48 hours, everything gets sorted. Some players are direct: boom, boom, boom. Others take time. The approach adapts, the support is tailored. This is what Villa offers, you choose how to use it. What matters most is that players know the club cares. Phil, the comfort blanket, travels home and away. When a player comes down to breakfast and asks 'Did you sort that?' the answer is 'Yes. Don't worry.' If something's happened at home, it's 'Phil will sort it now.' In one of the games at Villa Park, a player saw Phil in the tunnel, phone in hand, walking towards him. 'Everything all right?' Phil was just checking the scores. They know he's the conduit.

Early on, something else became clear. Sharon's vision for the department was for staff to receive the same level of care as the players. Staff should only be thinking about doing their jobs well. And one more thing: support has to be uniform. One of the challenges in elite football is consistency of messaging. Imagine the football department sends a clear instruction to a player but then the player walks into another part of the club and hears a different message, or worse, a softened one designed to placate. That kind of inconsistency creates confusion, even bias. So at Villa, it's been made clear: every department must sing from the same song sheet. Now, when a player comes into the Player Care office to vent, he will hear the same thing he heard from the manager. Even if the easy route would be to sympathise, 'Yeah, I can't believe he didn't start you,' that's not what happens. Instead, it's: 'What do you think you can do to change that?' If the conversation turns into something worth feeding back, Phil will ask: 'Are you comfortable with me sharing this with the staff?' If the footballer agrees, the message is passed on. There was one player who needed more help than most. Unai Emery showed remarkable patience, knowing he came from a very different background and could be a handful. Welcome to the unpredictable, explosive world of Jhon Durán.

The idea of rules, of following instructions just didn't exist in his upbringing and his mind hadn't been shaped in the same structured way as others. So, he needed special treatment. When he parked his car properly in the right space, Phil would make a point of saying, 'Well done, Jhon! Good lad.' And if he didn't, the message was equally clear: 'Come on, Jhon, you've got to understand, this is someone else's space. The other player will be irritated and that tension carries into the dressing room.' It was about education. His English is passable, in fact he was not particularly bothered about learning when he arrived in Birmingham, but communication isn't just about language. He knew Phil was there for him, even though others – like Sophia and Matt that work in the same department – would do the translating when needed.

Much of the work with Durán went beyond the player. It extended to his family. When his parents came over, Phil and Sofia sat down with them as well. Because it wasn't just Jhon who was learning; the family was, too. They talked openly. If Jhon went home and complained, *I'm being picked on*, Phil and Sofia could offer perspective. *No, he's not.* Or if he said, *The manager said this in the changing room*, Phil and Sofia might have replied, *Yes, but I was there, and I didn't hear it that way.* That kind of transparency helps avoid misunderstandings that can spiral.

To an outsider, all of this might seem over the top, but it is necessary and the manager wants it like that. He's tolerant, reflecting an understanding of cultural differences. Because at this level, diversity is the norm. The higher you go in football, the more varied the backgrounds. And the staff need to be able to read those differences, support the player and still hold the line. The Player Care department is filled with people shaped by all kinds of life experiences – whether that's their ethnicity, upbringing or the challenges they've faced in sport and society. That mixture of perspectives helps ensure that Villa's support structures aren't just professional.

Jhon Durán was born in Zaragoza, Colombia, a remote mountain town in the department of Antioquia, nestled some 250 kilometres north of Medellín, the country's second-largest city. For many families, daily life is a matter of making do and, yes, football is a way out. At eleven, Durán left that world behind. He moved to Medellín after being invited to join the youth academy at Envigado FC. Medellín presented its own challenges. The city is intense, fragmented and tough. The teenager saw things we would never see in a lifetime. He settled in a modest district with his grandfather, until the club eventually helped move his family into a small apartment. But he struggled with the demands of training and school. There were days he simply didn't show up. He'd be home, a few blocks away, listening to music and drifting. Coaches stepped in, meeting teachers, creating academic plans and making personal promises so Jhon could remain eligible to play. He tested every boundary.

All that because his talent was undeniable. On the pitch, he was electric, raw, impulsive, sometimes difficult, but different. Envigado, the city known as the 'Cantera de Héroes' (Quarry of Heroes) for producing the likes of James Rodríguez and Juan Fernando Quintero, recognised his potential immediately. He debuted professionally at just fifteen and soon became the second-youngest goalscorer in Colombia's top-flight.

Jhon Durán caught the eye of Chicago Fire head coach Sebastian Pelzer, a former Blackburn player, during a Colombian league match. Pelzer had come to watch someone else, but Durán's pace and aerial power stood out. He saw Premier League potential. In January 2021, Durán became the youngest international signing in MLS history, staying on loan at Envigado until he turned eighteen. As usual with Durán, the start in the States was rocky. Covid protocols meant he couldn't be with his family, and he struggled to settle, but he eventually found his best version, finishing as the club's top scorer that season with seven goals. That form caught the attention of European clubs. Aston Villa, acting on a recommendation from a club coach who had seen clips of the young striker, moved quickly. In January 2023, Unai Emery made Durán his second signing, for an initial £14.75 million, rising to £18 million with add-ons.

Durán's challenge went beyond club care. Rodri would admit it without hesitation: Jhon Durán was one of the most complex cases he'd ever worked with. From the moment he arrived, Durán was closed off. He gave the impression that nothing mattered, that he was ready to fight anyone at any time, that he knew everything already. It made building any kind of connection incredibly difficult. The coaching staff understood what was needed to improve him, they just had to find a way in. Some players have to be brought in gradually, offering solutions to their difficulties. You can't just walk in and say: 'I know more than you.' That only raises defences. The approach had to be subtle: present yourself as someone who's there to help. For players who switch off after 5 minutes, that might mean giving them exactly 5 minutes of video packed with information. It's about reinforcing what they're already doing well. If they want to learn more, you offer the tools.

In Durán's case, Rodri realised the only way to get through was with firm messaging. Clear instructions. No grey areas. 'This is what the manager wants.' There was another tacit message sent constantly too: 'Jhon, you have to respect me.' Even if that respect had to be earned day by day. Rodri had an advantage: connections in Colombian football. Friends like Yerry Mina helped bridge the gap. When Durán linked up with the national team, he'd hear good things about Rodri from teammates. That helped shift his perspective. The tone softened. The door opened, just a little.

Still, that first year after his arrival in January 2023 remained incredibly tough. On the pitch, Durán made an early impression in England, hitting the crossbar with a stunning strike against Manchester City in just his second Premier League appearance. But after that glimpse, his minutes under Unai Emery were limited, reduced to brief cameos across the 2022–23 season and much of the next. Brilliance came alongside volatility. His behaviour drew attention, he played to the camera, exaggerated expressions and let frustration spill out in animated gestures. On and off the pitch. Some players tried to help him adapt, but it was difficult. From the start, he resisted. Durán could be aggressively petulant during small-sided games and often showed arrogance towards younger academy players. He struggled to train consistently. At times, Durán arrived late and disrupted team meetings. He had a car accident. It seemed like every day brought a new problem.

He was pushing the limits of the squad's discipline, standards firmly upheld by senior players. In Bodymoor Heath he was compared to the NBA legend Dennis Rodman. The chaos and the genius, wrapped in the same frame. Like Rodman, Durán can be disruptive, impulsive, emotional. But like Rodman, when he's locked in, he smashes it in training, changes games. He bends them to his will. Rodri knew they needed to have a different kind of conversation, one that spoke to something deeper, something personal. Eventually, a key moment arrived.

Twelve months after his arrival, Durán approached Rodri and asked to watch some video analysis. It was the first time he'd done so. They sat down, started talking and something changed. Durán admitted he'd been stupid, now understanding what Rodri had been saying and how he could benefit. It marked a turning point. He became more open, more responsive. But Durán was still Durán, mercurial and unpredictable.

Mauricio Pochettino, Chelsea's manager at the time, was keen and had approved a move for Durán. Just before Villa's FA Cup tie against Chelsea in January 2024, the player congratulated fellow Colombian Mayra Ramírez on joining Chelsea's women's team, posting three blue hearts on Instagram. Why not get rid of him? There was only one reason why Villa wanted to keep him: Unai Emery.

The staff often found themselves frustrated, viewing many of his missteps as entirely avoidable. Unai saw beyond the chaos. He thought Jhon was a maverick. A physical marvel, gifted in ways that defy convention. Blistering pace, aerial ability, the left foot, his touch, passing, finishing, a sense for space and timing that seemed instinctive, not taught. Movements that split defenders open. All of it, raw. Natural. Off the street. In any top European side where he played regularly, he would score a minimum of twenty goals a season. No one had seen anything quite like him. Unai knew he would eventually be worth €100 million. Durán was a rough diamond no one truly saw, until Unai made it his mission to uncover it. Under someone else, he might have been out on loan at a club like Espanyol or Getafe. Unai kept telling his staff, 'He's going to be the best striker in the world.'

'There are moments of love and hate,' Jhon Durán said of his relationship with Unai Emery. He admitted to frequent clashes: 'We argue constantly, it's normal. He has his point of view, I have mine, and I've never been someone who stays quiet.'

Despite Chelsea's early interest – and they weren't the only club circling – Durán was persuaded to stay after key conversations with senior figures at Villa. His shirt number was changed to number 9, and he was assured by Unai that more minutes would follow. Durán is sharper than many give him credit for. His biggest challenge is retaining tactical information but what sets him apart is his unshakable self-belief, especially in front of goal. Misses don't linger. He's unaffected by disappointment, his short-term memory seemingly reset every 10 seconds. One moment he might fall out with someone or come across as rude, or miss a clear chance, the next he's fine again.

You could see in the way he celebrated goals that Durán knew how good he was. He was ambitious, even demanding with teammates. He would get angry if Rogers did not pass him the ball. His teammates might react to his petulance, but Jhon would respond, with words or a gesture that meant, *You can talk to me how you like, but don't think I'll back down.* That, to Unai, was the edge of competitiveness, but arrogance could be a weapon or a liability, depending on how it was channelled. The manager had countless conversations with Durán: about life, about family, about where his career could go, about maturity and responsibility. From the beginning, he emphasised that last concept, both individual and collective, as a non-negotiable part of life at the club. With Durán, that meant guiding not just the footballer, but the person.

'Jhon has a process,' Unai would often repeat. Jhon moved from Lichfield to an apartment in the same block as Emery, a shift unlikely to be coincidence. Whether arranged by the club or not, it reflected the effort to support him. It wasn't a father–son dynamic, but there was clear intent to keep him close and grounded. 'I'm not your father, but I have to say things to you like your father would,' he would tell the player. 'I have to try to instil values that you accept. Respect, for example, you know what it is, but you have to show it through actions. There are twenty players in the squad and you stand out, make sure what stands out is your football, not your behaviour.'

He had a soft spot for Durán and admitted as much. Managing him reminded Unai of his work with other talented but volatile players. When Durán's behaviour caused friction in the dressing room, Unai stood his ground. He asked the captains to back his decision to keep the player involved. 'I know you're right,' he told them. 'But I have a responsibility to develop him and so do you. Help me.' The frustration for Unai came from Durán's impatience, typical of young players who want everything now, and his inconsistency. Durán would follow him with full commitment one day, then only partially the next, and there were some days when Unai felt he wasn't being followed at all. To Jhon himself, Unai's message was always direct: 'Be Michael Jordan, not Rodman.' In those meetings behind closed doors, in Unai's office, he told him plainly: 'My goal for you is to be the best striker in the world. The biggest clubs will want you. If you stay on this path with me, you can get there.'

After a slow and often frustrating start to life at Aston Villa, Jhon Durán began to find his voice on the pitch. By the end of the 2023–24 season, he had started to silence critics with goals. Durán scored three times in the Europa Conference League, including in the qualifiers, and added five more in the Premier League. But it was one dramatic evening in May, under the lights at Villa Park, that best captured who he is, when Villa were hosting Liverpool in their final home match and chasing a Champions League spot. When Liverpool went ahead 1–3, the Colombian was sent to warm up. What happened next was pure Durán.

He came on in the 79th minute. Tactically, he was all over the place, miles from where Unai wanted him. The manager was shouting at him, demanding positional discipline. Durán ignored it. He refused to engage. It was one of the angriest moments anyone at the club had seen from Emery. Furious, Unai stormed out of the dugout and shouted to the sports science staff to get another attacking player ready. It looked like Durán was about to be subbed off just minutes after coming on. Then, in the 85th minute, he scored. A powerful, instinctive finish. 2–3. Three minutes later, Durán did it again. 3–3. Brilliant, infuriating, decisive. That cameo – less than 15 minutes – not only earned Villa a crucial point, but it also helped Durán secure a place in Colombia's Copa América squad.

Chelsea, again, were especially keen to sign him in the run-up to the 30 June financial deadline, when Aston Villa were under pressure to comply with Profit and Sustainability Rules. He was even given permission to explore the move. But in football, word travels fast. Everyone has contacts and as the London club quietly

asked around about his habits, personality and day-to-day behaviour they began to hear things that raised red flags. Despite
scoring five goals in twenty-three Premier League appearances the
previous season, concerns began to surface. Chelsea had room for
gambles, but this felt like more than that. There was a growing
sense that the energy required to support and contain him might
outweigh the upside. Meanwhile, Jhon frequently unfollowed
Villa on Instagram and deleted posts related to the club. Then,
in July 2024, during an Instagram Live from Colombia, Durán
made a crossed-arms gesture that resembled West Ham's crossed
hammers symbol. The timing was no coincidence. West Ham had
shown interest earlier that year, initially offering £4 million, a bid
that was considered but ultimately dismissed. Durán made no
secret of his desire to move to a 'big team'. That summer, West
Ham returned with a far more serious proposal: £30 million plus
teenage midfielder Lewis Orford. Villa rejected it again.

That summer, many teammates had had enough of him. Most
believed he would leave, but Villa stood firm, refusing to sell. Unai
had started seeing real change just before the new season was
about to start. Despite some chaos in his decision-making, Durán
had absorbed lessons. He no longer needed them repeated. Or so it
seemed. And as Durán grew, Unai made something else clear: all
the progress he had made, he didn't want that to benefit someone
else. Ironically, Duran was the match-winner against West Ham
on the opening day of the 2024–25 season, scoring late on in a 1–2
away win for Villa. Two months later, he signed a five-and-a-half-
year deal, with wages brought in line with first-team standards, up
from one of the lowest in the squad.

And yet, every morning, Durán still woke up as what he was: a
twenty-year-old. 'Jhon,' Emery once told him after a spectacular
goal, 'you're going to end up at Real Madrid, Barcelona . . . or in a

prison.' A joke but with Durán, the extremes are never far apart. Inside Jhon Durán's mind, the picture must have been complex. There's the talent, the ambition and the burning drive to succeed but also the noise: agents, money, family, the weight of his up-bringing. He comes from a place where the idea of making it isn't about lifting trophies but lifting others. What did he really want: glory on the pitch or financial security? He had to decide what kind of future he envisioned and show it, not in words, but in how he trained, how he played, how he lived. Because in elite football, intention isn't enough. The pull between ambition and protection, glory and safety, isn't clear-cut. And Durán, at twenty, was still figuring it out.

Despite featuring only briefly against Costa Rica that summer with Colombia in the Copa América, Jhon Durán began the new Premier League season just as he had ended the last, exploding off the bench and turning matches on their heads. He scored late winners against West Ham, Leicester and Everton. Then came the Champions League – and something extraordinary.

12

BAYERN MUNICH:

ALL OUR HEROES ARE VILLANS

The match before the Bayern Munich game brought a tension heightened by the expectation that accompanied Unai's regime. Villa had started the season well – fifth in the table with four wins in six games – but Unai felt the team had approached the trip to Ipswich as if it would take care of itself. Ipswich, still without a win in the Premier League by the end of September, were treated like a side to be swept away. The intensity and demand dropped. In the second half, with Villa leading 1–2, 20 minutes passed where nothing happened. It drove Unai mad. He didn't want his team to just let time pass, clinging to the lead. He wanted them to impose themselves. If Ipswich equalised, so be it but at least try to dominate. Instead, they lost control. And then, they lost 2 points anyway. A disappointing 2–2 draw away from home. Diego Carlos became the scapegoat among fans for his defensive mistakes – one of which, trying and failing to block a runner near the halfway line, led to a goal. After the final whistle, the dressing room was a funeral. The coach ride back to Birmingham passed in silence. Unai was livid.

'After a game,' Unai explains, 'the first thing I usually do is watch it back, quickly. That day, we had 3 hours on the bus. I ate something . . . but I didn't want to see it straight away. A bit later, still on the bus, I watched the first half.' Back at Bodymoor Heath, he spent 1-to-2 hours in his office – in what felt like a mini-crisis meeting with his staff – until 10 p.m. on a Sunday night.

'We're still picking up points, Unai. Want us to prepare something for tomorrow?' one assistant asked, looking at the bright side.

'We have to accept we're in a process,' Unai replied. 'Some things still aren't clicking – and they're punishing us.'

At home, he tried again: 'I told myself I'd watch the rest later … but I didn't. I was tired. I just sat for a while, doing nothing in particular. But I woke up early, by 7.30 a.m. I was already in and that's when I watched the second half. That's when I drew my conclusions. I knew I had to speak to the players.'

That Monday morning, everything changed. The normal plan – light recovery for new starters, tactical work for the rest – was thrown out of the window. The football world is increasingly shaped by algorithms and ruled by sports science. Sometimes it seems football is beginning to serve the science, instead of the science serving football. The tail wagging the dog. That Monday offered another look at that dilemma: for Unai, the game – its emotion, its consequences, its demands – had to come first.

Normally, the day after a match follows a clear protocol. Players who had played more than 60 minutes go through compensatory work, while the rest train more intensively. But there were too many details that had unsettled Unai – moments when the defensive line hadn't stayed compact enough, or failed to adjust in relation to the ball. The height of the line. When to cover. How to react to a switch of play.

So, everyone was going to work together.

'Today, boots on. Everyone runs. No recovery.' Results often shape the job. On another day, if Villa had held on to win 1–2 with the exact same performance, Unai might still have been angry but perhaps it wouldn't have led to a Monday like this. It wouldn't have prompted immediate changes. But Bayern Munich loomed and Manchester United after that. The tone had to shift. It felt like a pivotal moment in the season. Before the session, he gathered the squad.

'Listen – I told you, this draw, this result – it's part of our process. We're building something as a team. This is a step. And we have to keep building. Yesterday's result is a consequence of that process. But let me be clear: I don't want to be like Manchester United or Newcastle last year. Playing the Champions League . . . and then out. Playing for the league . . . and then out. No. If you're not willing to follow the line I set – that the league is the priority – then you're not in the right place. The league comes first. Always.

'Yesterday, we played at 50 per cent. Before the match, I prepared two videos for you – fifteen hours of work. I pushed you hard. Usually, you follow me. But this time . . . this time, you didn't. We were lucky. We could have lost. I told you: this, this and this. And in the end – you let me down.'

He said more. He told them that at a club aiming for top ten, a point away from home could be seen as a good result. But that mentality had changed. That wasn't good enough anymore. It was a different kind of message from Unai, a refreshing one. So, they all went to the pitch to work on the basics reinforcing the principles that should never be forgotten. They put some time on the ball too, correcting poor choices in transitions, positional issues when attacking crosses, sequences that hadn't clicked. The training lasted around 40 minutes.

Unai spoke to Diego Carlos personally. The words were sharp, direct, personal. 'You've played at a high level. You've been in the Europa League. And now you stop doing the things you used to do? Come on. Don't piss me off.' But he didn't punish him. Then they ate. And the work continued for the coaches, through the afternoon and into the evening, as usual. Unai went back to his office to study Bayern Munich and prepare a new video. As he worked, Damià poked his head through the door: both owners would be at Villa Park for the Champions League encounter.

By the start of the 2024–25 season, just as Aston Villa were about to step back on to the grandest stage of all, preparing for their first Champions League campaign in forty-two years, with a group-stage opener against Swiss side Young Boys, there had been enough shared experiences, conversations and decisions between Unai Emery, his inner circle and the club's ownership to take a clear measure of where things stood. While the team was in the United States for preseason, Wes Edens called Damià. He wanted to host a gathering at his penthouse in Manhattan. When asked how many people could come, assuming it would just be the captains or the manager, Edens replied, 'Everyone.' And by that, he meant the chefs, kit staff, security personnel . . . he opened his home to all. Whether the terrace, the dining room or the spectacular views, his penthouse is truly impactful. He even brought out the NBA trophy the Milwaukee Bucks won in 2021 so everyone could take a photo.

Damià describes the relationship with the owners, Nassef Sawiris and Wes Edens, as having been nothing short of extraordinary since day one. Naturally, there have been moments of disagreement but always within a framework of mutual respect. Neither of them has ever got involved in tactical matters or specific transfer decisions. Their focus is firmly on resource management.

With Wes, Damià is the main point of contact, largely due to language reasons, and speaks with him a couple of times a week by phone, but he also communicates directly with Unai and Monchi when needed. After matches, he often sends Damià a message, usually a graphic or a photo. He visits Birmingham two or three times a year and hosts regular meetings in the US. The 2024 summer trip with the visit to his apartment marked the fifth time Damià had met him there – sometimes alone, sometimes accompanied by Unai or Monchi.

Visits to Wes are informal and comprise dinner together or time spent in his office talking about the state of the club, the broader picture of English football. They're about understanding what's on his mind and helping Wes understand what's on theirs from the football side. It is important that owners feel part of the decision-making. What's striking is how closely Wes follows the club – not just the first team but academy players too, often knowing them by name and position. His background in American sports offers a clear blueprint that Damià has studied closely: the success of the Milwaukee Bucks took place despite lacking the financial scale and TV revenue of the league's biggest franchises, built on structure and elite talent, with the Bucks now boasting two of the NBA's top ten players. But Edens, seeing the work of Unai, has appreciated more than ever a third, essential element to that formula: a commitment to precision.

Wes has often told Damià how surprising he finds the European model of high transfer fees. In US sports, trades and free agency dominate – multi-million-dollar payments for players simply don't exist. Villa, by contrast, have been one of the Premier League's most conservative clubs in net spend since Unai's arrival, ranking nineteenth, while also making major sales like Moussa Diaby and Douglas Luiz.

Nassef is deeply involved in day-to-day operations, not just at the club but across all his businesses, especially for important matters. This includes commercial activities and sponsorship discussions.

Sawiris treats Aston Villa almost as a personal project, he is always reachable and responds immediately, day or night. He shares a WhatsApp group with Damià and Monchi. He's accessible, it's not unusual to call him one day and then be meeting with him in London the next. He's consistently attentive to the team's needs and if an investment is required, even something as specific as new physiotherapy equipment or a new member of the medical team, his answer is invariably supportive. When he visits Villa Park, he makes a point of greeting everyone and engaging with staff across all levels. But he keeps his feelings inside, he doesn't like to speak very much during matches.

A third American partner has joined the ownership group since Unai's arrival, the Philadelphia-based Atairos group, led by former executives of Comcast, one of the largest broadcasters in the world. While the manager has had less direct contact with them, their role within the structure is significant. They contribute with vast media and business expertise, rooted in their background at Comcast.

In two and a half years, neither Nassef nor Wes, themselves fully aligned in vision and approach, have raised their voice or shown frustration. There's been no crisis. Their expectations are felt not through pressure but through support and the responsibility the staff take on themselves.

The transfer market is where tensions arise, when the football side has had to firmly defend its position while the owners protect their investment. Deals can be complex or risky, and the timing rarely fits perfectly – ideally, you'd sell before buying but that's not always possible. When it's transfer window time, there's no inter-mediary. Damià, Nassef and Monchi communicate directly and constantly. There's no need for formal protocols during this period because everything moves with urgency. Plus, since Premier

League club owners speak to one another, Nassef sometimes plays the good cop or the bad cop in negotiations with rivals, depending on what's needed.

After the first eighteen months working with Unai, both owners would admit that the Basque has reshaped their view of how a football club operates. It reinforced the importance of aligning leadership with long-term vision and the value of stability. Once they find the right manager, they came to realise, everything else flows from there. That's why they committed to Unai until 2029 and, hopefully, they think it will extend even beyond that. Their idea of success has evolved. It's no longer defined solely by trophies or league position. With Aston Villa, they see success in how the club grows. Unai admits, half-jokingly, that Nassef has to put up with him more than most. 'When we lose, I can be unbearable,' he says, with Nassef sometimes on the receiving end. There have been moments when, after a defeat, Nassef has tried to offer encouragement, praising the performance, only for Unai to snap back with a comment like 'That's not enough.' For all their mutual respect, Emery doesn't hide his own uncompromising view of football: if you don't win, it's not good enough.

Damià, caught somewhere in the middle, has had to play peacemaker more than once. 'You've scared Nassef off again,' he's joked to Unai. 'They come to help, and you react like that.' But both owners were always going to be present for the Bayern Munich game at Villa Park in early October – the centrepiece of Aston Villa's 150th anniversary celebrations. Surviving members of the 1982 European Cup-winning team, that won the final against the same German team, were invited to dinner the night before and shown around Bodymoor Heath, several of whom had not seen it before. But there was one painful absence. On 16 September, news of Gary Shaw's death reached supporters gathered in Bern for the first Aston Villa Champions League match in 41 years, against Young Boys. He was only sixty-three. Shaw's passing was sudden, unexpected and deeply felt – especially by fans who had grown up idolising him. Weeks later, at night in the training ground stories were shared as a way to soften the grief. Gary had been the youngest member of that legendary 1982 side. A homegrown talent. A brilliant, fluid forward whose career was cut short by injuries that, today, might have been managed. In 1982, he was crowned Young European Footballer of the Year. The golden boy of his generation. He once recalled a story from the 1983 European Super Cup, when Villa faced Barcelona. After a 1–0 loss in the first leg at the Camp Nou, Maradona approached Shaw at full-time and asked for his shirt. Shaw wanted to oblige, but the Villa kit man wouldn't allow it – the club simply didn't have enough shirts to spare. In the return leg at Villa Park, Villa beat Barça 3–0.

The Bayern game was more than just the second Champions League fixture in the new league format. It was a chance to test, in real time, the club's new standing. What was Aston Villa's true status as an institution? Was the team genuinely competitive at this level? In the press conference in Bodymoor Heath to preview the match, Unai Emery was calm. It wasn't marked by grand speeches or overt nostalgia; Unai rarely works that way. But he of course understood what the moment meant. 'We have players with European experience,' he stated. 'And some of them will make their Champions League debut tomorrow. That's great for them, for the club and for me. I've been in Europe for sixteen years in a row. The most important thing is consistency throughout the season. Tomorrow is a special match, but I am preparing the match the same as I did on Sunday against Ipswich.'

The build-up hadn't been entirely smooth. Whispers of a potential January move for Diego Carlos to Fenerbahçe had begun to surface, fuelled by his high-profile error against Ipswich. Villa's defensive record was under scrutiny too, with just one clean sheet in eight games that had come away in the victory to Young Boys in their European opener. The discipline and cohesion that defined the previous season still felt just out of reach. Unai's decision was not to protect Diego but to trust him – to give him the biggest game of the season. 'If he plays well,' he reasoned to his staff, 'I get him back for the cause.'

After the press conference, Unai joined the team. There was only one meeting, but it lasted around an 1 hour and 20 minutes. It required a lot of detail. The message, as always, was layered. 'In football, there are three types of opponents: those at your level, those below and those above,' Unai stated. 'When you play against superior teams, like Bayern, you know you have to admit they have more alternatives than you, give your maximum and, sometimes, surprise them.' The video session was split in two: about 40 minutes on how to attack Bayern and another 40 on how to defend. As Unai spoke, he sketched out Bayern's different positioning structures. Every scenario was analysed. How to hurt them. Where they could hurt Villa. What each player's position should be at every moment. He highlighted their goalkeeper's advanced role and comfort on the ball. Unai recalled the 1–0 win against Bayern with Villarreal, when Manuel Neuer twice came out of his goal to play the ball. On one occasion, Gerard Moreno nearly scored from midfield.

Another insight stood out. Villa planned to press hard when Joshua Kimmich and Dayot Upamecano received the ball, Unai believed they were vulnerable in duels. A third point: 'We know that when they push up without the ball, they defended in one-on-one situations,' he explained. So, Villa would try to exploit that with long balls, second balls and aggressive runs from deep. The plan wasn't to sit off or play it safe all the time. 'We tried to convey that, regardless of their status, our idea was to face them head-on,' Unai said.

At the heart of it was one of Unai's core principles: 'If I lose once, I don't want to lose twice.' Meaning: if you lose, you lose but not because you convinced yourself you had no chance or by changing your way of playing. 'Always with respect, but making it clear we're not here by accident.'

'When you face a team like Bayern,' he said, perhaps to prepare himself, 'you have to take many key decisions. The great coaches, like Guardiola, always find a way to win, even when it seems impossible.' But Emery knew that even with the best-laid plans, many things still had to go their way: a goalkeeper's miraculous save, a defensive block at the last second, a moment of clarity in front of goal. 'Above all,' he added, 'you need a high level of defensive commitment, that allows your strengths in attack to be exploited.'

Wes flew in from New York with his family the morning of the match, arriving at 7 a.m. and had organised to return straight after the game. Also in attendance were UEFA president Aleksander Čeferin, Giorgio Marchetti – UEFA's director of competitions and the man who runs the Champions League draw, and the CEO of Adidas, Bjørn Gulden, – who spent time speaking with Unai Emery. Adidas would later sign Unai as a brand ambassador, another indication of his growing global profile. And, of course, Prince William.

Since Unai's arrival, Prince William has visited Villa Park and Bodymoor Heath multiple times, joined staff for meals and taken time to speak with players – especially familiar faces like Watkins, McGinn and Mings. His manner is always discreet and respectful. He speaks regularly with Damià about signings and team news, sends messages of support and has developed a genuine rapport with the manager. 'He's on top of everything,' said Unai. 'He usually tells Damià to pass on encouragement. It is admirable and I think it's because he's English. They're loyal to their club, it becomes part of their lifestyle, not just a hobby.' The prince and Unai talk football: ideas, opponents, specific players. 'It's a very natural, football-focused conversation,' said Damià. 'He sits with us in the canteen when he visits and chats like a member of the board.' He describes him as humble and fully informed. Before Thomas Tuchel named his first England squad, the prince crossed paths with the international manager and pushed hard – and with conviction – for the inclusion of Aston Villa's standout players.

The whole day, there was a weight in the air for the prince, for Nassef and Wes, for Villa supporters – not just anticipation but something deeper. A quiet, collective recognition: this is where the club belongs. Nobody wanted to shout it, but it felt that way. After years adrift from Europe's elite, Villa had found their way back.

Where you're from isn't something you choose, it's something you're born into. At some point in life, consciously or not, you choose to claim it. You accept its contradictions, its scars and worn edges. You carry its past, with all its weight. More often than not, an emotional bond, passed on or embraced, to the local football club comes with it. To follow Aston Villa is to tie your sense of self to something older and larger than you – 150 years of stories, stitched into the fabric of Birmingham as surely as the canals that cut through the city, the red brick terraces that line its streets and the factories that once powered the world.

Football offers its own reasoning. One season ends and you grieve it, whatever came. Then, another begins and with it the dangerous promise of starting again. That's what makes it different and keeps people believing. The Villa fan knows this cycle, has lived through it. This is what the Villa fan understood: that following your club meant accepting vulnerability, risking disappointment in exchange for the hope – however fragile – of joy. But that evening in early October they were ready to think differently about the club and even create new memories that would overwrite what came before. That was why they all wanted to beat Bayern. And for the prestige that came with such a win too.

Back in 1982, when Villa beat the German giant in the European Cup final, it should have been the happiest night of supporter Howard Hodgson's life. But grief shadowed it. Just weeks earlier, his three-year-old brother, Charles, had drowned in a tragic accident. Still, he and his father travelled to the semi-final second leg in Brussels against Anderlecht. They knew many of the players personally. Sid Cowans, Villa's elegant midfielder, wept when told what had happened. He promised to wave to them after the match – and he did. Dennis Mortimer, the captain, gave Howard his sweatbands. 'I never took them off,' Howard said. They didn't make it to the final in Rotterdam. Instead, they went to Jerusalem. They watched the final on television, far from home. And, even from there, they felt it. 'We believed Charles was our guardian angel that night,' said Howard. 'That he wouldn't let Bayern score.'

And they didn't.

All those years later, on their return to the greatest club tournament, it felt like fate when Aston Villa drew Bayern – and Juventus too, their last European opponent in the competition, the season after winning it. So, it was a day to savour. Every minute of it.

Earlier, at work, someone asked Villa fan Adam Barrett if he was worried Villa might suffer the same fate as Celtic, beaten 7–1 by Dortmund the night before. 'Don't be stupid,' he said. 'We've got Unai Emery.' Normally, most fans have a beer near the ground and get to their seats minutes before the game starts, that is the English way. On this occasion the majority came early to Villa

Park to soak in the moment. To claim the day. 'It felt more like a family gathering for a special occasion than a football match,' said Barrett.

Ben Moore got there 4 hours before kick-off. 'The anticipation was unreal,' he enthuses. Adam Britton hadn't planned to be there. He'd spoken out about the £97 ticket price. 'It was ridiculous,' he said. 'It prices people out.' But as the game drew closer, he couldn't stay away. 'I've watched us play Stevenage, Peterborough ... and now I wasn't going to see us play Bayern? I nearly spent £500 on hospitality.' He was lucky, someone offered him a face-value ticket. He took half a day off work, drove to the stadium, arrived just before the gates opened a couple of hours before kick-off. He expected a half-empty ground. It was already packed. 'There was a buzz. Not arrogance – just magic. Like we knew.'

Dave Powell and his son Billy came from the Catalan village of Calonge, where they've lived for the past ten years. Villa runs deep in their blood – three generations of Powells have held season tickets. Dave's father first took him to Villa Park when he was just six or seven, raising him on stories of the golden era. But Dave has lived some big peaks himself – the only major trophy he's never witnessed is the FA Cup. And from those matches and trips came the stories he now passes on to Billy, the kind he never tires of telling. When Billy was born, Dave's first words were: 'Son, we've just signed Olof Mellberg.' The family moved to Spain thinking they'd only make it back a couple of times each season, no point in renewing the season tickets. But once Villa returned to Europe, everything changed. They became season ticket holders again and have travelled to most European matches since. They've fallen in love with all things Spanish and, naturally, with Unai, whom they understand better than the average Villa fan.

They were at Villa Park for the Conference League semi-final against Olympiacos, watching in awe as fans lined the players' walk from the coach to the stadium, flares lighting the route past the fan zone. And of course, they were there when it happened again – that first Champions League night. As the team bus arrived, they joined hundreds of others forming a thunderous, fiery guard of honour – a blaze of claret that carried them all the way to the stadium gates.

'When the players arrived and we heard the roar, it really hit home,' Ben Moore said. Then the Bayern bus pulled up. Their stars stepped off. The scale of the night suddenly felt enormous. For Gemma Taylor-Whitehead, it was all too much. 'I had tears in my eyes,' she said. 'I'd only heard stories from my dad about 1982. I never thought I'd see us play Champions League football at Villa Park.'

On the *Claret and Blue* podcast, Mat Kendrick described his rare decision to walk the perimeter of Villa Park with his son before the match. 'I felt like a tourist. We were soaking it in, talking to people, taking pictures. It was the Champions League. The real thing.' For the FIFA generation, this was the dream. For their parents, a time machine.

Nick Sanders first stepped inside Villa Park in 1994, hand in hand with his dad – a man who had followed Villa home and away since 1971. The first photo of Nick as a baby shows him wrapped in the same scarf his father took to Rotterdam. Against Bayern, that same scarf was with him again. 'When I walked out holding the "All Our Heroes Are Villans" banner, wrapped in that scarf, all I could think about was my dad.' Gary Shaw's death had added another emotional thread. 'From Spink to Martínez, Withe to Watkins, Shaw to Tielemans . . . It's all one story.' The commemorative programme bore Gary's name; his name printed on the day's squad list.

A flag waited on every seat.

The prince wasn't just a guest of honour, he was part of it. He visited the dressing room 30 minutes before kick-off, just as Unai was delivering his team talk, greeting the players one by one.

Unai wanted the owners in the tunnel. For him, it's part of how you build identity. Nassef and Wes understand that instinctively. They know when to be visible and when to step back, and that night, their presence struck exactly the right chord. Standing alongside them were members of the 1982 European Cup-winning team, gathered around the replica trophy that now stands in the middle of the tunnel. Past and present, side by side. Chris Heck, president of business operations, hosted VIPs in the chairman's suite and also came down to the pitch to distribute Aston Villa's 150th-anniversary commemorative medals.

As is tradition before every big European night, Damià, Monchi and Unai posed for their pre-match photo – a ritual before the noise. They shared a few thoughts on Diego Carlos and the talk surrounding him. As Unai had said the day before, he was in the starting eleven – part of a team that had arrived at this peak from very different routes. In goal, World Cup winner Emiliano Martínez. Unai Emery has an emotional connection with the position of goalkeeper, a crucial figure in his structure, and Emi Martínez is the ideal conduit. Today, few goalkeepers in world football occupy a role as central – tactically and psychologically – as Martínez does under Unai Emery. From their time at Arsenal, where he showed raw ambition and mental steel, Emery recognised a player who demanded more of himself than most. A short loan at Reading saved their season; a year later, he was Emery's first-choice keeper. Emi is excrutiatingly self-critical. He holds himself to high standards and expects the same of those around him. He demands and he leads. In team meetings, on the pitch, even at casual meals, he vocalises goals. Whether it's pushing for a clean sheet or tracking a rival's points, he brings objectives into the everyday. That season Emi wanted to play the FA Cup final in Wembley and impress in Europe.

He's a cultural anchor in the dressing room. As a South American, he doesn't need long team meetings to focus, but he respects that others might. From his position as a veteran, one of the leaders, and as a goalkeeper who lives slightly apart from the group – starting and finishing training at different times, wearing different clothes – he reads the mood, senses tension. If he sees Unai more anxious than usual, he'll quietly say to him, 'Míster, we're good. We can win the next game.' He absorbs pressure and redistributes it as confidence. He's also technically obsessive. Whether it's analysing positioning, aerial dominance or distribution, he welcomes scrutiny. With goalkeeper coach Javi García, he's pushed further. 'He helped me unlock my weapons,' Emi Martínez says – long balls, calm build-up under pressure, choosing when to draw a press. He was already a fine shot-stopper; now, he controls games. He once said his achievements with Argentina wouldn't have been possible without the foundation laid at Villa.

Emi Martínez often has the most touches on the pitch. He holds the ball. Waits. Feels the opposition. 'Sometimes Unai would shout: "Not yet, wait another half metre, another second",' the goalkeeper laughs. But he knows he has the manager's trust, even in the tiniest details – like timing, decision-making, space – something that is rare. He was the one who slowed the game down at the start of the Unai era, drawing frustration from fans. But he understood he had to go through it. In Unai, he has found more than a coach. 'He came to my house for coffee recently,' Martínez recalls. 'We talked about the club, football, what he's given me. Those moments stay with you.'

In the mini crisis meeting after Ipswich, the coaches reflected about the position of Ezri Konsa. Where best to use him against Bayern? As a right-back he would be up against the pace and trickery of Serge Gnabry on the wing. By this point, Konsa had earned his place as a centre-back – not just at Villa but with the national team too. And yet, Unai and his coaches still saw him as capable of fulfilling both roles. There's a belief within Villa that Konsa has the potential to reach extraordinary heights – even, as one coach puts it, 'Real Madrid level'. But that can only happen if he refuses to settle for simply being very good. As players grow in stature within a team, they naturally want to play in the position where they feel most confident, most secure. For Konsa, that position is clearly at the heart of defence.

Unai understood Konsa's perspective, but sometimes, for the good of the team, it's better to sacrifice a bit of a player's strength in one position if that area is already well covered. His athleticism, his ability to turn and recover, his reading of the game – all of it makes him arguably the best suited for the hybrid role that Villa sometimes require. The previous season, Villa had beaten Arsenal twice, and Manchester City too, playing him at right-back. The problem is the player doesn't always see it that way. In any case, when asked to play there Konsa's response is always the same: a dependable 'Yes, of course.' But in that role not all of his qualities are always fully on show – and that's the manager's dilemma.

The Ipswich game exposed the problem. Konsa, usually a model of composure, appeared to play within himself, retreating rather than stepping out, reacting rather than imposing. Two days later, he was challenged directly. He was reminded that someone of his ability cannot afford that level of performance – hesitating rather than committing. If others don't follow, that's their problem. As a full-back too, there are non-negotiables. If you're already wide, you must commit to stopping the winger – don't get caught in no man's land. Even if the cross still comes, make sure you've done everything in your power to stop it.

Unai Emery has little patience for wasted potential, and when he senses a player holding something back, the tension can rise. There have been moments, even publicly, when Emery and Konsa have clashed. One such flashpoint came during a narrow 1–0 win over Fulham at Villa Park. After Konsa lost the ball and allowed a dangerous counter-attack, Emery's frustration boiled over. The two exchanged sharp words on the touchline. 'I have no problem with players showing anger. We speak a lot about how important it is to focus for 90 minutes in our game plan, to feel comfortable. But if someone is relaxing then we are going to lose. When we lost balls in the first half, in the dressing room I told them: "I can't accept how we are managing the game!"'

Konsa's response that day does not reflect what he feels for Unai and what he has done for him. Ezri Konsa, twenty-seven, has risen from Newham's streets to the Champions League with Aston Villa. A product of grassroots side Senrab, he began at Charlton, moved to Brentford and joined Villa in 2019. After a dip in form under Steven Gerrard, he has thrived under Emery, becoming one of Villa's most trusted and used players. In 2024, he earned an England call-up, starting in the Euro 2024 quarter-final against Switzerland, and made his Champions League debut. The last time Ezri Konsa crossed paths with Harry Kane, now leading the line for Bayern Munich, was with the England squad. As they chatted, Konsa couldn't resist asking with a smile: 'You ready for Villa Park in October?'

Finally, Unai decided Konsa would start at right-back and asked him to be more intense. That choice meant Matty Cash – the usual occupant of that position and one of the players who has developed most under Unai – remained on the bench. When Matty Cash first arrived at Aston Villa from Nottingham Forest in September 2020, his game was instinctive. A converted winger, he saw every gap as an invitation to burst forward. 'I was always pass and run. That was my game,' he admits. But the demands of Champions League football – and of Unai Emery – make the game more tactical. Early on, curious and eager to impress, he looked up Villarreal clips and noticed that Emery's full-backs – particularly the right-backs – played with more restraint. 'I thought, *Oh no*,' he jokes. Cash had to rewire the way he thought about space. And two years later, the change is visible. He no longer chases every run. He chooses them. 'It's not just playing now, you have to read, think, time it. It's about being a smart footballer.'

One mistake stayed in his mind and became a turning point. Against Chelsea, he tried to play a one-two in midfield, leaving his side exposed to a counter-attack that ended in a goal. Emery didn't berate him – he dissected the moment in video, calmly explaining that sometimes 'pass and support' is better than 'pass and run'. Cash now always checks: if we lose the ball, am I in position to defend? He still attacks – a cutback for Ollie Watkins's goal against Brighton came after he timed a run into space perfectly – but it's now calculated and rehearsed in training. 'He'll show us the full picture, all eleven players, where we should be. If we're not there, he'll let us know.' That intensity was difficult at first. Pau Torres remembers how some teammates struggled to read Emery's passion. 'They'd come to me asking, "Is he angry? Did I do something wrong?" Like Matty. And I'd tell them that if he's pressing you, it means he trusts you. He wants more.' The night before matches, in the quiet of the hotel, Emery often reminds the squad of what it takes. Sometimes, he'll hold up a message from friends out partying: 'That will come – but first, the work.' Then he will explain what they have to do. His team talks settle the nerves. 'They bring clarity. You walk out feeling ready,' Cash says.

For the Bayern match, Pau Torres was going to be second centre-back next to Diego Carlos. When he joined Aston Villa in the summer of 2023, it wasn't with the guarantee of a starting place. Unai Emery was clear from the outset: the team had finished the previous season strongly, and he intended to reward that continuity. 'I'll give you the opportunity when I see you're ready,' Unai told Pau. That chance arrived sooner than expected. On the opening day of the Premier League season, Tyrone Mings went down with a knee injury just 25 minutes into the match at Newcastle. Torres, still adjusting to his new environment, got the call. He did what he always does – kept calm, did what he had worked on in preseason. But Villa lost 5–1, a bruising introduction. *Welcome to the Premier League*, he thought.

It was the start of a steady integration. At Villarreal, Pau Torres had played in a deeper defensive line alongside the veteran Raúl Albiol. At Villa, Emery wanted something more aggressive – a higher line, pressing harder, squeezing the pitch. Initially, it left gaps. Opponents exploited them. Midfielders would pivot and launch balls into space without even looking – forwards were already running. Pau and the others felt exposed. So, they adapted. Players spoke openly in the dressing room, shared their concerns and the coaching staff listened. The line dropped a few yards. Not too deep, not too high – just enough to feel in control. In high-level games like Liverpool away, where timing and precision were ruthless, that slight adjustment helped. 'They didn't get in behind once,' Pau remembers. 'Their danger came from counter-attacks, not through our line.' Over time, the tactical nuances grew more complex. Opponents adjusted. Presses became smarter, designed to block Villa's build-up from the back. Pau had to analyse in real time, learn how to identify space, when to risk a pass, when to step in. With Rodri, he now spends time before each match dissecting how to beat the press and how to win his individual duels.

Pau has always been impressed with the timing of Unai's speeches. Pau remembers two. One, away at Chelsea, where the manager stopped mid-talk, stood in front of each player, looked them in the eye, and asked: 'Are you convinced we'll win?' One by one, they had to answer. Loud. Clear. They won 0–1. The other came after a defeat to Nottingham Forest. Spurs were flying, 5 or 6 points ahead. In the post-match meeting, Emery didn't dwell on the loss. He showed the table, pointed at Tottenham and said, 'That's our rival. If we overtake them, we make the Champions League.' They did.

Off the pitch, Unai's usual attention to detail showed early, checking that Pau was settled, asking about his home life and family. Pau noticed a shift too: Unai was growing into his role at Villa. He had brought the same obsessive care from Villarreal, but in England his presence felt more defined. He was no longer just a well-respected coach but the leader of a club with bigger expectations, ready to face teams like Bayern Munich on equal terms.

In the left-back position, Lucas Digne. The previous summer, he was expected to leave, just waiting for the move to go through. Then, ahead of a preseason friendly, Unai told him he wanted him to play – and to give it everything. That week, things changed. 'You're not going,' Unai told him. Just like that. Against Bayern he needed to be better than his erratic performance against Ipswich, where he got a yellow card and had to be replaced. He needed to be consistent, to attack when it was necessary, to defend most of the time. To make good decisions. Unai thought he could.

Youri Tielemans, who was having a very solid season, and Amadou Onana, signed from Everton that summer for £50 million, would occupy the centre of midfield. Onana came to fill the considerable void left by Douglas Luiz's move to Juventus. Tall, athletic and tactically curious, the Belgian midfielder had always possessed raw talent. But what Unai Emery offered was something more refined. Onana himself admitted as much: Emery was improving aspects of his game he hadn't even known existed before joining. 'I think I'm a completely different player from last season. He's one of the best in the business.' At Villa he's had more time on the ball, more responsibility, similar to his role in the Belgium national team. That suits him. His start at Villa was impressive: two goals in his first three games. But there was no resting on early form.

Ahead of the holding midfielders, the trio of Jaden Philogene, Morgan Rogers, and Jacob Ramsey carried the attacking thrust. For Philogene, it was a chance to prove he belonged at this level – if he backed his instincts, attacked the Bayern defence with confidence and balanced it with the discipline Emery demands. Rogers and Ramsey, each on their own ascent, offered energy and the kind of unpredictability that could unsettle even a side like Bayern.

Leading the line was Ollie Watkins: first choice, undisputed and in the kind of form that made him undroppable. He was on his way to becoming Aston Villa's all-time top Premier League goalscorer, chasing down Gabby Agbonlahor's record of seventy-four. Jhon Durán, for all his promise, hadn't yet earned the right to start.

On the bench, among others, Leon Bailey and Boubacar Kamara. Leon Bailey reached his best level under Unai Emery the previous season, featuring in thirty-five Premier League games, scoring ten goals and providing nine assists. This season, though, was going to be tougher despite being Villa's best dribbler. Others around him had improved, and his position was now under pressure. Boubacar Kamara, bought from Marseille in 2022, is one of the most admired players at Aston Villa. Before suffering a major setback in February 2024 – an ACL injury that ruled him out for over six months – he had become a vital part of Unai Emery's midfield structure. Emery has long believed that Kamara possesses the rare blend of intelligence, calmness under pressure and personality required to dictate the rhythm of a top-level side.

At first glance, Kamara doesn't grab attention: there's an awkwardness to his running, his unkempt hair, his quiet, almost detached demeanour. But the more you watch, the more you see how he controls matches, always asking for the ball, making sharp decisions, winning duels. He's stable, selfless, tactically fluent and at the same time disciplined. He's one of the few who hasn't needed much individual work. Give him an instruction – drop between the centre-backs during the build-up, shift into a double pivot, press to the left – and he executes without fuss. He doesn't engage much in back-and-forths. He listens. Then he does it. That rare type of soldier. Kamara doesn't attract much press attention, but those close to the team know the truth: when fully fit, he's among the most complete midfielders in the league. Emery knows it too – and he couldn't wait to have him back at his best.

Tyrone Mings didn't want to get in the way. Sidelined through injury, he's never liked having outsiders hover around matchdays. They already have enough people in and around the dressing room. That night, he showed up at Villa Park quietly, gave a quick interview to TNT pitchside, stepped into the changing room for no more than 30 seconds and left it to those who would actually be stepping on to the pitch. He didn't go to many games while injured – maybe two or three – but this one felt different. Something was building. You could feel it in the stands, in the atmosphere, in the noise around the match. But, funnily enough, perhaps not in the dressing room. 'There,' he said, 'it's business as usual.' He himself couldn't fully enjoy it. 'Did I enjoy it? Not really. It was a great occasion, but I was not happy sitting in the stands. Nervous? I probably felt that I wanted the team to give a good account of ourselves. I hoped that we stayed in the game. I hoped that the fans went away thinking: *Wow, what a great atmosphere, what a great evening.*'

The Bayern Munich starting eleven was largely what Villa had anticipated, though there was real surprise that young Jamal Musiala wasn't included. He had played every game and was often the one finding pockets of space and making the difference. Still, French international Michael Olise was there to provide quality in the final third. So, the idea was clear: in medium and low blocks, the focus had to be on owning your zone – defending your space first, then stepping out aggressively when the moment was right in one-to-one marking. The goal was to make Bayern uncomfortable. But with a team like this – so many attacking options, so much tactical fluidity – it's inevitable that they pull you apart at times. Their constant positional rotations create overloads, and in those moments, you can't always maintain your structure. The plan wasn't to defend deep, but sometimes you're forced into it. Villa knew they wouldn't dominate possession – Bayern were simply too good at it and had an exceptional pressure high up the pitch – but the aim was to press when possible and look for direct transitions. If Watkins could isolate Upamecano, there were opportunities to be found in behind. Playing out from the back depended on how Emi Martínez saw the field.

In the final meeting before the game, Unai Emery stayed calm. No shouting, no drama. He made a few quick tactical adjustments after hearing Bayern's line-up, then tried to strip the moment of excess emotion. He didn't want the team paralysed by the occasion. Yes, it was Bayern Munich. Yes, the world was watching. But for Emery, this wasn't a one-off spectacle. It was the standard. This, he told them, cannot feel like a reward. It's not a prize. Others might see it that way – fans, pundits, opponents – but not us. Because teams who treat it like a prize are the ones who vanish. They arrive in Europe once, light up the stage briefly and fade. That's not who we are.' He spoke of Atlético Madrid under Simeone, of Liverpool, Arsenal, Manchester City – teams who turned qualification into ritual. He wanted Villa to belong to that world. To stay. That's why the last result, the draw against Ipswich, had stung so much. Because it might be the difference between coming back . . . or not. 'We came here to stay,' he said. 'With ups and downs, yes, but to stay.' This was a step.

The roar when the players stepped on to the pitch was deafening. Then the Champions League anthem began. And suddenly, silence. Villa Park held its breath. For a second. No one moved. No one spoke. Shivers ran down spines. No one wanted the moment to end. It felt too precious – like if they blinked, someone might call it off. 'There's been an admin error,' they'd say. 'You're meant to be in the Europa League.' Then came another roar, louder than before. 'It's the loudest I've ever heard Villa Park,' Emi Martínez said afterwards. His ears rang for minutes.

The opening was careful. Cautious. 'We played the occasion, not the opposition,' says Adam Barrett. Bayern started with all the initiative and nearly 70 per cent possession but couldn't find Olise or Kane. Defensively Villa adjusted their height intelligently from the start – when they tried to press high, Bayern very occasionally broke through, exposing Villa's back line. Recognising this, Villa dropped deeper as the match wore on, prioritising solidity and closing passing lanes effectively.

Unai's players kept drawing Bayern forward with patient build-up, using Emi Martínez to create overloads. As Bayern marked aggressively, when their forwards committed, Villa exploited the gaps, finding the spare man and attacking quickly through wide areas or direct balls into Watkins and the wingers. It worked. Twice, Watkins spun centre-back Upamecano and was hauled down – one challenge went unpunished despite it being a possible red; the second earned only a yellow. Villa sensed the weakness.

Pau Torres scored from a set-piece. The Holte End erupted. Then VAR – the goal was disallowed for offside. A moment's release taken away but the momentum was shifting. Watkins and Rogers pressed. Tielemans stayed calm. As Mings put it, 'You realise we're causing them just as many problems as they're causing us.' Bayern tried to control the tempo, but Villa never cracked. Even with 600 passes, Bayern weren't hurting anyone. After 27 minutes, Jacob Ramsey – making his Champions League home debut as a proud Villa academy graduate – pulled up with a muscle problem. Leon Bailey came on in his place.

At half-time, still goalless, Unai Emery praised the team's defensive performance, particularly Diego Carlos and Pau Torres who he felt were at their peak. His message was simple: keep up the intensity. Villa were holding their own against world-class forwards, and Emery wanted that physical level sustained. Tactically, only small tweaks were needed unless Bayern shifted shape.

Emi Martínez had made saves on a couple of occasions, and he was needed in the second half too. Musiala, who had been brought on at half-time by the German side, had a double chance, but Unai stayed calm. He wanted quicker reactions in transition and more patience with the ball and was telling the players exactly that from the technical area but he liked the shape and was very impressed by Konsa's leadership.

Leon Bailey's substitution for Ian Maatsen after just 33 minutes on the pitch wasn't a punishment. Putting him on was a calculated risk that, ultimately, had to be managed. Bailey had only recently returned from a hamstring injury and was still not fully fit. In the days before the match, he missed part of training due to an infection and swollen lymph nodes and scans revealed a small abductor issue. While not serious, it came with the risk of aggravation. The player wanted to help and pushed to be available – just as he had done against Ipswich, when he played through discomfort for over an hour. Leon Bailey remembered Unai's words from that previous time when having been a sub he was replaced too: 'This isn't personal. It's not a humiliation. I treat you all equally, and if I sub you off, it's because at that moment I believe it's best for the team.'

The constant noise of the fans added to the occasion – loud, defiant. They made the evening worthy of the Champions League. At the 70-minute mark, Jhon Durán was about to come on for Ollie Watkins. Before sending him on, Unai Emery pulled him aside and fixed him with a look. 'You know why I'm putting you on, don't you?' he asked.

'Yes,' Durán replied.

'To win us the game.'

The substitution was perilous because, with the physical intensity of the match, if another substitution was made and then Jhon or another player picked up an injury it would have meant playing with a man down.

Tension rose. What could the player that fans called Captain Chaos do here?

Jhon confirmed in the way he approached his minutes on the

pitch, that he doesn't feel pressure, quite the opposite, he thrives on it.

Then, minute 79.

A move starts with a ball that Emi catches with his hands, and from there, he throws it straight to Pau Torres. From high in the Upper Holte End, Adam Barrett saw it early. Torres with the perfect weighted pass. Supporter Will Forrest had grown up on stories of his grandad travelling to Rotterdam, the stand bouncing as Peter Withe's shot went in. Now, Will was in the Holte End with his own son wondering what Jhon was going to do with that ball from Torres.

25 yards out from the Bayern goal, the striker stretched his arm out and swung his left foot with his first touch. He had not even looked at the goalkeeper, Manuel Neuer, who was away from his line. The strike was clean.

The net rippled. The place exploded.

Aston Villa 1. Bayern Munich 0.

Delirium. Disbelief. Movement in every direction. 'The ground shook,' says Barrett.

When the ball hit the net, Will's son didn't speak. 'He was speechless,' Will recalls. 'His face was pure joy.'

Sam stood still. Hands on head. Mouth open. 'I couldn't believe my eyes.'

Limbs. Everywhere. What the kids call 'ultimate limbs'.

Another number 9. Another 1–0. From Withe to Duran. It felt like fate.

You have to appreciate Jhon Durán's talent in that situation, he did not have time to properly control the ball. If the move had developed on the right side, he might not have attempted the same finish, even with the keeper just as far off his line. He would have needed to use his right foot, but he's very comfortable finishing on his stronger left foot.

Durán's winning goal – his fourteenth for the club, ten of them as a substitute – came on the back of tactical instructions issued by Unai and Rodri, who had shown that exact move to the Villa strikers, which Durán eventually executed. But Durán admitted that his lob was instinctive, saying he didn't see Neuer off his line, 'I put my hand out to check if Upamecano was there. Then I struck it. I don't need to watch it again. I've got it in my head.' A crucial goal on the biggest of stages. Durán wasn't just a handful, he was a weapon of mass destruction. He had just written himself into European folklore.

In the Holte End, a chant: 'Gary Shaw, Gary Shaw.' A moving tribute.

In the final minutes, as Bayern pushed and Villa – roared on by the stands – closed every gap, Harry Kane had a chance, an aerial ball, headed on the edge of the six-yard box. But Emi Martínez produced a huge save. The visitors appealed for a penalty after a supposed handball by Pau Torres. VAR reviewed it, the referee waved it away.

From a physical standpoint, the data from the match for Villa was excellent – both aerobic output and high-intensity efforts were where they needed to be in such a demanding match. You only hit those levels if you've had to defend a lot without the ball – and do it well. Bayern's expected goals, a statistic that measures the quality of a chance, were higher than Villa's, which was expected. With teams like Bayern's, a lot of things need to go right – and they did: but specifically you require Bayern to miss a few chances, because with their quality, chances are inevitable. As for Villa, while they couldn't turn their attacking moments into truly clear chances, there were four or five transitions where, if they'd found the final pass, they might've created a one-on-one chance.

Overall, it went largely to plan. Now, all that was left was the whistle. When it came, no one moved from their place. Fans just shouted, hugged, jumped. Eyes opened, heads shaking. Massive smiles. Many turned to strangers offering handshakes, hugs, stunned smiles. A shared disbelief. Villa had done it again. Bayern came into the game with a forty-two-match unbeaten run in the Champions League group stage. They left with nothing.

Gemma called it 'One of the best nights I've ever experienced at Villa Park.' Ben Moore turned to the fan next to him and asked, 'Did that really happen?' Adam Britton video-called his sons. 'They were jealous for not having there, but proud. I am jealous of them! They've only ever seen the rise. They don't remember relegation. They've only seen the progress.'

Emery cut a calm figure on the touchline. Rather than go wild or start demonstratively fist-pumping towards the Holte End, the Villa boss merely shook hands with his opposite number Vincent Kompany. He then strode purposefully down the touchline, applauding fans who serenaded him along the way. After a quick hug with a staff member, Emery then made his way down the tunnel, high-fiving a few fans as he did so.

Villa's record against Bayern: Played 2. Won 2. Scored 2. Conceded 0.

It was six years to the day since a fan hurled a cabbage at Steve Bruce in protest during a 3–3 draw against Preston North End in the Championship. Six years since the start of the rebuild. Bruce sacked. Smith arrived. Promotion. Gerrard. Then Unai. And now – this. That chronology hit some. Nick Sanders put it best: 'This was more than a win. It was a thank you – to Unai, to the players, to the owners but mostly to those who came before. The legends. The believers.'

Sam stayed frozen in place until the stewards ushered him out. When he came out, people were still walking around with their hands on their heads. On the *Claret and Blue* podcast, Kendrick couldn't stop talking about the goal. 'I've watched it a hundred times,' he said. 'The pass. The finish. It's not just a brilliant goal, it's a moment that will live for ever.' He even wrote lyrics: 'Jhon Duran is on my mind . . . and he's Villa's number nine.'

Mat – who had lived the drama of Phil King's winning penalty against Inter Milan in the 1990 UEFA Cup; the thrilling nights of the same competition against Inter in 1994 and Ajax in 2008; O'Neill's 2–1 win over Chelsea in the Premier League in 2009 – said this one topped them all. 'I think that was the best night I've ever had at Villa Park. And I've had a few.'

As for Adam Britton, who almost stayed home: 'No matter what happens next, we'll always have that night.'

It may not be Rotterdam. These players may never carry the same weight as the legends of 1982, that was a European Cup win. But what they did – what Emery's Villa did – was remind a new generation of what's possible. There was no champagne, no rousing speeches in the dressing room. Just handshakes. Unai waited at the door to greet every player, as he always does. English teams expect some words from the manager right after a game. Generally, not with Unai. They know that unless it's a crisis or a disaster, Emery prefers to wait, to reflect. 'In Spain,' says one coach, 'in coaching schools they tell you never to talk straight after a game. But here you adapt.' On this occasion Unai decided to say only a couple of words. One sentence, really: 'Next, Manchester United.' That was it.

Then came Prince William down to the dressing room with Villa's co-owners. His Royal Highness had spent the match singing, shouting and cheering – so much so that he lost his voice. The prince had a quiet word with the manager. 'I told him the best moments we can have are days like today,' said Emery. 'And that we have to enjoy the journey, because when you reach the end, whatever it is, it's what we're doing along the way, each day, each match, that matters most.'

The press conference carried a distinctive respectful winning feeling and a relief as Unai had established that he was moulding a team that could reach the heights he wanted.

'Before the match, winning wasn't the only objective. It was about how closely we could compete, and we did. We had to defend more than usual and improve on the last game. I'm proud of how we're growing, raising our level and our demands. Lucas Digne, for instance. In a game that demanded defensive discipline, he was solid, while going forward when he could – exactly what was needed.

'In the end, you can win or lose. Sometimes it comes down to a save from Emi or a flash of talent – like Durán's goal, which reminded me of one he scored against Hibernian last year. That day, after getting a pass from Pau, he drove past the goalkeeper. This time, we had discussed how Neuer offers you the option to beat him by lobbing him. That's his instinct. We have two strong strikers. Watkins is always consistent. Durán is improving, getting closer to starting. Having them both together on the pitch is a new challenge I welcome, meanwhile both are winning us points.'

'The atmosphere was amazing. There's a real connection between the team and our fans. They're feeding us energy. Now, the objective is clear: reach the next round and push for a top-four finish in this new Champions League format.'

The players headed home to their families. But the staff? That's when they start what they call '*el sanedrín del larguero*', a homage to a Spanish radio football debate show. No families, just football brains staying back to analyse, vent, laugh and, if needed but not that night, mourn. 'That night,' Pablo said, 'we'd just eliminated Bayern again, like Villarreal did in the Champions League quarter-final. So yeah, we stayed a while.'

And yet no one got carried away. 'The risk now,' said Damià, 'is people think we're Bayern Munich. And we're not. We have to value what we've done, but if we relax, or think we're already there, we'll mess it up.' Unai asked Damià to proofread a message before posting it to Instagram, his first in a long time. It read:

Too many feelings inside, but I can explain in one word what happened tonight ... PERFECT! Prince William, Wes and Nassef, great players, the coaching staff, the 82 heroes, the media ... the whole club having a beautiful night. Tomorrow back to work with energy and recharged! BUT tonight ... I just came back to social media to say from the heart: Thank you! To every Villa fan. We know your sacrifices, personal effort, how much you must work to be able to come to VP or watch us on TV. I hope you enjoy as much as you deserve. See you and need you fresh on Sunday! UP THE VILLA!

'That match made me feel good,' Unai said later. 'The players trust me. If I say something is black, they believe me. Even if they doubt it for a second, they trust that it's for their benefit. What's best for me is best for them too. I'm selfish like that.'

Damià had to remind them about the time. 'When we've gone off-piste chatting nonsense, and it's getting late, I say: "Come on lads, we've won, let's go home."' He's always the first out the door. The coaches arrived back home around half twelve. Unai, with the echo of a thunderous night still pulsing in the air, now alone in his flat, was already plotting the message for the next morning. 'Lads,' he planned to say, 'we're playing a team people think are terrible. I'm telling you, if we don't clench like we did against Bayern, they'll beat us.'

13

THE ARCHITECTS:

HOW TO BUILD A SQUAD

Ahead of the Manchester United game, Unai Emery was asked how he had managed to transform the team to make them capable of beating Bayern Munich. 'Mentality is built every day. In how we train, how we talk, how we eat together. If we relax even once, we're going the wrong way.'

The subsequent 0–0 draw against United, even more than the victory against the German giants, revealed where the team was two months into the season. On the touchline, Emery could be seen correcting Ollie Watkins during a break in play, urging him not to hang back when their rivals went long, reminding him of his job when the second ball drops. Inside the dressing room at half-time, the tone was sharp. Too many rushed decisions. 'Games that become end to end like that one,' Emery told them, 'often take more than they give.' There were chances – Jaden Philogene's miss in the 90th minute, a Marcus Rashford header brilliantly saved by Emiliano Martínez – and even a potential penalty for Villa that wasn't awarded after a VAR review for handball, but the draw was fair, as Unai admitted to the media.

Behind the scenes, however, the analysis was clear. There was fatigue, loss of energy. The Champions League represented a new level of demand and there was more of it as the new league format included two more games in the first phase, matches in January and a possible extra knockout stage in February. Injuries to McGinn, Konsa, Ramsey and Onana had disrupted the rhythm. Onana, for instance, had trained the day before United but he felt a sprint might tear something. In the last training session, they had worked on build-ups where he had a specific role. That's what makes these weeks so brutal. You build a plan, only to tear it up hours before kick-off if something occurs. There were only a few options on the bench.

Overall, the feeling was still of progress, but could it be sustained, and how would everyone respond, if for the first time at Villa under Unai the trajectory was not upwards? Was everyone asking too much of a squad that only two years prior were trying to avoid relegation? Half of the players were still there.

Six weeks later, by late November, something had shifted. The season had taken shape, but not in the way Aston Villa had imagined. Still within reach of the top four, still alive in Europe, but the flow had become jagged. A string of draws, narrow defeats, and missed opportunities – Bournemouth, Crystal Palace, Spurs, Chelsea, Forest – revealed more than a bad patch. For Emery and his staff, it became a time to observe, analyse and, above all, understand.

With Bournemouth, there was a late collapse. Villa dominated, led 1–0, and should have won comfortably. But one defensive lapse in the final minutes cost them 2 points. That game, more than any other, left a mark on Unai. He wanted to kill them all. The frustration internally was enormous. The performance had been enough to win. The focus, hadn't. As Emery later admitted to staff: he hoped those points were not needed at the end to qualify for Europe. The 1–2 defeat to Crystal Palace in the League Cup had already felt like a checkpoint. A disappointing result, yes, but it marked the return of Tyrone Mings and Boubacar Kamara after sixteen months and nine months out respectively and the first Premier League start for Emiliano Buendía in over a year. Managers have to choose their priorities in the season, and the League Cup was not top of the list.

Spurs away followed. A 4–1 defeat that looked worse than it felt. A defeat at the Tottenham Hotspur Stadium can happen, and in fact Unai felt they had played better than the previous two visits, two Villa wins. But it still raised alarms. Two goals conceded from their own corners exposed imbalances in transition. The second half saw the return of an experiment: Durán and Watkins together. It didn't work. Durán's raw power and instinct remained unrefined and though he had driven Villa to lead the Premier League in goals from the bench (ten goals, seven assists in 2024), against Spurs he barely touched the ball. The tactical trade-off – gain in chaos, loss in structure – was once again on display.

Post-match, Unai spoke to the players. Despite the result, he decided to identify the good points. They had gone back to resembling the team he wanted. He spoke about resilience, about knowing how to defend well in difficult stadiums and about the need to learn from defeat. He said that if they wanted to be in the same conversation as a team like Tottenham – who, he thought, could finish in the top six or seven – they would need consistency across all thirty-eight games.

After a defeat against Liverpool the best team in the division (2–0), then came the 2–2 home draw against Palace – another missed chance at Villa Park, another set of regrets. Unai's team had 71 per cent possession, controlled long stretches, but the goals they conceded were preventable. In the first half, Tielemans missed a penalty and within seconds, Palace scored on the break. The pain wasn't just in the timing. It had happened before, at Anfield, also following a set-piece. Strategy was producing goals from corners and wide free kicks, but it was also exposing them. They had spent the week adjusting defensive transitions after corners. Goals like that – ones you've tried to prevent – always cut deeper.

Tielemans felt the weight of the moment. Missing a penalty is hard enough but conceding a goal a few seconds later made it even harder to process. Unai doesn't fully trust penalty practice in training, as the pressure of fifty thousand people can't be replicated. But Villa do analyse penalties in detail – stats, success rates, histories. Youri had missed a few recently, but his overall record remained solid. Still, after the departure of Douglas Luiz, the club lacked a clear specialist this season. Emotionally stable and fiercely professional, Tielemans struggled with the unwanted swing. At half-time, the dressing room was tense. The message from Unai was direct: forget the frustration, reset mentally and go again. The team did – within a minute of the restart, they had a clear chance to equalise.

The second Palace goal was, as usual, the final frame in a sequence of unnoticed moments that accumulate until they fracture the structure. It began with Villa's short corner, three men back, McGinn stepped up instead of dropping back, leading to one pass through the middle, a run, a cut-back and the inevitable finish.

Two more points were dropped at home, a game that Unai expected to win. After the 0–0 with Juventus – a strong result that confirmed Villa's progress in Europe – came the 3–0 defeat to Chelsea. A reality check. Villa were still just 4 points off fourth, but the table was deceptive. They had gone eight games without a win.

Inside the club, there was no panic, instead a sense of clarity formed. Some players seemed to be reaching their limit. Not a lack of effort, but of ability. In team meetings, the question wasn't just who's off form, but why? What had changed? Could it be recovered? Was it physical? Tactical? Emotional? Then coaches had to analyse personalities and decide who could be pushed, who could be supported and who couldn't. Next: how do we get their form back? Does he need more coaching? Less? Encouragement? Distance? More video analysis? More pressure?

Case by case. Everyone needed a different approach.

Watkins wasn't quite himself, recovering from a summer knee problem. Buendía, after sixteen months out, struggled to regain the right pace. Bailey lacked physical preparation. Morgan Rogers was the only attacker in strong form. Jadon Philogene had been backed publicly and privately but couldn't sustain his level. Diego Carlos was perhaps the biggest disappointment. Emery had invested emotionally in him. When the centre-back flirted with a move to Fulham in the summer, he was withdrawn from training for weeks. Then, when the move collapsed, Emery welcomed him back, played him, trusted him. But again, Carlos seemed distant. 'What do you want, Diego?' Unai asked him. The answer was unclear. Unai put his faith in certain players, so it hurt more when it was his players who faltered. Diego Carlos was one. Jhon Durán also seemed distracted.

Players who had delivered last season weren't hitting the same numbers. The attacking output, collectively, had dipped. With it, defensive pressure increased. Emi Martínez's save percentage had dropped.

Margins everywhere had narrowed.

Home wins at the start of December against Brentford and Southampton gave the team a breather. Next, RB Leipzig in Europe. After European nights, there was almost always a dip in energy. After winning in Germany, Villa lost 2–1 to Forest. Following their first six Champions League fixtures, the record read: one win, two draws and three defeats. Emery gathered his players. The result had stung, not just because it was a poor performance but because it confirmed a trend. So, he set a new internal target: finish above Forest. At the time, Forest were nearly 10 points ahead. The message wasn't public. A long shot but also a point of reference.

In the Premier League, Villa were 4 points from fourth but in twelfth place, a fair reflection of the season. The previous campaign, Villa were something of a surprise. Opponents approached them with uncertainty. Now, they were seen as a top-seven contender, and teams faced them with a very different mindset. The table said they were close, but Emery looked at something else entirely – at what needed to change before the margins turned against them completely – who could stay, who had to go.

Unai often reflects on what makes a squad truly competitive. At Sevilla, his best season came with three high-level strikers – Gameiro, Bacca and Aspas – even if one of them, mostly Aspas, ended up playing less than he perhaps deserved. At PSG, he would tell Nasser Al-Khelaifi that what brings real peace of mind is seeing important players ready to come on at any time in a game. Frustration is inevitable, and Unai sensed that from those on the bench at Villa. However, it's difficult to accept for a manager when the options on the bench don't quite match the demands of the moment.

There had been enough meetings about what the squad needed. As the market was about to open in January, it was time for the fixers to act.

During the day, when Unai needs to disappear from the world, he retreats to his office. That's where he goes to plan, to review, to reset. From the heart of Bodymoor Heath, a wide view opens on to the training pitches. Every office faces the grass: Unai's, Damià's, the coaches', the analysts', the data department's. The architecture is deliberate. This side of the complex belongs to the first team, the professional engine of the club. At the other side of the estate, tucked into its own corner, lies a smaller, separate training ground, where the Under 23s and the women's team go about their work.

Unai's room sits quietly between two others. On one side, Damià Vidagany. On the other, Monchi, president of football operations. His Praetorian Guard. The men who watch with him, think with him, protect the space around him, shield him from distractions, manage the landscape around him, choose how to channel information to him. The inner circle.

The notion that Unai Emery is some distant overseer, perched on an exercise bike, just watching games? It's a myth. He's on the pitch, fully present, but his awareness stretches far beyond. He reads, thanks to the fountain of information that are Damià and Monchi, as well as his assistants, sensing the rhythm of the club like a conductor feels the swell of an orchestra.

Damià and Monchi oversee everything from recruitment and squad planning to long-term strategy and the overall direction of the project. Their job is to build a footballing framework strong enough to absorb dips in form and agile enough to address weaknesses quickly.

More specifically, Monchi anchors the scouting and recruitment side. His world is talent, profiles, markets. Damià, in contrast, deals in connections and solutions. Under the official title of director of football operations, he moves between departments and across hierarchies, providing Unai and Monchi with responses to the constant demands of building a modern football club at speed. One moment he's with the owners, the next with the academy, the kit manager, the analytics team. He's the thread that ties everything together.

He doesn't offer technical advice. His role, as he sees it, is to build a space where people lift each other, challenge each other, care for each other. A family with a shared direction. Everyone needs to believe in the project and have the same picture of what that looked like. Football is volatile by nature, but you can't allow the changing winds of form to shift the course of the boat. In the moments when doubt creeps in, where the temptation is to blame, fracture or look for fault, someone has to keep the family together. Damià steps into that role, quietly.

He grew up in the northern Valencian town of Llíria, where he played semi-professional basketball for over a decade. His career took him from journalism to Valencia FC, where Unai Emery quickly saw he was far more than a media officer. The two men were in their thirties and they were both stepping into unfamiliar roles in the corridors of Mestalla. Damià defended Unai because he saw a capable man under pressure from forces that had little to do with football in a civil war of conflicting interests. Despite Damià's efforts, Unai left Valencia misunderstood. Old wounds reopened years later.

It was the first leg of the Europa League semi-final against Valencia. Unai, now Sevilla manager, walked out to inspect the pitch and was met with insults from Valencia's ultras. It hurt. In Damià's view, that bitterness had been deliberately cultivated by some corners of the media. The second leg was one of the most dramatic nights Mestalla had seen. Sevilla's Mbia scored with seconds to go, the goal that put Unai's team through on away goals. The manager celebrated wildly. Damià, watching from the stands, felt torn in half. Professionally, it was one of the worst nights of his life. Personally, he was pleased for Unai. Because that moment changed everything in his career. Monchi, Emery's boss at the time, would later admit that had Unai lost that tie, his Sevilla era might have ended there, the pressure could have been too much. Damià wasn't angry. It was football. Valencia hadn't been robbed; they had simply lacked the experience to manage the final minutes. That was all. Many others did not forgive or forget the manager's reaction. However, in Valencia today, seeing how the club never reached those heights again, the view of Unai has shifted somewhat. There are still those who criticise him for not winning titles with what they call the best squad in the club's history, but Damià disagrees. 'The attack may have been elite, but after the departures of Ayala and Albiol, the defence was stretched thin.'

'Unai,' Damià says now, 'is still the same man.' Passionate. Demanding of himself and others. Back then, people misunderstood his energy, how he lived matches like an air marshal guiding aircraft. With age has come balance. He's learnt to breathe, to hold back, to wait. There's a calm in him now, a touch of Carlo Ancelotti, without losing the fire inside. What hasn't changed is his simplicity. In contract negotiations, he doesn't ask about the car or the house. All he wants is the right environment to work. For someone who's won as much as he has, that humility remains rare.

After Valencia, Damià Vidagany eventually found his way to Aston Villa. His first task, as he saw it, was not to act, but to listen and observe. He didn't take anyone's version of events as gospel. Instead, he began trying to understand the dynamics of a club that, from the outside, seemed adrift. He looked at relationships: between the players and the sporting directors, between departments, between the pitch and the boardroom. What emerged was clear. The players weren't the problem. John McGinn, for example, stood out immediately as a good man, a strong captain and someone with presence and respect. The real issue was structural. There was a visible disconnect between the executive and the dressing room, that bred misunderstanding and tension.

The job was not to tear everything down, but to fill a blank page. There were good people already inside the building. Johan Lange, the sporting director, for instance, had talent and decency but lacked the leadership Villa needed at that moment. Above him, CEO Christian Purslow had become too remote from the players, too far from the pulse of the group. The aim was to build a structure where the manager's only battle was football. Choosing a starting eleven is already a weekly war. Everything else, such as contracts, grievances and internal politics would fall to Damià and Johan, and eventually Monchi. So much so that involving Unai in anything outside that realm became, from the start, a logistical challenge.

At Bodymoor Heath, Damià and Monchi move through the building in sync. 'Batman and Robin,' as Damià likes to say. With Villa's structure evolving quickly, the small team around the manager must be fast and responsive. Monchi, still limited in English, relies on Damià to stitch the gap, just as he does for Unai in press conferences, stepping in when something isn't understood or when the answer should come from him not the manager.

Monchi has had to adjust to a new reality. Once the highly visible architect of Sevilla's success, where both triumph and failure landed at his feet in a club fuelled by passion and scrutiny, he now operates differently. At Aston Villa, he is no longer the main face of the project but a crucial cog in the machine. Before the offices, the gymnasiums, the pristine pitches and data hubs of Bodymoor Heath, there was just a desk with no drawers. That's where Monchi began at Sevilla, the club where he had spent much of his goal-keeping career. It was the year 2000, and he was handed the title of sporting director at a time when the role was still emerging within football and in a club that had little structure or room for it. 'There was nothing,' he recalls. No database, no scouting department, no blueprint to follow. Not even a drawer to file a single sheet of paper. From there he began building a method.

He focused on two pillars: gather as much information as possible and stay very close to the people that win football matches – the coaches and players. That principle never changed. In those early years, when Sevilla were still clawing their way back, if one of his strikers – Frédéric Kanouté or Luís Fabiano – were going through a dry spell, Monchi would be present. 'I always stood by the one who wasn't scoring,' he says. 'The one who was didn't need me.' The same went for coaches. The role of the manager is a lot like that of a goalkeeper: often solitary. There are moments when he feels alone, and that's exactly when Monchi had to be there.

Three types of players formed the foundation of the club's model. First, those raised in the academy: Sergio Ramos, Jesús Navas, Antonio Puerta, José Antonio Reyes. Second, the under-valued signings who exploded in Sevilla's colours: Dani Alves, Éver Banega, Ivan Rakitić. And third, those whose best years came at Sevilla, like Kanouté. All done with the necessary passion and patience. Alves, who won everything with FC Barcelona after he was sold, took eighteen months to find his best version. But Monchi wasn't just scouting talent. He was everywhere. On team buses. In the canteen. On the phone with families. He spoke to fans, managed tensions. He became the glue. 'At first it felt like an obligation,' he says. 'Later, it became devotion.' He worked long days, out of a belief that everything touching the first team should be within his grasp. Meanwhile, he made a net gain for the club of around €250 million.

Seventeen years passed. As success arrived in the form of

promotions, European titles and transfer market masterclasses, so did the weight of expectation. He left for Roma but came back two years later. Over time, the burden grew heavy. 'The last two years at Sevilla were very, very hard,' Monchi says. He had become responsible for every rise and fall. Even in seasons where Sevilla qualified for the Champions League or lifted another European trophy, something inside him was beginning to fade. There was a moment, a press conference, where the tears came. Damià remembers it vividly. 'That's when I thought: he has to leave. No job, no matter how much you love a club, should hurt you like that.' Monchi agreed. It wasn't the kind of tiredness you sleep off, but the recognition that a cycle had ended. 'I realised I could no longer get people to buy into my message,' he says.

His arrival in Birmingham began with a phone call in December 2022. On the surface, it was about Ludwig Augustinsson, who Aston Villa were looking to offload. Damià had reached out to Monchi to see if Sevilla would be interested in a deal. Underneath this, it was a quiet first feeler. Damià asked how Monchi was doing, whether the Villa project might interest him. At the time, Sevilla's form was improving, and Monchi had recovered some strength. Besides, the press were reporting that Villa was pursuing former Barcelona and Mallorca CEO, Mateu Alemany. That seemed to close the door. Then Alemany said no. Damià called again.

By then, Sevilla were in the quarter-finals of the Europa League, and Monchi couldn't consider walking away. He gave an honest answer, admitting that if they won the final, he might leave as his relationship with the club was strained, but if they lost, walking away would feel impossible, staying to rebuild a broken project would be the only option. Unai really wanted him and wasn't sure he would leave Sevilla. Monchi had turned him down before at both PSG and Arsenal. A couple of weeks before the Sevilla–Roma

Europa League final, Unai called him. They spoke for 45 minutes, Monchi sat on the stairs of Sevilla's training ground. He repeated what he'd told Damià but added he had spoken to the club. If he wanted to leave, they wouldn't stand in his way. Unai explained the vision, how he wanted to form a triumvirate: himself, Damià and Monchi. But Monchi was focused on the final. Sevilla won on penalties, their seventh Europa League trophy. So, Damià called again. Monchi was now open to joining Villa. That was a Thursday. On Saturday, Sevilla played their final league game away at Real Sociedad. Monchi had already told the club he wanted to speak with them about his final decision. He met with the Sevilla president and vice president and made his position clear: he was ready to move on. Then the story leaked. The press reported Villa's interest and negotiations grew tense. A video call followed with Nassef Sawiris, Unai and Damià. Sevilla demanded a release clause of €3 million, which Monchi wasn't going to pay himself. Damià flew to Seville to negotiate in person, but the club, hurt and angry, refused to receive him. 'It was a disaster,' Monchi said. At one point, even Unai lost faith. 'He's going to leave us hanging again,' he told Damià. Eventually, the two clubs reached an agreement. Monchi was officially announced as president of football operations at Aston Villa on 16 June 2023.

His first full meeting with Unai and the coaching staff as Villa's sporting lead took place in a fitting location: one of Unai's own restaurants, in Valencia. Not long after, the three – Unai, Monchi and Damià – travelled to Nice to meet with Nassef Sawiris. The setting? His yacht. By then, the triangle was complete. Seven years after their time together at Sevilla, Unai Emery and Monchi reunited. Their relationship was never just easy. 'We both have strong characters,' Monchi says. 'We're loyal to our ideas. I don't believe in calm seas between a sporting director and a coach. I believe in respect and in demanding more from each other.'

At Villa, Monchi found a more evolved version of the manager he knew, still obsessive but with a sharper, modern footballing vision and one of the best coaching staffs around. 'He hasn't become conservative with success. His game is more advanced, more aggressive. He listens more. He decides but he listens.' Monchi got to work straight away. When Unai Emery and his team arrived at Aston Villa, they found a club that had been spending heavily but with little return. Over the three seasons prior to their arrival, Villa operated like a machine for losing money: investing big, selling poorly and drifting without a clear identity in the market.

That changed, fast. In the three years since, including the half-season when only Àlex Moreno and Jhon Durán were signed, Villa have ranked twelfth in the Premier League for net spend. The numbers tell a new story: yes, they still spend but now they sell smartly. Douglas Luiz was sold for €50 million. Moussa Diaby's transfer in the summer of 2024, worth €60 million, was one of the highest in Europe. Even after two years of restructuring, turning over half the squad, Villa still operates on a tighter wage bill than the Premier League's top seven. The strategy is clear: not just acquiring talent but building players into assets. In the past, there was the outlier of Jack Grealish, a £100 million anomaly. Today, the model is to develop players who may not be global superstars but who carry genuine market value. It's about sustainability. When necessary, that includes shaking the tree, refreshing the squad by quietly replacing those who fall out of form, ensuring the ecosystem doesn't stagnate.

The process begins with Unai but not with fixed demands. 'He's not excessively specific,' Damià says. Instead, he outlines a player profile and broad traits, relying on his staff to map the market.

When Unai first arrived, Villa needed pace in attack. Names like Nico Williams and Pedro Neto were considered. However, his main priority was searching for a player to occupy that key role between midfield and attack, someone who could link and elevate play. A number 10. The first attempt was working with Philippe Coutinho but persistent injuries meant he could never return to his peak, despite him trying hard. Then came Youri Tielemans, who had the technical quality and vision to operate in that space but his best version emerged deeper, as a number 8.

Unai admired what Mikel Arteta had achieved at Arsenal with Martin Ødegaard: a technically gifted playmaker who gave the team fluency and direction in the final third. Marco Asensio fitted that vision. Elegant on the ball, intelligent between the lines, capable of interpreting spaces like few others. The idea of playing him with Tielemans, McGinn and Rogers became an obsession. In Villa's structure, the plan would often involve Rogers shifting to the right flank. The full-back typically stayed deep, almost as a third centre-back during build-up but now he would add depth to match the new shape. That positioning granted Rogers the space to drift inside, so Asensio could operate in the pockets, connecting play.

When things began to unravel in Paris, Asensio, who was very aware of the appreciation Unai had for him, decided to join Villa. Asensio quickly showed why he had won three Champions Leagues. Talent, of course, but also his personality. He was organised, punctual, ambitious, respectful and committed.

What traits does Unai value most? Physicality is a given in the Premier League but beyond that, decision-making is everything. 'I just want the player to be good,' says Unai. He looks for footballers who consistently make the right choices, repeatedly, at speed. That's a recent evolution in his approach: a more intellectual demand on the player. Talent is not enough if the player lacks clarity under pressure. Douglas Luiz, for all his ability, was replaced on the pitch by someone with better reading of the game: Youri Tielemans.

Tactically, the profiles vary and always in relation to what the team needs or lacks. If the left-back is a runner, maybe the right-back is more technical. If the midfield needs a duellist, you pair him with a distributor. Sometimes a forward isn't fast but plays better because the wingers fly. Centre-backs? In the Premier League, height is almost mandatory. You rarely find a centre-back under 1.90 metres, Manchester United's Lisandro Martínez being the exception. But they have to have ability in ball progression, tempo, win duels. A goalkeeper? Shot-stopping matters, of course, but playing with his feet comes first.

Character is important, but only once the player is inside the building. 'You can ask around, but you never fully know until you live with the player,' Unai says. He admires high-performance personalities like Cristiano Ronaldo and Michael Jordan. People with a sharp edge. 'You need a bit of arrogance to bring out your strengths,' he says. 'It makes you difficult sometimes, but it also makes you powerful.'

Always, the goal is to thread a line between immediate impact and long-term value. Monchi wants players who can grow and yield a return. Unai wants players who can deliver now. Damià, as ever, sits in between, balancing the short term and the long term. It is about creating what Emery calls 'the wheel'. Raise the level of a player, sell him at a profit, reinvest in two more. It's the same model that brought sustained success at Sevilla. However, it's not all spreadsheets. There's a structured system for tracking players. The scouting team filters them. They work through thousands of data points, videos and reports, but the final decision is always human. 'The data helps you remove the noise,' Monchi says, 'but the eye still decides. A match produces eight million data points. Only a few matter. There's a book I always recommend.' *The Signal and the Noise*. That's the core of the job: finding the signal, eliminating the smoke. 'Data is here to stay. It will shape coaches, technical staff, club strategies, business models. Those who succeed will be the ones who know how to use each thing for what it's worth.'

When the time is right, Monchi would present Unai with around twenty options, divided into three categories: established players in top leagues (who are harder to reach), players from smaller leagues with potential to make the jump and young talents on the verge of breaking through. Depending on the position and the team's needs, they choose who and what to prioritise. The options are then discussed with Unai's coaching staff and a second filter is applied. From there, they narrow it down to a final shortlist.

Even with all this, Villa know the odds. No club escapes the law of averages. In modern football, a 70 per cent success rate in transfers is about the maximum. And if the cost of the signing is €10 million+, according to *The Times*, almost half of them fail to start even half their team's matches. Only 54 per cent can be considered successful. Sometimes, complications arise. Take the case of Juan Foyth, the Argentinian centre-back at Villarreal, for example. He was a serious target, but the deal fell through due to personal decisions. Sometimes players are unwilling to come unless they're guaranteed a starting role.

If Emery and Monchi want a player, Damià does everything he can to make it happen. He then speaks to Nassef Sawiris and explains that, with Unai's backing, these are the signings they need and this is the investment required. The figure would be approximate, because nothing could be confirmed until the deals were done. The ownership sets a price cap, and once the green light is given, negotiations begin in earnest. A WhatsApp group with

Nassef Sawiris, Damià and Monchi keeps the lines open. During the transfer window, they are often in contact twelve times a day. For, say, an incoming winger priced at £20–25 million, the process is to try to buy low and decide quickly when the true number firms up. If negotiations exceed the planned expenditure, Unai will step in to make the case directly to Nassef. He trusts Unai deeply but expects clear justification and whether the goal is profit from player trading or sporting gains like finishing fifth instead of eighth. They debate, challenge, disagree but always with respect.

The summer of 2024 brought everything to the fore and tested the transfer 'factory'. The day that Aston Villa secured Champions League qualification was one of jubilation across the club. For some, it did not last long. Damià and Monchi were already thinking about the next battle. They had known for months that PSR would cast a long shadow over their summer. Both Everton and Nottingham Forest had already been sanctioned with points deductions for breaches. Villa had to avoid the same fate.

The previous January, the Premier League clarified that clubs had until 30 June to complete transactions that could help them balance their financial results for the 2023–24 season. So once Champions League football was confirmed it began a tense and chaotic process, shared informally by seven or eight clubs who were all exploring how to meet PSR requirements. Everyone understood the stakes. 'It was,' Damià recalls, 'a period of persistent pressure.' Accounting gymnastics followed. They sketched deals that collapsed at the last minute. Players were offered on loan or for sale, but other clubs saw through the desperation. Villa even made decisions that made little sporting sense but were necessary to stay compliant. Selling academy players offers instant profit on the books because their accounting value is zero. 'I had six or seven days off that summer,' Damià says. 'I remember being at a water park in Cullera with my kids, glued to the phone, unable to go in the water. That's how intense it was.'

Everton needed to balance their own books. They didn't want academy midfielder Tim Iroegbunam but agreed to buy him if Villa purchased someone for the same value. Everton had a young winger, Lewis Dobbin, who'd scored twice in the Premier League. He wasn't a high-profile target for Unai but was a player with market potential. Villa agreed. Still, the deal left them short of the £35 million in capital gains they needed. In parallel, Villa was negotiating with Chelsea over Jhon Durán. The London club valued him at £45 million. In return, Villa would get Conor Gallagher. But Gallagher refused the move and the deal collapsed. Eventually, Villa arranged a swap with Chelsea: Ian Maatsen came to Villa and Omari Kellyman, a promising academy talent, went the other way. Villa overpaid slightly for Maatsen, but the Kellyman sale generated £20 million of pure profit. Combined, the two deals moved Villa closer to the final figure that would leave them in the clear. Or so they thought.

In 2023, Villa recorded £15 million in profit from Cameron Archer's conditional sale to Sheffield United, as he was a homegrown player. However, when Sheffield were relegated, the obligation to buy was voided and Archer returned to Villa. The Premier League ruled that the deal no longer counted under PSR, turning Villa's £35 million target into £50 million – with just a week to respond. 'It was like *Lethal Weapon*,' Damià says. 'We were defusing a bomb with four wires and no idea which one to cut.'

Douglas Luiz had been instrumental for the club, but under Unai's intense tactical and physical demands, even Luiz had begun to feel his limits. He was tiring. When Juventus showed interest, Villa pushed hard but Juventus would only proceed if

Weston McKennie was part of the deal, a player Unai didn't want. An incredible athlete but tactically unreliable. Still, Villa was in a bind. A handshake agreement took place between Monchi and Juventus's sporting director in Milan on 15 May. Then McKennie's agent demanded more money than he was earning in Italy, citing tax differences. Italy's favourable 25 per cent flat rate meant Villa would pay significantly more. Villa decided not to take the American. However, the deal leaked. Italian media announced Douglas Luiz to Juventus as if it were done. It wasn't. Negotiations stalled. The whole transfer saga dragged on until 29 June. Villa had one more day to register a capital gain large enough to avoid a 15-point deduction. Time was running out.

Monchi and Damià worked side by side through it all. 'We had never argued,' Damià says. 'But this time, there was real friction.' Damià wanted to walk away from the negotiations with Juventus to actually put the Italian team under pressure. He told Monchi, 'Let's move on. They've already announced the deal. They're Juventus. They can't back out over a few million.' Monchi insisted patience and continuous conversation would pay off. In the end, he was right – eventually, the last-minute sale of Douglas Luiz, plus the transfers of Kellyman and Iroegbunam closed the gap.

By July 2024, Villa had spent around £150 million, more than any club in Europe. At the end of the summer, they had signed eight new players and ten left the club, including Moussa Diaby. Signed from Leverkusen for £51.9 million, he had not become the undeniable star Villa hoped for, but his presence had elevated Leon Bailey to become one of the best wingers in the league. Still, financially, Diaby's amortisation and wages accounted for £16 million a year. Selling him generated only £8–9 million in capital gain but slashed £10 million in recurring costs.

On top of everything else, Damià and Monchi were dealing

with two puzzles. The Premier League allows no more than £105 million in losses across three years. UEFA, on the other hand, demands that spending be capped at 90 per cent of revenue in year one of European competition, 80 per cent in year two and 70 per cent in year three. Villa was entering year two. The very players they needed to sell for Premier League compliance, those with high amortisation, were not the ones they needed to sell to meet UEFA's limits. That's because the Premier League cares about accounting losses, so selling players with expensive contracts helps reduce the books. In contrast, UEFA looks at how much you're spending compared to what you're earning. To meet their rules, clubs benefit more from selling homegrown players, like Omari Kellyman, who cost very little to keep but count as pure profit when sold, even though they don't help much with the Premier League rules.

Beyond the tension lay a deeper frustration. Villa had owners with wealth but not the freedom to manufacture sponsorship deals like Manchester City and Newcastle, whose backers can inflate income through state-linked companies. 'Our owners want a return,' says Damià. 'They're not here to lose money and they don't invent sponsors to cover losses. They want to grow the club's value the right way. This system protects the status quo,' Damià says. 'We had to make decisions that hurt. But eventually we found a way.'

After an unstable start to the 2024–25 season, Villa needed something in the winter market to steady things. However, Financial Fair Play rules stayed tight, which meant there wasn't much room to manoeuvre. Any spending in January would have to be added to the amount they'd need to raise through sales in the summer. 'If we spend another £10 million now between wages and transfer costs, that £10 million gets added to what we already need to raise to comply,' Damià explained in January. Unless the club managed to offset it with a January sale.

By the time those words were spoken, Monchi and Damià had already spent a month in meetings sounding out potential signings. Now the real work was about to begin. It was the moment to secure an agreement with the player, then move on to negotiating with the club. Damià explained: 'When we started planning the window, there was one clear rule: one out, one in.' Every player who left had to be replaced. The challenge was to bring in someone better – or at least with more potential – than the one going out. That's the theory, of course. Then it has to be proved on the pitch. The second consideration was financial: whoever came in had to help them improve economically. 'We wanted to finish the window in profit,' Damià says. And the third, just as important, was commitment. Usually, when a player leaves, especially in January, it's because they don't show the level of commitment his coach or his club expects.

'That 2024 winter window was madness,' Monchi recalls. 'Every deal came with complications. Diego Carlos was one of the most difficult. You can't imagine what that was like. Then there was Jhon Durán – in the summer, we could have sold him for £40 million, but Unai insisted we keep him. We were suddenly offered around £70 million for him. The rest of the club had doubts, but Unai believed in him and that doubled his value.' In the middle of all that, Arsenal appeared with an offer for Ollie Watkins. It came too late but turning down an offer for the striker, a well-known Arsenal fan himself, was no small matter.

Centre back Loïc Badé was almost done then fell through when Sevilla pulled out at the last minute as the player was unsure about the move. That caught Villa completely off-guard. 'Suddenly we were left asking – now what?' Monchi says. 'At the same time, Unai was keen to bring in a number ten, with Buendía set to leave, but as Buendía's form improved, the plan shifted again . . . until it was eventually decided to let him go to Bayer Leverkusen.'

Winger Jaden Philogene had a good game against Bayern Munich – he started and even shut down Alphonso Davies – but that was the exception. After that, he faded. He played it safe, stopped taking risks, dropped out of the starting eleven and picked up muscle injuries. When the opportunity came for him to regain confidence elsewhere, the club took it. Villa had been following forward Donyell Malen, an established, high-level player, for a year and a half and had tried to sign him from Borussia Dortmund in two previous windows. In the end, he agreed to come. So, they let Jaden go to Ipswich: £20 million, plus £3 million in add-ons.

Balancing all those variables made the window chaotic. At one point, Villa had agreed several outgoings but were still missing a number 10, a centre-back, a full-back and a striker – and the market wasn't offering many real options. Then, the injuries came: Pau Torres, Tyrone Mings. All of it added more pressure. In the final five days of January, things reached a critical point. Having got Malen in the bag, they had four clear targets for those roles in mind. One of them was Marcus Rashford. It started with Unai saying: 'Hey, I read Rashford might be available – that Barcelona want him but are struggling with wages.'

'We asked ourselves: *Does he fit our profile?* Maybe he could play as a number nine or out wide,' Monchi recalls. The next question was whether he'd even consider coming to Villa. Damià made the first call to Omar Berrada, United's CEO, who he knows well. The club's initial response was positive. That was already a big sign. Then there was the small matter of convincing Marcus. That's where Unai stepped in – and he's very convincing in these situations. He decided to reach out to Rashford personally – they had never spoken before. That conversation was key. Unai got it spot on.

There was talk of Chelsea's João Félix too. Unai liked both, but there was only room for one. The Portuguese maverick has long been a dream signing for Unai. But from the very start, it was clear that the only way to bring him in was to buy him outright from Chelsea and the terms they set made it obvious they had no intention of selling him to Villa. Financially, it simply didn't make sense. Chelsea was asking for €60 million plus add-ons – just six months after they had paid €50 million for a player who hadn't even featured for them. They refused to loan him to Villa either, choosing instead to send him to AC Milan.

In the end, Rashford became the priority. 'Unai convinced him,' Monchi says. 'We reached a financial agreement, which wasn't easy either. It was all done in two days. We also brought in Marco Asensio from PSG, who was desperate to work under Unai. Andrés García of Levante was a market opportunity. But we still needed a centre-back.'

Damià reflects: 'For me, this window showed that Aston Villa can now attract top talent – something unthinkable two years ago. We've become a threat to the big clubs. They're less willing to loan us players. Manchester United don't yet see us as direct competition – hence Rashford, in very specific circumstances. But PSG and Chelsea already do. We're more pragmatic. Leverkusen could face us, but if Unai doesn't have room for Buendía, it makes no sense to block a move just because of a possible future clash.'

Chelsea didn't use centre-back Axel Disasi often, but they still wouldn't loan him to Aston Villa until the last minutes of the market. 'That says it all,' Damià adds. The loans of Asensio, Rashford and Disasi allowed Villa to compete at the highest level without committing to long-term contracts. A calculated push. It had been a month where anxieties grew, white hairs doubled. Every transfer tested every aspect of the club and each one had an inside story.

Marco Asensio had learnt of Unai's interest through Rodri, with whom he worked doing individual sessions back in Madrid. Emery had even flown across Spain to visit him two years earlier, knocking on his door with Rodri, Damià and Johan Lange, but they couldn't convince him. He chose PSG – when they call, it's hard to say no. Now, things were different. Asensio had spent the better part of a decade winning everything at Real Madrid – four Champions League titles, fifteen trophies in total – but rarely from centre stage. Despite moments of brilliance, he never started more than 55 per cent of LaLiga games in any season. He scored in a Champions League final, yes, but he also watched three from the bench. At PSG, it was the same story: flashes of talent but it did not feel like home. When Khvicha Kvaratskhelia arrived in January 2025, it was clear where he stood in the pecking order.

Unai saw more. 'Sometimes you go for players who are hurt,' he said, 'not because they lack quality – they've already shown they have it – but because circumstances have wounded them. Rashford was wounded. Asensio too.' In November, when Asensio's minutes at PSG disappeared, Unai was already laying the groundwork. This time, Emery didn't just knock once – he called almost every day. 'We talked about family life, the city of Paris, Mallorca – things we shared,' Asensio says. 'That kind of closeness builds trust. I had the sense I'd fit his style of football.' He had offers from bigger clubs but eventually called to say he had chosen Villa, as Unai offered him something rare: a chance to play as a number 10 – the position in which he had first blossomed at Mallorca but never truly occupied at Madrid or Paris. Even though it was an expensive deal for a loan, the club's ownership immediately saw the value.

Asensio isn't a sprinter, nor a duellist. He covers ground – 12 kilometres per match – but at a pace that suits his game: subtle, technical, clever in tight spaces. There are always risks with his fitness. He's a player who has to be managed. In return, what he offers is quality, as could be seen very quickly in Bodymoor Heath. At the training sessions, he ran hard, stayed silent. 'I'm not some-one who speaks much,' Asensio admits. 'But when teammates see you giving 100 per cent, in training and in matches, they say: "This guy came here to win." And that's how bonds start to form.'

One of those was with Marcus Rashford. They arrived within days of each other, trained side by side and quickly clicked on the pitch. 'Playing with Marcus is easy,' Asensio says. 'He loves to run into space, to take players on. I'm more about assisting, timing, being in the right moment. We just found each other.' Asensio's start was electric. He made his debut in early February against Spurs in the FA Cup alongside Rashford in the 66th minute. He combined flashes of skill, like the occasional Marseille turn – a quick spin to evade pressure by dragging the ball with both feet – with real defensive intensity, verticality in his runs and a growing quality in decision-making that made him stand out. It was diffi-cult not to get very excited about the two arrivals.

'For us,' Damià says, 'Rashford was from another galaxy.' He seemed destined for Barcelona, who have a way of holding on to players through loyalty alone, even without a formal offer or the finances to sign them, keeping them tied till the last second. Convincing him to stay in England felt just as unlikely. Rashford was so deeply associated with Manchester United. Unai asked Damià to try and approach him anyway.

'We might be the Premier League club with the most England

internationals at the moment,' Damià notes. 'So before moving forward, I spoke with them – gathered everything I could.' What came back was clear: Rashford is a football obsessive. He's gone through a period of huge media attention, huge pressure. Here, the same attention that lifts you up is the one that crushes you. But there were no signs of ego. No sense that he was big-headed or detached. Just a player with good values who still wanted to be a top footballer. Some at Manchester United say Rashford had to be convinced to consider Aston Villa at first, but the club told him it would be a good platform to reach Barcelona if things went well.

The turning point came on Friday 31 January, just three days before the window closed. Rashford spoke with Unai – and everything changed. 'Maybe we expected someone withdrawn, protective, disconnected from the game,' Damià says. 'But what we found was a boy – almost like an academy kid – excited to play, to learn, to train, to love football again.'

Unai told him: 'Talk to your teammates. Ask the ones who've worked with me. Find out how I train, how demanding I am, how many videos I show. Get all the info. If you still want to come after that, then you're my player. If you've got nowhere to go, we'll take you in and help you feel at home.' In Unai, Rashford found the hunger and belief to win trophies again. Unai shared with him a dream to compete at the highest level with Aston Villa, to go all the way in the Champions League, the domestic cups, even to reach a European final like Villarreal did. That ambition lit something in Rashford. Unai reminded him that he had everything to become one of the best in the world, but that he needed to rediscover his fire. Rashford, in turn, admitted that the passion was still there, but at Manchester United it had become difficult to feel like himself again.

It was a pure football conversation, one between a world-class manager and a world-class player, stripped of everything but the game. This is what Aston Villa promised him: an environment focused only on football. No media presentation. No interviews. No branding. 'He was not going to be a commercial asset for us,' Damià adds. 'His contribution will be on the pitch.' Rashford was all in.

Villa knew the £40 million option to buy him was going to be difficult to execute – his salary package is simply beyond what Aston Villa can realistically afford. Villa covered more than 70 per cent of his wages as it was seen as a rare market opportunity: he would help the team, and the team would help him find his best level again. The staff knew the stakes. 'Rashford's risking a lot,' one coach told Unai. 'If it goes badly, people will say: "Not even at Villa." But if it goes even half as well, for £40 million, every top club will want him again.' When he arrived, Unai sat down with him straight away to make him feel comfortable and wanted, both tactically and emotionally. The goal was to maximise his traits in a system that suited him.

Everyone was pleasantly surprised. Rashford was quiet, respectful and hardworking, but there was a clear shyness about him, almost a wall. He didn't open up easily, and having just arrived, it took time to truly connect with him. There was something vulnerable about Marcus. Damià adds: 'You want to help him.' Still, he showed his curiosity, engaged when watching video clips, he responded with interesting questions. He was not a gladiator in training, but he wasn't lazy either. He arrived early, did his injury prevention work, stayed after training, did his post-match routines.

By 10 February, just seven days after his arrival, Rashford was already making an impression in training. They ran an eight versus eight match. The score was 3–3 when Pako Ayestarán turned to Unai and asked: 'Where should I put Rashford?'

'Wherever you want,' Unai replied.

Pako placed him as a number 9. 'Move as a nine, Marcus. One minute left to the end of the game.'

'No, no – give me five,' Rashford said. He scored. His team won. Little by little, he was rediscovering his love for the game.

What happened with Diego Carlos was a real blow. After a lot of tension around the potential move he wanted to Fulham the previous summer, with Unai managing to bring him back into the core group, in Emery's view Diego never abandoned the idea of leaving. To Emery, it felt like he checked out ahead of his last game with the club, the 2–2 draw with Brighton at home on 30 December, another disappointing result. After that, he sat down with Unai, Monchi and Damià and told them he no longer wanted to play for Villa, despite the fact neither he nor the club had a deal with Fenerbahçe. It looked like Diego was prioritising his future – he wanted a long-term contract given his age, thirty-one at the time, but it shouldn't have come at the cost of disconnecting from the club that was paying him. However, according to those who knew him at the club, he is someone who, once he has something in his head, doesn't see any other path. It was a difficult few weeks. Unai protected him publicly, saying he wasn't training because he didn't feel well, but then Diego posted on social media that he wasn't injured – probably thinking more about what José Mourinho, manager of the Turkish side, might think.

The final – and most difficult – deal of the window was Axel Disasi. This one didn't rest with the executives; the final say came from the clubs' owners. Despite a good relationship between them, negotiations dragged on and required real diplomacy. Unai had been clear from the start: it wasn't about signing *a* centre-back, it was about signing *the* centre-back – someone who could elevate the squad, not simply fill a gap. Dozens of names were considered and some fell through. As Diego Carlos prepared to leave, Chelsea reached out. Disasi might be available. Monchi and Unai both agreed he was the right fit. But just as quickly, Chelsea reversed course. They didn't want to strengthen a potential rival. What followed were two weeks of tension, persistence and clarity from the player's side.

Disasi turned down Borussia Dortmund, Napoli and Tottenham – all with stronger contractual offers – simply to wait for Aston Villa. Disasi even gave up a significant amount of money to make it happen. As Monchi put it, in twenty-five years as a sporting director, few had ever shown that level of resolve. For Disasi it was Aston Villa or nothing. He and Unai had already spoken. He'd fallen in love with the project. Even as Chelsea tried to push him elsewhere – to any club but Villa – he stood firm.

Inside Chelsea, frustration grew. The owner was furious, convinced that Monchi and his team were undermining the situation. Demands came from the London club, telling the player there was no deal. Villa's ownership approached Chelsea to try to smooth things over. In the end, it was Disasi, with his brother by his side, who held the line. Their insistence made the move possible, even as Chelsea resisted until the very end. The deal was completed just minutes before the window shut, with an official extension filed for two extra hours. Once at the club, Disasi settled quickly. Villa Park and its energy and atmosphere, the sense of something building – all of it confirmed what he had felt from a distance. And now he knew every match would offer a new peak to conquer. And he felt ready.

Villa brought in five players that January, but UEFA rules meant only three could be registered for the Champions League. Rashford, Asensio and Disasi were included, which left two players out:

Andrés García – purchased from Levante in the Segunda División in Spain – was going to be given time to adapt, and Malen. Malen's finishing stands out. He can score high or low, with placement or power, and has the instinct to make his shots unpredictable — a rare trait. Few players Unai has worked with have had such variety in the final third. Since arriving, he'd had a handful of starts, a few half-chances, but no goals. Morgan Rogers or Ollie Watkins were doing well in his position, and his opportunities remained limited. The staff were happy with his attitude. But Diego Carlos had just left, two centre-backs had suffered injuries around Christmas and Disasi had in his contract his involvement in the Champions League. When Unai Emery called Donyell Malen into his office to explain his omission from the Champions League squad in early February, he didn't flinch. No false comfort. He acknowledged the frustration, how could he not? Malen had come to Villa for European nights under the lights. 'The loanees,' Emery told him, 'they're for now. You? You're for what's coming.

'I am happy with you,' he told Malen. 'Your adaptation is going well. You arrived here last month not playing. The first objective was to get you fit, then to adapt to our structure and to show you you can be versatile. You've played as a striker, on the right side. Now you have to focus on yourself, on improving. Because we need you.'

Then came the line Malen would remember: 'You always have to be ready for the moment the train passes.'

The FA Cup was still alive. The Premier League still had chapters left to write. His moment was coming. An unhappy Malen responded with maturity. No complaints, no disruption. He understood the situation and kept working.

Finally, in that arduous January there was the Jhon Durán case. A few days after the historic Bayern game, in October 2024, Jhon

Durán had signed a new contract with Aston Villa, extending his stay until June 2030. The club made that commitment because they thought that even if he never matched the concentration and work ethic of players like Lucas Digne or Ollie Watkins, he had the raw talent to become a global superstar. Internally, everyone knew this story had more chapters.

In the Champions League win over Bologna at Villa Park, Durán scored and then showed visible frustration when subbed off. It wasn't the first time his emotions got the better of him. Emery may not have noticed it in the moment, he had been focused on giving instructions during a triple substitution, but once the assistants caught it, the verdict was softer: 'He's twenty. He still doesn't understand certain things. It was a bit childish.'

In a later interview, Youri Tielemans was shown the footage of that outburst and laughed. The team had come to see him differently. They were starting to accept the package. Durán became Villa's top scorer, scoring the winner against Southampton in only his fourth league start, he had earned the right to be the chosen striker. Harmony, briefly, seemed possible. But with that came another challenge: how to make Durán and Ollie Watkins work together. Unai tried to fit them into the same system but the balance was fragile. Tactically, it required countless adjustments – positioning, pressing, timing, spacing – and both players needed to understand and accept the structure. Emery admitted a few times it was not working at that point. He blamed himself, not the players but quietly wondered if the idea was costing more than it gave. As Unai once said: 'Watkins does the job, then shines. Durán still has to learn to do the job.'

He held one-on-one meetings with both forwards to keep them aligned. They respected each other but lived in different stages of their careers: Watkins, consistent and professional; Durán, volatile and still learning the craft. For eighteen months, Unai had continued a kind of paternal role with Durán off the pitch. He visited him at home, offered support and affection but also demanded high standards. There were moments of real tension, heated exchanges in the dressing room, times when he had to draw clear lines and tell Durán what he wouldn't tolerate. Every confrontation was calculated, measured by how Durán might react. If things got too intense, Unai knew when to pull back. And Durán responded. He even accepted that dynamic when criticised in front of the group. He would stand there, silent, fixing his eyes on Unai with a look of defiance. *Yes, look at me with that sour face, I don't care*, Unai would think. Afterwards, when the heat of the moment passed, they were both affectionate again, walking over, offering a hug.

By December, however, Emery began to feel Durán slipping. His commitment faded. He seemed distracted, confused, more distant in training. The transfer market was about to open. There were rumours, agents in his ear. Sensing the moment, Unai addressed the squad. He spoke about values, respect, adapting to English football regardless of background, recognising a rare chance to compete at the highest level. 'Maybe we won't play in the Champions League again as we are doing this season,' he warned. 'But we will if we are all focused.' It was a firm message to the Colombian.

A key turning point in Jhon Durán's season came at the end of the year. On 26 December 2024, away at Newcastle. The game was tough for Villa. They came in confident after beating Manchester City and started well, but Durán's harsh red card after 32 minutes for violent conduct disrupted everything. Durán went in to win the ball, there was a tussle and the Newcastle player landed awkwardly, twisting his ankle. On the replay, you can see Durán lifts his studs, but there's no intent to harm. If he'd meant it, it would have been obvious. Unai sat down and said, 'If I can't do anything, I'll just wait for VAR.'

As Durán walked off, he told Pablo: 'That's not a red. I didn't do anything.' That calm tone said a lot. If he'd felt guilty, he would've admitted it. He's aggressive but honest too. Pablo told referee Anthony Taylor it was too harsh, but Taylor stood by his decision. Playing with ten men against a physical side like Newcastle was a huge blow. Unai had taken a risk starting him over Watkins, who wasn't in top form, and the decision backfired. Villa were coming off five straight away defeats in the league. Playing away is always harder, Unai is very conscious of it. People often say there's no real difference between home and away but there is. The home side always has an extra edge, whether it's the crowd, the pitch or the atmosphere. Very few teams in the world perform better away than at home. Newcastle won clearly.

The fallout after the match was immediate. Villa appealed the decision, but the suspension was upheld. Durán was ruled out for three Premier League matches. Monchi and Damià publicly criticised the ruling on social media. But despite their protests, the appeal went nowhere, and it hid a situation that seemed clear. Durán was more out than in. Interest from Paris Saint-Germain and Saudi Arabia had reached him. Unai, trying to recentre him, allowed Durán to return to Colombia over the Christmas period to clear his head. But when he came back, he was even more un-focused. The connection was fading.

The team responded after the Newcastle loss. A draw at Brighton they deserved to win, then victories over Leicester and West Ham (FA Cup tie). They came from behind in the second half, to win both games 2–1. Emery was pleased to mark Villa's 150th anniversary with an FA Cup win. But form remained inconsistent as they lost against Monaco away in the Champions League in January. Emery was furious, he felt players let him down, but he also admitted his own tactical mistake in pairing Durán with Watkins. Privately, he had also come to a different conclusion: everything he could do for Durán in Birmingham, he had already done.

There had been real progress, moments of explosive quality and a deep emotional investment from Emery, along with warning signs. Durán's moods had fluctuated of late: when he was scoring, he was happy; when he wasn't playing, he couldn't understand why and refused to accept he had a teammate like Ollie Watkins ahead of him: constant, methodical, hardworking. In key matches, Durán would withdraw. Despite being told he would start, he'd sometimes claim to be in pain, or unwell, just before important fixtures. In some instances, Emery pushed him to play anyway, and he did. In others, he let it go.

It was then that the manager understood Durán's ceiling. The commitment wasn't consistent, and when the offers came in, Emery led the decision to sell. He had helped build the player's value and profile. The club had maximised his development and, now, his market worth. When the proposal finally arrived from Al-Nassr, the manager backed the move. For Durán, the destination didn't matter that much. On the evening of the Champions League encounter against Celtic, 29 January, the long-running speculation over his future reached its peak. Al-Nassr had everything agreed with Jhon Durán, who started on the bench and was seen warming up before half-time, giving a thumbs-up to nearby fans. He was not really there anymore.

Just 2 hours before kick-off, news also broke of Arsenal's approach for Ollie Watkins, which Villa swiftly rejected.

Faced with the long, demanding road to sporting glory or the shortcut to financial security, Jhon Durán had chosen the letter. Perhaps he never truly saw Unai as a mentor. To him, Emery was a good coach, but he had chosen not to listen to his guidance. Many came to believe that football didn't truly move him, that he enjoyed playing, yes, but didn't love the profession.

So, his departure felt natural. With Cristiano Ronaldo alongside him, the ultimate example of a player who lives for football, the hope was that Durán will take inspiration. When Emery sees a player like that, who has everything to reach the top, but something is clearly missing, when he cannot help, he feels a little sadness.

14

THE FORTRESS & ITS PULSE:

VILLA PARK, THE CITY, THE FANS

If we open the curtain on places where the cameras can't reach, we find a world full of moments that shape a match. In the final days of December 2024, Aston Villa travelled to St James' Park and left with one of their heaviest defeats of the season, a bruising and emotionally charged 3–0 loss. Villa had arrived in good form, but Newcastle struck after just 2 minutes. People often look for simple answers to questions such as: why do certain patterns repeat? Early goals were being conceded often. Football rarely gives clear explanations. The previous season, Villa were vulnerable early in the second half. Now they were scoring often in that same stretch. The preparation is the same, but in football you cannot control everything that happens. And that is its magic, isn't it?

Still, what lingered longest from that night wasn't just the sending-off of Jhon Durán half an hour in, or even the 3–0 scoreline. The most talked about situation came from the tension that erupted at half-time, with a confrontation in the tunnel involving players and staff from both sides. The source of that hostility was clear. At the centre of it stood Newcastle's assistant manager, Jason Tindall. His behaviour throughout the match had been deliberately provocative, with appeals, exaggerated gestures and constant attempts to sway the officials. It felt orchestrated.

The Premier League is rightly celebrated for its intensity and the intervention of authorities is reduced to the minimum but that approach shouldn't be exploited. In European competitions, only one coach is allowed to stand on the touchline; here, multiple staff members routinely push the boundaries, and the fourth official often lets it go. The result is a volatile touchline environment that rewards disruption. Unai sees no value in that kind of forced behaviour. There's no honour in provocation. What do you really take home, even if you succeed?

On the positive side, this was a period when Boubacar Kamara quietly re-established himself at the heart of Villa's midfield after returning from injury. That is never easy, but he effortlessly brought back his calmness, positional discipline and authority. Alongside him, Youri Tielemans was beginning to consistently influence games. His partnership with Kamara offered a balance: one anchored the midfield, the other connected with those in front of him, swapping the role when required.

Yet it was Morgan Rogers who stood out most. Week by week, he was becoming one of Villa's most consistent performers. He always wanted the ball, even in tight spaces. He was physically strong, willing to adapt. The 2–2 draw away to Arsenal on 18 January marked a clear point of evolution when Unai pushed the full-back wider, freeing Rogers to start from the right and drift centrally, almost as a second striker. It suited him. Unai was asking players to take responsibility in more complex roles. In that game, Kai Havertz scored a goal and the Villa bench felt something strange had happened before the ball went in. As players began to celebrate, Mikel Merino walked over to the German forward, who covered his mouth and said something. The replay on the assistants' iPads did not offer a clear angle, but from Merino's and Havertz's body language, Villa assistants understood what the goalscorer was saying: *I touched the ball with my hand.* Logically, the Arsenal players did not volunteer that information but eventually the goal was ruled out for handball. It's the kind of minor incident that, in another era, might have sparked a conversation between managers afterwards – laughed about over a post-match drink or brought up while watching each other's interviews on Sky, smiling at the half-truths.

But that world has almost disappeared. Unai rarely talks to managers after games now. Nobody does. When he was at Arsenal, he would invite some to his office, like Eddie Howe, Rafa Benítez, Roy Hodgson, and they shared stories or subtle jibes over team selection. Hodgson, then at Crystal Palace, once told Unai after their game, played before Arsenal's Europa League final: 'When I saw the team you put out, I thought, *OK, we've got a chance.*' It was said with a grin. Palace had just beaten them. Now, even when there's supposed to be a connection, as with Arteta, there's little beyond the pre-match handshake. Both are too focused, too competitive, too immersed in their own world. Bournemouth's Andoni Iraola, another Basque and someone who wants to live the Premier League experience to the full, is possibly the exception: 'Unai is one of the few managers I always spend time with before and even after matches. We always find a moment to talk about the game, about how the season is going. And for me, it's a real pleasure, even when the result matters, when points are gained or lost. Being able to speak honestly, with sincerity, about our players, other teams ... it's something I genuinely value.'

Away at Monaco, it was a different kind of challenge for Villa. The Stade Louis II has always carried a strange emptiness. The stands sit far from the pitch, the noise disperses. 'It's like you're not really playing a big match,' is how assistant Pablo Villa describes it. 'Everything feels too far away.' The emotions had to come from within. Getting a draw would leave everything in Villa's hands to finish in the top eight, avoid a round and go directly to the last 16. So, before the match, Emery had tried to focus the players' minds. He spoke to them not only as a coach but as a companion on a journey, someone who had carried past experiences – failures and triumphs alike – into this very moment. He reminded them how they'd started this path.

'How did we begin this?' he asked the group.

'Against Bayern Munich,' came the hesitant reply from Kamara.

'What?' Unai responded, dramatically shocked. The midfielder had finally understood Emery's intention. 'Oh sorry, it all started last season.'

'That is right,' Unai confirmed and then he spoke of Legia Warsaw, a defeat in Poland, a European away night that had slipped through their fingers. Of how hard it is to win away on the continent, especially when the atmosphere feels like a training ground. He reminded them of the return to Europe after forty-two years, the heights of beating Young Boys, and how well they competed in Leipzig – two away wins.

In Monaco, Villa started slowly, another early goal conceded. It came from the first corner they faced, Wilfried Singo heading in and putting a team that hadn't won a match all calendar year ahead. They had scored nine goals from set-pieces during the campaign. Villa had made a series of mistakes that gave away the corner, again. And the team could not come back. 'We didn't play a terrible game,' Unai reflected later. 'But the defeat . . . I got very frustrated. I showed it. I felt very negative.' It was the sense of losing control over a direct qualification to the last sixteen, without the need of an extra round in February. 'That night . . .' he said, 'I thought: *That's it. We've blown it. No more top eight.*'

He was angry. Not with his players or himself but with everything. He didn't raise his voice in the dressing room. He never does. 'What's the point?' he says. 'If I chose the players, the system, the approach, then I'm responsible.' The frustration poured out. In the press conference, he admitted he'd made mistakes. 'The last 20–25, when we had both Watkins and Durán on the pitch, we lost our positioning.' They had been vulnerable on the counter, Monaco could've scored again. And then came the dig. 'Some of the players are not following the plan,' he said bluntly. Only a handful escaped criticism: Kamara, Tielemans, Konsa, Cash, Mings and Martínez. Morgan Rogers, who was ill, was spared. The rest were unnamed, but it was clear where he felt the cracks had appeared.

On the coach on the way to the airport, he sat by the window and stared out, not really seeing. Everything had narrowed to a single thought: *We had it in our hands.* The silence on the plane home was thick. In the hours that followed, Damià tried to offer comfort, to point out that other results might still help them qualify in the top eight. Unai didn't want to hear it. Not that night. 'I always try to find something positive,' he said later. 'Always. But that day . . . nothing.'

A tired team faced West Ham next in the league, another draw at Villa Park against a team that was struggling to find some form. Unai, suspended, had spent the game in the stands. Current regulations allow a suspended coach to lead the pre-match build-up and speak at half-time – just not to enter the technical area during the game. Just as well. During the match, he stayed in contact with the bench via assistant Jaime Arias, seated near him. The communication was minimal, focused mainly on substitutions – like bringing on Maatsen after Mings's injury – and small tactical adjustments, such as defending crosses more compactly.

409

From the stands, he took advantage of the elevated view to observe structure and distances more clearly. He corrected some. It was a revealing angle from which to watch the game. Generally, in the dugout, you cannot perceive everything, distances are difficult to appreciate. Two screens are available – one with a wide tactical view, the other showing the television feed. While some coaches rely on these to review key incidents, Emery rarely looks at them. During VAR reviews, the same – he typically stays seated. There is not much he can do at that point.

Celtic was next at Villa Park, the last European league game, with the need to win and wait for other results to confirm the desired Champions League top eight finish, was a night that captured everything this Aston Villa side had been building towards. Against a backdrop of transfer drama, with Jhon Duran almost gone and Arsenal wanting Watkins, Unai pushed the players before going out onto the pitch: 'Now we have to think bigger. We were not expected to be top eight, but we have the chance, and when you have the chance, you go for it.' Damià left his seat to check on Matty Cash, who had gone off injured earlier in the first half. 'In moments like that,' he later said, 'you want the player to feel the club is close. When a guy is hurt, his mind starts to spin: *What if I'm out? What if I miss the rest of the season?* So it's important to be there.'

By half-time, the mood had darkened – after Villa had scored the first two goals, the match was level at 2–2, the crowd became restless, the players looked rattled. Inside the dressing room, Unai Emery's message had a bit of an edge. 'We're better than this,' he told the group, pacing slowly. 'We're playing their game. Too much *shoot, shoot, shoot*, too much *go-go-go*, too much noise from the stands. You need to play with your head. We win when we think, that's who we are.'

Damià did not return to the chairman's suite, he stayed in the tunnel, watching the match unfold on a small screen just off the corridor. That second half was one of the most mature performances of the season. Villa had recalibrated. Fans saw a goal from Ollie Watkins that put them in front again, a first senior hat-trick for Morgan Rogers, the third goal in the 91st minute, a missed penalty, dazzling moves, stunning saves and relentless noise from the stands. Unai Emery's side edged past the Scottish visitors (4–2).

Unai met Damià in the tunnel after the final whistle. 'Wait,' Damià told him, 'the Atalanta game isn't over.' They needed to drop points. Unai didn't respond. He walked straight past, heading to the changing room.

What happened next was one of those memorable moments you rarely get in football. The entire stadium seemed to pause. Eyes turned to mobile screens to wait for the Atalanta result. And then it came: confirmation. They had drawn. Villa had finished eighth, they were into the round of 16! 'It was beautiful,' Damià says. 'The way the whole place celebrated, but first holding their breath, together. Then there was this explosion. Just this release, this realisation. You could see the players, the fans, everyone, we had done something very unexpected.'

Back in the dressing room, Unai's tone had changed. He congratulated the players, reminded them what they'd achieved. 'When you think about who's out,' Damià explains, 'it hits harder. Bayern, Man City, PSG, Real Madrid, AC Milan – all out of the top eight. And Villa, with their flat caps and corduroy trousers, are in.'

The celebrations were brief. Unai turned to the squad: 'This is big. But we go again. Wolverhampton is next.'

'That's the next step,' Damià admits. 'To build that habit of winning. Of not dropping intensity. Of making this normal.'

And then, almost as if looping back to a moment that had

haunted him for weeks, Unai addressed the group once more. 'Now do you understand,' he said, 'why I was so angry in Monaco?

'Monaco,' he told the players, 'was our moment. We nearly let it go.'

Aston Villa had earned around £75 million from their European campaign. That included £42 million in prize money, approximately £16 million from gate receipts and £16 million from UEFA's new value pillar – a fund based on TV market size and past European performance.

Unai was happy with the squad he had to work with after the transfer window closed, but good results had to keep coming. Villa arrived at Wolverhampton with heavy legs and a light bench. Unai hoped for at least a Sunday slot. The Premier League said no. It's become a pattern: requests made, logic presented and yet, silence or rejection in return. Guardiola and Klopp had long since voiced similar frustrations, and this was just the latest example of a league unwilling to protect its clubs in Europe. On 1 February, the 2–0 defeat against Wolves, who hovered above the relegation zone, hurt. Another bad result after a European night. On their first attack, they scored. Yes, again, it had happened seventeen times during the campaign. Emi Martínez blamed himself. He felt he could have done more. At half-time, Emery made four changes, an unusual move. Malen, Bailey, Onana and Maatsen came on for Andrés García, Watkins, Digne and Ramsey. It was a necessary decision. Players were visibly spent, and with the prospect of having to play six games in the next nineteen days between the 9–28 February the risk of burnout was real. Many remembered with anger that Diego Carlos had removed himself from the equation.

The defeat left Villa with a goal difference sat at -3, unusually poor for a team in the hunt for Champions League places. The pattern was clear: early blows, frantic chases, late rallies. And while some of those rallies had delivered points, the cost was rising. The margins were getting thinner. They were eighth in the table, just 2 points off Manchester City in fourth and within reach of Arsenal and Nottingham Forest. Chelsea were also in the equation. With a fifth Champions League spot likely, the race remained open.

Throughout the first half of the season, Emery kept repeating his target. 'Let's stay close to Forest. To Chelsea. If we're near them at the end, we'll have a chance.' He reminded the players often that success was built on winning the games they *had* to win – especially at home. But there had been a home draw to Ipswich. Another slip against Bournemouth. *Maybe this year isn't ours*, he wondered, *maybe we just try to enjoy what we can in Europe*. The momentum brought by good wins against Brentford, City, Everton, was snapped by Wolves.

And then he thought, *that was it*. That defeat was the final stretch. They were still alive in three competitions. So, it was time to reset the tone.

After a short break, they gathered again at Bodymoor Heath. Taking advantage of the new arrivals, Unai decided to mark a change of gear. He stood in front of the squad. He let silence take over. And then, he spoke.

'Three and a half months.'

The words were measured. Players held their breath. 'That's what we have. Three and a half months.'

He stood still, looking at the group.

'The first year, we were dead. You know it. We clawed back. We finished strong. Conference League.'

A pause.

'Last season – no Mings, no Buendía, no Kamara. Injuries everywhere. We lost to Olympiacos, yes, so we had to prioritise the league. And we made the Champions League.'

His voice sharpened.

'This year we started strong. Very strong. And then came the problems. Injuries. Mistakes. And some players . . . betrayed us.'

'But we are still here. Still alive. Still fighting. Three competitions. Still standing.'

He looked around.

'What we've done so far? Not enough. From you. From me. From *anyone*.'

'Now – now is when the work begins.'

'No more excuses. No. More. Excuses. Three and a half months.'

'That's all. Forget what came before.'

'We can turn this into a magnificent season.'

'But it's up to us.'

And then he walked out. Rashford and Asensio were set for their Villa Park debuts in the FA Cup fourth round against Spurs.

Everyone wanted to be there.

Birmingham is the UK's second city and the beating heart of the West Midlands. An area of contrasts, it is an urban maze where Victorian grandeur collides with modernity. Navigating its streets can feel like an intricate puzzle, with a tangle of ring roads, underpasses and pedestrianised zones that leave even locals second-guessing their routes. The Spaghetti Junction, a web of intertwining motorways, is a symbol of the city's complexity. Beneath this labyrinthine layout lies a place that needs and enjoys reinvention. The canals, once the lifeblood of the Industrial Revolution, thread between new developments and historic red-brick warehouses that now house cocktail bars, cafés, creative studios and restaurants. Outside the Bullring, Birmingham's central shopping district and one of the busiest retail hubs in Europe, the iconic bubble-clad Selfridges building shows the intention to do things differently. A few metres away, the 2.2-metre bronze charging bull – officially titled *The Guardian* – reminds passers-by of Birmingham's strength and defiant spirit.

Aston Villa is a core part of Birmingham's story. The club and the city have grown side by side, sometimes in harmony, often at a distance. 'Historically, because Villa won a lot in the late 1800s, we've always carried that legacy,' says Adam Benkwitz, a Villa fan and academic who studied the socio-historical development of football in the city. 'There's always been this perception among Villa fans that we are the successful club, especially compared to Birmingham City, who see themselves as the underdogs. Even when we haven't lived up to it, the feeling remains. We're the "big" club. Villa is often associated with being more middle class. Especially when you consider fans like Prince William, Tom Hanks, Mervyn King, David Cameron. Meanwhile, Birmingham City fans play up to a working-class identity. There's a toughness there, a connection to street culture, to the Zulus, a notorious hooligan firm of the 1980s.'

Mat Kendrick, Villa's long-time correspondent and a fan since childhood, sees the relationship of the club and the city in more emotional terms. 'Villa lets Brummies hold their heads high,' he says. 'We're self-deprecating people. But Villa, especially the 1982 history, gives us something to compete with anyone. We're European champions. That matters. My dad was a bus driver, worked in the Rover plant. We're not flashy, but Villa gives us pride.' His dad actually supported Wolves, whereas his mother's side leaned towards the Blues. It was a chance encounter, a brass band playing at a Villa friendly in the mid-1980s, that turned his head. 'We walked up to the ground under the floodlights. There were maybe five hundred people, but that was it. That was the moment.' As a teenager, Mat stood in the Holte End, and he often moved to the ideal place so he could catch glimpses of himself on *Match of the Day*. 'The view was awful, but you felt part of something.' Now, he sits in the Trinity Road Stand. A different time, a different perspective. 'You mature. You start to see the game in new ways.'

Villa supporters wrestle with a kind of emotional duality: pride in history and culture but also a deep-seated disappointment with how that history has faded. 'One word to define Villa?' Adam says. 'Frustration. Frustration at unfulfilled potential. There's this whole generation of white, working-class, sixty–sixty-five-year-olds who lived the wins. And we haven't got back there. We only flirt with success. Newcastle winning the League Cup recently didn't help, we're now one of the longest-suffering major clubs without a trophy. We're next on that conveyor belt.'

'I was four when Villa won the European Cup,' Kendrick continues. 'So it wasn't on my radar. By the time I discovered football, Villa were rebuilding under Graham Taylor. Some of my favourite players, like Dwight Yorke, Paul McGrath and David Platt, came into the club then. Villa won two League Cups: in 1994 against Man United and in 1996 against Leeds. For a teenager, that felt like we won trophies every couple of years. But we haven't won one since then, and now I'm forty-six.'

There's this baggage from years of broken promises. 'I'm sometimes jealous when you see these fans who are just like non-stop supporting their team the whole time,' Adam admits. 'Villa fans can be brilliant when things are going well, but they're quick to turn when they're not. On matchdays, it can turn in seconds, a misplaced pass, and suddenly you feel it in the stands. There's not a lot of patience.'

There's no space for long-term thinking in today's world. Even at clubs like Arsenal or Chelsea. Everyone wants more, faster. So even now, when the owners are delivering and Unai is succeeding, that anxiety has to go somewhere. Lately it landed on the commercial side, on people like Chris Heck, on ticket prices, on the experience. Adam agrees. 'You criticise what you can: the cost of going, the matchday experience, the feeling many have of being milked.'

Chris Heck, the club's president of business operations, became a lightning rod for that tension during his tenure at the club. Heck's role in reshaping the commercial side – revising ticket prices, pushing new branding, rethinking how Villa sells itself – provoked unease. For some, he represented necessary modernisation. For others, he's symbolic of the club drifting further from its roots. 'There's pride in the name, sure,' Adam says. 'But not always a strong sense of local belonging.' Attempts have been made to change that, such as campaigns with local boy Jacob Ramsey, local references in marketing. But, Adam adds, 'It's often more about Birmingham as a brand than about the people. It's one thing to reference Ozzy Osbourne. It's another to engage with the street next to the Holte End.'

'Birmingham's often seen as a figure of fun, not the brightest or most glamorous of places,' Kendrick remarks. 'But we have pockets of creativity and brilliance. We're proud of anything that puts us on the map. Birmingham has a vibrant music scene: UB40, Black Sabbath. There's a Walk of Stars on Broad Street with stars for famous Brummies like Ozzy Osbourne and Frank Skinner. Historically, Matthew Boulton from the 1700s was an industrial pioneer.'

However, those are things that had been said about Birmingham for decades, almost as if no one had recently answered the question: what is Birmingham now? And, by extension, what is Aston Villa? The way fans see the club, and the city itself, has been shifting.

More change is coming too: a new high-speed rail line, major re-development around Digbeth and the Smithfield site, and the continued pull of a growing creative and tech scene. Birmingham is also one of the most multicultural cities in Europe. Since the 1950s, wave after wave of immigrants from South Asia, the Caribbean, Ireland and Eastern Europe have made Birmingham their home. Areas like Sparkhill, Handsworth, Small Heath and Aston became synonymous with new British identities. Today, over half the population identifies as Black, Asian or minority ethnic. That has transformed the sounds and smells of the area. The balti, a dish synonymous with the city, reflects its rich multiculturalism, while Digbeth's street art and music venues showcase a rebellious streak that keeps Birmingham at the cutting edge of British culture.

Football has been slow to adapt. Villa Park, while grand and historic, has at times felt like it stood still while the streets around it changed. That gap between club and city is still visible. 'Villa Park is expensive now,' Adam says. 'It's shifting the demographic, more middle class, less local. And I think that's why Villa still struggles to feel like Birmingham's club.' Despite its global profile and historic success, Villa hasn't always felt rooted in its immediate surroundings.

Villa Park, the home of Aston Villa Football Club since 1897, sits in the heart of Witton, a district in Birmingham that has undergone profound demographic and cultural changes over more than a century. At the time Villa Park was built, Witton was semi-rural, with a small population and large estates like Witton Hall. In the nineteenth century, the area had few residents – census data shows just 157 people in 1841 – and the community was predominantly white British. The arrival of the football ground spurred residential development and small industries, drawing more people to it, particularly working-class families. The area grew steadily through the early twentieth century, with much of the housing stock being Victorian and Edwardian terraces, built for local workers.

The most dramatic shift came after the Second World War. With labour shortages in Britain's industrial cities, large numbers of immigrants from Commonwealth countries – especially India, Pakistan and Bangladesh – arrived in Birmingham from the 1950s onwards. Aston, directly adjacent to Witton, became one of the central hubs for South Asian communities. By the 1990s, Aston had a majority-Asian population. The 2011 census recorded that over 50 per cent of Aston's population was of Pakistani descent, with growing Bangladeshi and Indian communities. While Witton-specific data is limited, its close proximity to Aston and similar housing profile suggest it experienced parallel changes.

The arrival of South Asian communities brought profound cultural shifts to the area surrounding Villa Park. Mosques, temples and gurdwaras were established. The local economy was transformed by Asian-owned businesses: from corner shops and curry houses to textile and wholesale stores. Events like Eid, Diwali and Vaisakhi added vibrancy to the area, creating a multicultural public life. Despite occasional tensions in earlier decades, the area has gradually grown into one of Birmingham's most culturally diverse districts. The club has made conscious efforts to engage with the evolving community around it. The Aston Villa Foundation, formerly Villa in the Community, has run inclusion initiatives, football coaching for local kids, education support and health programmes, aiming to build stronger ties between the club and its largely South Asian neighbourhood. But there is still plenty to do.

'That district is incredibly diverse,' Adam explains. 'Large Bangladeshi communities. There are four generations of Villa fans there, from the grandad that came from abroad, but many residents don't feel connected to the club at all. In fact, they see it as a nuisance. On matchdays, some businesses thrive, like pubs and takeaways, but parking and transport are awful. The Aston Villa Foundation has struggled to get buy-in for local school programmes. Not all the community around Villa Park see the club as theirs.'

Villa's fanbase is still majority white and often from outside the immediate area, but there are signs of change. Second- and third-generation immigrants are more likely to support local teams. In that context, the Punjabi Villans give South Asian Villa fans a voice and presence. They've been recognised nationally and won awards, and the club has supported their growth. Many Punjabi-speaking families settled in Birmingham from the Punjab region of India and Pakistan, since becoming an integral part of the city's social, cultural and economic fabric. The balti cuisine has Punjabi roots, and you'll find Punjabi dishes like samosas, parathas, and tandoori specialities in local eateries. Punjabi is one of the most widely spoken languages in Birmingham.

Before matches at Villa Park, the habits have changed. What was once a familiar British ritual of pint, game then curry, has quietly reordered itself. Now it's pint and curry then the game. In pubs like The Grove, you can feel that shift in full. These are no longer just watering holes, they're gathering places where the clatter of cutlery and the aroma of spice mix with the hum of pre-match nerves. This is where the Punjabi Villans meet and the conversation flows easily. Over food and beers, stories begin to surface.

In 1969, a five-year-old named Nim Gill stepped off a plane from India and into a new life in Smethwick, an industrial town in the West Midlands. 'My father came over after the war, like many Indians did, to help rebuild the country,' Nim recalls. 'Britain was damaged, and they needed workers. The steel factories were huge but there weren't enough hands.' Many of those hands came from Punjab, in northern India. Nim's father was part of a wave of Punjabi immigrants who answered Britain's call, many on work permits, or 'vouchers', as they were known. 'My dad came first,' he says, 'and then the rest of us followed, about seven or eight years later.'

They brought little with them but a reputation. 'Historically, Punjabis – especially North Indians – were seen as hardworking but also resourceful,' Sunjeet Jheeta explains. 'Going back to the empire days, the British viewed us as tough, even troublesome, but always willing to graft. Though, they also saw us as uneducated, because many of us were farmers.' That perception remained. Early immigrants were funnelled into the hardest jobs: steel, metal, foundry work. 'Because of that,' the fan continues, 'Punjabi communities settled in very concentrated pockets in Smethwick, Small Heath, Coventry, parts of West London. And especially the Black Country, bordering Birmingham.'

'I lived just four miles from Villa Park, and half a mile from The Hawthorns,' Nim says. 'My school was basically in West Bromwich Albion's backyard. Behind the school field was their training ground.' You can picture boys peeking through wooden slats in a fence. 'We used to sneak a look at the players, like Cyrille Regis, Laurie Cunningham, Johnny Giles. Sometimes when the ball came over, we'd "borrow" it. My friends and I ended up with so many footballs,' he laughs.

In the shadow of steelworks and stadium floodlights, football slowly became part of that life. For many second-generation Punjabis in the Midlands, football wasn't a tradition passed down through uncles or fathers, like wrestling or kabaddi had been. Ball sports weren't a thing in their relatives' culture. Even those that succeeded were not considered heroes. Nim recalls his uncle, Junaid Singh, known as 'The Wall', who had been a star in India.

'He played in the 1964 Olympics, met Pelé, met Eusébio. Got the Arjuna Award. I didn't even know about all that as a kid. It was only when I was fifteen or sixteen, when he came to England with a team, that I began to understand who he was.'

When the kids started getting into football, they were looked at like they were mad. Screaming at the telly, obsessed with a game that didn't belong to them. It wasn't played in proper football kits on grass pitches, but on pavements and playgrounds, between walls and lamp posts. On other occasions, jackets or kerbs made the goalposts. For many, supporting a football team didn't come naturally. 'I don't think it's unfair to say that, for a lot of Punjabi people, there wasn't a strong connection to a club, at least not until we made a conscious decision,' Nim says. 'Instead, it was with Brazil, Italy, Spain, teams on TV. Players like Romário or Baggio. That's what drew us in.'

Nim tells a story that still brings a flicker of awe to his voice. 'I came from a big family, but I didn't have a football shirt, I used to play in my school clothes. One day, this lad came to watch us play. He was older, bigger. He called me over and said, "Nim, I've got something for you." He handed me a shirt. It was the most beautiful thing I'd ever seen: claret and blue, crew neck, blue stripes, the round badge in the middle. That was it. From that moment on, I was Villa. I must've been nine.'

There's a phrase on the terraces: *Villa fans are chosen. We don't choose.*

Being a Punjabi football fan still meant building something from scratch. 'We're the first generation to live football as a lifestyle,' says Onkar Bhamber, in his fifties. 'And now, we know our place here. We know we add value.' The first match Onkar ever attended wasn't one that he remembers with joy. 'We lived in Kingstanding,' he explains. 'My dad took me to a Villa game when I was seven. I didn't see a thing, he smuggled me in under his coat and smuggled me out the same way.' He laughs, but there's an edge in his voice. 'He did it so I wouldn't have to experience the trouble. Because back then, there was always trouble.' For many Punjabi fans, going to football in the 1970s, 1980s and even into the 1990s and 2000s, was a risk. Onkar remembers it all too clearly. 'When I was a kid, someone threw a brick through our window. It had "Paki" written on it. My family were more offended that it didn't say "Sikh"!' he chuckles. 'But that was life. Racism, violence, it was just something you dealt with.'

Looking different could make you a target. Wearing a topknot, having brown skin, these were enough to mark someone out in the crowd. The Holte End, like many stands across the country, was not a space where everyone felt safe. As a result, some stayed away altogether, or only dared to attend one or two matches across an entire decade. The risk simply outweighed the love. Gurdev Singh Jheeta grew up in Small Heath, right by St Andrew's, Birmingham City's ground. 'We saw violence all the time. The Blues had the Zulus, who just went around fighting. My dad wouldn't let me go. First time I saw a match, I was in school, about fourteen. Then nothing again until I was twenty-one.'

Onkar tells a story of a young friend at a Villa–Arsenal game in 1990. 'He was about thirteen, on his own. Arsenal fans were about to start on him until some Villa lads came round the corner and backed him up. Got rid of the Arsenal lot. He was relieved. But then one of the Villa fans turned to him and said, "F*** off, you're still a f***ing Paki. We only helped you because you're one of us."'

It's this reality that partly explains why British Asian footballers have been so few. 'Our parents didn't see sport as a path,' adds Harry Purewal, in his fifties. 'They didn't see money in it. They didn't see safety in it. Asian kids are expected to choose education over sport. You've got to be a doctor or a dentist, not a footballer. But that's changing now.'

Back then they were told, *Football is not for us*. Some crossed that line. Nim sums it up: 'That moment when you go, despite what everyone tells you – that you'll get battered, you'll get racially abused – and then you go ... and it's fun. You don't get beaten up. You think: *I might go again next week*. And then you're in.' If alienation defined the early experience, community has become the latest answer. And for fifteen years it has had a name: Punjabi Villans. What began as a few friends organising lift-shares and meet-ups has become a visible, welcoming, culturally rooted group that has reshaped what it means to be a football fan at Villa Park. 'We just wanted camaraderie on matchdays. Now we raise thousands for charity, we support new fans and we're part of the club's wider identity,' Dev Jheeta says.

One moment changed everything: the flag.

Irish fan Von Symeou steps in. 'I didn't really know the group back then, but when I saw that Punjabi Villans banner inside the ground for the first time, it was a big deal. It was symbolic. That's when I became aware of them.'

Jag Kalaar, in his sixties, adds: 'That flag brought us together. It wasn't just a piece of fabric, it was a declaration. A statement: *We're here. We belong.*'

The group didn't stop at visibility. They are on the fans' advisory board and on the committee for Villa's 150th anniversary. 'We're there to contribute. To shape the future of the club. Pricing, accessibility, community, these are the things we're being asked about now. And we're being heard.'

They started reaching out to others who had once been excluded. Sunjeet Jheeta shares a story: 'A couple of months ago, we invited a man who hadn't been to Villa Park in twenty years. He used to go regularly but stopped because of everything we've talked about. We had a spare ticket and said, "Come with us." He came. Even now, he still texts me: "I can still hear the voices. I can still feel the sound."'

'A bunch of brown lads, chatting football in a pub with a Punjabi Villans flag above our heads. Who'd have thought?' Nim says, who adds they now have a mix of people with them everywhere they go, white, brown, women, children. 'It's all come full circle.'

Darren Smith, who sits in the Trinity with his son Luke, and alongside Nim and his friends Amarjit and James, says: 'The Punjabi Villans lads are absolutely great company, always accommodating and a right laugh. We travel all over with them. Have you seen the dances they put on socials before games?'

Women have often had to climb an entirely different set of stairs. 'When I was growing up, I got into football through my brother,' Jass Gill, in her thirties, says. 'But he didn't go to games or anything. And all the lads I knew were Man United fans. I just thought, *Sod it*. I was at university, had my student loan. I wanted to go to a game. So, I bought a ticket. Went by myself. I didn't know anybody.' To walk alone into a stadium where you know no one, surrounded by noise, aggression, testosterone and tribal loyalty, without the inherited map of family ties or matchday rituals, takes something beyond courage. 'It was intimidating,' she admits. 'But I loved the club. And I thought: *If I wait for someone to go with, I'll never go.*'

Over time, the solitary decision became something else. 'The last few years have been transformative. I joined the Punjabi Villans, messaged a few people and now some of my closest friends are from the group. They've helped me in my life. It feels like a Villa family.' Still, she knows her experience is not yet the norm.

'There are loads of women who support Villa, but do they feel comfortable enough to go? Not always. Things like social media, seeing other women post about going to games, that helps. Now I sit with people who look out for me. If someone harasses you, they step in. You feel safe.' She pauses. 'As a woman, you still don't see loads of us on our own, but I don't feel alone anymore.' The most radical thing, sometimes, is simply turning up. Punjabis are no longer on the fringes. Nim's wife Bal and his sister Andi are regular fixtures in the Trinity stand. Others bring their mums, women who never imagined they would find themselves in the thick of it all. And of course, the little ones too, five or six years old, learning early that the space in Villa Park is theirs as much as anyone's.

Football also creates new narratives when you least expect it. 'Something changed when we got relegated,' Onkar says. 'It felt like a reset. We had a Villa fan as captain. A Villa fan as manager. Relegation brought people in who hadn't been before. Tickets were available. Seats were empty. And those who came, they stayed. Even through the bad times.'

'And I'll be honest,' he adds, 'looking back, I'm glad we lost that play-off final to Fulham. If we'd gone up then, it could've all gone wrong. Instead, we got the right owners, ones who backed the club properly.'

In any case, in the recent history of the club, no decision – they all say – has had a greater impact than the arrival of Unai Emery. 'For the first time ever, I think we love the manager more than any individual player. We have total faith in him. We have accepted his style, we are learning about football by listening to him,' Nim says.

The rest nod in agreement. 'As long as we keep Unai,' one says, 'we don't care who we lose. We trust him.'

It's time to go to the game. Beers are finished, dishes stacked, tables cleared. The pub empties. Out they go: those who remember, however faintly, arriving in this country as children. Their sons, who were once turned away from football but found their way back. Their friends, Irish, English, from everywhere. Their daughters, who bring new fans. And the next generation, who are brown, claret and blue.

Together, they travel to Villa Park.

Aston Villa's remarkable rise under Unai Emery has required careful management in an unforgiving financial landscape. The truth is simple: Aston Villa do not generate enough commercial revenue to match their current sporting ambitions. Ticketing represents at most 15 per cent of total income. Sponsorships account for another 20 per cent and although there's been a modest uplift since Emery's arrival, it hasn't significantly changed. The bulk of income comes, as with most Premier League clubs, from broadcasting rights – domestic and European. That revenue stream has grown with the return to European competition, but it remains the only area showing significant gains.

In terms of transfer business, the perception from outside doesn't match reality. Villa's net spend between 2023 and 2025 places them fifteenth in the Premier League. Only Everton, Leicester, Luton, Sheffield United and Brighton have spent less. While clubs like Chelsea have posted negative net spends of over £400 million, Villa's is just £42 million. They've sold smart and bought selectively.

UEFA's European Club Finance and Investment Landscape report has laid it bare: Villa recorded a £119.6 million loss for the 2022–23 season and another £80 million loss in 2023–24 – the wage bill climbed to £246 million and remained just under the 90 per cent revenue limit. Villa's wage-to-revenue ratio was seventeenth in Europe last season, as well as far too close to the safety line – and came into a sharper focus as the limit got reduced to 80 per cent, with loan players like Marco Asensio and Marcus Rashford on the wage bill – Villa covered around 75 per cent of the Manchester United player's wages – which stood at more than £325,000 per week – and up to 90 per cent depending on performance-based bonuses.

Aston Villa are punching well above their financial weight. With annual revenue of around £280 million, they sit well below the likes of Tottenham and Chelsea (they more than double Villa's figure). Even further ahead are Liverpool, Arsenal, Manchester United and Manchester City, each generating well over £700 million a year. The club's income is too low for its ambitions. Because much of its recent investment has gone not into transfer fees but into retaining top players – locking them into long-term deals with improved salaries – Villa's wage bill has grown, but the highest earner at the club still makes only a third of what Manchester United's top player earns. In relative terms, wages are high – currently around 89 per cent of total income – but in absolute terms, they're still modest.

The recent past hasn't helped. The money earned from Jack Grealish's sale, around £100 million, was mostly spent on players who didn't deliver consistent returns. Buendía, Danny Ings, Diego Carlos, Axel Tuanzebe, Leon Bailey. Some are gone; some are still trying to find form. In contrast, Emery's signings have been smarter and leaner: Youri Tielemans came on a free. Pau Torres cost £25 million, less than the £29 million spent on Diego Carlos. Morgan Rogers arrived for £8 million. Amadou Onana for £13 million. There has been no blank cheque. Players like Coutinho, Buendía and Carlos have been offloaded to reduce the wage bill and avoid further amortised costs.

Still, those amortised costs linger. Coutinho, for example, no longer drew a salary, but his remaining book value means Villa still registered around £6 million in annual amortisation against their accounts. The club expects a significant improvement in the financial picture within two years – when high-cost, underperforming contracts expire and more revenue comes in. The £75 million-plus Champions League income helps offset much of the risk, but it is a serious gamble hinging on consistent European qualification.

Villa is working the diplomatic avenue to improve their situation. As UEFA expected them to breach their Financial Fair Play (FFP) rules, a two-year settlement has reportedly been reached. They have also asked the body for specific exceptions to current FFP rules. For instance, when a player is ruled out for the season, their wages still count towards the FFP salary limit, but clubs often need to sign a replacement. Villa is arguing for flexibility, especially at a time when they're investing in infrastructure, personnel and operational scale – much like opening a restaurant, the first phase is always heavier on costs. UEFA understands that for clubs in transition, these issues can distort the balance. But, they say, rules are rules. In the Premier League, failure to comply with FFP leads to points deductions. In Europe, it could mean exclusion from competitions. There is no room for manoeuvre. The club is consciously walking a tightrope.

So, while financial balance is found, will Villa need to sell players?

Yes, but not only because, at times, they're forced to. Selling is part of elite football. Even top clubs sell to regenerate. Emery is demanding. A few years under his leadership is intense. Players need to be refreshed. Selling and reinvesting is the natural rhythm of a competitive project. The losses don't alarm the club. They're part of a larger strategy. The owners bought Villa for £80 million.

Today, it's worth close to £1 billion. Losses only matter if you breach FFP and cannot find a way out of that. What matters more is the long-term value of the club – and that it continues to grow. Simply 'spending more' isn't an option. Under the current model, owners cannot just inject £100 million per year to fund transfers. That money must be backed by equivalent revenue growth. Otherwise, penalties follow. So where does that growth come from? Some of it will come from consistent European qualification but monetising sporting success isn't instant. You don't earn more the moment you qualify. Revenues lag behind results. Success must be sustained.

There has also been occasional internal discussion about relocating to a purpose-built stadium near the NEC, with better transport links and commercial potential. But for most fans, the idea of leaving Villa Park – especially for a less central, more corporate-feeling site – is unthinkable. For now, Villa Park remains at the heart of the club's identity and planning. However, if long-term ambitions outgrow the site or redevelopment continues to stall, the debate could return. So, what's the plan for now? In late 2023, Aston Villa put plans to demolish and rebuild the North Stand on hold, concerned about the disruption it would cause. Unai Emery did not want to hear about weakening the noise and energy of Villa Park; as he constantly repeats – he needs it. The growth had to come 'not via brick and mortar, but via the squad,' he told Damià. But expansion was never abandoned. The club announced in May 2025 that rather than tearing the North Stand down entirely, Villa will instead upgrade and extend the existing structure, allowing capacity to increase without reducing seating during the build. The goal remains a stadium of over 50,000 seats in time for Euro 2028, with phased work potentially continuing towards 52,500.

This evolution is tied closely to local transport infrastructure and improvement to cope with matchday crowds. The redevelopment of Witton Station – just minutes from Villa Park – is essential, with UEFA stipulating that a majority of Euro 2028 attendees must arrive via public transport. Backed by local authorities and tied to regional regeneration goals, the project is expected to inject over £100 million in its first phase and deliver long-term economic benefits to the area.

Meanwhile, the club's business leadership – particularly under Chris Heck – has improved fan experience, upgraded matchday offerings and modernised operations. When Chris Heck was appointed president of business operations at Aston Villa in 2023, the club was in a period of rapid transformation. The task for Heck was to match that progress off the pitch, to turn promise into a sustainable, elite-level business operation, to grow revenue significantly and modernise the club's commercial strategy. Heck arrived with a 33-year career in US sport behind him, having held senior roles in the NBA and MLS. He brought with him energy, a belief in creative disruption, and big thinking. In some areas, his impact was immediate.

Unai Emery's transformation on the pitch and the owners' long-term vision off it were evidence that Aston Villa was no longer a peripheral club. Heck gambled on that belief. He pointed out to clients the club's enormous demand, 41,000 on the season ticket waiting list, proof that Villa had outgrown its old commercial identity. 'Let's stop apologising for what we were,' he said, 'and start acting like a disruptor.' He had a blunt mission: clean up a series of outdated, undervalued contracts that were holding the club back financially. As Heck put it, the first six months were about 'getting rid of bad contracts while signing new ones.' He identified four key areas dragging the club down: merchandising, food and beverage, the kit deal and front-of-shirt sponsorship. He made it his goal to either renegotiate or replace each one.

Heck's message to partners was direct. He emphasised international ambition, especially in meetings with potential kit suppliers. The then-partner, a UK-based manufacturer with limited international distribution, was told that Villa wanted more, to be a global brand. He offered to buy out the final year of the deal, but the process turned sour, with the company reportedly delaying timelines and blocking a smooth exit, forcing the club to pay a large sum to terminate the agreement. Still, Heck moved fast. By December 2023, just six months into his role, he had cleared, with the crucial help of Nassef Sawiris, the path for a new kit deal with Adidas and was on planes meeting potential players. 'We wouldn't do a deal under one million pounds,' he told agencies in the UK, Europe and North America, refusing to accept the 'small club, small money' logic often imposed on teams outside the traditional elite. He went as far as telling existing sponsors they needed to 'pay more or leave'. Most left. But those who stayed, like sleeve sponsor Trade Nation, doubled their investment. The new front-of-shirt deal doubled the value of the previous one, from £8 million to over £16 million.

Sponsorship revenue rose from £19 million to £42 million in a single year. Heck also envisioned a more modern Villa Park – through incremental upgrades that could unlock revenue without displacing fans or tearing at the fabric of the stadium. A masterplan was drawn up that reimagined the club's hospitality offerings, introduced 18 new premium areas (representing five thousand seats at various price levels) and established a new tier of experience built around history and atmosphere. Working with the design firm 20.20, Heck helped initiate a wholesale redesign of seven key spaces at Villa Park in time for the club's 150th anniversary. The renovations paid tribute. The Oak Room, for instance, revived the legacy of English football's first ever stadium restaurant. The Aston Lounge, named after the area that gave the club its name, fused rich textures with pitch-facing loges and tapestry walls featuring iconic club moments. The Legends Lounge opened out into the parkland, offering a kind of retreat from the intensity of matchday. A former police holding cell in the North Stand – once built to contain rowdy fans – was converted into a high-end hospitality suite: The Cells.

He also introduced The Warehouse, a bold new project in an industrial space beside the stadium to be transformed into a four-thousand-capacity concert venue and the UK's largest supporters' beer hall on matchdays. Set to open in full for the 2025–26 season, the venue is part of a long-term strategy to turn Villa Park into a year-round destination, capable of generating revenue beyond football. At the same time, Villa's retail operation was improved. The club opened a 10,000-square-foot superstore next to the stadium – doubling its footprint. According to club figures, retail revenue tripled in the first year of the shop, jumping from £9 million to £30 million. In May 2025, a new flagship store was opened in the Bullring shopping centre.

But some of these developments came with complications. Around 900 season ticket holders were displaced as part of the hospitality expansion, not all the new VIP boxes were sold and high ticket prices for Champions League matches sparked frustration among fans. Heck defended the pricing structure by pointing to demand and market comparisons, but the communication around it caused friction. When Aston Villa released ticket prices for their Champions League campaign – ranging from £85 to £97, with season ticket holders offered discounted rates – fan response was swift and deeply divided. Supporter groups branded them 'out of touch', the Aston Villa Supporters' Trust warned of alienating lifelong fans and the Football Supporters' Association accused the club of exploiting loyalty at a historic moment. Plenty of social media reaction showed the discontent but, as some noted, excitement about Unai Emery's success muted public dissent.

For many fans, the cost of ambition was starting to hit close to home. Others accept the wider reality. 'We're trying to compete with clubs who generate three times our revenue,' says Adam Britton, a lifelong fan. 'But our sponsorship is just 20 per cent. We have six sponsors. United and Liverpool have twenty-five. If we keep squeezing fans without growing commercial partnerships, people will walk away.' He credits recent hires and retail gains but argues the real solution lies in better strategic deals, not ticket hikes. The club's defence was clear: to comply with Profit and Sustainability Rules, revenue must increase across all areas – including ticketing. For now, the direction is clear. Ticket prices are unlikely to fall. Villa's finances – and the structure of European football – make further increases almost inevitable.

Similarly, a controversial attempt to redesign the club crest – favouring a circular badge reminiscent of Chelsea's – triggered backlash from supporter groups and led to intervention from the Football Association. The proposal was eventually withdrawn and a new crest, shaped as a traditional shield and incorporating the club's yellow lion and founding year, was approved after wider consultation. Heck claimed credit for the correction but for many it raised questions about cultural sensitivity from the business department and from himself.

Internally, tensions also surfaced. Heck's approach – direct, numbers driven and at times unyielding – was different to the more collaborative, football-first ethos that had developed under Emery, Monchi and Damià. While he had clear responsibility over business operations, the club's hierarchy was unequivocal: decisions affecting the football team, from friendlies to player marketing, required sign-off from football leadership. As one senior figure put it, 'You can't treat this like the NBA. Here, forty-two thousand people believe this club belongs to them. It's not entertainment – it's identity.'

He also faced pressures most fans wouldn't see. Living alone in the UK for much of his tenure, Heck stayed in hotels for months at a time, shuttling between Villa Park, the training ground and meetings in London, where Aston Villa have an office. His family remained in the United States – his wife of thirty years managing life back home, his youngest child entering college and his older children living in New York. He worked long days, slept little and exercised regularly to manage the stress. It was clear, even to those who admired his drive, that his time at Villa was not built to last. Despite outlining a four-year growth plan, Heck left the club at the end of his second full season.

In June 2025, Aston Villa appointed Francesco Calvo as president of business operations. Calvo had previously held senior commercial roles at Juventus, Barcelona and Roma. His arrival signals a more integrated approach, one built on alignment between the football and business sides of the club, as well as a leadership style more attuned to the sensitivities of English football culture. Chris Heck left behind a stadium in the process of transformation, he brought urgency and disruption to a club with deep traditions, but he also left unfinished business. Commercially, the club was making progress but was still some way behind the top tier.

In modern football, a club's identity is no longer forged solely on the pitch. It takes shape in how ideas and personalities are communicated to the fans. Unlike at many European clubs, where a rotating cast of executives, players and content creators share the narrative load, Villa speaks mostly through one voice: that of the manager. Emery is the team's narrator.

Behind the scenes, each press appearance is prepared with care by Tommy Jordan, the club's long-serving head of communications who has lived through three owners, seven managers and four CEOs. Emery receives briefing sheets ahead of time, listing anticipated questions and likely storylines, not to stage-manage the message but to help him deliver it clearly in his second language. Whether Villa are winning or losing, his tone remains steady. He avoids excuses. Emery rarely gives one-on-one interviews, just a handful, sometimes to Spanish outlets or while on tour. 'He doesn't do many,' says Tommy Jordan. 'Unai is always respectful and generous with his time but doing media is time he's not using to prepare for games – and he doesn't like to waste that.' Yet, he never shortens his answers. 'He ensures every question gets a proper response.'

For the head of comms, two of Unai's qualities stand out most: 'his openness with team news and his respect for officials.' Emery doesn't believe in withholding information for the sake of advantage. Most of the rival tactical preparation, in his view, is already done by Friday. If someone asks for team news in the press conference, regularly on that day, even if the players are off, they receive it. 'He doesn't try to leave things out,' says Jordan. 'If someone asks for team news, they'll get team news.'

One visible marker of Emery's growth in English football is the once-parodied 'Good evening' greeting. Now he says it properly but still begins with it. His English has improved markedly since his first Premier League spell, thanks in no small part to his inner circle, including Damià. He sits next to him in press conferences, offering reassurance. In previous jobs, Emery's natural eloquence could lead him into meandering responses, drifting into complex answers. With Damià's support, the message is now cleaner. 'We've tried to bring consistency to his messaging,' Damià explains. 'I say to him: "Look, Unai, people now see you as a serious, hard-working man who makes the decisions he has to make, who never says anything foolish in a press conference. You're not afraid to say when the other team has played better, or when they deserved more, something many managers never admit. You don't criticise the referee, even when the decisions go against you. That's a sign of maturity." He is now more cautious.'

Villa's wider communication strategy has matured in tandem with the team's rise but managing fan expectation is a fragile task. One good week and supporters dream of top-four finishes; one loss, and everything is called into question. 'Externally, fans are excited after recent seasons,' says Jordan. 'Realistically, they'd probably hope for a finish around seventh or higher, maybe getting close to winning a title. Managing those expectations is tricky.'

What remains clear is that Emery distances himself from media noise. He rarely uses social media. He doesn't read the British press. He doesn't follow fan content. He understands their power, he knows they shape perception, influence mood. There is genuine quality in the fan-generated content surrounding Villa – blogs, videos, podcasts – that reflects well the highs (and lows) of this new era. But the analysis that emerges from these spaces often feels distinct from journalism. The podcasting fan is not just offering an opinion; they are building an audience. The tone tends to swing with emotion, sharp bursts of optimism or frustration that speak more to expectation than to the actual football. It's also about carving out an identity within a crowded ecosystem of creators, which inevitably colours the narrative. While this content contributes to the atmosphere around the club, it is logical that it rarely captures the methodical, unseen work that defines the project.

The Aston Villa 'message' gets communicated not just through traditional media but through direct dialogue with supporters such as fan advisory board meetings, for instance. After a recent dip in results, some labelled it 'a poor run of form'. Performance data told a different story, spells of dominance, missed chances, control. 'I had to push back and say: "It's not poor form. If you watch the games, we played well for large stretches,"' Tommy explains.

Tommy Jordan remembers the moment he knew he was going to work with a different regime to anything he had previously known. He was watching Emery's first week of training from his office window. He noticed the staff asking Emi Martínez to have a huge number of touches on the ball, practising patterns again and again. Coaches led pressing drills themselves to demonstrate correct angles. It was just days before a difficult home match against Manchester United. The plan came to life. Villa won. Tommy became a believer. 'They all worked so hard. The club's data science team is exceptional. Arjav Trivedi, for example, has a background in geoscience!' But he knew the style would have to be explained properly. Emery also understood that the fanbase needed to be educated, so they could help or push players. He wants to share experiences with them, it is what makes football better, more intense, memorable. Still at times, their restlessness frustrates him. 'What do they want?' he's been known to ask. 'To crash into each other? Box-to-box football? That's always failed us.'

'Interestingly,' Tommy adds, 'Emery has never been one to lament the modern schedule.' While many coaches crave week-long training blocks, he talks instead of 'coaching through games'. 'He's not bothered about having Saturday-to-Saturday preparation,' says Jordan. 'He doesn't make excuses if he only has one or two sessions. He works with what he's got.'

Off the pitch, the manager joined once or twice the dinners of assistants, and kit, communications and player support teams. 'You definitely feel his presence, it changes the tone a bit.' Tommy Jordan smiles. They tried all kinds of places together, Brazilian steakhouses, tapas bars, Indian restaurants, even the local pub. 'Analyst Victor Mañas even hosted us at his house with Spanish food,' he says. During a winning streak, the group joked about keeping the dinners going as a superstition, but it's harder now. The schedule has allowed for just one such meal a season. When they do happen, the warmth remains.

One of Jordan's favourite parts of the job is going to European games. Upon landing, it's usually a small group travelling together: Tommy, Emery, Monchi, Damià, Tom Otrebski from the media team and occasionally a player doing interviews. On those trips, Emery often recalls past visits to that city. 'He remembers every score, every goal, every detail,' Jordan says. 'Monchi and Damià do the same. It's fascinating and shows just how much European experience this staff has.' Sometimes after games, Unai takes time to check on club people, encouraging them to rest, enjoy family time, take pride in their work.

Yet, a certain distance with the fans remains. A mystique. Emery had been avoiding the post-game theatrical gestures seen elsewhere. His long-held rule, head straight to the dressing room at full-time, stays in place. It is a form of self-protection, built over time. He respects the supporters, he really appreciates away fans, but he believes the pitch belongs to the players once the whistle blows. Still, he has started to question that. English football, he recognises, is different. The emotion is more immediate. When he briefly addressed the crowd with a simple 'Up the Villa' after securing Champions League qualification, the moment landed. 'Maybe I should get used to it,' he admitted. He also enjoys the walk from the bus and through the fan zone at Villa Park. The players like it too. The fans want more of that. He knows it would bridge the gap but only if it remains authentic.

Out in public, he rarely engages. Sometimes, people stop him in the streets to say thank you. In Birmingham, Mallorca, Valencia, he encounters fans who ask for photos.

Inevitably, that is when you find a fish out of water.

Unai wants to use all that extraordinary energy that fans bring to Villa Park to convert the stadium into a fortress. 'It's a target. We want to feel comfortable and strong at home,' he says. He already managed to get a very impressive home run in the Premier League between March and December 2023, when Aston Villa won fifteen consecutive league matches at Villa Park. This streak equalled a club record set in 1983 and featured dominant performances against top sides, including a 6–1 demolition of Brighton, a 4–1 win over West Ham and a controlled 1–0 victory against Manchester City. The run played a crucial role in Villa's surge towards Champions League qualification and helped re-establish Villa Park as one of the most formidable home grounds in English football. It came to an end with a 1–1 draw against Sheffield United in December 2023. The 2024–25 season was also showing a very strong Villa at home, their unbeaten run was on the way to becoming another record, despite the annoying draws. The push from the stands helped the team beat Spurs in the FA Cup on 9 February. Villa went 2–0 up and held on, despite a late goal from the away side. It felt like a stable performance with a stellar appearance from the bench from the debutants, Marco Asensio and Marcus Rashford. Aston Villa hadn't reached the last

16 of the Cup in a decade. If they beat Cardiff next, they would get there.

After Spurs, five games in thirteen days, from 15–28 February. Pablo explains the reality: 'It's hard. After every game, you have to compensate. Players who didn't play need sprints, intensity. The ones that did, rest but not too much. Small details, daily.' The strain showed against Ipswich at home. Villa played over 50 minutes with an extra man but still drew 1–1. They dominated with twenty-five shots and fifteen corners. Rashford hit the bar, Watkins scored the rebound. After the Ipswich match there was a brief moment of friction between the managers, two coaches that respect each other hugely. Unai believes the handshake should come first, a gesture of respect before any celebration. Waiting while Kieran McKenna took in the applause didn't sit right with him. Inside the changing room, Unai told the players, 'It's the kind of game I want from us.' The performance pleased him. The result didn't.

Then Villa hosted Liverpool. A team flying under Arne Slot, top of the Premier League table, with a reborn Salah. Liverpool played a sleek, positional game with more control than under Jurgen Klopp, the dominating football model of our times that Unai used too. It was the fifth game in a row that Villa didn't win – but they held their own. The major flaw? The defence. A blind pass from Andrés García was punished by Salah. That made it 1–0. Villa had now made twelve errors directly leading to goals, the second-worst in the league. Unai's team went in at half-time 2–1 up with goals from Tielemans and Watkins. The shape was good. The patterns worked. The final 2–2 result was fair.

Then three matches in six days. The most crucial was Crystal Palace away, but first, Chelsea at home. Asensio stepped up. Two goals. Minute 56. Minute 88. A 2–1 win. Villa had started poorly – conceded a soft goal, no control but they reacted well. The second half brought energy. Urgency. The crowd lifted them, and Villa lifted the crowd. 'Europe back on track,' Unai said. The final match of the month: Cardiff in the FA Cup. Unai asked for respect: 'Guys, Cardiff deserved it. This is a historic competition. We are favourites. We have to act like it.'

From his first training sessions, Marco Asensio had stood out. His touch was assured. He moved with the quiet confidence of someone who sees spaces before they open, a top-level player. One moment in the FA Cup captured it perfectly. Asensio had seen a gap between Ollie Watkins and the Cardiff defender. It was not more than a yard. When Marco received the ball, with barely a second to spare, he knew what he was going to do. The pass slid through effortlessly. The weight was immaculate, allowing Watkins to meet it in stride and break free, one-on-one with the goalkeeper that almost opened up the scoresheet. Finally, the goals came in the second half, both from Marco. The first one from a back pass from Rashford. The second one after controlling a cross from the right-hand side inside the box. Final result: 2–0. Clean. Controlled.

In between the victories over Chelsea and Cardiff, though? A 4–1 defeat at Crystal Palace. The final whistle at Selhurst Park felt like a punch to the ribs. In the locker room, players were slumped in their seats. Shirts soaked, heads down. Robin Olsen, who had come on at half-time to replace an injured Emi Martínez and conceded three, looked shattered. Emery stood in front of them and spoke. Quietly at first. Then raising his voice slightly, to emphasise his points. He wasn't about to tell them off. He reminded them that the season wasn't over. That the road was still open. That they were advancing in the FA Cup. That the Champions League knockout stage was just around the corner. That new players were still bedding in. That adaptation takes time. He finished with a line that felt like a plea: 'We will get where we want to get to.'

They had flown down to London, but the return was by bus – a quiet 4-hour journey north. Emery sat in silence for most of it, lost in his own analysis of the game and of the team. What it was. What it wasn't. Where the cracks were. The first half hour had been clean, controlled. No corners conceded. No real danger. Then came a corner that shouldn't have been – and it all unravelled. Two more goals came from throw-ins. That's about basics. Underneath it all, the same old fragility. Again, the opponent's first shot on target had gone in – the eighteenth time this had happened. Again, they looked exposed through the spine. Onana and Kamara, their most promising midfield pairing, had barely played together. Kamara had been forced to drop into defence to cover for injuries. When they had played together – against Arsenal and City – the shape held. Without them, everything felt patchy. Vulnerable. Three clean sheets in twenty-eight league games. Still, a negative goal difference. Most matches turned into battles of will, of chasing late equalisers or winners. The cost, physically and emotionally, was mounting. Villa weren't bad but they were brittle. And brittle doesn't last.

The next morning at Bodymoor Heath was subdued. The building always felt different after a heavy defeat. Conversations were short. Emery said almost nothing. He had already watched the match back. Twice. Knew where the problems were. Knew they weren't all tactical. He spent two days like a lion nursing a wound. His tone shifted. He became withdrawn. Frustration lingered. The kind that eats away silently. Not angry at individuals but the deeper ache of being unable to change patterns. They had tried to answer the question months ago – could this group handle adversity? But the answer still hadn't come. Or perhaps it had, and no one wanted to say it out loud. This is when culture is truly tested – not in success but in loss.

Most players would accept anything as belief is easiest when you are winning, which Villa mostly were. As Michael Caulfield, one of the UK's leading sports psychologists, puts it: 'At the minute he could make them have cold showers, hot showers, training with trainers, training with boots, with studs, take away the ketchup, give them back ketchup ... it's fine. But when you've lost eight, nine, ten, eleven and it really has gone horribly not well, that's when you find out whether the regime works or not.'

'I find it very hard to lose,' Unai admits. 'I'm a terrible loser. I wasn't like this before – the pressure to coach and to win in order to survive has made me this way, but it has got worse with more responsibility. It's made me very tough on myself. Sometimes I'm tough on everything around me, because when I lose, I don't respond. I ask myself why I made one decision and not another. I ask what I did wrong. I suffer, especially the next morning – that's the worst, waking up after a defeat. I go into mourning. I spend the whole day thinking, turning the game over in my mind. Two days later everything rebalances. What I always try to do is move forward.'

There is a line often attributed to Giulio Andreotti, the seven-time Italian prime minister, when asked whether power corrodes those who wield it. His reply was sharp: 'Power wears out those who don't have it.' The same is true of defeat. Winning may carry its own risks – arrogance, vanity, a sense of moral superiority – but defeat, if not absorbed, poisons everything. You either find a way to live with it, or you spend a year cursing the woodwork, the referee, the penalty that might have been. 'I accept the past, I accept the present and I want the future,' Unai tells himself often.

Next it was a trip to Bruges for the first leg of the Champions League last 16. The city became a stage for Villa fans. Strangers converged in the beautiful European setting, swapping stories of journeys from Ireland, Calonge, Bedford – all roads leading to Birmingham and then to this away day. Many wandered among the thousands of claret and blue shirts with a look of disbelief – *Here we are, we can't believe it.* Some had been in Athens. Others in Leipzig. Some were returning to Bruges, scene of a Tyrone Mings error in the league phase. And, after a 3–1 win against Club Brugge, just four days later they were off again. Another away trip. This time to Brentford. In the build-up to the match, Unai spoke of Robin Olsen, who stayed in the line-up, deserving a clean sheet. After Palace, Olsen, who conceded three goals after coming on, needed support. 'Unai was kind with him,' Damià recalls. 'Monchi and I made sure he felt backed. He wasn't to blame for that loss, and we told him so. Everybody did. We said he had to keep working and that the opportunity he deserved would come. And it did at Brentford, two weeks later.'

Olsen had been close to leaving the club in January. Copenhagen made an offer but not once did he pressure the club to let him go. 'On the contrary,' says Damià. 'He understood that what Copenhagen were proposing didn't solve anything for Aston Villa. He knew that if he left, we'd need to replace him. He put Aston Villa ahead of his own future. Robin is the kind of guy who shows up when he's needed, even in the difficult role of backing up Emi Martínez. He's deeply respected in the dressing room.' Football, at its best, rewards integrity. 'If you connect the dots, when you work hard you realise that football always gives you the chance for a sweet victory after a bitter moment,' comments Damià.

Unai knew that anything less than victory at Brentford could cost them Europe. The path was narrowing fast. There was no room for error in the three competitions. So, he made that clear to the players. 'Unai approached the Brentford match with a sense of urgency,' recalls Monchi. 'We *had* to win. There was no other option. He told the players: "If we don't win at Brentford, we can forget everything." He treated it like a final.' Something intangible happened that day, a moment of grace. 'There was a kind of magic at Brentford,' says Damià. 'Robin had a brilliant match. We won 1–0. It was beautiful, it definitively left behind the tough week we had gone through.'

In mid-March, after the Champions League second-leg match against Brugge, Villa entered an eighteen-day stretch without fixtures. From Sunday 16 to Friday 21 March, the squad travelled to Dubai – a pause in the middle of the storm, a moment to take stock. The squad was depleted. Between injuries and late call-ups to national teams, only seven first-team players made the trip. Even so, the group trained well. They held three sessions, played a friendly – useful for players like Torres and Onana returning from injury – and regained rhythm and confidence. 'We used those days to work on defensive structures,' said Rodri. 'We focused on the midfield, especially with Kamara and Onana. Asensio was also there. It was a chance for the new players to understand the model.'

Monchi recalls one moment in Dubai that captured Unai's way of thinking. Looking ahead to the coming stretch – Preston, Brighton, Nottingham Forest – he laid it out with clarity: 'Against Preston, if we're as focused as we were against Brentford, we'll win, because we're better. Brighton will demand more from us than Brentford, so we'll have to be better. Nottingham are stronger than Brighton, so we'll need to raise our performance level again. And against PSG, in the Champions League semis, it'll take everything, and more.' Simple words, almost too simple. But it painted the picture of what was ahead.

In Dubai, Lander Emery made his debut with the Aston Villa first team during the friendly against Al Ain. As a boy, he'd imagined it. 'I thought about it when I was little, playing for my dad. There was always that little "What if . . .?"' Lander says. 'But as I got older, I've tried to follow my own path, stay focused on what I need to do.' The summer before, he was meant to travel with the team to the USA but an injury the day before departure kept him grounded. 'It was a huge disappointment,' he says. 'Just being there, even if I didn't play, would've been an unforgettable experience.' So when the Dubai trip came, he grabbed the opportunity with both hands. 'Honestly, I didn't expect to play. I went to train, to absorb everything.'

Lander had joined the first team squad in certain games and had occasionally done the walk from the bus, through the fan zone, to the stadium. He always strode in a determined manner, serious, as if he was meant to be there. Emi Martínez was noticing his focus: 'Lander's already doing Pilates and other stuff, to improve physically. Hopefully, he develops well as a goalkeeper. I try to help him out when he trains with us.'

Unai and Javi García, Villa's goalkeeping coach, had spoken before the match. Javi asked him, 'Shall we put Lander on for 15 minutes?'

Unai replied: 'You decide. You've got the plan with Olie.'

Without telling Lander or anyone else, they agreed to give him the final 15 minutes, replacing Oliwier 'Olie' Zych, the young Polish goalkeeper who Lander had trained closely with and got to know well and who was going to start the match. Lander found out at half-time. 'Javi told me I'd play 15 minutes. I stayed calm. I knew why I was there. If I didn't play, fine, but once I knew I would, I focused completely. I didn't even think about my dad being the coach. I didn't process it that way.'

Around minute 72, Pako was next to Javi and Unai, and said, 'Come on, let the boy go on.'

And he did. 'We kept the moment professional. I'm Unai's son, yes, but in that moment, I was just a keeper that had just come on. After the match, my dad shook my hand.' Later, in the quiet of the hotel room, the meaning set in for Lander. 'It was only when I saw the photos that I realised how special the whole thing had been. Even if it was just a friendly. I'll carry that with me forever.'

Unai was careful not to overstate things. 'I hardly ever mention Lander. I distance myself – maybe too much – just to avoid any sense of favouritism. I told Javi early on that if he doesn't meet the level, I don't want him blocking someone who does. But the truth is, he's good. He doesn't stand out too much, and he fits in. Plays well with his feet. He trains seriously. Benito used to ask me, "Why can't Lander play for the Villa reserve team?" Eventually, we made that happen. He's aware his contract ends this summer, and he's taken a lot from his time here. Javi's a great coach, and Lander's learnt more than he probably realises.

'When he goes away, it'll sting a bit.'

15

THE TREE & THE LEOPARD:

THE ESSENCE OF A CLUB

The meeting took place the day after a meteorite landed just outside Birmingham. They were all greeted by Danielle at reception, one by one, ushered in with the usual warmth. 'Please, take a seat. Sharon will be with you shortly to take you to Unai's office.' Rafa Benítez arrived early. When Sharon appeared, Pep Guardiola had just walked in, accompanied by Luis Enrique, who asked, if possible, to see the facilities. 'Yes, of course!' Sharon exclaimed. Pep Segura started a quiet conversation with Pep Gumbau, the coach of Villa's reserves, who had just entered from inside the building. Outside, Thomas Frank, Andoni Iraola and Nuno Espírito Santo stepped out of a taxi that had dropped them at the entrance of the first team building.

Sharon welcomed each one without fuss and led them up to the first floor, past a row of offices and a sweeping view of the gym below. Paul Heckingbottom, eager to uncover the mysteries of Bodymoor Heath, had chosen to arrive even earlier and now joined the group. They moved past cubicles designed for private calls or focused work, passed more offices where assistants sat glued to their screens. Heads turned when they saw the managers making their way to Emery's office. Sharon paused at the door. 'Unai, your guests have arrived.'

Sharon Barnhurst doesn't normally take on that role, but Phil Roscoe was away that day. She is the head of football administration, in short, general club secretary and, as is so often the case with those in that position, she is so much more. Sharon is a tree. Her roots in the club are deep, she is quiet, tough. She has been offering shade and shelter to those around her, season after season. Damià couldn't be more clear: 'She's extraordinary. A good person, a true professional. And this is the moment she's felt most valued at the club.'

'Sharon is my line manager,' adds Phil Roscoe. 'She lets me get on with my job, I respect her massively for that. It takes the right kind of ego to step back that way.' Sharon doesn't seek the spotlight, but everyone agrees, she deserves a voice of her own.

My name is Sharon Barnhurst. I was born in Sutton Coldfield, seven miles from Villa Park. I've been at the club for over thirty-six years. I started here when I was eighteen. I answered an ad in a local newspaper. My brother and my dad, who are big supporters of the club, encouraged me to apply for the role of office junior. My first thought was, I don't know how to get there, the offices were at Villa Park. Silly really. But I went for the job, got it. Back then there were only about twenty-five people working at the club. It was really small. Now there are over a thousand employees, if you count matchday staff. At first, I was making tea, doing photocopying, sorting tickets, a bit of everything.

Then I moved to work for the commercial manager, sending out matchday invitations to sponsors and general commercial administration. Doug Ellis was chairman and owner at the time, and later, I worked directly for him. He had a PA called Marion Stringer, who was his right-hand woman, the big force behind him. Steve Stride, who was the general club secretary and a director of the club, was another key figure. They were Mr Ellis's closest advisers. Mr Ellis was quite a ruthless leader, very hands-on. He was in the office every day, signing every cheque, reviewing every invoice. He even knew the cost of paperclips! People were a bit scared of him, so Marion and Steve acted as buffers. They made him more reasonable, softened his approach and advised him.

I worked alongside Marion. It was very interesting, we did everything. Marion and I had so many responsibilities. Nowadays there are lots of new departments and someone to cover everything. Back then, Mr Ellis (yes, I still refer to him that way!) had many other businesses, a yacht, a villa in Mallorca and other personal matters we managed for him. On the football side, we helped with player contracts and transfers. I typed up the paperwork. When I started, it was just typewriters, no computers. We didn't have a legal department in those days. A transfer agreement might be one page long; now they're twenty pages plus! We also answered most of the correspondence coming into the club, including complaints. Everything was done by normal mail then, no emails. I remember when we got our first fax machine; everyone crowded around, learning how to use it!

It felt like family, very close-knit. You couldn't plan anything because every day was different. On the football side, I was booking hotels and organising team travel. Gradually, I started doing more work for Steve Stride, I attended FA and Premier League conferences, keeping up with football governance, rules and regulations. It's constantly evolving, and you have to stay on top of it. When Steve retired in 2008, I was promoted and became club secretary.

On top of doing the football administration, I was also doing team operations, but it soon became evident that particular aspect required additional focus, so we brought on board a team operations manager to cover travel and logistics. How did I even manage to do all that? Also in my team is Maxine Hammond, who has been at the club for as long as I have, an unsung hero who also shares my work ethic and desire to do things to the best of her ability. I recently also brought Dan Mole on board and to add someone of his calibre and knowledge was long overdue. He was running Walsall Football Club, doing everything as their club secretary. I was drowning in workload, so I thought, I need a mini-me, another safe pair of hands. It also helps that he is a huge Aston Villa supporter.

Then there is Phil Roscoe, who heads up our player care department and has taken it to a fantastic level, and Paul Carter who has recently taken over the role of first team operations manager. Also, Sofia Allen. She came in on work experience because she's a native Spanish speaker, born and raised in Menorca, and fluent in Portuguese too. When Diego Carlos joined and didn't speak a word of English, I asked her to help him settle in. She blossomed in the role, and we decided to keep her on. Once I was happy with the team around me I 'rebranded' the department. We used to have football administration, player care and football operations as separate entities. When Unai and his staff arrived, they had similar needs to the players: housing, schools, cars, etc. So, I combined everything under a 'first team support' umbrella. Now, whether it's a coach, a player or the manager, they all draw from the same resources. It's more efficient and ensures everyone gets the best support.

Very little impresses me these days. In football, people like to overdramatise everything. 'It's a disaster!' And I'm like, 'It's not a disaster.' I'm always open, honest and reasonable. I think I gain people's trust because I'm straightforward and trust-worthy. I have always known my place in the ecosystem. I've never commented to a manager or sporting director on how a player performed or made technical decisions. I've watched every home match in thirty-six years, but I keep my opinions to myself unless someone specifically asks. Then I'll give a strong opinion. What is the essence of Villa? I think it goes back to its history and heritage, and the people who've worked here over the years. Many of them aren't in it for themselves, they love Aston Villa. Even if they don't like the manager, chairman or their boss, they still want the club to do well. They respect the people above them because they care about the club. People make an organisation. Yes, we need to make money to pay the players and keep things running, but it's the people who make the club what it is. Have you met Pam? You have to meet Pam!

I'm responsible for player registrations and it can get quite fraught on deadline day if lots of transactions are taking place. I remember telling one of our previous CEOs on deadline day not to panic. People were running in and out, asking, 'Is it done yet? Is it sorted?' Meanwhile, I was calmly working through it and said, 'Don't panic unless I start to panic.' He smiled and left the room. I think Monchi and Damià have a lot of trust in me because they see me as a calming influence. I once did a psychological profile test that categorised people as red, blue, green or yellow. I came out very green: calming, thoughtful, discreet. Many people in football are red, meaning they're high energy, react quickly and can get worked up when there's a problem. I've learnt that if a business is run entirely by reds in a boardroom, it'll crash. You need a mix of all the colours to balance things out. My green perfectly balances out the red in certain situations.

I realised I'm the type of person who, when given a task or a contract to review, prefers to step away and think about it properly before responding. I used to see that as a weakness, but now I understand it's a strength. I want to consider things carefully. One of the words often used to describe me is disarming. When I walk into a room, whether it's a player coming to sign or something more formal, people can be very professional and tense. I'll say something light-hearted to bring the tension down. It's not a conscious effort; I just prefer people to feel relaxed and maybe even have a laugh. I think it comes down to age and experience. There is another way in which experience shows too. These days, if the chairman, sporting director or manager asks something of me, I don't hesitate to speak up if I disagree. A younger version of me might have simply followed instructions without question, but now I trust my judgement. I've reached a point in my career where I'm confident in standing my ground.

All the Spanish guys are really nice people. They integrated into the existing staff quite quickly. A few of them stayed locally at first. Phil Roscoe was great at organising things because many didn't have their families with them straight away. They were living alone in rented accommodation near the training ground. On Thursday nights, we'd all go out for a curry at the local curry house. Food and drink always bring people together, don't they? Austin MacPhee, our set-piece coach, once organised an evening at a little pub near where he lives out in the countryside. That was lovely too, a different atmosphere, but the same feeling of togetherness. Damià often talks about the soul of the club, and he believes, as I do, it's in the people who work here.

There was always a bit of concern with so many new people coming in. Not so much for me, I've seen it all. Unai is my seventeenth manager. I've 'survived' multiple owners, CEOs and managers. Every time someone new comes in, it's like starting a new job. You have to prove yourself all over again and adapt to their ways of working. My approach is simple with new people: 'Take me as I am. I'll back you, I'll be honest with you, I'll earn your trust and you'll earn mine.' It worked out well.

On the sporting side, there's definitely worry. It's a revolving door in football. For example, Phil was initially brought in by Steven Gerrard. I made it clear from the start that he's not Steven Gerrard's man, he's Aston Villa's man. He does a great job and, thankfully, the new management team gave everyone a fair chance. Obviously, Unai brought a lot of his own staff in, and some of Steven Gerrard's staff ended up leaving. But I think everyone else was given a chance to prove themselves. If you work hard and show you're on the journey, you get to stay on the train.

I don't deal with Unai daily. When he needs to know something I might be the point of contact because people assume, 'Sharon will know'. My office overlooks the training pitches, and I remember seeing Unai for the first time right in the middle of it all. You can see him out there now, fully immersed in coaching. I'm not technical, but there's so much passion and hard work in what he does. It raises everyone's game. Some people struggle to adapt to the pace of change or the intensity, and they fall away. Using the same analogy as before, I'll never forget what one of our former staff members said: 'Aston Villa is like a speeding train. You can get thrown off, but the train keeps moving.' Unai's definitely an engine. Always moving. He rarely stops, except maybe for a quick moment in the canteen or in his office.

My regular interactions are more with Damià and Monchi. They're incredibly unified. If Unai wants a player or even something like new floodlights at the training ground – those just went up yesterday – they'll move heaven and earth to make it happen for him. As a woman in football, I have found that sometimes you don't have a voice. But with Damià and Monchi, I do. They treat me as an equal, ask for my opinion and respect it. If I tell them, 'No, we can't do this', they listen. If there is a way to make something work, I'll find it. But if not, I will go back and say, 'This is how we can do it instead.' The Premier League recently did a study on women in the work-force. They interviewed me and some women on the business side. The report mentioned that women often feel unwelcome in a training ground environment. That upset me. I spoke to the women who felt that way. The training ground is an elite environment, intense and focused. It's not like a traditional office atmosphere. I think some people struggle to understand the dynamic and the intensity of this environment. The nature of elite-level football is not for everyone.

And the Pam mentioned by Sharon? Pam Bridgewater's life is stitched into the fabric of Aston Villa. Her connection goes back generations. Her grandparents owned a large house on Trinity Road, just by the stadium. 'They used to host six players at a time, including Pongo Waring and Frankie Broome ... those are the two my mum always mentioned,' Pam recalls. She's not sure if they were young hopefuls or professionals, but either way, it was part of a long-gone era when players lodged in spare rooms a stone's throw from the pitch. 'I've got a fabulous story about meeting my husband,' she says with a smile. 'His name's David Bridgewater, but everyone just calls him Bridge.' Their story began in the most

Villa of settings: an away game in London. Pam used to organise coaches for fans. 'When we played in London, we stayed over, and that's how we met in a hotel lift. That's what happens at away games,' she laughs.

Her own role at the club evolved over time. During the pandemic, when her usual duties disappeared, the club created a position just for her. Today, she works as a co-ordinator for the Under 21s in the smaller building next to the main one in the training ground and helps out in countless other ways. She still travels with the team. Her husband Bridge handles all the logistics like hotels, flights and payments. 'He doesn't always tell me what it costs,' she admits. 'Although last time, we had two nights in a hotel . . . probably more than half the budget on just one trip!'

When asked about the best moment in the club's history, she doesn't hesitate: 'The European Cup final was magical. I just want all those days back.' She was there, of course, staying in Rotterdam, wearing a cowboy hat adorned with a Villa badge during the match. 'It gave me a migraine,' she laughs. 'Everyone else went out to celebrate, and I had to stay in the hotel.' Of the current regime, she says this: 'These are good days.' She hasn't met Unai yet but senses something is different. If Sharon is a kind of lighthouse, showing the way, Pam is the clocktower in Bodymoor Heath.

'Who wants coffee?' Unai asked, already fiddling with the machine. 'I'm really into coffee, I have four or five a day. And this machine makes a good one.'

Pep Guardiola asked for an espresso. Nuno Espírito Santo wanted his with a splash of milk. Andoni Iraola stepped in to help Unai prepare the cups, he has the same machine at his own training ground. Thomas Frank just wanted water. Paul Heckingbottom requested an Americano. Luis Enrique stood at the glass wall, chatting about the facilities – he probably hadn't even heard the coffee offer. Pep Segura, once Barcelona's sporting director and still one of the best readers of football's currents, sat quietly on the sofa, taking in the whole scene. Rafa Benítez went for a white coffee.

Unai moved around filling the air with conversation, trying to make everyone feel at ease. 'That table over there, I used to have it on the other side of the room,' he said. 'It's not a big office, but you can see the pitches. We all can. Sit down, sit down.'

Unai turned to Pep: 'You know, I listen to you a lot on YouTube or wherever I can find you. You and Arteta. I understand you both perfectly, and it helps me pick up football vocabulary. I watch a lot of sports documentaries too, all in English. I pick things up in them.'

Pep smiled. 'You're still learning? It is me that has to pick things up from you. Don't forget December.'

Unai shook his head. 'That was one night. A good one. But you're still the "*puto amo*".'

They are talking about the 2-1 Villa win at Villa Park, 21 December 2024. Emery's side had allowed Guardiola's champions just two shots, both within the first 11 minutes. After that, it had been pure suffocation. 'You played a four-two-four out of possession,' Pep said now, scratching his head. 'I thought, *He's matching us. He's gaining duels.* I told my staff: "We're in trouble".'

Unai nodded. 'You did not have Rodri that day, that helped us.'

'Again, like the 1–0 defeat the season before,' said Pep. 'You always exploit any available gap.'

That performance twelve months earlier, in December 2023, against a City that were reigning European and Premier League champions, and who would end up winning the league, represented a statement for Unai's Aston Villa, a signature moment. The score flattered City. Everything Emery had built clicked into place that night. Pep smiled, that mix of admiration and mischief in his voice. 'I love your consistency, bloody hell! Wherever you go, you find a way, you get petrol from under some stones. Three Europa Leagues in a row, *uff*. What I love is how you lift the team in the hard moments. And if you have to defend a knockout tie with six at the back for 90 minutes, you do it. And then, when the moment comes to chase a game, you create chance after chance. You're a great strategist on set-pieces, too. Let's see how things go in April, when we face each other again.'

'There is always a lot of video-watching and a lot of thinking before facing you,' Unai continued. 'I played four central midfielders on both occasions. Last December we pressed high but only with one trigger. If the pass wasn't perfect, we went for the ball. Otherwise, we waited. Onana holding. Tielemans between the lines. Rogers and Durán pinning back the full-backs. And when you pressed us high, we went long into the wide channels.'

'That second goal, by Rogers was brilliant,' Pep admitted. 'You dragged us to one side, then attacked the lane we'd abandoned. It is hard to play you. You go to McGinn, he avoids our pressure. You go to Rogers, he dribbles you. On days like these, you lose not because you fail but because the opponent gets it absolutely right.'

'My first idea is always to control the game.' Unai had nervously finished his coffee and was preparing a new one. 'If you play without control, the other team can take over. Against teams like your City, we know it'll be a challenge, and you'll probably have your moments, but my goal is always to impose our pace. When we can't, we adapt to yours but keep it tight, try to slow it down where we can and look for the moment to hurt you. I have no problem in saying this, Pep, in public or private. You are the best, a genius, there's no one like you.'

'No, no,' Pep said, shaking his head gently. 'You're as good as I am. The difference is, you haven't had the kind of teams I've had. Those squads that win almost everything. That's the only difference. I have a lot of respect for you.'

'After playing you so many times – and you beating me so often, the bastard that you are – I've studied you in detail for years, Pep. Especially since we started facing each other when I was at Arsenal. But even before as well. At Almería, I showed my players two full days' worth of videos about Barcelona under you. I told them, "I know I am overdoing it, I know, but I love the way Barcelona plays, and I wanted to share it." When you analyse someone that deeply, over time, you begin to understand the thinking behind it.'

Damià sometimes wonders if Unai talks about his admiration for Pep a little too often. Maybe he repeats it because, in some way, it helps him place himself, measure where he stands. It's his way of staying grounded, of giving himself a reality check before the ego has a chance to grow.

'You know,' Unai said, 'I used to keep my distance from you at coaching summits. Everyone wanted a photo, a word, a moment. I stayed neutral. If you wanted to talk, I'd talk. If not, that was fine too. I didn't want to be just another one of those people.'

'But we always talked,' Pep replied. 'Even back at Valencia. You always had ideas.'

Unai looked down, almost sheepishly. 'Maybe I respect you too much. I always say: you and Simeone are the two I admire most. People say, "But they're so different!" And I say, "Yes, but they win." Both of you, in your own way, have real courage. You, in how you build the game; Simeone, in how he competes. You're both leaders. And to lead, you need more than authority. You need humility, empathy. Not just imposing things. I try to explain everything to my players. And with you, Pep, I sense that same humility. Some say it's false humility. I don't think so.'

He paused, then added: 'I deeply admire those who build competitive projects. You stand above the rest when it matters most. You don't copy, you invent your own path, and you've done it the hard way: with the ball. You were the first to truly occupy space in structured ways. You're not afraid of radical decisions. You had the guts to drop Ibrahimović for Messi. You got rid of the handbrake and built your masterpiece. You're a coach who creates artworks.'

Unai's tone softened. 'I can see you're suffering. You're not used to losing, but you'll rise again. You always find a way. And I'll never forget one call from you.'

'Which one?' Pep asked.

'After we lost 6–1 at the Camp Nou. You called me the next day. We spoke for 15, maybe 20 minutes. You told me how hard it is to beat Barça or Madrid. That stayed with me.

'But you've made me suffer, Pep,' Unai said with a half-smile. 'One day we were losing 3–0 to your City at half-time. I told my players, "The game's over, understand? If we have to play dead, we play dead." I'm a terrible loser. One time when I was at Arsenal, you kind of smiled at me when you shook my hand, and it felt like a punch in the gut. I had already told you about it, last year, after that 1–0.'

'Yes, yes,' Pep said, a bit embarrassed, as everyone laughed. 'I told you then and I tell you again, Unai, I'm sorry.'

'By the way,' Pep added, 'the 2–1 of this season didn't feel like the same match as the 1–0 twelve months earlier. Your team has improved.'

Thomas Frank interjected. 'That's what I love about your coaching, Unai. You evolve. But it's not random. It's not copy-paste from Pep or Arteta, or any other coach that plays the positional game.

You watch, you digest, you create something new. And players improve under you. I've seen it – Watkins, Kamara, McGinn. They've all jumped a level. You also inherited well, credit to the previous sporting director, Johan Lange. What you've done is build on that base. Just pure coaching.'

Luis Enrique added: 'I think you were the best and most organised team we faced in the season.'

'What you are doing is extraordinary, Luis,' Unai said. 'Coaching Madrid or Barça or PSG is a balancing act between the players' happiness and maximum effort. That is why it is so hard to do what Zidane did. And that is why it is so admirable what you did at Barcelona and now at PSG. Like Guardiola and Simeone, you are the best in the art of having their players happy while asking the most of them. Am I at that level? Not yet. I am not there yet. But I think I can get to that level.'

Unai told the group he had changed his approach after Villarreal's 4–1 defeat to Quique Setién's Barcelona at the Madrigal. 'I said to myself, *Unai, this can't go on. It's over.* That's when I started to use more positional structures in our play, the kind of things you've always done, Pep.'

Pep Segura nodded. 'This summer, Xabi Alonso will be confirmed as Real Madrid manager. Even Madrid is heading in that direction. It's the clearest sign yet of the evolution that is taking place. The best teams in the Champions League play that way. Barcelona, Liverpool, Bayern and your PSG, Luis. Even Liverpool, Manchester United. These kinds of managers, system builders, have reached the top clubs.'

'Still,' said Thomas Frank, 'there's a risk to that. You Pep, and you two, Unai and Luis, you have full control over your teams and even clubs. Full control means full responsibility. It's your system, your vision and if you leave, what remains?'

Unai answered. 'That's what I think about now. Continuity. Not just in tactics but culture too. That is the legacy. But that control allows you to grow.'

Nuno agreed. 'I think you, Unai, have found the perfect ecosystem here in England. A club that suits you. That lets you build the team you want.'

'I give you an example of that ability to grow,' said Andoni Iraola, turning to Unai. 'Facing your teams is one of the hardest things there is. Like Pep's, and I haven't gone up against you yet, Lucho, but I imagine what it is like. After you two, no one causes more problems than Unai. Because with most teams, you kind of know what to expect. But you, Unai, you've got a defined idea, yes, but you twist it every game. You find the adjustment. You target weaknesses. You believe you'll win and, usually, you do. You dominate every aspect of the game. To create so many layers, you need to have control over a lot of matters.'

Nuno Espírito Santo nodded. 'Preparing to play against you, Unai, has always been complicated. You are exceptional. A strategist. You create different games within the same game. You get players to buy into a clear idea, that's rare these days. Trying to anticipate your moves is a serious challenge for any coach.'

Thomas Frank leaned in. 'What I always look for in top coaches is structure. On and off the ball. With you, it's clear. Your teams are consistent. Very well organised.'

Iraola picked up again: 'Your teams are always strong without the ball. Compact. You don't allow games to get stretched. For teams like us, who want high-tempo, open football, you always manage to drag the game on to whatever you want to do, you slow it down to stop us. It's always a headache to play against you.'

Paul Heckingbottom, who had to face Villa in the FA Cup with Preston North End, added his perspective. 'Your teams are so stable, Unai. Every player seems to know their role exactly. And you've improved that squad every window. But from our point of view, preparing to play you? We couldn't commit to a plan until we saw the front line. Was it going to be Bailey out wide? Rashford on the left? Watkins, Asensio, Rogers as a nine or a ten? Each option changed everything.' He shook his head, half-smiling. 'As a coach, I'd love to set my team up knowing exactly how we're going to win the ball back. But before seeing your line-up, I couldn't be 100 per cent sure. That's frustrating but also a credit to how flexible and unpredictable you are.'

Thomas Frank spoke again. 'And you compete in Europe, too. That's impressive. Though this season I think it'll be a bit tougher to qualify again. Maybe Champions League, more likely Europa League. I hope you make it, I really like the work you are doing.'

Then Pep said what they all thought. 'You've done an incredible job at Aston Villa, Unai. You've taken them up there, to the top. When a coach succeeds in so many different places, in so many different ways, there's a reason. You're a big-club coach. A coach who should be aiming to win leagues and Champions Leagues.'

No one disagreed.

'To reach that height, you need a lot of help,' Unai said, trying to change the subject. 'I used to solve everything myself. Not anymore.'

'It's what Pep's done,' said Segura. 'At City, the club surrounded you with people who think like you. The CEO Ferran Soriano, the director of football Txiki Begiristain, they smooth the path. Before you even speak, they've read your mind. The difference between Manchester United and City is not the oil. It is the people running the club.'

'It is true that you need more help than ever,' Pep added, 'you burn out. I used to watch five videos of the rival. Now, just one. I have a team that filters what I need. Otherwise, I'd collapse.'

'It's what we all face,' said Thomas Frank. 'The grind, the repetition. Eventually, you start to see everything as a problem to solve. Even dinner.'

The room laughed, knowingly. They all understand that without rest, delegating, without some breathers, the likes of Unai or any of those in the room simply would no longer be able to do their job. They would fall over. The human body and mind have developed and evolved but not that much. We've got better nutrition, better medication, better health awareness, better everything, but everyone has a limited resource. As far back as 1974, Bill Shankly retired as Liverpool manager because he was completely and utterly exhausted. In elite football management, the Premier League in particular, there's no escape.

'I think, Unai, you have that love and passion that, in this profession, you either have or you can't do the job – that passion to not go under,' says Pep. 'In the tough moments, you're really strong. That's why you're able to change dynamics so quickly.'

'Pep, you're like me,' Unai replies. 'A coach who I think can also be exhausting. You've said it yourself. We have to change players because we push so hard. I'm seeing it in the *All or Nothing* documentary. I didn't realise how intensely you push. You've just won a Champions League match and you're already talking about Crystal Palace or whatever!'

Thomas Frank puts it plainly: 'Our sports psychologist Michael Caulfield told me that football is maybe the most popular pastime in human history. And these days, we're expected to comment on everything. Covid, Brexit, potholes, the price of hamburgers. By the end of each season, everyone is exhausted.'

The conversation moved to City's defeat against PSG in Europe, the sense that PSG looked more balanced without Mbappé and that they now seemed genuine favourites to win the Champions League, with a team fully shaped in Luis Enrique's image.

Unai shared a lesson. 'You told me, Pep, a key thing: to win the Champions League, Barcelona had to break from two crucial moments in the club's history, wins that took them to the final: Bakero's last-minute header in Kaiserslautern, Iniesta's goal at Stamford Bridge. PSG has still not found that goal, that moment that breaks the mould. Having its "Bakero's goal". Even when you don't deserve it at all. But, boom! You score that goal, you win the Champions League and you have that moment, it takes you to the next level. Now Luis, you have the chance to break that final barrier.'

'Who wins normally, Unai?'

Rafa Benítez had broken the flow with the pointed question. The managers, men used to being listened to, now turned their attention towards two of their own. What began as a challenge from Rafa became something more: a spontaneous debate between him and Unai.

Unai Emery was certain. 'The team that plays better. That's clear.'

Rafa Benítez shook his head. 'No. The team with the better players wins. That's the truth.'

Unai Emery: 'That's part of it, of course, but the coach plays a key role. Choosing the right players is part of our job but also improving them. You pick someone not just for what he is now but for what you know you can make of him.'

Rafa Benítez: 'Maybe, but the best players fill the winning teams. Over time, for managers, what also matters is experience. When you're young, you think you can fix everything, outwork every problem. Then reality hits. There are things you can't control. The players, the board, the promises they break. You're expected to deliver results, but you're not given the tools. And when it goes wrong, it's your fault.'

Unai Emery: 'At first, it's about winning and being competitive straight away. Then, it becomes about how to win. You start building something. For me, coaching today is multidirectional. It's not just the pitch. It's the group. It's the individual player. It's the conversation before kick-off that changes a mindset. It's dealing with the sporting director. Sometimes even the owner. You have to be present everywhere. All that helps you win more often.'

Rafa Benítez: 'And still, nine times out of ten, the team with better players wins. You can plan for every detail, but if your striker can't finish and theirs can, what then?'

Unai Emery: 'In a single match, maybe, but not over time. If you win once by scoring from your only chance when the other team had created ten, fine, you won. Stretch that over weeks, months, seasons . . . it doesn't hold. You need structure. A system. A method that creates your own luck.'

Thomas Frank leaned back slightly in his chair, eyes half on the window, half on the room. He tried to reduce the tension. 'I heard something from Caulfield recently. He was talking about coaches like us, especially the ones at the very top. He called us addicts. But I guess you have to overwork so you don't get caught.'

Luis Enrique chuckled. 'He's not wrong. You have to be obsessed. You can't do this job otherwise. The pressure, the hours, the scrutiny . . . You'd burn out if you didn't love it in a strange, unhealthy way.'

Thomas Frank added 'And it's constant. It's not just passion, it's addiction to the pursuit. To the next win. To the idea of the perfect team. That perfect moment when everything clicks. You chase it, and you never stop. Caulfield also said something else. That we're afraid. Not just of losing matches but of failing. That fear is behind the obsession. We've worked too hard to get here. No one gave us this. You fight your way up, through the lower leagues, through bad squads, sackings, short contracts. When you finally get here, you'll do anything to stay.'

There was a pause.

Unai spoke up. 'I agree. That fear pushes you. At Villarreal, at Sevilla, even here, I always felt that urgency. Like if you don't deliver now, you disappear.'

Iraola glanced back out at the pitch. 'It's cultural too. In Spain, in my generation, you were told: if you work hard, if you behave, if you take responsibility, you'll get ahead. And so, when you're finally in charge, you carry that voice with you. You never switch it off.'

Frank smiled. 'Exactly. And Caulfield said something else that stuck with me. He said rest, holidays, time off, they almost feel like the enemy to people like us. You take a day off and you start worrying that someone else is working harder, planning more, getting ahead.'

Nuno nodded slowly. 'It's dangerous, isn't it? You stop seeing people who aren't working with you as friends and start seeing them as distractions. Even family.'

Unai added, 'That's why what Pep said resonated. Remember? You said in that interview on *Match of the Day* just before the October break: "Everyone needs a few days off." It's so true.'

Nuno, quieter now, added one last thought. 'Caulfield's right. We don't slow down. We go until someone else stops us. A sacking, an illness, a moment when the machine breaks. Until then, we will just keep going.'

Unai looked around the table. 'That's why these moments matter. Would anyone like another coffee?'

*

What a conversation. It never happened, of course, it was just a fantasy, but it was made entirely of true words.

The 2024–25 season, in many ways, was encapsulated in the three games against Brugge. In the league match in November, there was a big mistake but also imbalances and frustration – recurring themes across a difficult end of the year – when dropped points and small errors began to add up. Then, the round of 16 against the Belgium side in March would test where they truly stood.

Club Brugge 1–0 Aston Villa, 6 November 2024

The fourth match of Villa's Champions League league phase. After beating Young Boys, Bayern and Bologna, Aston Villa arrived in Belgium as one of the surprises of the European season. And went home defeated.

Unai didn't react during the game. Not in the dressing room. It came after. On the team bus, he sat down and slammed his fist into the window. 'I was angry. So angry. The frustration was overwhelming.'

At half-time, Unai had told the players: 'We're where we want to be in the game – not especially brilliant but in control. We only allowed a couple of passes in behind, no real counter-attacks. If we keep this up and don't give anything away, it'll be a long game, not much will happen – and by the end, we'll have chances to win it.'

Tyrone Mings had started in his second official game since returning from a fourteen-month knee injury layoff. It was his Champions League debut. Five minutes into the second half, Emi Martínez played a short goal-kick to him inside the area. Mings bent down, picked the ball up with his hands and stood still. The whistle blew.

Another twist in Tyrone Mings's story, which has never been linear. He joined Ipswich Town in 2012 for just £10,000 from Southern League side Chippenham Town. He had been working as a mortgage adviser, squeezing training sessions between shifts. Two years later, Bournemouth signed him for £8 million. In 2019, Aston Villa made him their own for £20 million. When Unai Emery arrived at Villa Park, Mings was already a senior figure at the club. But it was, as he puts it, 'a moment where I needed to learn more.'

'With Unai, it was the first time I played under a manager who didn't speak English as their first language,' he says. 'So I was thinking about the benefits and complications that come with that. I didn't know too much about his philosophy or how he worked. I just knew he was intense and extremely successful.' Very quickly, there was connection, despite the risks. 'He told us things like: "take time on the ball, wait for the man that presses you to come closer," and I thought, *Yeah OK, we can do it, but it's going to take a while for the fans to get comfortable with that.*' Unai told him something that changed his perception of the game. 'You run to the right, to the left, you step into midfield. I need you to just do less, less is more.' It was a moment of recalibration. Mings had always leaned on his fitness and athleticism. Now, Emery was making him better and prolonging his career by asking him to forego useless efforts.

Before the Spanish coach arrived, Mings had lost the captaincy. Unai brought it up once, then moved on. 'He basically said it wasn't a big deal to him, so it shouldn't be a big deal to me. And it never was.' Mings understood the symbolism of the armband but also its limits. 'How people perform, how people act, is more important than wearing the armband. The leadership group, me, Ezri [Konsa], Ollie [Watkins], John [McGinn], Emi [Martínez], we're all part of that. It's not just matchday, it's what you do during the week. Are you helping people? Are you leading? Are you setting a good example?'

Then, came the injury. Fourteen months and the fear of not being able to return to elite football. For some, that kind of layoff becomes a form of exile. 'The club was brilliant,' Mings says. 'Especially Damià. He was absolutely superb. Anything I needed was never too much of a big deal.' Mings spent much of his rehab in the United States, removed from the daily intensity of the training ground. He preferred not to interfere, yet he never felt forgotten. 'The manager was always referencing me and Emi Buendía, also injured, in meetings, "They're still a part of this." We weren't available for selection, but we were part of the team.' When he returned, he brought more than just his body back. 'Tactically, I understand so much more now. Because of that, I'm always proud that I'm not scared to make decisions on the pitch, even if it's not what the manager wants. If you just do what the manager says and it doesn't work, players say, "Well, it's not my fault." But some footballers *want* to take responsibility. That's where big personalities are worth their weight in gold.'

There was confusion at first in Bruges when Mings got hold of the ball. Referee Tobias Stieler blew his whistle and stopped play just as Emi Martínez was preparing to retake the goal-kick. Then Stieler pointed to the penalty spot – prompting disbelief from the Villa players. Only the television replays made it clear: Mings had picked up the ball inside the area, not realising the kick had already been taken and the ball was in play. The VAR check confirmed it. You could read Unai's lips on the touchline. 'What a sh***y penalty!'

In the replay you can see Tyrone looking up to assess the press, checking whether the opposition is pressing with two or three players. If it's two, he has to drive the ball. If it's three, he would have to move wide to give options to Emi. That's the general structure, although there are small adjustments, but the basic idea is that they decide how to build from the back based on how many players are pressing.

'I thought the ball actually came from the stand or was sent by the ballboy. I just went and picked it up. It felt natural. Then I saw the referee . . . and I thought, oh well. But honestly, it didn't have much significance or any bearing on how I felt about the performance. I've learnt to put those things to the back of my mind. This is not something I have always had. I've probably learnt it through serious knee injuries and challenges in my career.'

Villa were penalised for the error, and Hans Vanaken converted from the spot. 1–0 to Brugge. Tyrone Mings was taken off for Pau Torres just 14 minutes later but not because of the incident. Both centre-backs were on yellow cards, and Mings was still not able to play 90 minutes at the highest level. Pau Torres's ability to find attacking teammates in tight spaces felt important, especially as it looked like the opposition would drop deeper. During the game, one coach shared this thought on the bench. 'The best players make fewer errors not because they're perfect but because they learn from them faster, and that's why they succeed.' None of the assistants spoke to Mings as he moved to the bench. 'What are you going to say then?' Pablo notes. Players did not know yet if the mistake had been made by the centre-back or the goalkeeper.

Villa were unable to turn the game around. It was their first European defeat of the season. Damià sought out the referee to challenge the decision. He pointed out that an almost identical incident had occurred the previous season in the Champions League quarter-final between Arsenal and Bayern Munich in London. Gabriel handled a pass from David Raya inside the box, not realising play had restarted. The referee did *not* give a penalty, allowing Arsenal to retake the goal-kick. Bayern's manager at the time, Thomas Tuchel, was furious and claimed the referee told his players it was 'a kid's mistake' and didn't warrant punishment. Damià asked why the same rule had been applied dissimilarly. The response? 'Each referee is different.' He also recalled how UEFA, in the Arsenal incident, backed the referee's decision, explaining that the action didn't violate the spirit of the game. 'Yes, technically it's a penalty,' Damià reflected, 'but it goes against the spirit. It's like a player coming on to the pitch wearing the wrong number. It doesn't affect the game.' The referee acknowledged his point but said that in this case, he had to consider how it would look to Club Brugge's fans if he *didn't* give the penalty. The suggestion was that if it had happened at Villa Park, it would not have been a penalty. Damià found the lack of consistency frustrating.

Meanwhile, on the way to the changing rooms, Mings shared that he felt he hadn't done anything wrong, in the same circumstances he would do the same again. But that kind of situation underlines the need for full awareness. Just as a goalkeeper checks all sides before taking a goal-kick, a defender has to read the entire moment: where the ball is, whether the game is live, what's happening around him. At this level, those assessments are essential. The coaching staff understood Mings's perspective, but they also reflected on the demands of concentration at the elite level. They all agreed: focus can elevate a limited player beyond his technical level or undo the best in a split second. Some players, even at the highest level, switch off. They remembered how surprising it was to discover that some professionals don't even follow football, as if detached from the game.

That's why what happened with Tyrone Mings was so striking. He's the opposite of careless: professional, committed, a model teammate, family man. It seemed unthinkable.

So they kept analysing. He'd been out for a long time. For the staff, this was the sixth or seventh time playing in Europe's top competition. It was his Champions League debut. The anthem, the pitch, the pressure, those things carry weight. It's easy to assume players can just slot in, perform, reset but standing in front of sixty or seventy thousand people every three days, that takes a toll. Mistakes happen, even to the most focused. Eventually, they concluded it was one of those surreal moments that simply defies preparation. They had spent countless hours on video analysis, fine-tuning everything. But no matter how meticulous you are, covering 100 per cent of the details is impossible.

Ezri Konsa addressed the incident in the media, pointing out the inconsistency: if it had been judged a deliberate handball, why wasn't Mings shown a second yellow? Still, he emphasised that it was a mistake the team would learn from. Inside the dressing room, the reaction was equally measured. The group didn't turn on Mings or use the error to undermine him. They protected him, not excessively, but enough. No one used the moment to cast doubt on his place or influence in the squad. Had it involved a player the others didn't fully trust, it might have been used to weaken his standing. With Mings, that was never in question.

Damià, straight after talking to the referee, spoke to Tyrone Mings and made it clear the mistake was serious but that the only option was to move forward. By then Mings was visibly upset, angry with himself, frustrated and deeply embarrassed. It hit him hard. But those around him knew he had the mental strength to handle it. Unai, who had not spoken to Mings at that point, was fuming, but not at the error. In the press conference, he called it 'the biggest mistake I witnessed in my career' though didn't go any further. He basically saw it for what it was, a moment of lost concentration that led to a goal. It happens in sport. Mistakes are always tactical. His responsibility, as he sees it, is to ensure that players are prepared to make the right decisions on the pitch. If something goes wrong, it starts with him, then the staff, then the players.

But after the defeat in Bruges, Unai was visibly shaken. He kept telling his assistants that he wasn't furious about the penalty incident itself. What unsettled him ran deeper: a sense that the team hadn't shown the collective strength required at this level to recover after the goal. They had prepared meticulously, controlling the first half without brilliance but with purpose. Then, suddenly, after conceding they didn't look like themselves. They looked uncertain. This wasn't just about one game. Emery knew that tougher tests were coming and Brugge was supposed to be the game that gave them breathing room in Europe. Instead, they left Belgium empty-handed and asking questions. It was one of those defeats that left him feeling alone in spite of the support around him. The kind of loss that strips football down to its rawest truth: the game doesn't care how hard you've worked.

As always with Emery, the emotion did not last long. The players, too, had begun to move on the next day at Bodymoor Heath. Some were seen laughing with Tyrone Mings before the session, preparing boots and tape like any other day. There was no trace of finger-pointing. At around 11 a.m., the whole squad gathered in the gym. Players, physios, analysts, staff, Monchi and Damià too. This is a ritual. The post-match reflection to take stock, to reset. Unai spoke. 'Mistakes like this happen when we stop taking the smallest details seriously,' he began, scanning the group. He didn't mention Tyrone by name. Instead, he focused on something he'd observed in training. A habit he'd seen countless times in the rondos, one he'd been trying to break for years. 'In the rondos,' he told them, his voice steady, 'you all have this bad habit of picking up the ball with your hands. I've been a coach for twenty years, fifteen straight doing rondos. One player starts and the game begins. The ball doesn't get picked up with the hands! Your hands are for pissing. Only the goalkeeper can use them. The ball gets placed in the middle at the start, once, and then we play. You lose it, you play it. That's how it works.' That would be the first time of many where he would tell Tyrone, half-jokingly, hands are for the toilet.

By the time the players left the gym that day, the focus had already moved. The recovery training was led by Pako. Unai kept to the periphery. He was already deep into preparing for their next match: Liverpool. Even though he likes to analyse games that have been lost, he did not use that Brugge defeat in his video analysis for the players. Not this time.

Club Brugge 1–3 Aston Villa, 4 March 2025

Four months later, by the time Aston Villa reached the Champions League round of 16, their season had begun to shift. The early months of inconsistency, with brilliant wins followed by frustrating draws, a growing injury list and a sense that something wasn't quite clicking, was being left behind. The arrivals of Marco Asensio and Marcus Rashford, and a returning Boubacar Kamara added experience and tactical variety. The defence started to show signs of the compact, high-line discipline that Emery demanded. In Europe, Villa were quietly among the best defensively, only two defeats in the competition, both by a single goal. The FA Cup was seen as an exciting adventure; they had reached the quarter-finals where they would face Preston North End.

In the league, there were still stumbles but their best version was returning. The race for Europe was intense with five Champions League places up for grabs and sixth place taking you to the Europa League. Arsenal and Liverpool were already clear at the top. Behind them, the field was crowded: Guardiola's City, Howe's Newcastle, Maresca's Chelsea but also Nuno's Forest, Silva's Fulham and Frank's Brentford. Six teams fighting for three remaining spots for the top European competition. Expectations were rising.

On the eve of the Brugge match, Unai was animated during the final internal coaches' meeting. He began shouting, trying to make a point. 'I haven't seen *E.T.*,' he declared. 'I don't watch films like you lot do. But football films? I've seen all of them. Every last one. I know how they end. He pointed across the room. 'Pako, you too. Don't come telling me anything different. We've lived this. We know the script. We have seen everything. We cannot think Brugge are just an inferior team!'

Everyone had been caught off-guard by Brugge's elimination of Atalanta, not just the result itself but the manner of it. They had been clearly superior. That tie made an impression on Unai and his assistants. The manager approached the preparation trying to get the group to forget about reputations. They were facing a team without big names but that could hurt them. Winning away in Europe is never easy, one of his most repetitive themes. Anyone who thought they'd walk into Bruges and come away comfortably was mistaken. If they couldn't win, they must not lose. To drive the point home, he used a phrase in French: '*Attention à la bicyclette*'. Meaning, beware of the thing that looks harmless. Beware of Club Brugge.

This was a match they *could not* lose if they wanted to get to

Villa Park with a chance of reaching the quarter-finals. The squad spent time analysing Brugge's previous round against the Italians. For the first time, they also reviewed Villa's own defeat in Belgium in the group stage. They looked at Brugge's transitions and studied their set-pieces.

Tyrone Mings started his third-ever Champions League match. 'I didn't walk into that stadium feeling any real difference,' he admits. Villa started well. Early pressure, a header from Mings found Leon Bailey with space and he lashed the opener into the net. It wasn't an accident that the ball had been directed towards Mings, Unai had spoken about it. For someone of his size, Mings has scored surprisingly few headers. Just one. And it's something Emery has been hard on him about.

Then came the equaliser. Maxim De Cuyper drawing Brugge level with a clean strike. Suddenly, the match began to mirror that first meeting. Not much separating the sides. Every detail counted. Hans Vanaken, who had scored the penalty in the group match, rose to meet a perfect cross, nodded the ball across goal. It was a goal. It *should* have been a goal. The keeper was beaten, the ball was dropping towards the far post. But Tyrone Mings, somehow, stretched out a leg like a pouncing leopard and clawed the ball off the line. A fraction more contact and he would have turned it into his own net. Instead, he flicked it wide, out of danger. Vanaken looked stunned. From the bench, the view was unclear. The staff thought the ball had simply gone wide. No one understood, in the moment, what Mings had done. It wasn't until they reached the dressing room and Pablo looked at the four camera angles. A fingertip of the boot. The tiniest touch. The save of many seasons. Fans online said it was the greatest goal-line clearance they'd ever seen.

Villa made four changes in the 64th minute. Kamara came on

for Bailey, Asensio for Rashford, Cash for Disasi and Ramsey for McGinn. Asensio had been carrying a small knock; Kamara was just returning from injury, but when your bench holds players of that level, you use them to elevate proceedings. It worked. Morgan Rogers, charging down the right, fired in a dangerous low cross. Brandon Mechele, lunging to intercept, turned it into his own net. 2–1. Moments later, a penalty. Matty Cash's heel was clipped by Christos Tzolis. Marco Asensio stepped up and converted. 3–1. Job done.

In the tunnel someone turned to Mings and asked how he'd done it. He just smiled. 'That stretch in the away end,' he said calmly. 'Probably I couldn't do it again. Big moments are what you're paid to do.' Damià said afterwards that the man of the match award, which had gone to Morgan Rogers, should have been given to Mings. 'It would have been absolute poetic justice.' He told Morgan as much, and Tyrone too. Football does offer second chances but only if you're ready to take them. Unai had seen this movie many times before.

Aston Villa 3–0 Club Brugge, 12 March 2025

A win in the second leg against Club Brugge would send Aston Villa into the quarter-finals of the European Cup for the first time since 1983. It would also bring with it a £10.55 million boost in UEFA prize money, plus another £3.75 million in gate receipts. That was in everyone's mind but wasn't necessarily what Unai Emery had spent the week talking about. He had warned the players repeatedly: in Europe, no lead is safe. No margin, no matter how comfortable it looks, can be trusted. He gave examples, he had a few himself. He reminded them that the second leg is always a new story.

For much of the opening spell at Villa Park, that story was tense. Villa barely touched the ball. Something wasn't clicking. Then, minute 16: the tie turned. Marcus Rashford, who had been lurking on the shoulder of young full-back Kyriani Sabbe, timed his run perfectly as Emi Martínez picked him out with a superb long ball. Clear through on goal, Rashford was brought down by Sabbe in desperation. The referee showed a straight red. Brugge were reduced to ten men.

Marco Asensio, who had been nursing minor injuries in the build-up to both legs, hadn't trained in the two days before the return fixture. Emery was cautious with him. 'The important thing is that you're available often,' he told him, 'that you're present all the way to the end of the season.' He came on at half-time. With less than 5 minutes on the pitch, a lovely ball from Leon Bailey found Asensio in stride and with a graceful swivel and half-volley, he lifted the ball over Simon Mignolet. 1–0 on the night. Then, shortly after Maatsen scored. 2–0. Tie effectively over. Asensio almost had another, controlling a ball over the top with a sublime first touch before his effort crashed off the post; but he wasn't done. Rashford drove down the left, cut the ball back, and Asensio arrived to sweep in his second and Villa's third. It was his seventh goal in claret and blue, a tally bettered only by PSG's Ousmane Dembélé across Europe's top five leagues since he landed in Birmingham. In less than 1 hour across two legs, he had scored three goals.

When the final whistle blew, Unai Emery finally let himself breathe. On the touchline he had been motionless, his face giving nothing away, but as the stands roared and flags waved, even he broke into a smile. They were in the quarter-finals of the Champions League! Things were falling into place. Although he was not quite as animated as Prince William in the directors' box.

'What an exciting end to the season we've got,' John McGinn said afterwards. 'We're giving these fans experiences they'll remember forever. We want to write our names into the club's history and make these nights happen more often.' The season was shaping up. Although whether it would turn out to be a good one, a bad one or possibly one without progression, the worst type, was still to be determined. The next two months would bring that judgement. 'We're very excited and motivated to play PSG,' Emery said.

He had not returned to Paris since he had left.

16

FORWARD, INTO THE STORM:

THE PSG FIXTURES

The Dubai training camp, held from 16 to 21 March during the international break, proved significant on several fronts. With Thomas Tuchel newly in charge of England, he used the opportunity to assess Aston Villa's English core. Morgan Rogers, Ezri Konsa and Marcus Rashford all started in a World Cup qualifier against Latvia – a clear sign of their growing stature. Meanwhile, Unai Emery, left with just eight senior players, worked closely with several promising youngsters from Josep Gombau's Under 21s. The standout was Kane Taylor, a 20-year-old winger who had recently joined from Manchester City, and who scored in a 3–1 friendly win over Al Ain.

By the time the group returned and internationals rejoined, the squad was close to full strength again, just in time for a daunting run-in: FA Cup and Champions League quarter-finals, as well as nine crucial league games.

Now that the players, as Monchi put it, 'all wanted to eat', hungry for minutes, Emery spoke of 'using the squad': choosing the right players at the right time based on form, focus, and freshness. Those that did not play shouldn't feel pushed aside. They were all going to be important. Emery saw twenty players with a genuine claim to start. For instance, with centre backs Konsa, Disasi, Mings and

Torres all at a similar level, competition was fierce.

Villa had rediscovered momentum, with four wins in all competitions. In the league they sat just 1 point behind Chelsea, who occupied fifth place and the final Champions League spot. UEFA's new European Performance Spots (EPS) grants two extra places each year to the best-performing leagues across the three European competitions. English clubs had excelled, and as a result, fifth place in the Premier League now came with a ticket to the Champions League. But, first, there was a trip to Lancashire to face Preston North End, a side enduring a difficult season in the Championship, in the FA Cup quarter-finals. Marcus Rashford, still without a goal after 11 appearances across all competitions, was handed a start. A month after his return to regular action in mid-February, he had already made his presence felt. Since coming off the bench for his debut, no Premier League player had created more chances, 13 in total. The staff urged him to take risks, attack defenders, to keep going even after setbacks, and make central runs to stretch defences. From the left, he'd already provided four near-identical assists for Asensio. As a striker, his movement in behind was just as dangerous, shown perfectly when Sabbe was sent off against Brugge.

Marcus Rashford had arrived at Aston Villa quietly, just as he preferred. His relationship with Unai Emery took shape over three conversations. The first was via FaceTime. At that point, they had never spoken to each other. Emery didn't want to hear about the reasons for his exit, only that if he was to join Villa, it had to be because he truly wanted to. When they finally met face to face at Bodymoor Heath, Unai explained to Rashford that his goal was to win back his place in the England squad. That box was ticked perhaps sooner than expected, as he was selected for the international fixtures in March 2025. The next step, Unai outlined, was even more ambitious: to restore his standing as one of the best players in the world. There was also one more conversation Unai planned to have. He had thought, more than once, about saying something that sat on the edge of challenge and provocation. Something like: 'Marcus, what you can't do is let someone like Bruno Fernandes walk into the room, take the armband, take the penalties and lead everything – just because he's the loudest.' Rashford is a good person, but he would have to show a little more fire.

At Villa, his attitude was exemplary: hard-working, respectful, punctual, committed. In football, every player responds differently to challenges. Some are expressive, riding emotional highs and lows depending on recent results. Others are more even-keeled. Rashford falls into that second category, stable, but also clearly ambitious. But he was difficult to reach, guarded. Little by little, coaches and staff began to chip away at the armour, earning his trust. They could sense they were heading in the right direction with him, but they had to see how he would react when pushed a bit further. After he returned from England duty, Rashford was paired with McGinn in Rodri's individual training after the main session. McGinn already understood the objectives behind each exercise, he knew exactly where the work with Marcus was heading. Rashford, by contrast, followed instructions, but he was not yet entirely aware of the purpose behind some of the drills. After the session he asked for more individual training.

Before the FA Cup match against Preston, Unai and Rodri sat down with Marcus for a detailed video analysis session. They showed him clips of his best moments at Manchester United, the kind of movements and decisions that had once made him unplayable. 'You could do this here too,' Unai told him. What struck Rashford was the attention to detail. The clips reflected hours of preparation. At that moment, something clicked. He felt seen, understood. The player's door opened a bit more.

In the days leading up to the match, Unai had shown the players video clips of the previous round against Cardiff to frame the unpredictability of cup football. 'Expect pressure, physicality, even the possibility of extra time or penalties. No complacency.' In England, the FA Cup holds a mystique that is often missing from domestic cups elsewhere. In the stands, the atmosphere feels different. A higher proportion of season ticket holders attend, the songs are louder. Pablo recalls a fan stopping him at the airport just days before, saying: 'I know winning the Champions League would be incredible, but my dad's dream is to see us win the FA Cup.' For many, Wembley is a memory in waiting.

Aston Villa's 0–3 win away at Deepdale secured the club's first appearance in the semi-finals of the competition in a decade. The victory was played out over a 13-minute spell of dominance in the second half. Rashford opened his account for the club in the 58th minute, guiding a precise left-footed strike low into the corner to give Villa the lead. Just 5 minutes later came a penalty which it looked like Asensio would take. He picked up the ball, placed it on the spot, but in the final moments he stepped aside. Rashford took responsibility and converted calmly, doubling his tally. At Villa, penalty duties are planned. Javi García, the goalkeeper coach, compiles detailed data on every taker and every opposing keeper. Since his arrival, Rashford, with the best conversion rate in the squad, was always first in the hierarchy, followed by Asensio, Tielemans, and Watkins. There are no heat-of-the-moment debates. Jacob Ramsey added a third shortly after, capping a dominant performance. After the match, the press focused heavily on Marcus Rashford, whose performance and two goals had turned heads. Media reports had highlighted that Villa held an option to buy him for £40 million, but added that only Champions League qualification would make his permanent signing a realistic outcome. Everyone around the club knew that Rashford dreamt of playing for Barcelona one day.

At the press conference, Unai was upbeat: 'Today he took a step forward.' When asked about the prospect of winning trophies, he insisted on an old idea: 'The priority is consistency in the Premier League.' Emery also pointed to the squad's strong condition: 'Today's bench showed we have options – crucial for Wednesday's demanding match at Brighton, and again on Saturday against Nottingham Forest.' Brighton & Hove Albion were led by Fabian Hürzeler, who at just 31 was the youngest permanent head coach in Premier League history, having replaced Roberto De Zerbi in June 2024. Sitting in 8th place with 47 points, two below Aston Villa, they remained firmly in the hunt for a European qualification spot, although their form had recently fluctuated. In the preview, Emery told the media that Villa were not only refreshed, but added that they were stronger than they had been at any stage of his reign. He was referring to their potential, which of course had to be confirmed.

A dozen players who could have started for almost any team would have to sit on the bench against Brighton. No one is promised minutes just to keep them happy. As Monchi joked: 'I once knew a coach who used to tell both goalkeepers they were going to start. All he managed to do was make both of them angry.' However, conversations can be had to add context to decisions. The day before the match, Unai chatted with Disasi, Rashford, and Cash, two players who ended up starting, and one who didn't. Meanwhile, Damiá and Monchi spoke with Malen. Before the midweek match at Brighton's AMEX Stadium, Unai addressed the players, making things clear. Firstly, to say it was the team that would take them to the target, not 11, 12 or 13 players. Secondly, if they lost that night, the gap to the Champions League places would grow to 5 points, and closing it would become extremely difficult. He opened the floor to the players. Tyrone Mings was one of the first to speak, acknowledging what everyone felt: they knew exactly what was at stake.

Tactically, the staff had anticipated Brighton's approach – a back five, and a retreat into a low block if Villa managed to bypass the initial press. That's exactly how it unfolded. But, as always, some aspects of the match couldn't be fully planned for. Brighton hit the post, Villa missed a clear chance, and there was a strong case for a Villa penalty that went uncalled. In the second half Rashford, leading the line in place of Ollie Watkins, found himself one-on-one with the goalkeeper and didn't waste the chance, his third goal in two games. It hadn't been Villa's most fluid performance, but that moment of quality made the difference.

Before this season, none of the Villa coaching staff had faced Brighton's young German manager, but from the first minute, his behaviour stood out. He was constantly on top of the fourth official, protesting every decision, big or small. At first, it was almost comical, even the officials seemed to shrug it off, but as the minutes went by, it became exhausting. There are coaches who choose to voice frustration when something decisive goes against them. That's understandable. But when the protests are from the opening whistle to the final minutes, it starts to feel per-formative. It becomes difficult to ignore. Eventually, it reaches a point where someone has to say something. Unai did. Hürzeler calmed down.

Asensio scored his 8th goal for the side. No Premier League player had more goals than Marco Asensio since he made his Aston Villa debut. Donyell Malen, coming on for the last 10 minutes, added to the scoreline, his first in claret and blue. 3–0 away. For the first time under Unai, it was the sixth win in a row for Villa. Villa moved to within 2 points of fifth-placed Newcastle, as the battle for European places below third-placed Nottingham Forest grew ever tighter. Three days later, it was Nuno Espírito Santo's Forest side, 4 points ahead of Villa, who were the rivals in Birmingham. The day before the match, Unai informed his assistants and players that he would be making eight changes, allowing the team to rehearse the new setup in training. These decisions are never simple. A player might naturally think: if I've earned my place, I want to play alongside the best. In this case, the changes were easier to accept, especially for the key players who were left out. When only one big name is dropped, it can feel personal. When several are rested together, it's clearly strategic. It also sends a powerful message of trust to those stepping in: this is your moment.

If Emery relied on Axel Disasi, now was the time for him to show it. The Chelsea loanee started alongside Mings, with the entire back four rotated. Malen came in, Marco Asensio continued to be managed carefully, playing 73 minutes, and Morgan Rogers started on the left, just behind a single striker, as usual. Rashford and Watkins continued to alternate roles, with Watkins starting and Rashford coming on in the 62nd minute. The match was uneven. Villa controlled possession as they often do, but showed dangerous verticality. One moment captured it: a ball played into space where the defender had a two-metre advantage, but Rashford accelerated past him and won it. If you did not look closely, you would have said it was Watkins making some of Marcus's moves, due to how similar their decisions were. With Ollie playing every Sunday and Wednesday for half of the campaign, such physical output was becoming difficult to sustain. Rashford now offered a viable alternative and Unai was starting to imagine them playing together. That combination hadn't yet been tested, but it was clearly on the horizon.

After the match, Emery had mixed feelings. He emphasised some positives from a tough game, mainly a solid first half with decent control, but admitted the second half lacked competitiveness. Still, he did not go any further, smart enough to keep that bullet in the chamber. With the 1–2 victory secured, it now meant Villa had won seven consecutive games across all competitions, a feat that nobody in Europe's top five leagues had managed during the campaign.

Next, a trip to Paris.

Marco Asensio arrived at Villa with a point to prove and a clear role to grow into.

What stood out most to the coaching staff was his talent in the small, decisive details. Pablo put it simply: 'Some things only Asensio can do.' A shot that looks routine becomes unsaveable because of how he strikes the ball. He makes the goalkeeper look worse than he is. It's not about dribbling past four players or juggling endlessly. It's about knowing exactly when to dribble past one, when to release the pass, when to slow the game down or speed it up. Every action has meaning. He's not the most physically dominant, he could not be a midfielder with a lot of space to cover, but he always makes the right decision. That, for them, is the essence of real talent. From the start, he worked closely with Rodri to shape his role as the team's connector, the player through whom the ball must pass. He had to understand where the passes would come from, how to receive under pressure, and how to accelerate Villa's play in the final third. Asensio was returning to the Parc des Princes, but he found out in advance that Unai preferred to start with

Ramsey, McGinn and Rogers behind Rashford. Watkins sat on the bench too.

The day before the match, preparation was spread across three meetings. The first took place at 10 a.m., lasting around 50 minutes. He asked the players which had been the toughest away match of the season. The worst defeats were obvious: Tottenham (4–1), Chelsea (3–0), and Newcastle (3–0, with a red card) were mentioned. Yet, the consensus was Arsenal away, a 2–2 draw full of intensity and competitive balance, had been the hardest game. Unai responded clearly: 'If you perform like you did against Arsenal, you will find solutions; if you respond like you did at Chelsea or Newcastle, you won't.'

'It's very difficult to press PSG,' Unai reflects looking back. 'Vitinha drops and everything builds through him. It's hard to take the ball off him. Even holding a mid-block is tough, they pull you deep. So our plan in Paris was to stop their progression early, to avoid sinking into a low block if we could. We also prepared the players mentally: if we have to defend deep, we must do it without fear. And all the while, think ahead: let's get to Villa Park alive.'

At 1 p.m., before flying to Paris, the second meeting began: a full tactical breakdown of the game plan through video analysis, lasting another hour. Here, Unai reminded the group that those who had been at the club longer had already come through games of this difficulty and stature, especially the win over Arsenal the previous season, which had helped secure Champions League qualification. That 0–2 victory was built on collective defensive resilience and the ability to strike at the right moment. Finally, at 6:30 p.m., the squad met again, this time to go over set-piece strategy.

Then, match day arrived. When supporters Dave and his son Billy, who had travelled all the way from Catalonia, sat near the

Seine, gazing at the Eiffel Tower, surrounded by Aston Villa shirts, their minds couldn't quite process what was happening. It felt surreal. Their club, in Paris. In the Champions League. Surrounded by thousands of strangers who made up the same blue and claret family. The walk to the Parc des Princes was something else: a slow, joyful march with two thousand fellow Villans lucky enough to have tickets, singing with the kind of pride that comes from years of waiting. Another thousand stayed behind in the city, finding corners of Paris to turn into temporary home ends: bars, cafés, squares.

Unai hadn't returned to Paris since his departure from PSG, and what he found moved him deeply. There was warmth from the club's staff, genuine affection from those who had worked alongside him. Within the corridors of PSG, many still speak of him as one of their most admired coaches, for his tireless work ethic, his passion, his humility, and the way he connected with people. The president in particular, Nasser Al-Khelaifi still holds him in high regard. For Unai, facing Luis Enrique is always a quiet return to the deepest wound of his career. That night in Barcelona still lingers: the chaos, the sixth goal in the dying seconds, the referee's decisions, the sense of something slipping away that had already been earned. Revisiting it now is also a form of perspective. A lot of good stuff has happened since, but football always brings you back to earth. Nobody should forget that.

Sawiris and Edens made a brief visit to the dressing room to greet the players before kick-off. Prince William was also there, in the tunnel alongside Damià, shaking hands with the squad, right up to the final moments before they stepped out. On the pitch, Unai took a moment to speak with Luis Enrique, expressing his admiration for the quality of his team, and for the way he had succeeded in making them play exactly the kind of football he envisioned. His PSG side had torn through Liverpool, Atlético Madrid, and Manchester City already.

Final result: PSG 3, Aston Villa 1. Villa struck first, with Morgan Rogers finishing off a well-worked move in the 35th minute to silence the Parc des Princes and give the visitors the lead. It was a fitting moment in a breakout season for the forward. In his first 14 months at the club, he racked up 65 appearances, scoring 17 goals and delivering 14 assists. That strike in Paris would be his final goal of the season, his 14th in all competitions, but confirmed his status as one of the brightest emerging talents in European football. He ended up being named PFA Young Player of the Year. PSG responded quickly: Désiré Doué levelled with a brilliant curling effort just before half-time. Early in the second half, Khvicha Kvaratskhelia fired PSG ahead with a powerful finish. Despite some superb saves from Emiliano Martínez, Emery's side were ultimately punished with a goal in stoppage time: Nuno Mendes gave the home side a two-goal cushion. One of Unai's assistants turned to him and muttered, 'That goal changes everything.'

As soon as the final whistle blew at the Parc des Princes, Unai Emery didn't rush to the media. He spent several minutes with his staff, gathered around a table in the small changing area adjoining the visitors' dressing room. All the public noise was gone. There was a shared sense of frustration, not anger. The match, in many respects, had gone as they expected: they had to defend deep in long periods, adjusting midfield lines to respond to the constant positional changes of Luis Enrique's side, which, they all admitted, had been the better team. With the score at 2–1, they still felt the tie could have been decided at Villa Park. Pablo told Unai that Villa had played a better game than either Manchester City or Liverpool had managed against PSG. Everyone spoke. No one was trying to be cold or over-analytical, it was an exercise of releasing adrenaline. Then Unai went to speak to the players. Whether the first leg ended 2–1 or 3–1, the task remained the same: they had to win. 'With 2–1, we needed a win. With 3–1, we still need a win. Win, win, win, and once we are winning, we score one more.'

'The result is big,' Unai said calmly in the press conference. 'But it forces us to go and win. PSG have experience, but we have Villa Park.' He repeated the phrase 'I believe' several times, the tie was not over. He wanted everyone to feel it, the players, the staff, the fans. Afterwards, Damià asked Tommy Jordan to build a small communications push around that message. Not to create artificial hype, but to amplify a feeling that already existed in the dressing room: that despite the 3–1 defeat, Aston Villa still had a real chance. Videos, short clips, social media – all aimed at making that belief visible.

Later that night, at the airport, conversations continued. The coaching staff were absorbing the match in fragments: the third goal, the timing, the choices, the substitutions, the runs not made, the half-second too late. Who performed at the expected level? Who didn't? Which details could be sharpened in the return leg? As they boarded the plane, Damiá shared a thought: yes, that late goal had made things harder, but it might also play to Villa's advantage. PSG might come to Birmingham just a little too relaxed.

Unai got to bed at 3:30 a.m. At 9:35 a.m. the next morning, he arrived at Bodymoor Heath. Training was at 12. In the gym, there was a short chat with the players. He felt the mood was a bit subdued. Maybe it was going to take more than words after last night's game to convince everyone Villa had a chance to still make it to the semi-finals. 'We'll think about PSG tomorrow,' Unai told them. That morning was about recovering, resetting. Still, he made a lone point about the game in Paris: 'I'm proud of how we competed. I feel the same disappointment you do. But we have

Villa Park. We've only lost twice at home all season, and even against Arsenal we could have won. We've been strong, reliable, tough. So, let's look for the opportunity.'

With that, the focus changed. Unai prohibited any further talk of PSG. Southampton was next. Every game, he reminded them, had to be treated like a set in a Grand Slam. You don't think about the one before or the one ahead. Just the one in front of you. Then work was distributed around. Asensio, despite only playing 30 minutes in Paris, had covered nearly 5 kilometres and logged almost 500 metres of high-intensity sprinting. On a normal day, a player with less than 45 minutes would train to top up their fitness, but his physical output had been so high, the staff gave him just a light warm-up with some small-possession work to balance his load. For others, there were compensatory recovery sessions like massages, strength work, or contrast therapy. If a player had taken a knock but hadn't played much recently, it was more important that he trained. If another had played three games in a row, rest took priority. Meanwhile, for those who hadn't featured or had only played limited minutes, the post-match routine included longer-distance game work, such as 11 vs. 11 matches with the academy, 9 vs. 9, or carefully structured position-specific drills to replicate match conditions.

At St Mary's, an already-relegated Southampton awaited, just three days after the bruising night in Paris. On paper, it looked like a straightforward fixture. In reality, it required focus. Emery kept seven players from the team that had started at the Parc des Princes, among them Marcus Rashford, leading the line again. Marco Asensio also returned to the starting XI. Villa dominated from the outset, but for a long stretch they couldn't make it count. With the score still 0–0 at half-time, Asensio then missed a penalty early in the second half. Villa had to wait until the 73rd minute to break through, with Ollie Watkins scoring 7 minutes after coming on for Rashford. Donyell Malen firing low, in his trademark fashion, added a second. In the 94th minute, Asensio had a second penalty saved, but this time John McGinn pounced on the rebound to seal the scoreline, the first occasion three substitutes had scored for Villa in a Premier League match. Had Rashford still been on the pitch, he would have taken the penalties, but Unai backed Asensio fully with his decision to take the second one. He told him as much.

The stats told the story of a side peaking at just the right time: four straight league wins, three consecutive away victories without conceding for the first time since November 2020, and a much-needed third win in the season following Champions League fixtures. Now it was time for the return leg against PSG, which became one for folklore, a memory of wonder and regret, like a symphony building towards a grand crescendo, only to end it on a dissonant note: unforgettable, but not completely satisfying.

There was no need for a big media campaign to stir emotion. The belief was already there, or at least growing. Inside Bodymoor Heath, the feeling was that fans were beginning to believe, they were expecting something special. The data seemed to support that optimism: since Unai Emery's arrival, no Premier League side had taken more points after falling behind. But perhaps the truest reflection of the mood was more modest, a hope for a performance that would make them proud, rather than a full-blown expectation of overturning a team like PSG. This Villa had not yet built enough of those memory-making matches.

For Unai, these nights are where real growth happens. He knew they were about to face the most in form team in Europe. With a two-goal deficit, there was only one route: a radically aggressive game plan. The defensive line would go man-to-man. So, if Dembélé dropped deep and sprinted 70 yards up the pitch, Pau Torres would follow him. Risky, yes, but it also meant leaving bodies higher up, ready to attack space when it opened. Villa would aim to keep the ball, take it off PSG, despite the fact that it would create spaces that the French team could take advantage of, but if Villa embraced the game and its immense possibilities better than PSG, they'd have their opportunity. Villa Park would help. When it roars, it's a beautiful, powerful stadium.

PSG had the weekend off. Villa had just two days to prepare after beating Southampton. Never mind. No excuses were to be used. In the days before the game, Emery gave those in the training ground hope. He delivered it in his video meetings, not with polished visuals, but with presence: with his voice, with his gestures, with his faith in the idea that something special was about to happen. He showed them the first leg in Paris, the good stuff that was produced – which there was plenty of. The players left that meeting thinking: 3–1 is possible. 'We can win,' one assistant shared. Then, on the eve of the match, the team analysed PSG's visit to Anfield and the amount of weaknesses the French team showed despite their narrow 1–0 win against Liverpool. PSG, like any team, become human away from home. The same assistant walked out of that room and said, 'It's not mad. I think we'll win 3–1, I genuinely feel it is likely it will happen.' That week, Emery was at his absolute best.

As kick-off neared, the noise inside Villa Park was electric. It went through bones. It lifted hairs. Although, the PSG faithful were also heard non-stop from the first minute. Then, for a few surreal seconds, an IT glitch played the Europa League anthem instead of the Champions League one. It pierced the moment, but only briefly. The game exploded into life. Villa pushed forward not carving clear chances, but showing they could find a pass, force a mistake. Unai was living every move as if there was 1 minute of play to go. Villa were aggressive, intense. PSG were uncomfortable. But then came the two goals by the away side. Two quick punches. On the Villa bench, heads dropped, they were 5–1 down on the aggregate with 1 hour of the match left. Pablo leant over and told Unai, 'They've scored two goals, both from more or less isolated moments, but we're playing the game we need to play.'

Unai replied, 'I'm not unhappy with what I'm seeing.'

In the 34th minute, Youri Tielemans struck. The noise of the first few minutes returned, with an edge. Now or never, many felt. PSG slowed things down. On the way to the dressing room, Unai's assistants noticed something: Luis Enrique's players, despite the scoreline, weren't enjoying themselves. Villa weren't letting them breathe, they had applied an infernal pace. Everyone on the pitch felt the scoreboard was misleading. Inside the dressing room, Unai reminded the players that the job wasn't impossible. 'It's in your hands now,' he told them. He was enjoying the match, he admitted, and urged them to keep going exactly as they were, even though it was very tough physically. Then, in a moment that stayed with everyone, he went around the room, quickly, one by one, asking each player: 'Are you enjoying it? Yes? And you? Yes? And you? And you? And you?' Heads nodded. Some of them were physically on the edge, but they were in it. 'If I see anyone suffer even a little physically, I'll make changes. We are where I want to take you. Now give me everything.'

No big speeches from Emi Martínez, no words from McGinn or the other captains, as had been the case in so many other games. Unai had already spread conviction through the room. Half-time was a kind of release. They were behind, but somehow it didn't matter anymore. There was nothing to lose. No one even imagined what was about to happen.

In the second half, McGinn, who had started the game, was the first to surge, a bundle of intensity, harrying everything on his way. Driving with the ball, with the confidence that a path would open up for him. It had to be him who represented on the pitch what everyone felt in the locker room. If you asked any Villa player who deserved to succeed the most, the answer would likely be: John McGinn. If they were asked who receives the most criticism from Unai Emery in team meetings, the answer this time would be unanimous: John McGinn. Every moment that John could have resolved better is dissected. And yet, McGinn takes it. Most of it. He is the perfect Emery player.

Released by Celtic at nine years old, he was told he wouldn't have the body to be a footballer. He then made his professional debut for St Mirren in a 5–0 defeat to Celtic, a trial by fire. Soon after, at 16, he helped knock Celtic out in the semi-finals of the Scottish League Cup. Then came the final: a win over Hearts, St Mirren's first trophy in 35 years. They haven't won one since. After three years at Hibernian, he signed for Aston Villa in 2018, and has been through the ups and downs of the club ever since. When Emery arrived, there was internal pressure to sell him. 'You need to get rid of McGinn. He can't be your captain,' Emery was told. One club executive even suggested he shouldn't be playing. Unai, curious, asked why. McGinn had inherited the armband during a difficult period, after Gerrard took it from Tyrone Mings. The club wanted change. Emery's response was emphatic: 'You're not telling me what to do.' McGinn stayed captain. He was handed a new five-year deal and became the heartbeat of Emery's Villa.

He is different, tenacious, humble. There is a depth to him. He debates, questions, challenges, and is never passive. He drives a regular car. He doesn't wear flashy watches. His leadership is subtle. Not the loudest in the room, but he is a man of honour, principled and Scottish to the core. He trains hard. He stays behind if he gets asked to, to help others adapt or improve. He speaks to everyone – French, Spanish, English teammates alike – and sits with different groups in the canteen. His parents are teachers, and it shows. He's smart. He understands the game. If Unai gives him two or three tactical points, he absorbs them and adapts. In fact, his development under Unai Emery may be the most striking of all the squad. He's played almost every position this season alone: centre-back, left-back, even up front. Strong and deceptively fast, he's not 'nice on the eye' but effective. 'If he looked different,' Alberto Benito once said, 'he'd be playing for Barcelona.'

Unai sees something of himself in McGinn: hard-working, fully committed, not the most gifted but giving everything he has. Reliable. Uncomplicated. That admiration between player and manager is real enough to clash. At the start of the season, Emery told him bluntly: 'You need to improve or you'll be playing for Celtic in two years.'

McGinn shot back: 'Bring in whoever you want, you'll still end up playing me.'

He was right. In a cup match against Everton, with no left-back available, McGinn was asked to play there. No problem. He struggled. Later, during Unai's team review, McGinn thought he was being accused of a lack of commitment. He was furious, not because he played badly, but because the implication, however unintended, cut deep. A coach tipped Unai off that McGinn had taken it personally. Unai explained to him he would never disrespect him, and that he understood what the captain was saying: If Unai put John in a position he had never played before, and didn't perform well, that was fine, he'd own it. But if Unai suggested that

John wasn't committed, that's different. That hurt. The two men shook hands. Case closed.

There have been games when he's played less, moments when others seemed more on form, but when it matters most, when the heat is on, Unai always turns to him. McGinn answers every time. And in Paris, in the 55th minute, McGinn answered. He picked up the ball in his own half and surged forward. Nobody quite believed he would be both the start and the end of the move. On the edge of the box, he struck a fierce, swerving shot that rose sharply over Gianluigi Donnarumma, who had no response for it. 'Oh my goodness me,' shouted the TV commentator, as Villa Park erupted in a single, thunderous voice. It was 2–2 on the night, 5–3 on aggregate.

Leading up to the goal, Unai had been throwing water bottles away, kicking them, jumping, shouting, but he celebrated without fuss. He had just spoken to Jacob Ramsey and Marco Asensio, with the intention of bringing them on. After the goal he decided to wait, and he was right in doing so. Villa unleashed a 15-minute spell that knocked PSG off balance. Rashford came close with a powerful effort that forced a strong save from Donnarumma. The England international was electric, picking up the ball on the right, dancing past two defenders, and cutting it back perfectly for Ezri Konsa to fire home. 3–2 to Villa. 2 minutes after McGinn's goal, Unai had the win he wanted. Now for an extra goal.

Unai headed the air in frustration when Tielemans forced another big save with a header. He turned wide-eyed to the bench, hands on his head, after Asensio missed a one-on-one. Konsa, Asensio again, Rashford . . . they all had chances. Villa created six clear openings to score a fourth. On another night, they might have put in one of those, maybe even two. But say it was just one more, PSG would have surely gone. They wouldn't have recovered. They were on the ropes. Minute 76. Watkins stood warming up, and anyone who's played the game could easily read his face, a touch sad, not so angry. He knew the moment was big but also that it might slip from him. Sometimes, coming on with half an hour left, you join the fast train that is the game, you find your timing. Other times, you enter too late or too cold, and the game moves past you. That night, for whatever reason, Watkins never quite caught the thread, it eluded him. In fact, Villa lost a bit of energy in the last 15 minutes, none of the substitutes made a big impact. It seemed PSG was about to survive. And then . . . Minute 94. Unai dropped to the floor when Ian Maatsen's volley was cleared off the line by centre-back Pancho. Final result: 3–2. The defeated PSG were semi-finalists.

No one inside Villa Park had ever lived through 45 minutes like those. Supporters loved that the team took risks, with the football on the pitch matching exactly what they craved: bravery, intensity, emotion from start to finish. When it was over, they didn't just leave with pride. Some stayed behind, unwilling to step too far from the place where, for a brief time, everything had felt unique and new. Many fans believed this performance was not the end of something, but the beginning. If you can score three goals and beat PSG, you can beat anyone. Four days later, they had to take 3 points from Newcastle to keep fighting for a top-five finish. The following Saturday, it was the FA Cup semi-final. In that context, the pain of elimination hurt a little less.

Matty Cash, still catching his breath, talked to the media, almost unable to concentrate. 'It feels like I've been hit by a truck,' he said, head and body exhausted. He had spent 95 minutes locking horns with the fast and tricky winger Bradley Barcola and others down the right flank, often left two-against-one. Villa had been so close, he was pleased with everyone's effort. Then he walked towards the changing room.

'We were proud of ourselves,' Morgan Rogers says looking back. 'Inside the locker room, we could look each other in the eye and say, "We've gone toe-to-toe with one of the best teams in the world. We've shown a great account of ourselves." We'd actually won the game when no one would have picked us to win. We all played so hard.'

Damià found Unai and pulled him into an embrace. 'This was your work,' he told him. 'You, the players, the staff, what you have built is incredible. We have been knocked out by the smallest margin.'

But Unai couldn't accept it. What he felt was hard to explain. Losing a game like this, after so much planning, so much emotional and physical investment, was like writing a whole chapter of a book – meticulously researched, carefully crafted – only for someone to tear the pages from your hands and burn them. History only remembers victory. He entered the dressing room with something between rage and grief. It was rage that took hold first. Some players hadn't even taken off their shirts when he stormed in and kicked a table, splitting a nail in the process. 'We've lost such an opportunity,' he spat. 'We had it. We had it!'. There was not an ounce of the vindication or satisfaction that others felt. Morgan Rogers's eyes widened, surprised and confused, and he wasn't the only one: 'He was so annoyed, so angry.' After a home match, there is food in the coaches' room and, with a win, someone might open a bottle of wine. This was a victory difficult to decipher, so there was no wine. Someone mentioned that Luis Enrique, battle-worn, told the media it was the toughest match PSG had faced all season, And a night they would never forget either.

Back at Bodymoor Heath, after two days off, Danielle Fulford, at reception, asked to hug Ezri Konsa when he arrived. 'They looked broken,' she says. 'I just felt I had to.' Unai, calmer now, gathered the group for a talk. He wanted to get them back on their feet. He knew, from experience, that the first game after a European elimination, especially when the team had performed well and brought so much attention and energy, could bring a dangerous dip. 'There are people congratulating me,' Unai told the group. 'That's not what I want. I don't want this to be treated like something exceptional. We lost. We didn't go through.'

McGinn chimed in. 'I want to play against Real Madrid and Barcelona again next year,' he said. And the manager started talking about the Newcastle game, another final two days later. Now, Unai looks back and allows himself a flicker of perspective. 'What a fixture that was,' he admits.

'For a coach, to be part of it, to take decisions, the atmosphere . . . It was so beautiful.'

17

CREATING MEMORIES:

THE FA CUP SEMI-FINAL & THE END OF THE SEASON

Jag, one of the voices behind the Punjabi Villans, had never imagined that his quest for a simple post-match fan reaction would end up spanning two continents and involve a handshake with a World Cup winner. But then again, football has a funny way of turning the ordinary into extraordinary. It was the night Villa lost to PSG in Paris. Jag, high on adrenaline and half-drenched from a light Parisian drizzle, was wandering near Notre-Dame on a mission. He wanted to capture the post-match thoughts of any Villa faithful for the Punjabi Villans' ever-growing fan group. And that's when he saw her – a lone figure on a bridge, wearing a claret and blue Villa top. In Paris. At night. On a bridge. Almost poetic. Naturally, he went over.

Her name was Mae. She was from Argentina of all places, and had travelled to Europe on her own little football pilgrimage. She hadn't managed to get a ticket for the PSG game but had found a bar full of Villa fans and watched it there, shouting at the screen like the rest of them. Turns out, she taught English back in Buenos Aires and had decided to sprinkle her Euro tour with as much Villa as she could. Jag, moved by her story, said something bold, probably without thinking it through: 'Come to England. We'll sort you a ticket.'

Good Friday, the day before the Newcastle game, and Mae had arrived. True to his word, Jag had come through. He got her a ticket by the dugout, the kind of seat where you feel like you should be nodding knowingly alongside the coaching staff. The ticket even included tunnel access. Mae arrived to the match early, wandered through the fan zone like it was Disneyland, and watched the players arrive, including Emi Martínez – fellow Argentinian, World Cup winner, idol – who walked past her in the corridor to the pitch. Then she sat down to watch the game of the season. Three points were required, but so many had been dropped at home after European nights.

Unai did what he always tries to do in moments of uncertainty: channel the emotion, pick the right team, make the right changes, and keep the energy high. His frustration hadn't faded, not so much from the memory of the heavy defeat to Newcastle, but from the tension that had followed. Assistant manager Jason Tindall's behaviour that night had helped spark friction between the benches, even leading to a brief spat in the tunnel. With Eddie Howe absent through illness, it was Tindall back in the technical area – and that alone seemed to sharpen Unai's focus. There are certain figures in football Unai finds difficult to ignore: those who project loudly without carrying full responsibility. He rarely comments on it, but in moments like this, it can drive him.

After the first leg against PSG, one thing in particular troubled Unai: the substitutes. For 70 minutes, Villa had played extraordinarily well, but after that, something had not quite clicked. Villa didn't create another chance until the final action of the match. Afterwards, Unai spoke with one of his assistants about how players enter a game, and what mindset they bring with them. In today's game, with the physical demands and five substitutions, a player can decide a match without starting. Although many still see not being in the XI as a mark against them, which unsettles Unai. Perhaps he hadn't yet fully convinced the squad that each player mattered. The manager often feels he has to constantly push those who aren't starting to come on with the right mindset – a common battle for modern coaches. Some come on subdued, disappointed not to have started, and still carrying that weight when they finally step onto the pitch. Others enter with anger, wanting to confront. Sadness drains. Anger fuels. It led to a wider reflection for Unai. In the days that followed, he wrote something on the board for all to see: 'Come on angry with me for not picking you.'

Ollie Watkins, who had played just 20 minutes across both PSG legs, started against Newcastle. What Unai values most in Ollie Watkins is that he's a fighter. He always gives everything he has. He's not a player whose game is built on natural flair or effortless talent, Watkins is about grafting. He's been vital for Villa over the past two seasons, even if there have been recent spells where he hasn't started. Watkins is a player who needs to feel confident and secure. Naturally, being on the bench can make a player question things, but not everything in football has a clear answer. Sometimes, things just shift. Doubt is natural, but managing it is part of a forward's evolution. At one point, Jhon Durán became more than just a back-up. Still young and full of potential, he offered something different when Watkins wasn't quite at his best. Later, Marcus Rashford arrived – just as Watkins was returning to top form – and brought new qualities. That level of competition is part of Villa's growth. The aim is to be among the Premier League's top six, and that may not be possible if relying on a single striker. Watkins is having to adapt to that new reality. In the match against Southampton, between the two PSG legs, Watkins started on the bench. He came on in the 66th minute and broke the deadlock just

7 minutes later in a game that had stalled. Performances like that show exactly what he brings – even in a supporting role.

Rodri recalls Watkins' growth and the work behind it. Rodri had learnt this from Unai: every player is different, and each one needs a tailored approach, sometimes technical, sometimes emotional. In the centre forward's case, it all began with some questions: what kind of striker is he? A player of finesse or brute force? Does he come with a sledgehammer or with a scalpel? If it's the sledgehammer, you have to tell him he can use it – but there are other tools too. He's not just a labourer on the pitch; he shouldn't rely solely on strength or physical battles. Maybe sometimes it's about being more precise, using a jeweller's hammer. With players who are all force, you have to show them they've got finesse too, even if they don't believe it at first, and then help them develop it through work. Other players naturally come with finesse. Fine. But they also need to bring something more. Teammates will give you the ball at exactly the right moment, but for that to happen, you need to earn their trust. Sometimes that takes a bit of the sledgehammer too.

Watkins was clearly one with the sledgehammer. So the task was to help him see that he didn't have to rely on strength alone. Watkins soon asked questions: 'Why this movement? Why that positioning?' That's when you know a player is starting to understand the game on a deeper level. That's when you can really go to work. Rodri goes back to a game against Crystal Palace, 5 matches into the first full season, which he claims best showcases Watkins' key strengths. Villa knew they'd face three centre-backs who left gaps between them. Rodri prepped Watkins to use those spaces, to hold off defenders, to wait for the right moment to spin. Watkins reacts fast, and that's a huge advantage. One particular move they trained came off in the match – Watkins broke free and provoked a penalty.

With Ollie open to change, Rodri gave him clear, direct instructions, such as how to read his teammates' passes, how to exploit defenders' habits, and how to prepare his body to receive in space. He's not the type to ask for help directly – sometimes it feels like admitting weakness. So, Rodri found ways to offer support without waiting for a request. 'When in doubt,' he'd tell him, 'just look at me.' Some players act like they know everything. Others, like Watkins, eventually hand you the keys. That blend of grit, learning and intelligence is what's taken his game to the next level. Now when Watkins goes to the England squad, he's in a different environment. Sometimes Ollie calls to ask Rodri, 'What's this defender like?' and they go over footage together.

The work on the player is part of a collective effort. Víctor analyses the opposition in depth, showing how they defend and attack. Unai designs the tactical adjustments. Rodri adds the fine-tuning – what Watkins' marker might do, where the spaces are, and how to exploit them. These conversations spill into warm-ups, end-of-session work, or small-sided games when others are resting. Even injury recovery time becomes a chance to sharpen specific details. Pablo plays a key role too. He knows when Watkins is a bit flat, and steps in with focused drills, like specific finishing situations so the player can gain some confidence, or just acts as a buffer between Unai and the player when needed.

After one of the rare defeats in the final stretch of the season, Watkins approached Unai the next morning. Unprompted, he apologised for the result and his performance. Unai told him there was no need. The team, collectively, hadn't been at the level required; they hadn't known how to win that game. But in that moment, what stood out was Watkins' humility. Yet, Unai thought to himself, sometimes he'd like to see a bit more ego, a touch more arrogance. Just enough to match the humility with bite. Unai, who often speaks of Watkins as 'a marvellous human being', had a direct conversation with him after the PSG fixture and before the Newcastle game. He urged him to assert himself, 'to be angry, to use the disappointment of not starting as fuel'. He used 'angry' a few times. He did not want to see him quiet or subdued, but to make a statement – just as he had done against Southampton. 'You need that pride,' Unai told him, 'that self-respect.' Watkins channelled his frustration for not starting the Champions League quarter-finals into a sensational performance, scoring after just 33 seconds in a 4–1 win over Newcastle, which Villa were dominating throughout. That goal equalled Gabriel Agbonlahor's Premier League club record of 74 goals. Since the start of the 2022–23 season, the Villa forward was one of only two players in Europe's top five leagues to record 50+ goals and 25+ assists. The other was Mo Salah.

Aston Villa's demolition of Newcastle was the kind of showing where everything clicked. From the first whistle, Villa were relentless: pressing high, with offensive intention, and punishing every weakness in a Newcastle side that looked overrun. Villa's coaches were particularly impressed by the players' personality on the day and against a side known for its physical power and intensity. What stood out wasn't just how they competed in the duels, but how they chose when to compete and when to take control. After winning the ball, instead of getting dragged into a scrappy, end-to-end battle, the team had the composure to put their foot on it and say: now we play – on our terms, not yours.

Watkins had set the tone not only with his early goal, but also hitting the woodwork twice and assisting Ian Maatsen's goal with hunger, the kind of reaction Unai demanded. The manager had targeted Newcastle's vulnerable right side – with the ageing legs of Fabian Schär and Kieran Trippier – and unleashed Watkins down that channel. The outcome was brutal. The substitutes came on and this time they made the difference – Jacob Ramsey and Amadou Onana combined for Villa's third and fourth goals.

In the dressing room afterwards, there was pride from Unai, yes, but also a hint of regret. This kind of form, this cohesion, this momentum – and now, the season was nearing its end. 'It's a shame there's no time to enjoy it,' he told his staff. There were signs that the team was alive, healthy, together. Look at how they celebrated the goals, someone pointed out, not just the scorers, but the whole bench, the backroom staff. There was a shared energy, a collective push. You can't fake that. It was one of the best matches of the season – alongside the win over Manchester City and the second leg against PSG. Villa's fifth consecutive Premier League win brought them within touching distance of the top five with five league games to go.

After the game, Ollie Watkins spoke candidly to Sky Sports. 'I'm not going to lie – I was fuming,' he said about not starting in both legs of the PSG fixture. 'I'm not one to sit quietly on the bench.'

Emery praised Watkins' reaction: 'It's fantastic to be angry – and fantastic to play like that.'

The world misunderstood what lay behind Watkins' words. When he said he was 'fuming' it wasn't a public outburst of frustration, it was the result of the conversation carefully managed by Unai. What unfolded on the pitch, and in Watkins' post-match comments, was not a player lashing out. He wasn't upset, no; he was angry.

Meanwhile, Mae was starstruck – first by the sight of Villa Park, then by what unfolded on the pitch: the commanding 4–1 win over the Geordies. After the final whistle, she waited patiently by the players' exit. Emi Martínez, spotting the Argentine flag on her, came over. Not only did he sign the Villa goalkeeper shirt she'd just bought from the club shop, he also handed her his actual match-day gloves, signed. From Birmingham, she continued her European tour, heading to Spain for a Real Madrid match. A few days later, she flew back home to Argentina, with Emi Martínez's gloves in her bag and 'Up the Villa' echoing constantly in her head.

The trip to the Etihad came at just the right time for Villa. City were third in the table, sitting on 61 points, but they had played a game more than Villa. They were 23 points adrift of league leaders Liverpool and enduring their most inconsistent season under Pep Guardiola. Villa, meanwhile, were seventh with 57 points and full of confidence. Unai had never won or even drawn at the Etihad – not with Arsenal, not with Sevilla, and not yet with Villa. This time felt different. In the dressing room, the message from Unai was ambitious: 'we're ready.' For the first time, there was a feeling they could go toe to toe with City. 'Face them. Beat them. We're in our best moment. They're not.' Unai presented the players with a very ambitious message.

Before kick-off, Pep and Unai shared a long embrace and exchanged a few private words. Guardiola's line-up was crowded with players tucked inside – designed to control the ball, squeeze space, dominate proceedings. The approach was to stay compact, be lethal on the counter, punish them with set pieces, press high when possible, or defend deep when they were forced to. The plan was anchored by strict defensive responsibilities. Full-backs had to be tracked. The shape would move into a back six at times. It was similar to what had worked so well against Bayern. Whatever happened on the scoreboard, the idea was to drag the game into Villa's world. Against teams like City, everything has to fall into place, but that's not exactly how it went. At least not all the time.

Within the first 20 seconds, a pass from Tielemans to Marcus

Rashford, a sharp cut inside past Rúben Dias, and then the forward struck the post. The match was low on chances – just as Unai had hoped. City went ahead but Rashford equalised from the penalty spot in the 18th minute, coolly converting after Bernardo Silva's opener. Of all the trips to the Etihad in recent memory, this was the one where they felt least under siege. Then came the biggest blow. Later in the second half, Rashford pulled up with a hamstring injury. It was Marcus' last game for Aston Villa.

In the final 20 minutes, with Marco Asensio on the pitch, Villa might have shown more personality by keeping the ball or stringing passes together, but, overall the match had followed the blueprint. Axel Disasi came on in the 61st minute. A substitution that caught the eye. Unai walked him all the way to the touchline, speaking intensely the entire time, pulling him close. Not once, but two or three times, he called him over again. It was the kind of detailed, personal handover that suggested some doubt lingered – not necessarily in Disasi's ability, but in his readiness. The Chelsea loanee had come to Villa with hopes of a bigger role, but it hadn't unfolded as expected. In training, there had been days when his body language betrayed his disappointment. He'd wanted more, and Unai knew this. That was precisely why he didn't want him stepping onto the pitch in a haze of doubt or detachment. Still, the decision was puzzling. Disasi is a centre-back by trade, occasionally used as a wide centre-half. Villa were defending deep and, as it had become six across the back line, Disasi could have slotted in as a third central defender. Yet, he was asked to replace Matty Cash and act as the right back for the rest of the game.

In the 94th minute, City found Jeremy Doku isolated on the left, one-on-one with Disasi. The Belgian winger, all sharp angles and bursts of pace, skipped past him far too easily. Disasi, caught flat-footed and wide on the flank, couldn't recover. Doku's low cross found Matheus Nunes, who finished at the near post. City got ahead with seconds to go. As always, to pin everything on that moment is to ignore what came before. There were earlier missteps. Villa had failed to keep the ball seconds before, opting to clear. Gvardiol had stepped out from the back and, driving with the ball, eliminated Malen, who went to press at the wrong time. Konsa and Kamara were then caught covering the same zone. Disasi's distance to the centre backs was not right. The image ends with one player, but the sequence is far more complex. Unai often says he'd rather lose a game and win a player. That sometimes, the pain of a defeat is worth it if it means a player will be stronger next time. But this one hurt. It showed how thin the margins can be when meeting a top team. City won, 2–1.

At the final whistle, Unai walked with his head down to the tunnel. Pablo could hardly contain himself. He kicked at the ground, agitated, pacing the edge of the technical area. The game had slipped away. It had happened too often this season. Near the changing rooms, Pep Guardiola and Unai chatted for around 15 minutes. There was mutual respect, and perhaps a hint of surprise in Pep's tone. For much of the final stretch, Villa had looked solid – unbreakable, even. They had frustrated City, held their ground, and still found moments to counter. Guardiola hadn't thrown everything forward. There was no storming of the gates. Yet, somehow, they'd found a way through. A more mature side, Unai thought, would have shut it down, settled for the point, and left. The numbers supported the feeling. Only Southampton had conceded more goals than Villa in the final 8 minutes of matches. A team still learning the hard truths of game management at the very highest level.

Villa returned to Birmingham by coach. Unai sat in his usual place – front left. After a disappointment, he can easily withdraw.

Beside him, Damià. Behind him, Pako Ayestarán. At one point, Unai stood and made his way to the back of the coach. There, in the last few rows, sat Alberto Benito and Rodri. He spent time speaking with them, searching for reassurance. That the plan had been right, even if the outcome wasn't. Sometimes, that's all a coach wants after a loss. Among the staff, there was agreement: to reach Europe again, they would probably not need to win all four of their remaining matches, but 10 points would be necessary. First Fulham, then Bournemouth, the toughest test as the final two opponents, Spurs and Manchester United, would be distracted by their Europa League final encounter in Bilbao. Qualifying for that competition was still a real possibility – and it wouldn't be a failure, despite the ultimate target being Champions League once again.

No one quite voiced the other scenario: falling short altogether and not playing in any European competition. As Villa's model isn't built yet on global brand strength or vast commercial revenues, its momentum comes from European competition. Missing out would be a blow to the project. Not to mention that Unai feeds his ambition from playing against the best. Still, as the coach moved south in the night, the mood slowly changed. Talk turned to Crystal Palace. To recovery. Fifty-two matches in, the staff knew the cycle well – pain gives way to planning. They arrived at Bodymoor Heath just after 2 a.m, before heading home for rest. By 10 a.m., Unai was already back at the training ground.

The dominant football model in Europe is the one used by Aston Villa. Five of the eight Champions League quarter-finalists and three of the four semi-finalists played structured, positional football, each a disciple, in their own way, of Pep Guardiola. This style offers control, instills confidence in players, and has become the most reliable route to the top. The next step in its evolution, including Unai Emery's version, is learning how to consistently break down deep, compact defenses. The response to the Pep Guardiola style is relatively easy to coach – stay together, hand over possession, learn to suffer – but it demands high-quality attackers to convert the few chances it creates. It won't necessarily earn a coach instant prestige if their dream is to lead a European giant, but it builds a competitive team.

Aston Villa had found their kryptonite in Crystal Palace, a mid-table Premier League side that were organised and had in Jean-Philippe Mateta, Ismaïla Sarr and Eberechi Eze, three offensive nightmares for any rival. That season Palace had frustrated Villa three times across all competitions: two losses and a draw. Now, as fate would have it, they were facing off again in the FA Cup semi-final.

Unai had just four days to prepare. Until that point, they couldn't fully focus on Palace, because in the space of eight days they had faced Paris Saint-Germain, Newcastle, and Manchester City, three of the most exhausting matches of the season. Crystal Palace, by contrast, had spent four weeks building to a single match marked on their calendar, their Alpha and Omega, the beginning and end of everything: the match against Villa. But the real conversation in Bodymoor Heath wasn't about tactics. It sparked a fascinating debate that quickly took over the media, the dressing room, and the fan base. Unai placed clear and consistent emphasis on the Premier League over the FA Cup or even the Champions League. He looks ahead, he is building a project, laying down bricks season by season. Meanwhile, players like Emi Martínez weren't afraid to voice their discord. 'I disagree,' he once said, raising his arm in one of the group chats. If you're a player, you want to win trophies, now. You're not playing for a legacy someone else might enjoy ten years down the line. You want medals, and the most accessible ones are the Carabao Cup, FA Cup, Conference League, and Europa League. Both perspectives are valid.

Supporters live for cup nights, but it is true from a club-building point of view, it offers relatively little. At Villa, Emery's wage bonus isn't tied to survival like in previous jobs, it is tied solely to European qualification. For lots of reasons, that's how the club measures success. Sustained participation in European competition is what drives brand growth. That's what brings money, what allows you to build a bigger stadium, upgrade facilities, charge more for hospitality, and access better players. Europe brings you progress. A title earns you a statue by the stadium. For most fans, that's a hard sell, especially when your team is just two games from lifting a trophy. The challenge was convincing players and supporters alike that, regardless of what happened in the FA Cup, the club's true priority had to remain the same.

At Wembley, the emotions on either side couldn't have been more different. A party for Palace, a final, and a tense, expectant air among the Villans, another hurdle, something to get through on the way to something bigger. The contrast was stark in the visual displays. Crystal Palace's fans unfurled a vast horizontal banner across the lower tier, stretching the width of the stand, with a romantic message in bold white letters: 'Take my hand, take my whole life too.' The words, drawn from Elvis Presley's *Can't Help Falling in Love*, were set against a deep red and blue background – the colours of the south London club. At the opposite end, Aston Villa fans displayed a large but more restrained banner across their section that read, 'Pride of the Midlands.' Inside the club, there was acknowledgement that Palace had won that particular battle – but no one, at any point, would use it to justify anything. There were far more relevant factors affecting team performance.

For instance, it seemed to be a psychological weight pressing down on the Villa end. It felt like a game they had to win, a semi-final they were expected to handle. Not winning was more than a missed opportunity. That creates a kind of internal paralysis, and when pressure tightens, and things don't go as expected, it spreads. It became a classic piece of football theatre: Villa were afraid of falling; Palace were thrilled by the chance to climb. Villa weren't at their level. Their movements were tense, their decisions cautious, as if every misplaced pass or missed tackle carried the weight of disaster. The crowd didn't freeze first, the team did. The problem wasn't from the stands to the pitch. It was from the pitch to the stands.

As expected, Oliver Glasner's side had lined up with a back five and a dense midfield. They conceded possession to Villa, and waited for the chance to spring into a quick transition, while they won every duel, stayed superbly organised, and waited for their moment. Every attack, every sprint and tackle crackled with energy. They knew exactly how to hurt Villa, a team that lacked a sixth gear, missing penetration, freshness, and sharpness in the final third. Palace are asymmetrical. You don't quite know how to approach them from a structural point of view, but if you bring the right energy, keep pushing, and trust in your quality, your better players – most of them at Villa occupying central areas – should make the difference. However, that's the trap. You can become lethargic against Palace. They give you time on the ball. Your players are in the middle; their players are in the middle. They're not pressing high, they're not chasing down your goalkeeper. If you're Villa, you slow down. Because you can't pass, and the only way through is to craft the perfect goal.

Unai had worked all week on a clear plan: keep the ball and deliver it when it could hurt Palace. Yet all three Palace goals came from losing possession. The players were told: take care of the ball. Still, in certain moments, the instinct to take a risk kicked in. Each loss had its own context, but all three were avoidable. And, on top of it, Palace's very first shot on target again ended up in the net. Eze. Aston Villa struggled to get back into the game, and one of Crystal Palace's defining traits is that once they take the lead, they become an extremely dangerous team. Then Ismaïla Sarr made a huge impact. He never quite broke through at Marseille, but now had nine goals and five assists that season. Against Villa alone: five goals and two assists. Two of those goals came on the day.

A new debate broke out in the stands: is it more important to stay true to your style, or to adapt and win? In the final 20 minutes, Villa improved, offering danger down the flanks – Leon Bailey and Matty Cash added thrust, same as Jacob Ramsey and Lucas Digne on the other side. It was too late. Villa lost 3–0. Five attempts now without a win against Palace. And on aggregate, the score reads 16–4.

The players were devastated, especially the British ones. They have grown up with the FA Cup. It still meant something personal. Morgan Rogers put it simply: 'It was one of them where we didn't need to speak about the game after. Structure and the way you want to play is one thing, but sometimes it's about your heart, your players just performing and delivering on the day. Our quality wasn't there. Our sharpness wasn't there.'

Unai Emery spoke briefly to the players. 'Today wasn't our day,' he told them. 'I take full responsibility for the defeat, lads, and I want you to know how proud I am of each and every one of you and of everything we've achieved so far.'

'Switch off,' he said. 'Go spend time with your families.' After five relentless weeks, the squad were given two full days off before training resumed on Tuesday.

Unlike the hollow victory against Paris Saint-Germain, where both Unai Emery and Damiá Vidagany had looked shattered in the press conference, this time Emery seemed more composed, but he didn't really fancy talking much. He repeated almost the same words four times in response to four different questions. His words seemed aimed not at the journalists in the room but at the supporters. 'Please,' he said, 'dominate your frustration. We are improving a lot. Maybe if the improvement had been slower, we'd all be happier with each small step. We need to take these experiences with us. To win trophies is, of course, something very important. Aston Villa has a history of winning trophies. We're trying to be part of that process. But what we are doing in the Premier League, gaining consistency, is the most important thing.'

'Palace were better than us.'

The question loomed: how deep did the faith in Unai's project run? The suspicion of club observers was that there would be a couple of days of raw frustration, a flurry of criticism and questions, but soon enough, fans will remember: no one ever promised this journey would only be an upward trajectory

Emery left Wembley with Rodri and Iosu on the way to the airport, noticeably quieter. There hadn't been standout performances, either individually or collectively. No one truly imposed themselves. Perhaps Bailey, when he came on, and a little from Maatsen. But beyond that, it looked like the players were simply drained, legs heavy, minds dulled. So you start to wonder: was it the pressure of a semi-final? Was it Wembley? Was it the weight of expectation? Because becoming a serious team means winning these kinds of matches. Maybe Villa just aren't there yet. Maybe they need more time.

Two days later, back at Bodymoor Heath, the mood started to shift. Emery spoke to the players for a little longer than usual. No video. He shared a story about when he had first arrived. At the time, none of the players wanted to come to Villa. That's why he holds Alex Moreno in such high regard: in December, a month after the new regime started, Moreno was the only one who said yes. Once Villa qualified for the Conference League, a few more started to join the club. But the real magnet, Emery explained, is consistency – results in the Premier League and regular presence in Europe. That's what puts you on the map. He admitted the cup semi-final defeat hurt, deeply, but not like the one against PSG. That one had cut him to the core. 'Europe has given me so much,' he said. 'Reaching the Champions League semi-finals with Villarreal, that's footballing glory, and we were close. We had done the work to be there. Watching that Champions League semi-final now, I was thinking: it could've been us out there today against Arsenal.'

'I want to keep growing with this club so that next year, we are there.'

Because Villa can't go from being a club that hasn't won anything since 1996, nearly 30 years without a major title, to expecting trophies overnight. Titles don't come as targets. They come as consequences of sustained presence at the elite level. As Damiá later reflected, 'The problem with football, and especially clubs with great histories, is that the curve of expectation always races ahead of the curve of success, no matter how fast the latter moves.' But what they felt on the streets, on social media and in the fan zone the following weekend wasn't bitterness. It was gratitude. 'It was beautiful,' Damià says. 'I went to the fan zone for the Fulham game, and people came up to me, thanking us – for Unai, for Monchi, for the project. One fan told me, "Thank you for saving my club." I was there with my son, and it felt like a wave of love for everything this club is becoming. I remember someone saying to me: "We always lose at West Ham." And then we went there and won. Arsenal? Same story. Now, in their last two home games against us, we've won and drawn. Newcastle? People say they're a bogey team, but they came to Villa Park and we beat them 4–1. When a team like Palace wins three and draws one out of four in a single season, well, you've just got to shut up and give them credit.'

But that is not the end of the story, is it?

On the journey between Bodymoor Heath and Villa Park, for the first game in May against Fulham, someone brought up Jhon Durán. Unai had already heard whispers about his situation in Saudi. Since his abrupt move to Al Nassr, where he played along-side Cristiano Ronaldo and Sadio Mané, things had unravelled. Despite scoring 12 goals in 18 matches, the team did not get a single trophy and he did not seem happy. Durán had also become embroiled in controversy with the Colombian national team, rumours of a falling-out with the coach, a withdrawal from the squad, and questions about his behaviour. Some close to the situation even spoke of a potential loan move back to Europe, Turkey maybe. While hearing all this, Unai kept shaking his head.

Stepping off the bus, the fan zone greeted the team with their usual wave of noise. Despite two consecutive defeats, the mood was far from despondent. Aston Villa were still in a strong position: 7th in the table, level on points with Chelsea, just two behind Newcastle in 5th. Only 4 points separated them from Manchester City in 3rd. Nottingham Forest were also still in the top four. Fulham, their opponents on the day, had only slim hopes of reaching Europe, but for Villa, a win would all but guarantee continental football next season. Only the competition – Champions League, Europa League, or Conference League – would remain to be decided. Villa had once trailed Nottingham Forest by 11 points and Chelsea by 10. Since January, every game had carried the mental weight of a knockout tie. Concentration had been absolute and had to continue to be so.

That is why the victory against Fulham was hugely important. A clean sheet, 3 points against a team that played well and forced Villa to take the game seriously. Unai's pupils again showed incredible mental strength. That day, Unai brought to the table a huge amount of energy. He was exhausted by the end. Happy, but completely drained. It also felt like the definitive performance of Youri Tielemans's season, not just because he scored the only goal of the match, but because of the complete nature of his display. His defensive work, his ability to suffer through fatigue, and his commitment to the team stood out. He picked up an injury while covering defensively, already running on empty. Tielemans's mentality that day was a perfect reflection of the team's ideal collective mindset. Youri Tielemans was eventually voted both Supporters' Player of the Season and Players' Player of the Season at Aston Villa. No surprise there. He had become the team's metronome, a player whose influence grew with every week.

His decision making had been shaped long ago, with cones on a training pitch at Anderlecht's Academy. 'We used to make games and play passes between cones,' he recalls. 'At first, they were wide open. But as you grew older, they got closer and closer. It taught you precision. Timing. The weight of the pass.' Today, when he threads a ball between two opponents or picks out a runner from deep, he remembers the cones. He arrived at the prestigious youth system very young, at just four or five years old. 'It's very well known for its playing style,' he says. 'Playing on the ground, moving the ball, finding space.' And technique: 'It's not about flicks and tricks. For me, technique is the basics, like control, passing to the right foot so your teammate can turn or play forward. That's what matters.'

He played eleven-a-side football when he was just ten, years ahead of most Academies. 'It gave me an edge,' he says. 'You understand spaces early.' As a boy, he even tried his hand in goal, until a coach noticed he kept dribbling the length of the pitch after conceding. 'The manager said: "Right, you're playing in the middle now."' He never left. He played as a number 10 in youth teams, always the one to make the final pass or take the shot – but as he matured, he played a bit deeper, as an eight. 'That taught me how to defend. In the academy, we didn't have to. We had the ball all the time. We were too good.' He rose through their system quickly, and by 16, he was doing preseason with Anderlecht's first team. After that, he never went back. Two league titles followed. A move to Monaco. Four and a half years at Leicester. Then, in 2023, Aston Villa.

At Villa, he found a style of football that felt like home. 'Unai offered the type of football I'm used to, having the ball at my feet, being able to dictate play.' Youri walked into a midfield that was already functioning well. Boubacar Kamara and Douglas Luiz were the preferred pair in the holding positions. 'There was no reason to change them,' he reflects now. So, Emery looked for another way to integrate Tielemans's intelligence – in the number 10 role, just behind the striker. 'The manager enjoys playing me there because I can understand the pressing side, when to close the middle, when to go. Offensively, I can find the pocket and link with the striker.' Emery also tailored the setup to his strengths. 'He understands what type of players I need around me when I play as a 10, more runners. I'm not the guy who's going to outpace everyone, but I can send the ball through.' Still, it's the number 8 role that feels most natural. 'That's my favourite position,' he says. 'I can help a lot in the build-up play, which is what we need with this manager, and sometimes I can join the attack too.'

Tielemans was not one of those players that needed a lot of explanation, but the methodology suited him. 'You understand a lot from those videos,' he says. 'Everyone can see where everyone needs to be to help the team.' Watching them when you are involved in the clips feels useful. 'But when you've not played and you have to sit through it . . . it feels really long.' Still, he has not seen anyone falling asleep. 'The manager never stays quiet. He talks, talks, talks – and sometimes he'll ask you a question about what's just happened. You've got to be ready.' There's humour, too. 'Sometimes we laugh because you see a player do something you'd never think of in the game, and it gets picked up,' he adds with a grin. 'I'm doing things well. I try not to be that stupid guy in the video.'

On the training ground, Emery's methods surprised him because of their simplicity. 'A warm-up, a passing drill, maybe some tactical focus. Then we go into possession and a game, but the key in those games is you stay in your position. Not everyone running everywhere, not two-touch or one-touch unless it's needed. As many touches as you want, but always in context.' That repetition, that structure, has changed the way Tielemans reads the game. 'When I receive the ball from the centre-half, my body is already in position. If the opponent's coming from one side, I know I can turn the other. I know who's in the pockets. I have two runners. Everything has been put in your head. It's just about looking up and picking the right pass.'

Emery's approach is built on control. 'He always says the game is 90 minutes. He's in no rush. If the attack is on, take it. If not, wait. Be patient. If you make a technical error, he won't punish you. He knows it can happen.' Then Tielemans smiles: 'His perfect game? We keep the ball for 90 minutes, we score in the 91st, we win the game, and we go home.'

An injury stopped his early progression and then he had to be patient. 'He made me realise it was part of the process. Even if I wasn't playing, I wasn't less important. My time would come, and when it did, I had to be ready.' That message stuck. 'I've always been the kind of player who needed one or two games to get going,' he says. 'But I realised I wouldn't get that. I had to take the opportunity the moment it came – 10 minutes, 15, whatever I was given.'

He wasn't alone in learning to wait. Jhon Durán comes to mind. Looking back after Durán's departure, Tielemans remembers him with warmth: 'He's young. One day, unbelievable. The next, it's like he's forgotten what he needs to do.' Then he adds something more reflective: 'It's interesting how, from the players' side, we understand things sometimes only when it's too late. When the manager is gone, or you've moved on somewhere else, you start thinking: that was good. Then you look around and ask: "What are we doing now? I miss what I had."'

For Tielemans, that maturity arrived early, helped by a solid up-bringing. 'I had a good education at home and at school. Finished my grades, got my diploma at 18. After that, professional football.' Today, he's very stable with his wife and three daughters. When his third child was born, in the thick of Villa's early-season fixture congestion, he asked for a short break. 'We had Conference League qualifiers and a very busy period, but Unai made it work. I had two days to be there for the birth, and then rejoined the team for the game. He's first class with those things. If he sees a player is fully committed, he's always willing to find a compromise.'

Tielemans missed the next match, away to Bournemouth, and with it the chance to join Ollie Watkins in celebrating a historic moment. Watkins' winner, the only goal of the game, was his 75th in the Premier League, making him Aston Villa's all-time top scorer in the competition, reaching the milestone in just 184 appearances. The match was, in theory, the toughest remaining test of the season, and it helped Villa have the best defensive form in the league over the previous eight matches. Villa had learnt how to suffer. And with more time between games, Emery and his staff had made subtle but crucial adjustments – especially on defending crosses, one of the crucial parts of Bournemouth's game. They added an extra midfielder next to the full-back to help defend wide areas. Small details that helped stop their rival.

Unai Emery's roar of *¡Vamos!*' (Come on!) as he disappeared down the tunnel was perhaps his most visceral of the season. It had been that kind of game: exhausting, tense. With two matches remaining, just 3 points separated Manchester City in third from Nottingham Forest in seventh in the tightest Champions League race in Premier League history. But Unai was celebrating something else. Villa had mathematically secured European football for a third consecutive season. According to Opta's global rankings, Villa had just become one of the top ten teams in the world, and for only the second time in the Premier League era, they were heading for a third season in a row with over 60 points. Unai Emery became the first manager in Aston Villa's history to collect 180 Premier League points in fewer than 100 games (99). Brian Little needed 120, Martin O'Neill 118, John Gregory 117.

For Unai, the challenge at the conclusion of the season was internal. Managing a squad where some players' futures were undecided and agents were beginning to circle. Ensuring no one switched off. To be honest, the dressing room had responded. After Pau Torres' difficult outing at Wembley against Crystal Palace, there was a case for starting Mings against Fulham, but Emery doesn't like to make changes that feel like a punishment. Pau played against the London outfit, the team kept a clean sheet. So, against Bournemouth, it had been Mings' turn again. Pau, Bailey, Durán, Malen, Mings, García, they had all conducted themselves impeccably. Managing this group, Unai admitted, was a joy. He said as much: 'I would be happy with the same squad next season.'

After a deserved 2–0 win over Spurs at home, Villa had gone 21 home games unbeaten in all competitions, stretching from March 2023 to April 2024, and Emery had surpassed a 51 per cent win rate at each of his last five clubs. There were reports of a £15 million release clause in his contract. In England, these are rare, only enforceable if mutually agreed. But Unai didn't sound like someone planning to leave. 'Nassef showed great respect for me,' he said. 'First, he signed me when no one else would. Then, he renewed and improved my contract. My obligation here is not just contractual, it's about building something for as long as we can.'

After the final home match against Tottenham, Emery took selfies with fans before heading upstairs to his press conference. He checked his phone. 'Chelsea won? OK, I expected it!' he smiled. 'It's not in our hands, but we are in the race.'

The day before the Manchester United game, the last one of the season, Real Unión were relegated to the Segunda Federación, the fourth tier of Spanish football. It happened on Saturday 24 May, with a 4–2 defeat to Bilbao Athletic at Lezama. The team had not fallen this low for twenty-six years, but, in truth, the drop had been a long time coming. The club had narrowly escaped relegation the previous two seasons. Albert Carbó was unable to reverse the team's decline, and the Emery family project at Real Unión now entered an uncertain new phase. What was built to lift the club into the second tier must now be reformulated – at least in the short term.

'It was very sad,' said Igor Emery. 'After saying goodbye to the fans at Lezama, the bus ride home was heavy. And when we arrived at the Gal stadium around midnight, the farewell was even harder.' A couple of days later, he held end-of-season meetings with the squad and staff. These were standard protocol—but this time, there was nothing standard about the context. People, not just staff or footballers, were going to lose their jobs. 'We have to stand up and get to work with clarity. The contracts of players that extended beyond this season, or those we had renewed, are cancelled by the relegation clause.' Head coach Albert Carbó, too, was only contracted until 30 June and he was replaced by Ramsés Gil, whose CV includes a promotion from the division Real Unión went down to.

Paradoxically, relegation, and a drastic reduction of expenses, might bring financial relief. Competing in Primera RFEF had been costly, there is not enough income, there wasn't enough support. The revenue model the project was built on kept running a deficit of over €1 million a season. That gap was plugged repeatedly through capital injections, including the most recent, in which V Sports, owners of Aston Villa, officially joined the club. Their sporting and financial agreement with Real Unión remains in place, unaffected by the relegation. 'The Emery family project at Real Unión goes far beyond the first team,' Igor explained. 'It's not dependent on results. The goal remains to return to professional football – but to do so as a healthier, better-run club. With stronger infrastructure, deeper social roots, and a more solid internal structure. We want to come back better prepared – in mentality, organisation, everything.'

For Unai, Real Unión is both something he tries to keep out of his head and something impossible to ignore. That night, it had to sit in the back of his mind. The next day, he had to win against Manchester United to keep Villa in the Champions League race. Despite back-to-back defeats in April that threatened to derail their momentum, Aston Villa rallied with vital wins over Fulham, Bournemouth and Spurs – and now faced a final day that could define everything. Champions League, Europa League or Conference League, all outcomes remained in play. Villa arrived at Old Trafford on 66 points, level with Chelsea and Newcastle in a three-way shootout for two remaining Champions League places. Manchester City, on 68, were nearly out of reach. For Unai Emery's side, the maths was simple: win, and hope either Newcastle or Chelsea slip. But Nottingham Forest, just a point behind Villa on 65, could push Emery's side to the Conference League. Chelsea travelled to Forest, City to Fulham. Newcastle hosted Everton.

During the week, the rondo told the story of the team. When Kamara and Onana were on the same side passing around, the ball moved smoothly between their feet. In the short-sided games, the pattern held: if they played together, their team won. Then the coaches moved Kamara to the other side – a team that, until then, had been chasing shadows – and instantly, everything changed. The passes became sharper, tempo lifted, and the losing side began to dominate. Tielemans was back from injury, but when Kamara and Onana are playing like this, how can you leave them out? So of course, they both started at Old Trafford.

Unai set out to control the game through possession. He chose players who could handle the ball under pressure, anticipating the possibility of Manchester United pressing high and man to man. Emery respects Ruben Amorim's United side, still hurt by their defeat in the Europa League final against Spurs four days earlier – but Unai could see their improvement. United did press Villa's build-up from the outset and unsettled them. The areas Villa had hoped to exploit never appeared. Attempts to go long – seeking Rogers, Watkins or McGinn – had little success. United struck the post, and Emi Martínez was called upon to make a couple of important saves. The duels were going United's way. Nothing flowed. Why is it that one day you win every duel – every single one – and the next, not a single one falls your way? When you ask why top players cost so much, there are at least two answers. They tend to give an eight out of ten performance in any type of match, and in a moment of difficulty, when the team is not performing, they give you that flash, that stamp of quality, be it defensively or offensively, that makes you go: 'Wow.' They are the type of player that changes a game.

Manchester United fans sang: 'Champions League, you're having a laugh.' Villa fans responded in kind: 'Europa League, you're having a laugh!'

Unai knew the game was not going the right way.

Just as the game began to settle a little, the moment came that changed everything. In the 45th minute, a long Bruno Fernandes ball over the top sent Rasmus Højlund through. Emi Martínez raced out of his area, mistimed his challenge, and blocked the forward outside the box. The referee didn't hesitate – straight red. Pablo came out of his seat to ask the fourth official if that did not deserve only a yellow instead. His protests were met with understanding but there was no VAR reprieve. Robin Olsen had to come on, and Marco Asensio was replaced. With a few seconds before half time, the forward went straight to the changing rooms.

At half-time, Unai had said it plainly: 'We're going to have one opportunity.' Because that's how these games work against a team with no urgency. The manager didn't want to know the other results during the game, unless something major happened; it would cloud his match analysis. He just wanted to win. But in the dressing room, he couldn't help himself. He quietly asked Pablo about them: only City had scored at Fulham. As things stood, Villa were heading for the Europa League – but a goal from Forest would drop them into the Conference. On the bright side, a Villa goal would lift them into the Champions League.

United's dominance remained clear in the second half, but as minutes went by it was starting to fade, just slightly. They were still pushing, they wanted to win, but they weren't baring their teeth. There was an untold sense of what the game meant for them: not that much, really. Watkins had the chance to slip it through to Jacob Ramsey, who would've been clean through, but instead of playing it inside, he chose the outside, and the keeper blocked the move. With the game still goalless in the 73rd minute, Morgan Rogers stole the ball from United goalkeeper Altay Bayındır and poked it into the net, but referee Thomas Bramall had already blown for a foul that hadn't occurred before the ball crossed the line – preventing any intervention from VAR.

Unai erupted. He sprinted up and down the touchline, well beyond his technical area, fingers pointing wildly in the air, swinging side to side, shouting over and over: 'No, no, no, no, no, no, no, no!' His key error was to judge that Bayındır had full control of the ball, with both hands on it, when Rogers challenged. Replays showed otherwise. The goal would have given Unai's team a 1–0 lead with 18 minutes to play. The Villa bench was stunned. Yes, the referee seemed like a decent man, but this was only his second year in the Premier League. Of the ten referees officiating that day, Brammall was the second least experienced. A referee doesn't need to favour anyone, but he does need to understand the weight of the moment. You could see that Manchester United had nothing riding on the match. For Villa, it could mean losing out on Champions League qualification and £75 million in revenue. At the very least, he should have waited for VAR support. The decision was inexplicable.

There is a red line Unai refuses to cross: the game must be played with integrity. He will not instruct his players to waste time, to exaggerate contact, or to provoke opponents. Respect for football is non-negotiable. He would rather lose honestly than win by deception. Even in moments of desperation. He once made that clear to Emi Martínez when the goalkeeper was wasting time. In return, he expects the game to be fair with him. Unai kept raising his arms, asking for an explanation. He couldn't believe what had just happened. The fourth official could only say, 'Nope, I don't understand it either.'

In the next move, Bruno Fernandes put a ball into the box behind Maatsen, headed in by Amad Diallo. 1-0 to Manchester United, a deserved lead with the bigger picture in mind, but with very cruel timing. Unai kept crossing his stretched arms and shaking his head. He felt overwhelmed by the unfairness of it all. A few minutes later, as the match approached the 80th minute, the analyst Moisés came over to Unai and said, 'Just so you know, Newcastle are losing at home. If we score, we're in the Champions League.'

Unai asked, 'What about Chelsea?'

'They're winning 1–0,' Moisés replied.

Unai nodded. After that, he didn't ask for any more updates. Incredibly enough, the Champions League was still possible. The frustration kept growing, as the referee could have signaled for a fault on Watkins, but especially when he then gave a fair penalty to Manchester United, with Maatsen stamping on the heels of Diallo. Unai, sat on the steps next to the bench, clapped and threw his hands in the air. 'Of course, of course, of course!'

2–0 to Manchester United.

Forget Champions League. The hope was now that Forest did not score a goal that would take Villa to the third European competition. The remaining Villa fans were singing in the final minutes: 'Europe, Europe, again.' There was already a shared feeling among many supporters, a kind of collective struggle with a paradox. Look how far we've come, but we could have gone even further. We're better than Palace, better than United. And yet . . . here we are. A mix of pride and frustration, of progress and the sense that something just slipped through their fingers.

At the final whistle, Unai stood frozen. He didn't know anything about Forest, about what the result meant. Just staring into space. Not moving. He started looking at the referee, expression blank. Damià, as always, waited for him in the tunnel. Unai never stayed behind to protest, or to celebrate. But this time, he was not heading towards the tunnel. The overriding feeling, for Damià, was of irritation. Who could have predicted Newcastle would lose at home to Everton? But that wasn't the heart of it. The deeper frustration came from how poorly the team had played. There was a kind of stiffness, a pressure that stopped them from flowing, and that – Damià thought – is something they'll have to learn from in the future. The internal analysis would be, in his view, tough but fair. 'These last three months,' he reflected, 'in which we've taken 37 points and played at a high level, they have to be the foundation for what we build next season, but we also need to understand what happened against Palace and United.'

Damià didn't believe there was any agenda against Aston Villa. The club had always shown respect to referees, even in extreme situations. Figures like Howard Webb, head of the referees in England, and Hugh Dallas, part of the referee assessment team, recognised and valued that approach, and keep mentioning it in the regular zooms they have with Damià. Yet it was hard to ignore the pattern: Villa had simply been the side most affected by serious refereeing mistakes this season.

All and all there was a strange contradiction in the air. Only two seasons age we were throwing people in the air for reaching the Conference League. Now 'I had the feeling that, despite qualifying for Europe for a third consecutive year, and making it to the Europa League, felt like falling short. That says something about the speed of the project,' Damià says. Meanwhile, Manchester United's manager, whose team had finished 24 points behind Villa and missed out on Europe entirely, was being cheered from the stands.

Players began to walk past, but still no sign of Unai. So Damià walked out towards the pitch. He passed by Emi Martínez who was visibly upset. He blamed himself for the defeat. Coming so close to a Champions League semi-final and falling short in the FA Cup, left a bitter taste on the player. He was unsure if that had been his last game for Villa. Tyrone Mings entered the changing room with a sense of regret. The team had grown, but maybe hadn't been quite good enough across the whole season. Certainly, they were not today. There was a hope that if they went on to win the Europa League, the story of this season would be felt differently.

As fans were trickling out of the stadium, they talked among themselves. 'I love all these players,' one said. 'Ideally, you'd just tweak the squad, improve one or two areas and go again.'

'Yeah, but that's not how it works here, is it?' another replied. 'Record gate receipts, sold out every game, quarter-finals of the Champions League, biggest kit deal, biggest sponsorships . . . and still, we're one of the only clubs, along with Newcastle, that has to sell to keep competing.'

Someone else nodded. 'I was at the awards night. Damiá Vidagany stood up and said, "It's going to be a difficult summer." How's that even right in this day and age?'

Damià saw Monchi coming straight from the VIP seats, weaving quickly through people as he made his way to Unai, who was still on the pitch, beginning to walk slowly towards the tunnel. Monchi had been deep in thought since the final whistle. The missed Champions League spot weighed heavily, especially in a season where neither United nor Tottenham had made the top five. Next year, teams like Everton, West Ham, Crystal Palace, Brentford, Fulham, Brighton . . . any one of them could have the kind of run Nottingham Forest had this year. There were easily seven or eight sides that did not make it into Europe but with enough potential to reach European places. This season, nine had done so. It was a sign of the quality Villa would face. However, it wasn't just about league positions. The challenge this summer was clear. Villa had signed a financial agreement with UEFA that included fines but gave them clearance to play in Europe. From here, the goal was to rebuild within limits. Over two years, the club had to reduce squad costs to no more than 70 per cent of total revenue. There were only two ways to get there: raise income or cut wage spend. Having two top earners in every position would no longer be viable.

When Monchi finally caught up with Unai, he gave him the news: Forest had lost, Villa had finished sixth. Europa League next season. City, Chelsea and Newcastle were in the Champions League. It was a bitter-sweet update. They'd made history again. No team outside the traditional top six had returned to the Champions League the following year since 2003, but over the past three seasons, only Villa, outside the top three, had consistently played in Europe. Still, the feeling was not celebratory.

Unai, who never speaks to referees, started accelerating, with his hands behind his back, towards referee Thomas Bramall, now leaving the pitch with his assistants. Damià joined the manager. They caught up with Bramall just as they reached the entrance to the tunnel and Unai began speaking to him directly. Thierry

Henry, watching the footage on television, could only think of one word: dignified behaviour from the frustrated manager.

'I think it was a very serious mistake,' Unai told the referee. 'I respect you, I believe in what you do, but come on . . .'

The referee admitted he had got it wrong.

Damià also had a quiet word with him, even though, deep down he believed the issue for Villa wasn't just the official's error. When a referee tells you he has made a mistake, you have to move on and reflect. Growth, he thought, wouldn't come from expecting referees to be flawless, but from Villa learning to play those high-pressure matches better – so that even if a referee did get it wrong, the outcome wouldn't depend on it. As the referee walked away, Damià turned to Unai and told him the club would be lodging a formal complaint with Howard Webb. Mostly about the inexperience of assigning Bramall to a fixture with so much at stake.

On the way to the changing room, Unai's head was a volcano of thoughts and emotions. Around him, people watched, uncertain, should they approach him or leave him alone, hug him or let him explode? No one quite knew. This season, he thought, will be remembered for the Champions League nights. The lights. The fireworks. The sheer noise. The Holte End. All of it majestic. The discussions with his closest people in all sorts of rooms, hotels, planes.

'I can't believe Real Unión went down. Lander could play with them next season, but that would mean . . . he won't be here with me. We didn't play well today. No Champions League next season. We were better with ten players than with eleven. Seven draws at home. We didn't do so well against the top seven sides. The demand now is to win a title, that is good. Am I pushing too much? If Forest scored, we were in the Conference League, and they didn't – that is good. No more time for corrections this season. Some players gave everything. Others, not enough. Tomorrow, I face them, one by one – who's still committed? Who's already gone, in mind or body? Then they will collect their things, go to different parts of the world. Some won't return. It will be very difficult to keep Marco Asensio or Marcus Rashford. How do I build again from this? The owners believed in me, I cannot fail them. Did I demand too much? Or not enough? Did I misread someone? Leave someone behind? I've never felt so close to this squad – and still, I wonder. This project we've spent three years building is wide awake. I need to find new motivations, refresh three or four things in the team. Three years from now, if I'm happy, what will have happened? I'll still have players raising their level, getting better, staying motivated. We'll have achieved collective goals: reaching a final, playing in Europe. If one year we miss Europe, like Newcastle, but return the next, it shouldn't weaken us. If it does, and that weakness becomes draining, then it's time to rethink. When the league starts, I'll say, "There are seven teams ahead of us by budget, that's just how it is." What will help us is being consistent across all thirty-eight league matches. Everyone has holiday plans, and I still don't. We created memories, but there are new heights to reach.'

'What do I even say to the guys now?'

Unai pressed his lips together as he entered the dressing room. He began by telling the players the season was over, that they had secured Europa League, fallen just one step short of the Champions League, and that he was deeply proud of them all. And something happened for the first time. And he could not stop it.

He started crying, and left the room.

ACKNOWLEDGEMENTS

In 1962, during a visit to NASA, President John F. Kennedy paused his tour when he spotted a janitor carrying a broom. He asked him, 'And what are you working on?' The janitor replied, 'I'm helping put a man on the Moon.' Kennedy later recalled this moment in his famous speech at Rice University, as a reminder that every role contributes to a greater mission.

Bodymoor Heath is football's version of NASA. Unai Emery has taken Aston Villa to the vanguard of modern football, and that requires relentless attention to detail – to relationships, to tactics, to constant improvement. It demands the commitment of everyone at the training ground. That's why as many of them as possible needed to have a voice – to help me build the fullest, closest picture of what this place truly is. You can't fully grasp that methodology from a clip on social media, a post-match interview, or even a documentary. Some of it is visible, but much of it is not. Being there for a full season – speaking with people, watching the work unfold – gets you closer to understanding what really goes on. The rest of my job is turning that experience into words, scenes, anecdotes, and quotes. My hope is that these pages reflect the depth of what I witnessed. This book would not have been possible without the knowledge and friendship of so many generous people.

First, to Unai Emery. Thank you for letting me interrupt what is an incredibly busy schedule, and for giving me access to your life, family, friends, even photographs, but your biggest help was by letting me walk around the most hermetic of worlds.

To Damià Vidagany, who has been much more than a guide. Thank you for your constant support, for helping me understand so many processes and relationships, and for making the complex feel a bit less so. Your insights have been central to this project. The same can be said of Monchi, who has a great memory for details and stories, and found time to share them.

To the Aston Villa staff, thank you for helping me understand this remarkable football club in transformation. To the ever-present Pablo Villa, who never said no; Antonio Rodríguez 'Rodri', whose understanding of individual growth left a deep mark; Austin McPhee, for always offering a different point of view; and Pako Ayestarán, whose perspective added another layer to Unai's regime. Javi García, Moisés De Hoyo, and Alberto Benito – each of you brought warmth and details that helped complete the picture.

A special mention for three people who shaped this book more than they may realise. To Sharon Barnhurst – the sharpest most empathic mind in any room and the toughest negotiator this book had to face. To Phil Roscoe, the quiet heartbeat behind player care. Your reflections reminded me what really matters inside a football club. And thank you for keeping me posted on the whereabouts of the bosses! And to Tommy Jordan, whose diplomacy guided this entire process from the background. Thank you for being the sounding board.

To the wider Villa family, your care for the players and the club is evident in every gesture. Elisa Ceñal, Tom Otrebski, Luke McNulty, Michael Bache, Chris Heck, thank you. Also, to Pam Bridgewater,

Sarah Rajani, Matt Lambert, Danielle Fulford, and Bashir Lebada – your efforts, seen and unseen, help hold everything together.

To the fans who spoke to me – thank you for your passion and memories. Adam Britton, Adam Baz Barrett, Joe Boone, Simon O'Regan, Ben Moore, Tracey James, Will Forrest, Gemma Taylor-Whitehead, Howard Hodgson, Luke Robinson, Sam Leonard, Nick Sanders, Harry Purewal, Gurdev Singh Jheeta, Nîmes Gill, Sunjeet Jheeta, Dev Jheeta, Onkar Bhamber, Jag Kalaar, Darren Smith, Jass Gill, Dave and Billy Powell – I hope this book has done justice to what this club means to you.

To the players, thank you for letting me see the person behind the professional. Matty Cash, Youri Tielemans, Pau Torres, Emi Buendía, Marco Asensio, Morgan Rogers, Emi Martínez, Tyrone Mings, and others that stopped to chat with me in corridors and the canteen.

To the people from Unai's past and present, who helped me paint the roots of this story: Lander Emery, thank you for your perspective as a son and as a sharp football mind in your own right. To the extraordinary Amelia Etxegoien, for sharing your son Unai with the world. To Igor Emery, Iosu Reta, Roberto Olabe, Mikel Etxarri, Iñaki Ibáñez, Pedro Reverte, Voro, Juan Carlos Carcedo, and Sander Westerveld – your memories and reflections shaped the most intimate parts of this book.

To the journalists and experts, thank you for offering your lenses. Mat Kendrick, your words echo the heartbeat of this city. Michael Caulfield, for your insight into the psychology of performance. Adam Benkwitz, who painted a very clear picture of the city of Birmingham and the relationship with the club. Conrado Valle and Miguel Ángel Vara, for your sharp look back. George Woffenden, Pep Segura, and Jay Tee, always there when needed.

At the very start of this journey, two books helped lay the

foundation for everything that followed. *Mentalidad ganadora* by Juan Carlos Cubeiro Villar offered a powerful lens into leadership. *Unai Emery, el maestro* by Romain Molina provided a valuable portrait of the man behind the method. My thanks to both authors for helping shape the questions.

Ah, by the way. That conversation between the top managers in Unai's office? It didn't actually happen. Not all together. Not in one room. Not like that. I owe you an apology if I momentarily misled you. But I hope you'll forgive me – because every word in that scene has, at some point, been said to me, or said by them in interviews or press conferences. I simply rearranged the furniture. The aim was insight – a way to bring these voices together so you could hear how they think, how they challenge one another. If it worked, you'll understand them better.

This book is a product of a shared love for football, for Aston Villa, and for storytelling. There are many more who supported this journey in ways large and small, many off the record and will remain so – your fingerprints are here.

Last but by no means least, there's a group of loyal friends who, every time I write a book, pitch a tent around me – to protect me, care for me, and turn the process into something collective. It might be pouring with rain, snowing, thundering, or unbearably hot – I wouldn't notice, because Maribel Herruzo always had everything ready for whenever I needed to hide away. William Glasswell brought me whatever I needed to survive. I really enjoyed your feedback, William, as I did Peter Lockyer's with his detailed emails after reading the first drafts of chapters. I sensed the enthusiasm from both of you and it helped massively. Brent Wilks, Yolanda and Gustavo Balagué, and my mother Maria Oliva kept me going when things got tough. My agent David Luxton would check in from time to time to see how things were progressing, and quietly fix anything that needed mending. And finally, the great editor that is Tierney Witty, who not only made the book much better, but upgraded the tent into a five-star hotel room.

OK. So, what's next?

ORION CREDITS

Seven Dials would like to thank everyone at Orion who worked on the publication of *RISE OF THE VILLANS*.

Agent
David Luxton

Manuscript Coordinator
Maribel Herruzo

Editor
Tierney Witty

Copy-editor
Clare Hubbard

Proofreader
Elise See Tai

Editorial Management
Pablo Pizarro Janczur
Jade Macé

Jane Hughes
Charlie Panayiotou

Audio
Paul Stark
Louise Richardson
Georgina Cutler-Ross

Contracts
Rachel Monte
Ellie Bowker

Design
Nick Shah
Jess Hart
Loveday May
Deborah Francis
Helen Ewing

Picture Research
Natalie Dawkins
Finance
Nick Gibson
Jasdip Nandra
Sue Baker
Tom Costello

Inventory
Jo Jacobs

Marketing
Tom Noble

Production
Hannah Cox
Katie Horrocks

Publicity
Sian Baldwin

Sales
David Murphy
Victoria Laws
Sammy Luton
Group Sales teams across
Digital, Field Sales,
International and Non-Trade

Operations
Group Sales Operations team

Rights
Rebecca Folland
Barney Duly
Tara Hiatt
Ben Fowler
Maddie Stephenson
Marie Henckel

RAISING READERS
Books Build Bright Futures

Dear Reader,

We'd love your attention for one more page to tell you about the crisis in children's reading, and what we can all do.

Studies have shown that reading for fun is the **single biggest predictor of a child's future life chances** – more than family circumstance, parents' educational background or income. It improves academic results, mental health, wealth, communication skills, ambition and happiness.[1]

The number of children reading for fun is in rapid decline. Young people have a lot of competition for their time. In 2024, 1 in 10 children and young people in the UK aged 5 to 18 did not own a single book at home.[2]

Hachette works extensively with schools, libraries and literacy charities, but here are some ways we can all raise more readers:

- Reading to children for just 10 minutes a day makes a difference
- Don't give up if children aren't regular readers – there will be books for them!
- Visit bookshops and libraries to get recommendations
- Encourage them to listen to audiobooks
- Support school libraries
- Give books as gifts

There's a lot more information about how to encourage children to read on our website: **www.RaisingReaders.co.uk**

Thank you for reading.

---

[1] National Literacy Trust, Book Ownership in 2024, November 2024
https://nlt.cdn.ngo/media/documents/Book_ownership_in_2024

[2] OECD. 2021. 21st-century readers: developing literacy skills in a digital world. Paris, France: OECD Publishing.
https://www.oecd.org/en/publications/21st-century-readers_a83d84cb-en.html